PROCLUS

Commentary on Plato's Timaeus

Proclus' Commentary on Plato's dialogue *Timaeus* is arguably the most important commentary on a text of Plato, offering unparalleled insights into eight centuries of Platonic interpretation. This edition offers the first new English translation of the work for nearly two centuries, building on significant recent advances in scholarship on Neoplatonic commentators. It provides an invaluable record of early interpretations of Plato's dialogue, while also presenting Proclus' own views on the meaning and significance of Platonic philosophy. The present volume, the first in the edition, deals with what may be seen as the prefatory material of the *Timaeus*, in which Socrates gives a summary of the political arrangements favoured in the *Republic*, and Critias tells the story of how news of the defeat of Atlantis by ancient Athens had been brought back to Greece from Egypt by the poet and politician Solon.

Harold Tarrant is Head of the School of Liberal Arts, University of Newcastle, Australia. He has published widely on Plato and ancient Platonism including *Scepticism or Platonism?* (1985) in the Cambridge Classical Studies series.

PROCLUS

Commentary on Plato's Timaeus

VOLUME I

Book 1: Proclus on the Socratic State and Atlantis

TRANSLATED WITH AN
INTRODUCTION AND NOTES BY

HAROLD TARRANT

University of Newcastle, New South Wales

With a general introduction by
Dirk Baltzly and Harold Tarrant

CAMBRIDGE UNIVERSITY PRESS
Cambridge, New York, Melbourne, Madrid, Cape Town,
Singapore, São Paulo, Delhi, Tokyo, Mexico City

Cambridge University Press
The Edinburgh Building, Cambridge CB2 8RU, UK

Published in the United States of America by Cambridge University Press, New York

www.cambridge.org
Information on this title: www.cambridge.org/9780521173995

© Harold Tarrant 2007

This publication is in copyright. Subject to statutory exception
and to the provisions of relevant collective licensing agreements,
no reproduction of any part may take place without the written
permission of Cambridge University Press.

First published 2007
First paperback edition 2011

A catalogue record for this publication is available from the British Library

ISBN 978-0-521-84659-2 Hardback
ISBN 978-0-521-17399-5 Paperback

Cambridge University Press has no responsibility for the persistence or accuracy of
URLs for external or third-party internet websites referred to in this publication, and
does not guarantee that any content on such websites is, or will remain, accurate or
appropriate.

Contents

Acknowledgements	*page* vii
Note on the translation	viii

General introduction to the *Commentary*	1
DIRK BALTZLY AND HAROLD TARRANT	
The importance of the *Timaeus* and its commentary tradition	1
Proclus' life and writings: some essential facts	2
Cultural context: Proclus and pagan practice in Athens	3
Proclus' writings	7
Intertextuality and interpretation in the Neoplatonic commentary tradition	10
Formal features of Proclus' commentary	13
The *skopos* of the *Timaeus*: theology and physiology	16

Introduction to Book 1	21
The structure of Book 1 of Proclus' commentary	21
Interpreting the *Timaeus* in antiquity	23
Proclus on general questions concerning the *Timaeus*	49
Proclus on the summary of the constitution in the *Timaeus*	53
Proclus and his predecessors on Atlantis	60

On the *Timaeus* of Plato: Book 1	85
Analytical table of contents	87
Translation	91

References	305
English–Greek glossary	312
Greek word index	318
General index	342

Acknowledgements

The project of which this is part was a cooperative one from the start, emerging from a mutual conviction that Proclus' great *Commentary on the Timaeus* is a work for which a modern English translation was particularly needed, and helped along by the shared belief that input from both classicists and philosophers was needed. The team of translators originally consisted of Dirk Baltzly of Monash University, David Runia (then working in the Netherlands), and myself, and was later expanded to include Michael Share. The input of my colleagues was very much appreciated. The project has been kindly supported by a three-year grant from the Australian Research Council, notionally for 2000–2002. The University of Newcastle (Australia) afforded me study leave for the second semester of 2001, and has also supported me with conference grants to attend various conferences crucial to my interests in the history of Platonism in antiquity. Furthermore, it supported a conference held in Newcastle in July 2002 on 'Plato's Ancient Readers', where many of the papers were related to Proclus.

The support of our research assistants, Dr Tim Buckley (on a wide range of matters) and Fiona Leigh (on the indexing), has been very much appreciated. So also has been input from the wider scholarly world, and particularly from my widely spread colleagues in the International Plato Society, the membership of which I have found invaluable. I may confidently predict that none of them will have saved me as many errors as I should have wished to avoid, but these are due to no fault but my own. Constant pressures as Head of School in a University trying to grapple with an ever-deepening deficit might have been an easier target to blame, but my admirable colleagues have been commendably happy to put up with inferior administration and welcomed the idea of a Head with active interests in research and publication. Their tolerance has been critically important, but is of course superseded by that of my wife, Judith, who has long been used to the perils of a husband obsessed with his latest publishing projects. I can confidently assert that I do not intend to desert her for Proclus!

Creative life is not an island, whether in the universe or the partial space of one's study. There are a great many others, both past and present, who have contributed in their own ways to this single reversion to the text of Proclus. To all that plurality I send my thanks.

Note on the translation

In this translation we have sought to render Proclus' text in a form that pays attention to contemporary ways of discussing and translating ancient philosophy, while trying to present the content as clearly as possible, and without misrepresenting what has been said or importing too much interpretation directly into the translation. We have not sought to reproduce Proclus' sentence structure where this seemed to us to create a barrier to smooth reading, for which reason line and page numbers will involve a degree of imprecision. We have found the French translation by A. J. Festugière an invaluable starting-point, and it is still a useful and largely faithful rendition of Proclus' Greek.[1] However, we consider it worthwhile to try to make the philosophical content and arguments of Proclus' text as plain as possible. Something of our intentions can be deduced from the translation and commentary that Tarrant produced cooperatively with Robin Jackson and Kim Lycos on Olympiodorus' *Commentary on the Gorgias*.[2]

We believe that the philosophy of late antiquity now stands where Hellenistic philosophy did in the early 1970s. It is, at least for the anglo-analytic tradition in the history of philosophy, the new unexplored territory.[3] The most impressive contribution to studies in this area in the past fifteen years has been the massive effort, coordinated by Richard Sorabji, to translate large portions of the Greek Commentators on Aristotle.[4] R. M. van den Berg has provided us with Proclus' *Hymns*, while John

---

[1] Festugière, (1966–8). We are enormously indebted to Festugière's fine work, even if we have somewhat different aims and emphases. Our notes on the text are not intended to engage so regularly with the text of the Chaldean Oracles, or the Orphic fragments, or the history of religion. We have preferred to comment on those features of Proclus' text that place it in the commentary tradition.

[2] Jackson et al. (1998).

[3] To be sure, some of the seminal texts for the study of Neoplatonism have been available for some time. These include: Dillon (1973), Dodds (1963), Morrow (1970), Morrow and Dillon (1987), O'Neill (1965). There are also the translations by Thomas Taylor (1758–1835). While these constitute a considerable achievement, given the manuscripts from which Taylor was working and the rate at which he completed them, they cannot compare well with modern scholarly editions.

[4] The *Ancient Commentators on Aristotle* (Duckworth and Cornell University Press). The first volume in the series, Christian Wildberg's translation of Philoponus' *Against Aristotle on the Eternity of the World*, appeared in 1987. There are a projected 60 volumes including

Note on the translation

Finamore and John Dillon have made Iamblichus' *De Anima* available in English.[5] Sorabji's Commentators series now includes an English translation of Proclus' essay on the existence of evil.[6] There is also a new edition of Proclus' eighteen arguments for the eternity of the world.[7] We hope that our efforts will add something to this foundation for the study of late antiquity. If we have resolved ambiguities in Proclus' text without consideration of all the possibilities, or failed to note the connections between a particular passage in the *Timaeus* commentary and another elsewhere, then we can only plead that our team is working to begin the conversation, not to provide the final word.

In all five volumes in this series, the text used is that of Diehl. His page numbers and line numbers are reproduced in the margins; the page numbers are in bold. Deviations from that text are recorded in the footnotes. On the whole, where there are not philological matters at issue, we have used transliterated forms of Greek words in order to make philosophical points available to an audience with limited or no knowledge of Greek.

Neoplatonism has a rich technical vocabulary that draws somewhat scholastic distinctions between, say, intelligible (*noêtos*) and intellectual (*noeros*) entities. To understand Neoplatonic philosophy it is necessary to have some grasp of these terms and their semantic associations, and there is no other way to do this than to observe how they are used. We mark some of the uses of these technical terms in the translation itself by giving the transliterated forms in parantheses. On the whole, we do this by giving the most common form of the word – that is, the nominative singular for nouns and the infinitive for verbs – even where in the corresponding Greek text the noun is in the dative, or the verb a finite form. This allows the Greekless reader to recognize occurrences of the same term, regardless of the form used in the specific context at hand. We have deviated from this practice where it is a specific form of the word that constitutes the technical term – for example, the passive participle of *metechein* for 'the participated' (*to metechomenon*) or comparative forms such as 'most complete' (*teleôtaton*). We have also made exceptions for technical terms using prepositions (e.g. *kat' aitian, kath'*

---

works from Alexander Aphrodisias, Themistius, Porphyry, Ammonius, Philoponus and Simplicius.

[5] Van den Berg (2001), Finamore and Dillon (2002). Other important, but somewhat less recent, additions to editions and modern language translations of key Neoplatonic texts include: Segonds (1985–6) and the completion of the *Platonic Theology*, Saffrey and Westerink (1968–97).

[6] Opsomer and Steel (2005).

[7] Lang and Macro (2001). Cf. the first translation of the reply to Proclus by the Christian Neoplatonist, Philoponus, Share (2005).

Note on the translation

hyparxin) and for adverbs that are terms of art for the Neoplatonists (e.g. *protôs, physikôs*). This policy is sure to leave everyone a little unhappy. Readers of Greek will find it jarring to read 'the soul's vehicles (*ochêma*)' where the plural 'vehicles' is followed by the singular form of the Greek noun. Equally, Greekless readers are liable to be puzzled by the differences between *metechein* and *metechomenon* or between *protôs* and *protos*. But policies that leave all parties a bit unhappy are often the best compromises. In any event, all students of the *Timaeus* will remember that a generated object such as a book is always a compromise between Reason and Necessity.

We use a similar system of transliteration to that adopted by the *Ancient Commentators on Aristotle* series. The salient points may be summarized as follows. We use the diaeresis for internal breathing, so that 'immaterial' is rendered *aÿlos*, not *ahylos*. We also use the diaeresis to indicate where a second vowel represents a new vowel sound, e.g. *aïdios*. Letters of the alphabet are much as one would expect. We use '*y*' for υ alone as in *physis* or *hypostasis*, but '*u*' for υ when it appears in diphthongs, e.g. *ousia* and *entautha*. We use '*ch*' for χ, as in *psychê*. We use '*rh*' for initial ρ as in *rhêtôr*; '*nk*' for γκ, as in *anankê*; and '*ng*' for γγ, as in *angelos*. The long vowels η and ω are, of course, represented by *ê* and *ô*, while iota subscripts are printed on the line immediately after the vowel as in *ôiogenês* for ᾠογενής. There is a Greek word index with each volume in the series. In order to enable readers with little or no Greek to use this word index, we have included an English–Greek glossary that matches our standard English translation for important terms, with its Greek correlate given both in transliterated form and in Greek. For example, 'procession: *proödos*, πρόοδος'.

The following abbreviations to other works of Proclus are used:

in Tim. = *Procli in Platonis Timaeum commentaria*, ed. E. Diehl, 3 vols. (Leipzig: Teubner, 1903–6)

in Remp. = *Procli in Platonis Rem publicam commentarii*, ed. W. Kroll, 2 vols. (Leipzig: Teubner, 1899–1901)

in Parm. = *Procli commentarius in Platonis Parmenidem* (*Procli philosophi Platonici opera inedita* pt. III), ed. V. Cousin (Paris: Durand, 1864; repr. Hildesheim: Olms, 1961)

in Alc. = *Proclus Diadochus: Commentary on the first Alcibiades of Plato*, ed. L. G. Westerink (Amsterdam: North-Holland, 1954). Also used is A. Segonds (ed.), *Proclus: Sur le premier Alcibiade de Platon*, vols. I et II (Paris, 1985–6).

in Crat. = *Procli Diadochi in Platonis Cratylum commentaria*, ed. G. Pasquali (Leipzig: Teubner, 1908)

Note on the translation

ET = The Elements of Theology, ed. E. R. Dodds, 2nd edition (Oxford: Clarendon Press, 1963)

Plat. Theol. = Proclus: Théologie Platonicienne, ed. H. D. Saffrey and L. G. Westerink, 6 vols. (Paris: Les Belles Lettres, 1968–97)

de Aet. = Proclus: on the Eternity of the World, ed. H. Lang and A. D. Macro (Berkeley: University of California Press, 2001)

Proclus frequently mentions previous commentaries on the *Timaeus*, those of Porphyry and Iamblichus, for which the abbreviation *in Tim.* is again used. Relevant fragments are found in

R. Sodano, *Porphyrii in Platonis Timaeum Fragmenta*, (Naples: Istituto della Stampa, 1964) and

John Dillon, *Iamblichi Chalcidensis in Platonis Dialogos Commentariorum Fragmenta*, (Leiden: E. J. Brill, 1973).

Proclus also frequently confirms his understanding of Plato's text by reference to two theological sources: the 'writings of Orpheus' and the Chaldean Oracles. For these texts, the following abbreviations are used:

Or. Chald. = Ruth Majercik, *The Chaldean Oracles: Text, Translation and Commentary* (Leiden: Brill, 1989)

Orph. fr. = Orphicorum fragmenta, ed. O. Kern. (Berlin: Weidmann, 1922)

Majercik uses the same numeration of the fragments as E. des Places in his Budé edition of the text.

References to the text of Proclus' *in Timaeum* (as also of *in Remp.* and *in Crat.*) are given by Teubner volume number, followed by page and line numbers, e.g. *in Tim.* II. 2.19. References to the *Platonic Theology* are given by Book, chapter, then page and line number in the Budé edition. References to the *Elements of Theology* are given by proposition number.

Proclus' commentary is punctuated only by the quotations from Plato's text upon which he comments: the lemmata. These quotations of Plato's text and subsequent repetitions of them in the discussion that immediately follows that lemma are in bold. We have also followed Festugière's practice of inserting section headings so as to reveal what we take to be the skeleton of Proclus' commentary. These headings are given in centred text, in italics. Within the body of the translation itself, we have used square brackets to indicate words that need perhaps to be supplied in order to make the sense of the Greek clear. Where we suppose that Greek words ought to be added to the text received in the manuscripts, the supplements are marked by angle brackets.

xi

General introduction to the Commentary

DIRK BALTZLY AND HAROLD TARRANT

THE IMPORTANCE OF THE *TIMAEUS* AND ITS COMMENTARY TRADITION

Proclus' *Commentary on the Timaeus* is arguably the most important text of ancient Neoplatonism. The *Timaeus* itself has proved to be the most important of all Plato's works from a historical perspective, for it remained a key text from the death of Plato, through Hellenistic philosophy, Philo of Alexandria, Middle Platonism, and the Christian fathers, down to the Neoplatonists, and well beyond. The fact that in the past century or so it has been effectively challenged by the *Republic* for the title of 'Plato's greatest work' means little in the 2500-year history of Platonism. The *Timaeus* was acknowledged as one of the two supreme texts of the Neoplatonist curriculum. The other was the *Parmenides*, which was of similar importance to many Neoplatonists, but less widely acknowledged as central to a Platonic education.

The commentary itself was usually the major vehicle of Neoplatonist teaching, even though much of what survives on Plato, unlike Aristotle, is not in this form. Interpretation of authoritative texts, including many of those of Plato, was a central part of a Neoplatonist's work. The commentary arose directly out of the reading of texts in the schools of philosophy, though some commentaries went on being used by subsequent generations, for which reason Proclus would have been conscious that he was not writing an ephemeral work, but one that could be used in other contexts.

The *Commentary on the Timaeus* is the culmination of centuries of interpretative work, with much earlier material embedded within it. From it we can see the kinds of debates about interpretation that flourished in a previous age, as well as the particular stance taken by the Athenian School under Proclus and Syrianus. From the historical point of view, this commentary is the richest that Proclus has left us. It also gives insights into the interpretation of other Platonic works, in particular the *Republic* and *Critias*, which Proclus believes to be part of the same Platonic sequence. It will often seem alien to us, employing unfamiliar exegetical and metaphysical assumptions. Yet in following his reasoning, and seeing how he argues for his views, we shall have new cause to question our own interpretative assumptions.

1

General introduction to the *Commentary*

PROCLUS' LIFE AND WRITINGS: SOME ESSENTIAL FACTS

We are reasonably well acquainted with the facts of Proclus' life through a surviving biography by his successor, Marinus.[1] The biography aims not merely to record the events of Proclus' life, but to show how his ascent through Neoplatonism's various grades of virtue enabled him to live a happy and blessed life. So it is partly a moral treatise and partly a pagan hagiography, like Porphyry's *Life of Plotinus*. Nonetheless, we may draw some relatively secure conclusions about Proclus' life.

He was very likely born in 411 and died in 485.[2] His father, Patricius, was a lawyer at court in Byzantium, but shortly after Proclus' birth took a post in Xanthus. This might well have been agreeable to his parents, since they were themselves Lycians. Siorvanes suggests that this choice might also have been related to a law of 415 that excluded pagans from imperial service and the army. While this is possible, there is no easy pathway from our knowledge that the law at a certain date forbade something to the conclusion that the prohibition was uniformly enforced.

Proclus was intended to follow his father into the law. He studied rhetoric and law both at Xanthus and then at Alexandria. It is an indication of his father's wealth and reputation that he was tutored by important men, such as Leonas of Isauria. At the behest of the governor of Alexandria, Theodorus, the young Proclus accompanied Leonas to Byzantium. There Marinus' hagiography records that Proclus had a vision of the goddess Athena who instructed him to leave rhetoric and law and pursue the study of philosophy (*VProc.* 9). It is possible that the climate had changed in Byzantium and that Proclus encountered Athenian Neoplatonism within the circle of the Empress Eudocia and her father, the pagan sophist Leontius. In any event, Proclus did not move immediately to Athens, but rather returned to Alexandria where he studied logic and mathematics with distinction. At the age of 19 he moved to Athens to study at the 'Academy'.

Proclus' talent was quickly recognized in Athens. Syrianus was at this time the acting head of the school, and with him Proclus embarked on the first part of the Neoplatonic curriculum – the works of Aristotle. Indeed, Proclus became such an intimate of Syrianus that he lived in his house, calling him 'father'. Syrianus persuaded the aging Plutarch of Athens, who had retired as head of the Academy, to instruct his star pupil

---

[1] For the Greek text see Boissonade (1966), and for an English translation, Edwards (2000).
[2] There is some uncertainty about the date of his birth. What Marinus tells us about the date of his death and the length of his life is incompatible with the horoscope that Marinus provides for Proclus. The issue is well discussed in Siorvanes (1996).

2

in Aristotle's psychology and Plato's *Phaedo* (*VProc.* 12). Such was Proclus' progress that at least some version of the work before us was written in his twenty-eighth year (*VProc.* 13). The date of Syrianus' death is not clear. Proclus became *Diadochos* or 'Platonic successor' either immediately afterwards or perhaps after a brief interlude in which Domninus assumed leadership.[3] Thus Proclus was head of the Academy for around fifty years.

Proclus lived a life of strict asceticism. He abstained entirely from sex, and ate meat only in the context of sacrifice where necessary for the sake of piety. His religious devotion apparently imposed considerable strains on his somewhat delicate constitution. His habits included ritual bathing in the sea year-round, all night vigils, and fasts. He died at seventy-five years of age, though for the last five years of his life he endured ill-health (*VProc.* 26). At his death Marinus tells us that he was 'judged worthy of the rites according to the ancestral custom of the Athenians' (*VProc.* 36, trans. Edwards). He was buried in a common tomb with his teacher, Syrianus, on the hill of Lycabettus.

CULTURAL CONTEXT: PROCLUS AND PAGAN PRACTICE IN ATHENS

One of the things that must strike any reader of Marinus' biography is the extent of Proclus' devotion to the gods. When contemporary readers imagine the office of 'Head of the Academy' it is easy to think of a professional academic – a slightly eccentric but harmless chap who spends a lot of time in the library and rather less lecturing. Certainly Proclus lectured, and wrote commentaries and essays – what university administrators might now characterize as 'research'. But we cannot get a clear picture either of the man or of Athenian Neoplatonism without some appreciation of the centrality of pagan religious practice in the life and perception of both.

It is a familiar point that 'pagan religion' was even less of a unitary thing than the religion of the Christians who adopted this single word to describe so much. This 'other' of Christianity was in fact a fairly disparate collection of localized cults. Central to the various cults was not a body of *doctrine* that one believed in, but rather a set of *practices* that one engaged in. Participation in one set of rites in no way prohibited participation in others. Moreover, people could participate in various rituals with various attitudes and degrees of understanding. It would be a mistake to suppose that, even in the fifth century, we can distinguish completely distinct groups of people – the Christian and pagan communities. Christians

---

[3] Cf. Diller (1957), 188 and Siorvanes (1996), 6.

General introduction to the *Commentary*

sought to incorporate traditional celebrations into the new religion.[4] Doubtless there were many hard-working men and women who didn't really care whether a particular feast was part of a pagan sacrifice or a saint's day. Who today would refuse a day off on religious or political grounds? The self-understanding among those who did not think of themselves as Christians differed too. The word 'Hellenes' is traditionally used of intellectuals who see the tradition of Greek language, poetry, drama, and philosophy (*paideia*) as the core of civilization. The traditions of pagan religious rituals were commonly integrated within this *paideia*. Radical 'Hellenists', like Julian the Apostate, were Hellenes who supposed not only that this integration should be pursued thoroughly and systematically, but that the empty, superficial, populist tide of Christianity ought to be vigorously resisted. Perhaps it is not too far wrong to see the Hellenes as like conservatives in the 'culture wars' in America in the 1980s and 90s. They supposed that empty, superficial post-modernism and deconstruction were assailing the eternal values of 'Western culture'. Attention lavished on the simple *koinê* Greek of New Testament writers might have been regarded by the Hellenes much as conservatives regard cultural studies PhD theses on Madonna or Mills and Boon novels. An important disanalogy with the culture wars of America was that the Christians had the law notionally on their side.

The Theodosian Code of 438 sought to codify laws in the eastern Roman Empire issued since 312. Among these were various proscriptions of pagan religious practices. An imperial decree in 391 notionally prohibited all pagan cults and closed their temples. But it is one thing to pass a law, and another to have it enforced with due diligence everywhere, as we still see in states with laws against sodomy or the possession of marijuana. Pagan religious practices in the fifth century were in a similar situation. Different cities took different attitudes and much depended on the degree of animosity to paganism, the energy and the influence of the local Christian population.[5] One of Marinus' anecdotes about Proclus' arrival in Athens is perhaps revealing about the extent to which Athenian pagans were closeted and the extent to which Proclus was not.

Marinus tells us that Proclus was met upon his arrival in Athens by a fellow Lycian, Nicolaus. On the way back up to the city, Proclus finds

---

[4] Trombley (1995), chapter 2.

[5] Marinus' biography of Proclus is one of the documents that historians appeal to in order to understand the progress toward the closure of the Academy in 529. We discuss below one episode from Marinus' biography that indicates some sort of dispute between Proclus and the Christians. Two other points seem salient. First, Marinus notes rather sadly that – at the time at which he is writing – the city no longer has the use of the temple of Asclepius (29). Second, he makes oblique reference to the removal of the great statue of Athena from the Parthenon (30). It is unclear whether this took place in Proclus' lifetime.

4

Proclus and pagan practice in Athens

that he is tired and they stop to rest. Nicolaus has a slave fetch water from a nearby spring where stood a statue of Socrates. Nicolaus, Marinus tells us, was struck by the fact that the newly arrived Proclus first drank the Attic water (a metaphor for eloquence) in a place sacred to Socrates. After making obeisance (*proskunêsas*), presumably worshipping the statue of Socrates, he continued on. Proclus' readiness to engage in this behaviour contrasts sharply with his initial introduction to the circle of Syrianus. As Proclus talked with Syrianus and Lachares, the sun set and the moon appeared for the first time in her new cycle.[6] The older men wanted to send their new acquaintance away in order that they might worship the goddess (*proskunein*) by themselves. But when Proclus saw the moon he took off his sandals[7] in front of these strangers and greeted the god. Both were struck by Proclus' *parrhêsia* – his paradigmatically Athenian frankness of speech and action – in doing so. Proclus' willingness to display his pagan piety openly contrasts with their initial desire to rid themselves of the stranger so that they might worship in private.

Proclus clearly did things that were forbidden by the law. He sacrificed, not merely cakes or wheat, but animals. Marinus tells us that, on the whole, Proclus abstained from eating meat except where it was necessary as part of the ritual for the sake of holiness (19). He performed ceremonies in which he invoked the aid of the gods for the healing of the sick. Marinus says that he interceded on behalf of ill friends by works and hymns (*ergois te kai hymnois*, 17). He is particularly associated with the cult of Asclepius, whose temple was near where Proclus lived. When Asclepigeneia, who was the wife of the archon Theagenes, fell sick, he 'worshipped Asclepius in the ancient manner' and successfully cured her. But apparently even Proclus knew his limits. Marinus says of this episode:

Such was the act he performed, yet in this as in every other case he evaded the notice of the mob, and offered no pretext to those who wished to plot against him. (*VProc.* 29, trans. Edwards)

But there must, nonetheless, have been limits. It appears that Proclus' devotion to the cults of the Greeks, Egyptians and Chaldeans caused

---

[6] Trombley supposes that the goddess that Proclus worships in this episode is Athena. Edwards supposes that the goddess in question is Artemis and/or Hecate, both of whom are associated with the moon. If the latter is correct, then the action is doubly bold. Hecate is associated with theurgy and magic. Magic was particularly likely to be suppressed and the penalty was death.

[7] As Edward's note ad loc. informs us, the removal of one's footware was not a feature of Greek ritual, though it is associated with Pythagorean sacrifice by Iamblichus. If the anecdote is true, perhaps Proclus thereby related his foreign and wonderful learning from Lycia. Cf. Iamblichus, *VPyth.* 85, 105.

General introduction to the *Commentary*

trouble for him at least once. Marinus gives a cryptic reference to a year in which he left Athens for Lydia.

[He] entered into the billowing tempest of affairs at a time when monstrous winds were blowing against the lawful way of life, yet he carried on a sober and undaunted existence even amid the perils; and once when he was critically harassed by certain giant birds of prey, he left Athens, just as he was, entrusting himself to the course of the world . . . (*VProc.* 15, trans. Edwards)

Saffrey has speculated that the 'tempest of affairs' might have been the closure of the temple of Asclepius and its conversion to a place of Christian worship.[8]

It would have been necessary for Proclus to be particularly circumspect about *theurgy*. For the Neoplatonists of the Athenian school, the theurgical virtues were the highest level of intellectual and moral perfection. The accomplished theurgist understands enough about the way in which various gods are manifested and symbolized through different physical substances in order to open himself to the ubiquitous presence of the divine in all things. It is a form of ritual magic in which the aim is to become united with the gods. However, theurgy was associated with other, less noble forms of magic. The laws forbidding sorcery were more stringently enforced, having had their origins in the reign of Constantine when there was a positive terror of the black arts.[9] The execution of the magician Maximus of Ephesus, associate of Julian the Apostate, in 371–2 set a bad precedent for Hellenes with Platonic leanings and an association with theurgy. Yet in the chapter on Proclus' theurgic expertise Marinus reports that he used his skills to end a drought in Attica, that he protected the city from earthquakes, and that he made use of the prophetic tripod.

One conclusion to draw from the evidence of pagan religious practice in Marinus' biography of Proclus is that Athenian Christians were

---

[8] Saffrey (1975), 555–7. It seems that Proclus was particularly devoted to the cult of Asclepius, as the episode with Theagenes' wife shows. Marinus even notes that Proclus' house was conveniently located in close proximity to the temple. So it is certainly possible that this is what Marinus alludes to. However, if Trombley is correct to place the closure of the temple in the period 481–5, this would mean that Proclus left Athens 'just as he was' in the last five years of his life during the period of his illness (Trombley (1995), 342–4). If the events related in §32 involving a visit to the temple of the sons of Asclepius near Adratta are supposed to take place during Proclus' year in Lydia then this seems odd. Marinus notes that he was deeply affected by the memories of what took place there, and perhaps this implies that the events were significantly in the past. Second, Marinus seems to imply that he put to good use what he learned of the gods of Lydia in the course of his career. But if the trip to Lydia happened in his twilight years, this seems hard to understand.

[9] Trombley (1995), 65.

6

Proclus' writings

relatively tolerant. This may be true, but we should also not overlook the rather special position that Proclus occupied. As the Platonic successor, he would have been a relatively important person in Athens. First, he would have been afforded slightly more latitude than the ordinary non-citizen for speaking his mind in public. The Athenians were apt to tolerate a certain amount of blunt speaking from the inheritors of Socrates' role.[10] Second, Proclus would have had the financial resources to back his favoured causes and Marinus tells us that he did much of this through his friend Archiadas, the grandson of Syrianus who was entrusted to Proclus' care after his teacher's death (*VProc.* 12, 14). In his capacity as *Diadochus*, Proclus would have had an income of 1,000 gold *solidi* a year–a sum that Siorvanes estimates as equivalent to over US$ 500,000 per annum.[11] The intellectual, cultural-historical and financial power of the Platonic successor is physically manifested in the dimensions of the 'Proclus house'. Near the temple of Asclepius on the southern side of the Acropolis is a large structure that some archaeologists believe to be the house used by Syrianus, Proclus and their Neoplatonic school (*VProc.* 29).[12]

So Proclus was no closeted academic happily writing books that few will read. He was a powerful man in a delicate political position. Neither should we think of Proclus' religiosity as an extraneous aspect of his Platonist role – as someone like Isaac Newton, who held a position at Cambridge because of his brilliance in mathematics and physics, but who happened to be interested in alchemy as well. Proclus' religious devotion and his practice of theurgy were not an incidental hobby, irrelevant to his role as a Platonist. Rather, it was partly *because* of his piety that he was deemed worthy of the job. For the Athenian Neoplatonists, the activity of teaching Plato and writing works of Platonic philosophy was itself a spiritual exercise. This has implications for the understanding of Proclus' *Timaeus* commentary. Shortly we examine the contrast between modern commentaries and those of the Neoplatonists, but we should first examine the breadth of Proclus' writings.

PROCLUS' WRITINGS

Marinus tells us that Proclus was a workhorse who wrote and lectured relentlessly. His surviving works alone bear this out. They divide into roughly four genres: commentaries; large systematic works; shorter

[10] See Edwards (2000), 78 for the tradition of 'parrhesia' or 'philosophic frankness' that comes with the role of the philosopher.
[11] Cf. Damascius *Phil. Hist.* 102, in Athanassiadi (1999), and Siorvanes (1996), 22.
[12] Karivieri (1994).

General introduction to the *Commentary*

monographs; and religious hymns and works dedicated to the exegesis of sacred texts other than Plato's.

Commentaries on Plato's dialogues dominate the first group. We have only a portion of Proclus' commentary on the *Timaeus* – it breaks off after 44c where the condition of the newly embodied soul is discussed. But even this portion runs to over one thousand pages in the Teubner edition of the Greek text.[13] Both his massive commentary on the *Parmenides* and his *Alcibiades I* commentary are also cut short.[14] A partial summary of his commentary on the *Cratylus* too has been preserved.[15] Proclus' *Republic* commentary is actually a collection of essays on topics relating to that dialogue.[16] The other surviving work in commentary form is on Book 1 of Euclid's *Elements*.[17] Among the Plato commentaries that are lost to us are works on *Gorgias*, *Phaedo*, *Phaedrus*, *Theaetetus* and *Philebus*. Probably there was also a *Sophist* commentary,[18] a *Theaetetus* commentary,[19] and a commentary on Plotinus.[20] There may also have been a commentary, or perhaps just an essay, on *Symposium*.[21]

Three of Proclus' systematic treatises survive. The best known is his *Elements of Theology*.[22] The least well known is his systematization of Aristotelian physics, the *Elements of Physics*.[23] The third is the massive *Platonic Theology* which attempts to chart the hierarchy of divinities from the highest to the lowest gods.[24]

We also possess three monographs from Proclus: *Ten Problems concerning Providence*, *On Evil*, and *On Fate*.[25] The contents of his work, *Eighteen Arguments on the Eternity of the World* can be reconstructed from Philoponus' criticisms in the latter's *Against Proclus on the Eternity of the World*.[26] There are also two astronomical works. The first, *Outline of the Astronomical Hypotheses*, is a critical examination of Ptolemy's astronomy.[27] The

---

[13] For the Greek text see Diehl (1965). For a French translation see Festugière (1966–8).
[14] In the introduction to his Morrow/Dillon translation of Proclus' *in Parm.*, Dillon suggests that this might be the consequence of an exhausted scribe!
[15] Duvick (forthcoming), Pasquali (1908).
[16] Greek text: Kroll (1899–1901). French translation: Festugière (1970).
[17] Morrow (1970). [18] Annick (1991), Guérard (1991).
[19] Cf. Marinus, *VProc.* 39 and *in Tim.* 1. 255.25. [20] Diller (1957), 198.
[21] A scholion to Proclus' *Republic* commentary at II. 371.14 gives the title 'On the speech of Diotima'.
[22] Greek text with English translation is provided in Dodds (1963).
[23] Ritzenfeld (1912), Boese (1958).
[24] Greek text with French translation is provided in Saffrey and Westerink (1968–97). With a certain amount of caution, one can also make use of the reprint of Taylor's 1816 translation of *Platonic Theology*, Taylor (1995). On the question of the completeness of the work as we have it, see Saffrey and Westerink vol. 6, xxxv–xliv.
[25] Isaac (1977), (1979), (1982). [26] Lang and Macro (2001).
[27] Manitius (1909).

8

Proclus' writings

other is a paraphrase of some difficult passages in Ptolemy's *Tetrabiblos*. There are a couple of lost works mentioned in the *Timaeus* commentary which we may assume would form similar short essays. One is an 'examination of the objections made by Aristotle to the *Timaeus*' (II. 278.27). At least part of this work is preserved in Simplicius' commentary on Aristotle's *On the heavens* (*in Cael.* 640–71). The other is a 'collection of mathematical theorems in the *Timaeus*' (II. 76.22).

We possess fragments of a variety of works that demonstrate Proclus' interest in the canon of pagan Neoplatonic religious texts, as well as in theurgic practices. Among these are the fragments of his commentary on the *Chaldean Oracles*.[28] The *Oracles* were a collection of hexameter verses composed by Julian the Chaldean – or perhaps his son, Julian the Theurgist – during the late second century AD. Previous Neoplatonists had accorded these a great importance. Proclus' chance to study the *Oracles* in depth with Syrianus was lost. The master set his two star pupils, Proclus and Domninus, the choice of reading either the *Oracles* or the Orphic poems with him.[29] They disagreed. While Proclus preferred the *Oracles*, Domninus opted for the works of Orpheus. Alas, Syrianus died shortly thereafter. Proclus, however, seems to have worked up his commentary on the *Oracles* from his study of Porphyry and Iamblichus (*VProc.* 26). Marinus also tells us that Proclus was further instructed in the theurgic rituals associated with the *Oracles* by Asclepigeneia, who was the daughter of Plutarch (*VProc.* 28). A portion of Proclus' work *On Sacrifice and Magic* survives.[30] In spite of his preference to study the *Oracles* rather than the Orphic writings, it appears that Proclus did not neglect these inspired texts either. The *Suda* attributes to him a commentary on the *Orphic Theology*, as well as a work entitled *On the agreement of Orpheus, Pythagoras and Plato with the books of the Chaldeans*.[31] Finally, we have a number of hymns to various gods from Proclus.[32]

In light of his pagan piety and the cultural context, we may regret that we have no record of any work on Christianity. Porphyry, of course,

---

[28] Text and French translation included in des Places (1971). English translation in Johnson (1988).

[29] The 'Orphic writings' that Proclus and the Neoplatonists quote most frequently, however, is the *Rhapsodic Theogony* which is mostly the product of the post-Hellenistic period. Comparisons with the Derveni papyrus suggest that they also encompass earlier material too. On the Orphic poems generally, see West (1983). We cite the fragments of Orphic writings that Proclus quotes by their numbers in Kern (1963).

[30] Greek text, Bidez (1928); French translation in Festugière and Massignon (1944).

[31] It is possible that Proclus' role here was to edit Syrianus' notes and perhaps to add some scholia. A work of the same title is attributed to both authors. Cf. Dodds (1963), xiv. On the question of originality in Proclus' works, see pp. 13–16 below.

[32] Cf. Vogt (1957), van den Berg (2001).

General introduction to the *Commentary*

wrote an infamous *Against the Christians* – in no fewer than fifteen books. Saffrey argued that we can discern coded references to Christians in Proclus' works.[33] But these are very subtle. Proclus' work *On the Eternity of the World* is often given the sub-title 'Against the Christians', but Lang and Marco argue convincingly that this is a later addition.[34] The more obvious targets of Proclus' arguments in this work are other Platonist philosophers, such as Plutarch, who supposed that the *Timaeus* implies a creation of the world in time. Of course, it may simply have been too dangerous by the mid-fifth century to write anything that was openly critical of Christian theology. This would perhaps explain the absence of any such work by Proclus, even though he was not much inclined toward compromise. It seems equally likely that Proclus cultivated the same frosty indifference to Christians that Plato displayed toward Democritus.

To conclude, just as we should not think of Proclus' religious devotion as distinct from his role as Platonic successor, so too we should not imagine that his works divide into two distinct kinds: sober exegesis of Platonic texts and enthusiastic writings on obscure, mystery religions. Proclus' version of the content of Platonic philosophy weaves what may seem to the modern reader to be quite disparate elements into a single synthesis which is pagan religious Platonism.

INTERTEXTUALITY AND INTERPRETATION IN THE NEOPLATONIC COMMENTARY TRADITION

The Neoplatonic commentaries on Plato differ in quite significant ways from the modern commentaries like that of Cornford or Taylor on Plato's *Timaeus*. One potentially misleading way to characterize the difference is to claim that for modern commentators the purpose of the commentary is simply to interpret Plato's text, while for the Neoplatonists, the commentary form serves as a vehicle for the elaboration of the commentator's own philosophical views. This *may*, in fact, be the correct way to contrast the content of, say, Cornford's commentary with that of Proclus, depending on what you take to be the distance between Neoplatonism and Plato's intended meaning. But it is exactly the wrong way to characterize the Neoplatonic commentators' own self-conception. The Neoplatonists would be shocked by such an imputation, not only because they would regard it as false, but because the idea of philosophical theorizing independently of a tradition of interpretation would be *hubris*. Thus, Damascius writes in *On first principles* (*Peri archôn*):

---

[33] Saffrey (1975).   [34] Lang and Macro (2001).

10

The Neoplatonic commentary tradition

And if I should have introduced any innovation (*kainotomoiên*) concerning these things, I would have dishonoured the divine Iamblichus, this man who was the finest interpreter of divine as well as intelligible matters. Therefore, following in the intellectual footsteps of the one who had thought about so many things, it seems right to me to at least propose that ... (I. 291.23–5, translated by Mossman Roueché in Sorabji (2004), II 45)

The activity of philosophy is the same as the act of interpreting Plato because the truth is to be found in Plato.[35] Proclus thinks that Plato was the one man to whom the entire truth about all matters of importance was entrusted by the gods (*Plat. Theol.* I. 6.2). Of course, Plato needs to be properly interpreted in order to yield this knowledge and Proclus belongs to a select band of Bacchic celebrants who have been initiated into divine vision (*epopteia*) of Plato (*Plat. Theol.* I. 6.16). These include Plotinus, Porphyry and Amelius, Iamblichus, Theodorus of Asine and Syrianus. Hence the commentary tradition makes frequent reference to previous interpreters of Plato.

What about philosophers other than Plato, particularly those who cannot be regarded – as Aristotle was[36] – as a follower of Plato? When we find agreement between Presocratic philosophers and Plato, this is not because Plato is influenced by them or takes on board any of their ideas, but because Plato philosophizes in such a way as to agree with any ancient intimation of the truth (*Plat. Theol.* I. 6.30.23). The exception to

---

[35] It is important to note that there may be a slight difference of opinion here between Iamblichus and Proclus on the one hand, and the Neoplatonists of the Alexandrian school on the other. Olympiodorus acknowledges the possibility that sometimes Plato might actually be wrong! Cf. Olymp. *in Gorg.* 41.9 and Tarrant (2000), 97.

[36] For Porphyry's role in establishing the place of Aristotle in the Neoplatonist tradition, see Hadot (1990). For Aristotle and Proclus' teacher, Syrianus, see Saffrey (1990). The Neoplatonists held slightly different views among themselves about the extent of this agreement or *symphônia* between Plato and Aristotle. Proclus and his teacher Syrianus belong to the end of the spectrum that is willing to acknowledge some pretty important sources of disagreement, for example on the theory of Forms. Iamblichus stands at the other end and is accused by later Neoplatonists of going too far and not recognizing *any* disagreement between Plato and Aristotle (Elias, *in Cat.* 123.1–3). Where Proclus does acknowledge that Plato and Aristotle differ on a substantive matter, Plato must be *defended*. This defence, if sufficiently sustained and thorough might make up a supplementary work. Proclus gave an extensive answer to Aristotle's criticisms of Plato's theory of the elements. His reply is preserved in Simplicius' commentary on *De Caelo* III (643.13 ff.). Diller (in *RE* [1893] q.v. Proklos) assigns this fragment to Proclus' 'Examination of Aristotle's refutations of the *Timaeus*' (cf. *in Tim.* I. 279.2). In his defence of Plato's views within the context of the *Timaeus* commentary itself, Proclus will frequently offer Aristotle a fig leaf. So, in the case of the fifth element, Proclus notes that if Aristotle means no more than that the kind of fire in the heavenly bodies is quite different from sublunary fire, and that he indicates this by calling it a fifth substance, then there is no real disagreement with Plato; cf. Baltzly (2002).

11

General introduction to the *Commentary*

this generalization is Pythagoras. Iamblichus had sought to portray *Plato* as a link in the chain running back to Pythagoras,[37] while Pythagoras, in turn, was initiated into the divine mysteries by Orpheus[38] (*Plat. Theol.* I.5.25.24–26.4). Thus we find several places in the *Timaeus* commentary where Proclus establishes the correctness of (his reading of) Plato's claims by showing how this agrees with something in the Orphic poems. There are two other sources unfamiliar to the modern student of Plato that Proclus draws upon for confirmation of what Plato means. The first is Homer. Proclus argued, particularly in his Fifth and Sixth Essays on Plato's *Republic*, that when Homer is read 'symbolically' what is meant is in agreement with Plato's divine philosophy.[39] Plato's criticisms of poetry in the *Republic* are actually directed only at 'mimetic' poetry, but Homer's works are the product of divine possession. The other, frequent source of a *confirmatio* for Proclus' reading of Plato will be the *Chaldean Oracles*.[40] Throughout the *Timaeus* commentary, Proclus is anxious to show how the truths symbolically encapsulated in these inspired works agree with Plato.

Two further points of comparison between Proclus' *Timaeus* commentary and that of apparently similar modern commentaries are worth noting. First, some, but not all, modern Plato scholars work with various hypotheses about Plato's philosophical development. Neither Proclus, nor any other ancient Platonist, considers genetic explanations of apparent differences in doctrine between dialogues. Thus Proclus feels perfectly free to cite other Platonic texts as confirmation of his reading of *Timaeus*. Second, few modern scholars of Plato work with as strong a view about the unity of each Platonic dialogue as Proclus and his fellow Neoplatonists. Iamblichus was perhaps the first to insist that each dialogue has a specific target or *skopos* toward which it is directed. *Every* aspect of the dialogue directs the reader toward this end when it is correctly interpreted. Thus there is no feature of a Platonic dialogue that is, in principle, too trivial or tangential to comment upon. Where it appears that there is no strong thematic unity between one part of a dialogue and later parts, such a unity must be discovered in analogical or allegorical readings.

Finally, it is important to keep in mind the different purposes for the composition of these commentaries. People study the texts of Plato and Aristotle for many reasons. The Neoplatonists studied them with the ultimate goal of union with God, the unitary source of all

---

[37] O' Meara (1989)   [38] Iamblichus, *VPyth.* 28.146, cf. Brisson (1987).
[39] Lamberton (1986), Sheppard (1980).   [40] Brisson (2000), Brisson (2003).

Formal features of Proclus' commentary

existing things.[41] They approached this goal systematically, reading philosophical works in a set order under the direction of a qualified teacher.[42] Students begin with the works of Aristotle, as Proclus himself did when he read them with his teacher, Plutarch of Athens.[43] Iamblichus likely introduced the order of the dialogues that Proclus supposes is the right one.[44] There are some doubts here because the text is corrupt, but it is clear that students began the study of Plato with *Alcibiades I*, *Gorgias*, *Phaedo*, *Cratylus*, *Theaetetus*, [probably *Sophist* and *Statesman*], then *Phaedrus*, *Symposium*, and *Philebus*. The final or crowning dialogues were *Timaeus* and *Parmenides*. The extant commentaries by Proclus on *Alcibiades I*, and then on *Parmenides* and *Timaeus*, thus represent very nearly the alpha and omega of Neoplatonic studies of the 'greater mysteries' of Plato.

This also means that the content of the *Timaeus* commentary is pitched to a very advanced audience in terms of the Neoplatonist curriculum. Proclus assumes that the audience for these lectures will be sufficiently familiar with the texts of Plato that they will immediately recognize allusions to them – or indeed to the *Oracles* or anything else in the Neoplatonic canon. Proclus also assumes that his audience is both familiar with, and convinced of, the fundamental correctness of the basic principles of Neoplatonic metaphysics. His *Timaeus* commentary therefore offers not so much an articulation and defence of these principles, but an application of them.

FORMAL FEATURES OF PROCLUS' COMMENTARY

The origin of Proclus' *Timaeus* commentary as a series of lectures also deserves some comment. The first implication to consider is that of authorship. Some Neoplatonic commentaries are explicitly said to be *apo phônês*. This means that the content of the commentary is derived

---

[41] Cf. Ammonius, *in Cat.* 6.9–16 and Sedley (1999b) for the Platonic antecedents of this specification of the goal or purpose of life and philosophy.

[42] Cf. Elias *in Cat.* 107.24 where he discusses Proclus' work 'Being led by one who knows' on the texts of Aristotle.

[43] Marinus, *VProc.* 28. The justification for beginning with Aristotle can be found in the introductions to the *Categories* commentaries beginning with Ammonius. Prior even to the logical works of Aristotle, a student could read Porphyry's *Introduction* or *Isagôgê* to the *Categories*. It is also possible that they might hear a course of lectures on an ethically uplifting work. Simplicius' commentary on Epictetus' *Handbook* or *Enchiridion* provides an example.

[44] *Anonymous Prolegomena to Platonic Philosophy*, 26

General introduction to the *Commentary*

from a lecture given by someone other than the compiler.[45] Such commentaries sometimes record the name of the compiler and note that he has included some observations of his own.[46] Proclus' commentaries are generally not of this sort.[47] However, there is good reason to believe that his *Timaeus* commentary in particular is significantly indebted to the lectures of his teacher, Syrianus, on the dialogue. First, there is a revealing remark in Proclus' biography by Marinus. Recall that Proclus first studied with the aging Plutarch of Athens. Marinus tells us that Plutarch 'exhorted him to write down what was said' in order that 'when these notes were filled out by him (*symplêrôthentôn autôi scholiôn*), there would be a commentary (*hypomnêmata*) on the *Phaedo* in Proclus' name' (Marinus, *VProc.* 12). The *Timaeus* commentary is not perhaps tied *quite* so closely to the content of someone else's teaching. Having read Aristotle and the *Phaedo* with Plutarch, Proclus was initiated into the greater mysteries (*mystagôgia*) of Plato by Syrianus. Here too he made rapid progress.

> Working day and night with tireless discipline and care, and writing down what was said (*ta legomena . . . apographomenos*) in a comprehensive yet discriminating manner, Proclus made such progress in a short time that, when he was still in his twenty-eighth year, he wrote a great many treatises, which were elegant and teeming with knowledge, especially the one on the *Timaeus*. (Marinus, *VProc.*13, trans. Edwards)

Consistent with this description of the circumstances of its composition, Proclus' *Timaeus* commentary frequently reports and endorses the opinion of 'our teacher' on some disputed point. Should we conclude that such ideas as are endorsed in the commentary, but not explicitly attributed to anyone, therefore belong to Syrianus, not Proclus? There are cases where the content in Proclus' works is not attributed, but where

---

[45] Praechter (1990), Richard (1950).

[46] For example, the works of Ammonius – son of Proclus' fellow pupil, Hermias, and eventually Proclus' own student as well – are particularly likely to be *apo phônês*. Only his commentary on Aristotle's *De Interpretatione* was written out by him. His commentaries on Porphyry's *Isagôgê*, Aristotle's *Categories* and *Prior Analytics* were transcribed by someone else but listed under Ammonius' name. Ammonius' lectures on *Metaphysics* appear as a commentary by Asclepius. His commentaries on *Prior Analytics*, *Posterior Analytics*, *On Generation and Corruption*, and *De Anima* appear under the name of Philoponus. In the case of the last three, Philoponus notes that the commentary includes some of his own additions.

[47] The exception here is the very incomplete *Cratylus* commentary. This comes down to us described as 'extracts from the *scholia* of Proclus on the *Cratylus*'. We have no idea who the extractor might have been.

Formal features of Proclus' commentary

we can find exactly the same views in some of Syrianus' surviving works.[48] On the other hand, Sorabji has argued persuasively that Proclus often modifies and extends some ideas found in Syrianus in important and interesting ways.[49] One possibility is that we should see a distinction between *scholia* and a commentary or *hypomnêmata*.[50] The notes from someone's lecture get 'filled out' to a greater or lesser extent. Once filled out, they constitute a commentary that can – but need not – be regarded as the work of the person who thus filled out the *scholia*. The filling out might be accomplished by incorporating material from other commentaries or by adding thoughts of one's own. The Neoplatonists' general attitude toward innovation, considered above, would militate against any tendency to highlight one's own contribution.[51]

Finally, the fact that Proclus' *Timaeus* commentary derives from lectures accounts for some of its structural features.[52] As the genre of Neoplatonic commentary evolves, it becomes increasingly rigid in its structure. This structure is clearly displayed in Olympiodorus' commentaries on *Gorgias* and *Alcibiades*. After the all important preliminary remarks in which the lecturer isolates the *skopos* or target of the dialogue, discusses characters and their symbolism and so on, there is a division of the text into sections (*tmêmata*). Each section is then further divided into a lesson (*praxis*) which may include a title. Each lesson begins with a text to be interpreted – the *lemma*. The general interpretation (*theôria*) follows. After this, various points in the *theôria* are often recapitulated in an examination of particular words or phrases from the text under discussion. This portion of the lesson is called the *lexis*. Proclus' commentary

---

[48] The commentary on the *Phaedrus* by Proclus' fellow pupil, Hermias, is increasingly treated as evidence for the views of Syrianus. In addition, there are portions of a commentary on Aristotle's *Metaphysics* (Books 3, 4, 13 and 14). Dodds' introduction to *ET* (p. xxiv) gives some examples of parallels between the *Metaphysics* commentary and Proclus. See also Sheppard (1980), 42.

[49] Sorabji (1988), 111–19.   [50] Lamberz (1987).

[51] David Blank considers the commentary of Ammonius on Aristotle's *De Interpretatione*. Ammonius' introductory remarks suggest that the commentary reflects the content of the notes he took from his reading of this text with Proclus. Comparison with the *De Int.* commentary of Boethius suggests that he has filled out the *scholia* from Proclus with material largely drawn from Porphyry's massive (and no longer extant) commentary on the same work. Ammonius acknowledges his indebtedness to Proclus at the beginning (1.6–12) and humbly comments that, if he has added anything to the clarification of Aristotle's very challenging text it will be 'thanks to the god of eloquence.' Cf. Blank (1996), 2–4.

[52] On the form of Proclus' commentary in contrast with that of later Neoplatonists, see Festugière (1971). For the theôria-lexis division in this commentary see now Martijn (2006), 152–5.

General introduction to the *Commentary*

on the *Timaeus* does not conform rigidly to this structure, though the outlines of it are certainly visible. Although there is no formal division into lessons the commentary does present the *lemma* to be commented on. The number of pages devoted to the discussion on different *lemmata* varies greatly. Frequently something like a general interpretation comes immediately after the *lemma*, followed by *lexis*. Sometimes, however, Proclus will examine key phrases within the *lemma* first. Moreover, the *lexis* seldom merely recapitulates the *theôria*. Proclus often takes up problems that are traditionally asked about particular phrases or the meaning of the whole passage under discussion. His general interpretation is often reinforced in sections where he invites the audience to consider the facts themselves (*ta pragmata*) independent of any connection with Plato's text. As one might expect, Proclus finds that such independent considerations confirm the truth of what he supposes Plato's text to mean.

THE *SKOPOS* OF THE *TIMAEUS*: THEOLOGY AND PHYSIOLOGY

The extant portion of Proclus' *in Timaeum* is divided into five books. These divisions mark more or less significant breaks in the text.

- Book 1 contains an introduction and exposition of the recapitulation of the *Republic*[53] and the myth of Atlantis.
- Book 2 covers *Timaeus* 27c–31b: from Timaeus' invocation to the gods to his conclusion that the generated cosmos is unique.
- Book 3 covers *Timaeus* 31b–37c. This content may be roughly divided between an account of the body of the world and an account of the generation of the soul from Being, Sameness and Difference; its form or shape, which mirrors the heavens; and its activities.
- Book 4 covers *Timaeus* 37c–40e and is the shortest of the five books. It opens with a discussion of time and the heavenly bodies. It concludes with a discussion of the traditional gods.
- Book 5 covers 40e–44d where the commentary breaks off. It takes up with the genealogy of the traditional gods, spends considerable time on the address of the Demiurge to the junior gods, and their distribution of souls into bodies. It concludes with a discussion of the difficulties faced by embodied souls and the structure of the human body.

---

[53] Proclus supposes that it recapitulates the *Republic* (I. 4.12). Against this, see Cornford (1957), 4–5.

16

The *skopos* of the *Timaeus:* theology and physiology

What, apart from the order of Plato's text, gives Proclus' commentary a structure of its own? As noted above, one thing that sets the tradition of Neoplatonic commentary apart from the modern commentary tradition is a strong presumption about the unity of every Platonic dialogue. Among the first tasks of any commentary is to articulate the *skopos* or thing at which the work to be examined aims. This strong unity assumption justifies a meticulous examination of every word in the text. There can be no purely extraneous elements in the dialogue, nor any unit of meaning so small that it plays no role in the overall plan of the work. Morever, the assumption of the single *skopos* for each work was also a way of placing limits on attempts to find significance in various aspects of Plato's texts. Attempts to find some unity in every Platonic dialogue often took the form of allegorical readings of the text. An illustration of how a specification of the *skopos* can legitimate one among a variety of possible allegories is provided in Proclus' *Parmenides* commentary.

The *skopos* of the *Parmenides* (*in Parm.* 641) is 'all things insofar as they are the offspring of one cause and are dependent upon this universal cause' (Syrianus) and 'insofar as they are thereby deified' (Proclus). This reading of the *skopos* bears out Proclus' allegorical interpretation of the introduction of the dialogue. Recall that the conversation is related fourth-hand. There is the conversation (i) that first took place between Parmenides, Zeno and Socrates; (ii) Pythodorus, a friend of Zeno, related it to Antiphon; (iii) Antiphon relates it to the Cephalus and the philosophers from Clazomenae; (iv) Cephalus relates this episode to some unknown person – it is this conversation that the reader 'overhears'. Proclus claims that (iv) symbolizes the enforming of sense objects, since the indefinite auditor is like the indefinite receptacle. (iii) symbolizes the procession of Forms into genera and species. (ii) corresponds to the procession of Forms into Soul – a correspondence that is confirmed by Antiphon's involvement with horses and the image of the soul as a chariot with two horses in *Phaedrus*. Finally, (i) corresponds to the structure of Nous: Parmenides, Zeno and Socrates standing for Being, Life and Intellect respectively (*in Parm.* 625.37–630.14). Doubtless there are any of a number of correspondences between the conversations and persons of this dialogue and various elements in Neoplatonic ontology. However, Proclus' insistence that the dialogue has as its goal or *skopos* to speak about all things insofar as they are products of the One is used to vindicate an allegorical reading which includes all the levels from *Nous* to the sensible realm (644.3 ff.).

So what is the *skopos* of the *Timaeus*? It is among the first things that Proclus tells us about the dialogue:

General introduction to the *Commentary*

> This whole dialogue, throughout its entire length, has physical inquiry (*physiologia*) as its target, examining the same matters simultaneously in images (*en eikosi*), and in originals (*en paradeigmasin*), in wholes (*en tois holois*) and in parts (*en tois meresi*). (*in Tim.* I. 1.17–20, trans. Tarrant)

Let us first consider what Proclus alleges the dialogue aims at and then discuss how it carries out this examination.

The claim that the *skopos* of the dialogue is *physiologia* might lead us to expect that it is not also a work replete with theological content. After all, for the Neoplatonists *physis* or Nature is either the lowest manifestation of Soul which is incapable of reverting upon its cause and so not separate from the matter that it informs (Plotinus III.8), or some principle of motion that inheres in body but which is distinct from soul (Simplicius, *in Phys.* 286.20 ff.). In either case, it is nearly at the bottom of the levels of being in Neoplatonic metaphysics. But Proclus divides the study of Nature into three parts. One part does investigate matter and material causes. A second part studies form as well, since this is more properly a cause. But *Plato's* study of Nature is of the highest kind since it postulates the true causes of these things: the productive, paradigmatic, and final causes (I. 2.1–9). So the proper investigation of Nature requires that we ascend back up the onto-causal ladder to the Demiurge, then the All-Perfect Living Thing upon which the Demiurge models the cosmos, and finally the Good for the sake of which it comes to be (I. 2.29–4.6). Thus, while the *skopos* of the *Timaeus* appears to be merely physiology, it is in fact a work of *theology*.

Let us now turn to the themes through which the dialogue investigates the *skopos*. These oppositions – images versus paradigms; universals or wholes versus parts or particulars – figure repeatedly in Proclus' attempt to impose an orderly architectonic upon the dialogue. The integration of the recapitulation of the *Republic* and the myth of Atlantis makes use of the first opposition. They are an investigation into the order (*taxis*) of the cosmos through *images* (I. 4.7). This understanding of the role of these episodes in Plato's dialogue is summarized again at the beginning of Book 2 of the commentary where Proclus begins the transition to the speech of Timaeus. The architecture of this book is harder to characterize in terms of the oppositions invoked in the statement of the *skopos*. In general we may say that it carries the investigation of the cosmos further through examining its *paradigms*: the Demiurge and the All-Perfect Living Being upon which the Demiurge models the realm of generation.

At the opening of Book 3, Proclus explicitly attempts to reimpose these oppositions on the text. He now describes the contents of Book 2 as providing an initial foundation (*hypostasis*) of the universe with reference

The *skopos* of the *Timaeus:* theology and physiology

to wholeness (*kath' holou*) that it has from its creation (II. 2.9). In virtue of this, it is made divine, possessed of intellect and ensouled through resembling the All-Perfect Living Being. But, Proclus tells us, Plato then goes on to provide us with a second foundation of the universe that creates a division of the universe into universal *parts* and intact *wholes*. By this, he says he means the psychic being and the corporeal being just considered in themselves. Thus, while Books 1–2 tend to pursue the *skopos* of the entire work through the theme of paradigms and images, Book 3 picks up the theme of wholes and parts that was introduced in the initial statement of the *skopos*. While Proclus returns to this theme time and again, the framework within which he organizes Plato's text from Book 3 onward consists in the idea that the Demiurge gives to his creation ten gifts. Recall that according to Plato's text, the Demiurge does not merely make a cosmos: he makes a *visible god* (34ab; 62e; 92c). Book 3 breaks Plato's account of the creation of the cosmos into ten stages corresponding to ten gifts that the Demiurge bestows on his creation which make it a god. These ten gifts organize Proclus' exposition of Plato's text not only in Book 3, but right through Book 4, where the last gift is bestowed (III. 98.12 ff.). They also hark back to the original statement and explication of the *skopos* in Book 1. As noted above, the *Timaeus*' investigation of physiology really entails an investigation of theology. Tracing the productive, paradigmatic and final causes of the universe takes us back to the Demiurge, the Form of Living Being itself and the Good. The organizing theme of the ten gifts of the Demiurge makes clear another way in which the *Timaeus* is a theological work. The ten gifts are properties that make the cosmos itself a god.[54] So the study of divine matters is implicated with physiology (properly understood), not merely because the real causes of the universe are transcendent divine ones, but because the product taken as a whole is itself a divinity.

In general, then, Proclus' commitment to the fundamentally physiological-cum-theological *skopos* of the *Timaeus* yields a commentary that moves at several levels. If the surviving fragments of Iamblichus' commentary on this portion of Plato's text are representative, then we may say that Iamblichus engaged with the dialogue primarily at a symbolic and allegorical level. To be sure, Proclus thinks that the *Timaeus* communicates many truths about the various ranks of hyper-cosmic gods, as well as those within the cosmos. It is, in this sense, a theological work. But it is also a work of physiology or natural science and at many points Proclus is keen to show that (what he takes to be) Plato's view is defensible as a contribution to Greek natural science and mathematics.

---

[54] Note that this additional factor in boosting the *Timaeus* into the realm of theology is noted in Proclus' introductory discussion of the *skopos* of the dialogue (I. 3.33–4.5).

19

General introduction to the *Commentary*

This tendency explains the dense, encyclopaedic character of Proclus' commentary. It surely moves at the level of high-flown Neoplatonic theology in some parts. But it also seeks to vindicate Platonic doctrine by means of arguments constructed from materials that are not solely the province of Neoplatonists. The mature Platonic philosopher should know these things as well because those who practise dialectic can defend their views against all objections (*Rep.* 534bc).[55] This is part of what is required in mastering dialectic. It is also characteristic of the dialectician that his view be *synoptic*: he must see the interconnections between things and be able to engage every subject at every level (*Rep.* 537c).[56] Proclus' commentary perhaps takes the form that it does – an exhaustive pursuit of physical matters back up to their divine causes – because he wishes to make sure that his Platonic pupils become genuine masters of dialectic. The character of Proclus' commentary would thus correspond to the place that it has in the Neoplatonic curriculum.

[55] See Proclus' account of the three forms of dialectic at *in Parm.* 989.13. As a master of the second form – that which involves recollection of true being – Socrates is able to engage in the other two forms which involve the refutation of false opinions.

[56] For the superiority of the synoptic mode of apprehension, see *in Parm.* 1026.18 and *in Tim.* I. 148.27.

Introduction to Book 1

THE STRUCTURE OF BOOK I OF PROCLUS' COMMENTARY

Book one covers the first 204 pages of the first volume of the Greek edition by E. Diehl. In the course of these two hundred pages Proclus introduces his treatment of the work as a whole in about thirteen pages. He then discusses just under fourteen pages of Burnet's Greek text of Plato, from 17a to 27b of the Stephanus edition that supplies the universal method of referring to Plato's text in modern times. That means that it is entirely given over to matters that precede Timaeus' treatment of the physical world, the part that has been so influential over two millennia, and the only part of interest to many scholars. In the course of these pages Socrates had provided a summary of some of the most prominent features of the state that had been proposed at length in the *Republic*, explaining that he would like to be able to picture that state in operation. And then Critias had explained the feast of words that others then present planned to offer Socrates in return, including a preliminary treatment of a story supposed to have been passed down to him by his grandfather, who had heard it from Solon, who had in turn heard it from an Egyptian priest. That story had been about a conflict between prehistoric Athens, the city of Athena, and Atlantis, once sacred to Poseidon.

There are many reasons for the length of Proclus' treatment of these pages, though the fact that he devoted a book to them seems from the closing statement to have been due to the fact that Porphyry and Iamblichus had also done so. The commentary tradition tended to absorb earlier material, reusing it and building upon it, so that while some issues receded in importance they tended not to be forgotten. Furthermore, Porphyry had been keen to promote the idea that Plato's prologues were always philosophically important, opposing here the view of Severus in particular. He returned to a version of a view that surfaces at one point in the anonymous *Theaetetus* commentary (IV. 23–6) where prologues are said to be useful for the guidance they can offer about appropriate ways to behave, both in pursuing one's studies and in a variety of other ways. However, Porphyry's idea of the prologues' moral relevance seems to have been fuller, more closely related to his psychology, and so leading on more naturally to much of the later material in a work such

Introduction to Book 1

as the *Timaeus*. Iamblichus, however, insisted on treating any dialogue as having a unity of purpose, and all material within it as contributing towards this, so that a dialogue with the natural world as a focus must have preliminary materials that enabled one to reflect upon the natural world, whether directly or indirectly. Proclus, following his master Syrianus, broadly accepted Iamblichus' position, but required that preliminary material be found to have a bearing not just on physics but also on the lower levels of theology. By this I mean those gods who by virtue of the creative, life-giving, or protective roles were somehow involved in processes affecting the natural world. Such lines of interpretation would inevitably take many pages to explain and defend.

This accounts for the length of the treatment, but what structure did Proclus afford to it? This may be best considered by looking at the opening of Book 2 (I. 205.4–12):

> The prelude of the *Timaeus* offers two principal themes, a summary of Socrates' constitution, and a brief narration of the battle of the Athenians against the Atlantines and the ensuing victory over them. Each of these accounts makes a very important contribution to the overall study of the cosmos. The structure of the constitution, though object of knowledge in its own right, fitted in primarily with the organization of the heaven, while the narration of the war and the victory offered us a symbol of cosmic rivalry.

So there are only two main parts of the book, divisible no doubt into multiple further parts, but seen by Proclus as reflections of the universe, in the former case of its structural unity, and in the latter case of the polar oppositions that pervade it. The role of each will be considered in greater detail in due course. Here, however, we shall consider the space that Proclus allots to them.

The absolute preliminaries begin at 14.4, and, while gradually leading into matters pertinent to the constitution, might be said to conclude at 28.14, while texts treating the individual aspects of this constitution are discussed from 33.1 until 55.26. Next Socrates' reasons for wanting to proceed further and the reactions of the others are discussed in detail from 55.27 to 74.25. The story of Athens and Atlantis is now introduced, and some aspect of it remains in central focus until 192.27, taking up well over half the book, before discussion of some further concluding lemmata occupies the last twelve pages.

In the course of this introduction we shall first examine the history of commentary on the *Timaeus* and related matters, since the importance of this commentary for the history of Platonic hermeneutics is unrivalled. Not only does it contain a great wealth of earlier interpretations, but it usually names the figures whom Proclus associates with them, in sharp contrast with his practice in the *Commentary on the Parmenides*. The

Interpreting the *Timaeus* in antiquity

interpreters' names that he offers range from Crantor, perhaps already writing at the end of the fourth century BC, to Proclus' own fifth-century AD companion, Domninus (110.1). Many scholars first encounter Proclus as a source for fragmentary material on the history of Platonism or of Platonic interpretation, and it seems appropriate to offer this history in the first volume of our translation. Following this study we shall turn our attention first to Proclus' general remarks about the *Timaeus*, the correct approach to it, and its relation to its sister-dialogues the *Republic* and *Critias* (*in Tim.* I. 1.4–14.3; 198.21–204.29). Then we shall devote a section each to his treatment of the summary of the *Republic* and of the myth of Atlantis. There will once again be considerable historical material in our discussion of Atlantis, as the evidence of Proclus has often been quite wrongly interpreted here. I shall argue that Proclus actually knew of no Platonist authorities who maintained that the account of Atlantis was historically true.

INTERPRETING THE *TIMAEUS* IN ANTIQUITY

Some observations on Plato

It is well known that Plato did little to make the interpreter's task easy. We have come to think of the history of philosophy as something akin to a history of well-reasoned belief concerning philosophic issues. Many in late antiquity seemed to agree, insofar as the history of philosophy was often seen in terms of doxography – of lists of successively held doctrines on key issues. However, this was not a major activity of Neoplatonists, who seem to have thought it more profitable to record the history of philosophy in terms of lives. In the lives of major philosophers, such as those of Pythagoras, Plato, Plotinus, and Proclus (written by Iamblichus, somebody close to Olympiodorus, Porphyry, and Marinus respectively), philosophy could be seen to be acting itself out, giving evidence of the consequences of doctrine for life, particularly moral and religious life. The lives of Diogenes Laertius had done something similar, though including summaries of the doctrine of some major figures.

Hence, not everybody thought that the object of studying a philosopher was the unearthing of that philosopher's views. More typically the goal was to uncover the truth, utilizing past writings in whatever way was conducive to intellectual progress. Some even acknowledged that the truth was dearer than Plato.[1] They were able to point to the words of Plato's own *Phaedo* (91c), where Socrates tells his followers not to

---

[1] This is the attitude of the School of Ammonius and Olympiodorus: Olymp. *in Gorg.* 41.9; Elias *in Cat.* 122–3; Tarrant (2000), 97–8.

Introduction to Book 1

bother about himself, but rather about the truth, and of *Alcibiades I* 114e, where Alcibiades is told not to trust something from another unless he can hear himself agreeing. While Proclus believed that Plato, as a source of inspired writings, was in inspired contact with the truth, this was not quite the same as making Plato's beliefs the goal. Nor did it mean that the discovery of Plato's conscious intentions as a writer was the key to the set of truths that his writings concealed.

The discovery of his own doctrines was never what Plato was encouraging. Recent work on the embedded poetics of early texts has shown that authors were encouraging a certain type of reading long before Plato, and laying claim to the truth in a variety of ways.[2] Plato, by contrast, was deliberately trying to undermine any suggestion that access to the poet's mind was access to the truth. This may be seen in the *Protagoras*, where for Socrates 'the poet's intentions have no existence if he is an inspired poet'.[3] Accordingly the task of the true interpreter is to establish the deeper inspired meaning of a poem, just as Socrates' own attempt to fathom the meaning of the Delphic Oracle is not concerned with the Pythian priestess' views (*Apology* 21a–b). Further legitimization of in-depth interpretation occurs at *Apology* 22b–c, which acknowledges the quality (and by implication the truth-value) of much poetry, while denying that the poets have knowledge themselves. The *Ion* also offers support for any interpreter who is more interested in the truth arising from a chain of inspiration than from the understanding of the mind of either a poet or his interpreter.

Examination of Plato's treatment of the poets immediately raises the possibility that he envisages a similar response to his own writings. Does he play a poet-like role himself, or is he to be distinguished from them as an author who has reasoned knowledge? Should we look for inspired meaning, or for his own reasoned opinions? The latter view would be widely preferred today, but the former has more support in the key text on composition, which also happened to be an important text of Neoplatonic theology. In stunning us with the idea that a sensible person's principal work will not be entrusted to writing (*Phaedrus* 276c–d), Plato makes a claim that applies to himself as well as to the poets. Insofar as it is *his* work, and he has *nous*, writing can achieve little. But consider the palinode from this very dialogue (256a–b), the most poetic passage in Plato that was enormously influential in generating in-depth interpretation among later Platonists. This very passage is not even represented as Socrates' own (244a); it commences by explaining the crazed inspiration of oracles, rites, and the poetic Muse; its content throughout invites

---

[2] See particularly Ledbetter (2003).   [3] Ledbetter (2003), 113.

Interpreting the *Timaeus* in antiquity

in-depth interpretation; and it ends with an injunction to philosophy. The reader is transported to the truth, not told it.

The sceptical reader will perhaps feel that we are using the evidence only of Plato's most poetic text, but even if we turn to the most prosaic of all, the *Laws*, we find the Athenian Stranger casting himself in the role of a serious dramatic poet (817b), and seeing the discussion that has preceded as being somehow inspired (811c). It may seem that in prescribing these texts to be learned and praised, like Homer, by Magnesia's teachers, and to be taught to their pupils, Plato's mouthpiece (if the Athenian can be legitimately so described) is asking that his views be adopted by successive generations. Yet on close inspection, the Athenian is not referring to views of his own, but to the discussion as a whole, and it is not doctrines but a paradigm of political discourse that is to be learned. Indeed the writing of dialogues within which he takes no overt part would not seem to be a natural activity for a writer who thought it important to communicate his own views to the public rather than approved ways for them to discover truths for themselves. If we approach Plato in the belief that our goal must be the discovery of his own doctrines then we approach him with an attitude that is ultimately inimical to his own purposes.

If this is true elsewhere in the corpus it must surely be true of the sequence, possibly unfinished, that constitutes the *Timaeus* and *Critias*. We are given some reasons for taking 'Timaeus' seriously (20a), but none for trusting 'Critias' or 'Hermocrates'. The truth-value of almost everything said is kept in doubt by remarks that make us think, and think inconclusively, about what is said. The character from whom the reader who seeks Plato's own views expects to find them, 'Socrates', remains largely a background figure, and never actually gets the opportunity to say what he thinks of Timaeus' cosmology. Surface meanings may regularly be found unsatisfying because 'Timaeus' is often economical in giving reasons for his statements, while enormous challenges await the reader who demands deeper answers and pursues further reasons himself.

Early responses

Plato's rivals, the tragedians, attempted to say something important about the human condition by retelling in their own manner stories that illuminate it. Their theatrical compositions in no way affirm the historic truth of what is depicted, and are frequently based on a newly invented version of the myth. That did not cause them to be called liars, even by a Plato who was happy to criticize them in *Republic* 2 for promoting a different kind of falsehood. Tragedians were still teachers.

25

Introduction to Book 1

Plato's immediate successors, Speusippus and Xenocrates, thought that the creation-story of the *Timaeus* was similarly unfettered by historical truth, in that it did not portray any actual creation.[4] It was designed to illustrate the workings of the world, and the narrative itself was a convenience. The figure of the creator-god was just a *deus ex machina* designed to advance the action. He was the intelligent designer without whom it would have been far more difficult to convey the message that the world is organized in accordance with an intelligent design. While similar figures might be detected in the myth of the *Statesman* (272e) or in the mixing cause of the *Philebus* (27b1), neither has the same paternal character and neither creates so much as organizes.

The voice of Aristotle alone suggested that Plato was seriously proposing an entity with a beginning in time, but no corresponding end.[5] Though at times not a friendly witness, Aristotle is nevertheless not to be dismissed, since he, if anybody, seriously engaged with many of the views that we have come to associate with Plato. Yet Aristotle's charge of inconsistency[6] would have some point even if Plato had not intended the creation-process literally, and Dillon notes in this context that he accused Plato of failing to employ a motive cause,[7] which would in a way imply a recognition that the creator-god is not to be taken at face value.

When discussing issues such as this, and in particular the creation of the soul at 35a–b, the early pupils of Plato seem not to have been preoccupied with what Plato *believed*, but rather with why he wrote what he did. Even Aristotle is not so much criticizing what Plato believed, but what he saw Plato promoting, whether by written or oral means. Plato's immediate successors, Speusippus and Xenocrates, may have discussed Pythagorean or other ancient belief when dealing with Plato's writings,[8] but that does not lead to a preoccupation with *Plato's* beliefs – beliefs that they may have had no commitment to themselves. In general it seems that their challenge was to present their founder Plato in the best possible light, and hence to find *meaning* that others could respond to in the text. They had to make Plato defensible in the light of challenges from hostile

---

[4] Tarrant (2000), 44–5; Speusippus fr. 95 I-P = fr. 61b T; Xenocrates frs. 153–8 I-P; evidence suggests that not only Crantor (below) but also Heraclides Ponticus and Polemo (Dillon (2003), 172–3) understood the *Timaeus* similarly.

[5] *Tim.* 32c, 41b etc.; *De Caelo* 1.12, 2.2.

[6] The inconsistency of postulating an entity that has been brought into being, yet is not subject to destruction.

[7] *Met.* 1.6, 988a7–14; Dillon (2003), 25 n.49.

[8] See for instance Speusippus in Proc. *in Parm.* 7.38–40; Xenocrates' definition of soul (in the *Timaeus*?) as 'self-moving number' is also foisted on Pythagoras (Stob. *Ecl.* 1.49.1), and Xenocrates seems generally to have tried to place his version of Platonism in the Pythagorean tradition, on which see Dillon (2003), 153–4.

Interpreting the *Timaeus* in antiquity

schools. Certainly the refusal to accept the words of a principal Platonic speaker such as 'Timaeus' at face value led directly to an acknowledgement that Plato's text required interpretation.

Interpretation first comes formally from Crantor, a senior figure of the Academy under Polemo, and a strong early influence on Arcesilaus who is held responsible for moving the Academy in a sceptical direction. Polemo himself, while something of a mystery who has left us few fragments with any philosophical meat in them, has recently been the focus of interest, as Sedley and Dillon have accepted that the picture of Old Academic beliefs found in Cicero *Academica* 1.24–32 reflects the official line of Polemo's Academy,[9] rather than being the result of Antiochus' stoicizing distortion of the evidence. The physics reduces the forces of the Platonic universe to a fundamental dualism: an active intelligent power and a passive, quasi-material one. The former is also known as the cosmic soul, providence, and necessity. If this was supposed to underlie Plato's own *Timaeus*, and it surely needed to be reconciled with it somehow if it was an official Academic position,[10] then it is clear that the basic active power of the universe was thought of as being none other than the world-soul itself, identical (perhaps in different circumstances) with both intelligence and the contrasting force of necessity (47e).

Whatever we make of the evidence for Polemo, Crantor worked with him, and is seen as the first commentator by Proclus in the present commentary (I. 76.1–2). It seems that a number of early exegetes did tend to follow his position, to judge from the way that both Plutarch (*Mor.* 1012d) and Proclus (I. 277.8–10) refer to 'those with Crantor'. Crantor (ibid.) explained the 'generation' of the universe in terms of its dependence on a cause other than itself. Plutarch (*Mor.* 1012f–1013a) confirms that he followed the standard Old Academic view that the *Timaeus* should not be read as postulating a creation in time, and offers his account of the mixing of the world-soul, which assumes (on the principle of cognition of like by like) that the soul must be mixed of the principal ingredients of the universe in order that it should be able to grasp all that constitutes the universe. As it needs to apprehend both intelligible and sensible elements in the universe, along with their similarities and differences, it requires these four ingredients within it. So the two primary ingredients in soul would seem to reflect a fundamental dualism in the universe.

A non-literal interpretation of the creation-process was accompanied by some observations on the status of the Atlantis story, some of which seem to support the view that it was historically true, while the rest

---

[9] Sedley (2002), cf. (1999a); Dillon (2003), 168–76.
[10] That would apply even if it were Antiochus' own work, for his own claim to Plato, and to the best known of Plato's works, was more open to challenge.

Introduction to Book 1

support a different view. Proclus puts Crantor at the head of the tradition that treats the story as *historia psile*. If this meant 'unadulterated history' then Crantor would be a literalist on this issue, but the *'psile'* is being used primarily to suggest the absence of any deep allegorical meaning such as Amelius, Origenes, Numenius, and Porphyry demand.[11]

Our information also assures us that Crantor did not dismiss the whole prologue as irrelevant to the main subject of the work. Sedley has recently argued that complaints about the non-integration of the prologues of Heraclides Ponticus and Theophrastus, found in Proclus *In Parmenidem* 659.20–3, go back to Crantor himself.[12] Of three basic attitudes to the interpretation of prologues discussed in that context – that they are irrelevant, that they relate to morally correct behaviour, and that they have a deep symbolic link with the principal theme – it seems clear that the first and last are not those of Crantor. It therefore seems logical to suppose that he was linking the prologue with Platonic ethics, including the ethics concerning the plagiarism charges. That view is also closely associated with Porphyry, and is still reflected in some of the content of the Proclus commentary.

The path to 'Middle Platonism'

There is then a considerable gap in our knowledge of Platonic commentary for quite some time. It may be that partial exegetical discussions of the *Timaeus* were preferred to any attempt to replace the work of Crantor. In his discussion of 24c5–7, Proclus has cause to mention 'Panaetius and certain others of the Platonics' (162.12–13), implying (presumably) that the Plato-loving Stoic from Rhodes had been involved in the interpretation of Plato, but the absence of any other reference to him in this commentary suggests that Panaetius had not contributed more generally to the exegesis of the dialogue. Posidonius, the Stoic who practised in Rhodes, is mentioned by Proclus at 3.125.14 in relation to the world-soul's movements at 40a7–b4. This reference, involving Rhodes, could be disregarded as evidence of any *Timaeus*-specific activities, but for some exegetical fragments in Plutarch, Sextus, and Theon of Smyrna.[13] All these have a bearing on Plato's discussion of the world-soul, involving its basic construction (35a–b), the seven numbers (35b–c), and like by

---

[11] The term *historia psile* would most naturally be derived from Porphyry, the champion of the allegorical interpretation of Atlantis. Hence we should perhaps be considering what this term might have signified for him rather than for Proclus, and the likely answer is that it was meant to cover any non-allegorical interpretation that took into account the story's claim to be true (20d7). I deal with this matter in my introduction to Atlantis.

[12] Sedley (1999a), 141.   [13] F141a, F85, and F291 EK.

Interpreting the *Timaeus* in antiquity

like cognition (37a–c) respectively. This last involved the close association of the world-soul with Pythagorean theory if one judges from its context in Sextus (*Math.* 7.93). Whereas a straightforward commentary on the *Timaeus* would have strongly suggested that the work was being studied within the unlikely context of a Stoic school, a treatise on the world-soul, emphasizing its Pythagorean background,[14] might suggest nothing more than an antiquarian inquisitiveness about the history of philosophy.

Whatever Posidonius had contributed to discussion of the *Timaeus*, it had been widely respected, and made him one of the philosophers whom Plutarch found it natural to refer to when writing his own work on the Platonic soul. Others were Xenocrates, Crantor, and Eudorus of Alexandria.[15] Eudorus remains a shadowy figure, with much of what we think we know about him little better than speculation. Given a late first-century BC date, this is not particularly surprising. He has left no mark in Proclus, and this perhaps reflects Porphyry's failure to take note of his views on the *Timaeus* beforehand. Even in Plutarch we find him drawn to the views of both Crantor and Xenocrates on the composition of the world-soul, but no view of his own is attributed to him on that issue. In general the period from around 50 BC to AD 50 is an age when important developments seem to have taken place: Cicero composes a translation of the *Timaeus*; a de-platonized version of the cosmology, intended to reflect early Pythagorism, arises under the name of Timaeus Locrus; Philo of Alexandria makes extensive use of the *Timaeus* in his own essay on the creation of the world in *Genesis*, and elsewhere;[16] Potamo of Alexandria revives the Plato-commentary under the banner of Eclecticism;[17] and Thrasyllus organizes the Platonic corpus. While none of these events can be linked straightforwardly to provide a broader picture, I think it should be noted that Philo uses the *Timaeus* in the context of what are, in effect, scriptural commentaries, in much the same way as Proclus will later use the religious texts of different traditions to elucidate those of Platonism. And just as Philo utilizes allegorical interpretation of his target texts, so Platonists will soon be using it in the service of understanding Plato.

In Plutarch of Chaeronea, the essayist and biographer who needs to be distinguished from Proclus' early teacher Plutarch of Athens, there is no evidence, I submit, that the Platonic commentary is taking over. Lively oral discussion takes place throughout his life, and is reflected

---

[14] A link that was probably already played up by Xenocrates; see Dillon (2003), 152–3.
[15] I leave aside those who were perhaps more mathematically inclined, such as Theodorus of Soli.
[16] On Philo see particularly the extensive treatment of Runia (1986).
[17] On Potamo, who wrote a *Commentary on the Republic*, see Tarrant (2000), 177–80.

Introduction to Book 1

in his dialogues. But this discussion seems usually to have been rather loosely focused, quite the opposite of a commentary on a key text. We get the feeling, both from Plutarch and from his mathematically-minded contemporary Theon of Smyrna, that more effort had been expended in recent times on Plato's mathematical passages than on straight philosophy. Plutarch himself was happy to tackle individual exegetical problems, but had no appetite for tackling whole dialogues.

A little reflection can help explain why this is so. Plutarch, while happy to engage in allegorical interpretation of Egyptian religion in the *De Iside*, tends to be a literalist in relation to Platonic texts. Thus at those points where a dialogue can be taken relatively straightforwardly, and still yield a meaning that agrees with the rest of the corpus, he probably sees no need for the exegete to intervene at all. Though he finds key passages in a number of dialogues that do require deeper interpretation, he still prefers to anchor his interpretations in the literal meaning of other passages. It is not simply that he stood out against the Old Academic trend, and accepted that Plato meant the creation process in the *Timaeus* to be taken seriously. It is rather that he admires Plato more when he is prepared to speak his mind, as he thinks is the case in the passage on the two souls in *Laws* 10.[18] Non-literal interpretation, at least where a literal one is an option, is for him a struggle for a way out, as we see from his response to Xenocrates and Crantor (especially *Mor.* 1013e). Consequently he will become in Proclus one of the most often used of the Middle Platonists for illustrating the pitfalls of literalism, outshone only by the pedantic Atticus.

The forerunners of Plotinus and Porphyry

The age of Plutarch probably coincides with the rise of the Platonic commentary among professional teachers of Platonism. He may have been fairly close in date to the anonymous *Theaetetus* commentator,[19] who besides his partly extant work on the *Theaetetus* seems to have written commentaries on the *Timaeus* (XXXV.12), the *Symposium* (LXX.12), and the *Phaedo* (XLVIII.10).[20] By his time it is clear that commentary was a natural activity for the Platonist teacher of philosophy, and the genre was already developing many of its enduring features. These include

---

[18] *Mor.* 370f; *Laws* 896e.

[19] Uncertainties persist, and I am not entirely persuaded to date this figure as early as I suggested in Tarrant (1983), even though my case received some support in the CFP edition of Bastianini and Sedley (1995).

[20] This is either a reference to a planned work, or to a work that will follow later in the works designed to be read by his readers.

30

Interpreting the *Timaeus* in antiquity

both the topics that are to be included in the introductory pages (somewhat curtailed in the papyrus), and the division of the text into *lemmata*, which attract about one or two columns of commentary. The lemmata themselves cover most of the text, though there are some omissions. Also worth mentioning is the commentator's shyness of naming rival interpreters, something that applies to the anonymous commentator on the *Parmenides*, to other Proclus commentaries and to Olympiodorus, but not really to *On the Timaeus*.

Also of importance are some basic attitudes to the text itself. It is assumed that Plato has something consistently worthwhile to offer, so that there will always be something to be said that can enhance his reputation. Consequently Plato cannot be seen as one whose views developed in such a way that anything would be completely superseded. Certainly he cannot come to see the error of his early ways, and a unitarian assumption will always control the discussion. Equally vital to the commentator is that the text should *require* exegesis, being in need of its defender and expounder. It is observed that in his investigations Plato does not simply state his views on the topic being investigated, but allows them to emerge in such a way that they become clear enough to the experienced reader (LIX.12–34). The author here distinguishes sharply between a Socrates (not Plato's) who would completely undermine the truth, and one who would conceal or omit it. Such concealment or omission, though compatible with *Theaetetus* 151d, would be the kind of complication that requires the skilled interpreter. Another feature is the development of key snippets of Platonic text that are thought vital for the interpretation of the work in hand: in this case mostly passages from the *Meno* and *Phaedo* as far as one can tell from the surviving pages. Similar developments clearly take place in relation to the *Timaeus*, though the key texts for comparison will be different.

The number of commentators in this period seems to have grown. Besides the papyrus fragments unrelated to the *Theaetetus* commentator,[21] for which only the date of the copy can generally be guessed, there are several persons referred to by Proclus and others. The Athens-based Platonists L. Calvenus Taurus (*fl. c.* AD 140) and Atticus (*fl. c.* AD 175) composed commentaries on the *Timaeus*,[22] as did Severus and either Numenius of Apamea or his close follower Cronius. Some of their work is reflected faithfully in the partially extant *Commentary on the Timaeus* of Calcidius, though it may it have been composed as late as the fourth

---

[21] Fragments exist of what seem to be commentaries on the *Alcibiades I*, *Phaedo*, and *Statesman* (nos. 5, 7, and 8 in *Corpus dei papiri filosofici* III).

[22] We also have a passing reference, from Proclus (*in Tim.* III. 247, 15), to a commentary by Atticus on the *Phaedrus*.

Introduction to Book 1

century. It seems more or less untouched by Neoplatonic influences, and employs other sources from the Middle Platonic period including the Peripatetic Adrastus. Evidence of commentaries on other dialogues is much thinner, though we know various views on some of them.[23]

On the whole, one would suppose that most of those who wrote commentaries on other dialogues also tackled the more popular *Timaeus*, though one cannot be sure. Such commentaries may have omitted the prologue (like Severus, *in Tim.* I. 204.17–18), or the later pages that are full of the details of what we might see as early anatomy. The failure of others to deal properly with this caused the great physician (and part-time Platonist) Galen to write his own commentary on this part, and some of the third book has survived in reasonable shape.[24] What one imagines would have concerned all philosophical commentators on the work is the account of the first principles of Timaeus' cosmology, including the nature of the demiurge and his model, and the soul, both cosmic and human.

In spite of a growing amount of evidence during this period for both commentaries and the interpretation of the *Timaeus*, we should always remember that this evidence does not cohere in such a way as to offer the unified picture that we should like. In particular one should perhaps bear the following difficulties in mind. First, while we have the names of several of those whose commentaries were employed by Plotinus (Porph. *VPlot.* 14), the relevant authors (Severus, Cronius, Numenius, Atticus, and Gaius)[25] have not left us any substantial example of their commentary. Consequently it is difficult to say what *type* of commentary had been available to Plotinus. Second, we have no substantial piece of commentary on the *Timaeus* from anybody before Porphyry whose main income was derived from Platonic teaching. So whereas we can say what at least one commentary on the *Theaetetus* looked like, we cannot simply assume that the same author's *Timaeus* commentary was similar in either scope or format. We could make substantial mistakes by assuming that Proclus' *Timaeus* commentary was going to be similar in scope to his *Alcibiades*

---

[23] A certain Democritus may have written commentaries on the *Alcibiades* and *Phaedo* (on details of which he is found offering views), while Eubulus (also mentioned at Porph. *VPlot.* 20) was said by Longinus to have written on the *Philebus* and *Gorgias*. Harpocration (Suda, s.v.) is supposed to have written a 24-book *Commentary on Plato*, on which see Dillon (1971).

[24] See Schröder (1934). There are other fragments also.

[25] There is at least a possibility here that Gaius' commentary was being read through Albinus' record; likewise, though Numenius may have written a commentary on the *Republic* or on the *Timaeus* rather than mere exegetic works, he may have been being read through the work of Cronius. It is otherwise hard to understand why Cronius should have been mentioned first.

Interpreting the *Timaeus* in antiquity

commentary or in format to his *Republic* commentary, or in assuming that Olympiodorus' *Phaedo* commentary would be similar to his *Gorgias* commentary. Third, though we have examples of commentary from Galen and Calcidius, they cannot suffice to give us a clear idea of what a professional Platonist of the time would have written. Fourth, while we have some reason to suspect that the genre involved much updating of the works of predecessors,[26] and this is even detectable in Proclus, we cannot assume too much similarity between commentaries on any single dialogue between, say, AD 50 and AD 250.

The two main matters that concern us concerning the commentaries and other exegetical works of the period are which commentators Proclus himself uses, and how he knows them. The short answer is that, of Middle Platonists, he refers mainly to Albinus, Atticus, Numenius, Plutarch, and Severus. Comparison with Porphyry's list of those read at Plotinus' gatherings (*VPlot.* 14) shows that Plutarch is the only addition, and this is not surprising if he did not write ordinary commentaries. Besides, Proclus' understanding of Plutarch is perhaps not profound,[27] and in the present commentary Plutarch's name mainly occurs in relation to that of Atticus,[28] who may well have been using Plutarch himself. The thesis that Plutarch is important because Atticus had thought he was important is at least arguable. The only omission is Cronius, whose importance there may have been more as a reporter of Numenius' views, and who does find a place in the *Commentary on the Republic*.

The significant references to Middle Platonists in Book I of the *Commentary on the Timaeus* are as follows:

	Platonist	Others in the context
20.21	Atticus	Others of that age
77.6/23	Numenius	Amelius, Origenes, Porphyry
83.26	Numenius	Origenes, Longinus
97.30	Atticus	Theopompus
204.17	Severus	Longinus, Porphyry, Iamblichus

[26] See Longinus on the work of Euclides, Democritus, and Proclinus at Porph *VPlot.* 20; in later times compare the commentaries on Aristotle's *Categories* from Ammonius' school (under the names of Ammonius himself, Olympiodorus, Philoponus, Elias, and Simplicius), and also Arethas' scholia on the *Categories* (Share 1994).

[27] See on this matter Opsomer (2001a). The evidence suggests to me an incautious assumption on Proclus' part that Plutarch tends to agree with Atticus, rather than any lack of familiarity with Plutarch's writings.

[28] I. 326.1, 381.26–7, 384.4, II. 153.29, III. 212.8.

33

Introduction to Book 1

While I have no confidence that Proclus' knowledge of these authors is uniform, the vast majority of references can be explained in terms of their importance in the age of Porphyry. Certainly it should not be assumed that Proclus has their works open in front of him, and it is plausible that they had become routinely associated with certain positions by Neoplatonist commentators from Porphyry on. It is worth noting here that at 77.6–8 Porphyry will be found to be consciously making part use of the view of Numenius, while at 204.16–20 it is highly likely that Longinus had already remarked on Severus' refusal to tackle any of the prologue.

Whatever we may suppose to be Proclus' means of knowing the Middle Platonists, his level of respect for them was not great.[29] To anybody trained in the more elaborate speculations of post-Iamblichan interpretation, with its extensive literary and religious background, the Middle Platonists would generally have seemed remarkably unsophisticated (as they have sometimes seemed today),[30] and Proclus' attraction to symbolic meanings entails that the more literal interpretations of straightforward Middle Platonists would have seemed to him to imply a lack of depth. Atticus in particular is viewed with little respect, since, like Philo and Plutarch before him, he seems to have reverted with something of a fundamentalist fervour to a literal reading of creation and creator.

However, Middle Platonism was by no means united either in its beliefs or in its approaches to Platonic exegesis. What we refer to by a single convenient label actually embraced many shades of opinion. Ironically, it seems that the second-century interpreter in whom the Neoplatonists found most to interest them was the Neopythagorean Numenius, in part because Numenius analysed texts in such a way as to find a plurality of metaphysical entities where some might not have suspected any complications, and in part because of the imaginative nature of his interpretation of myths and stories. The Atlantis-interpretation found in the present volume is a case in point. Though Proclus himself failed to see the attraction of Numenius, it is clear that Porphyry had done so.

The diversity of Middle Platonism should warn us against trying to see any homogeneous approach to commentary during this period. In particular I feel that I have been too hasty in the past in assuming that there ought to be a close correlation between the different products of the time. Besides commentaries, known to us mainly via small fragments and occasionally as something bigger but still incomplete, the

---

[29] Whittaker (1987) refers in relation to the reference to Albinus and Gaius at *in Tim*. I. 340.23ff. to 'Proclus' lack of interest in the Middle Platonists'.

[30] Part of the function of Tarrant (1983) was to try and see Anon. *Tht.* in a way that better appreciated its merits, against Dillon (1977), 270.

34

Interpreting the *Timaeus* in antiquity

period produced doxographical handbooks (such as Alcinous' *Handbook* and Apuleius' *On Plato's Doctrines*), introductory works designed to assist readers of Plato (such as Albinus' *Introduction* and Theon's *Mathematics Useful for Reading Plato*), and a great variety of treatises. Plutarch and others (including Numenius) also produced dialogues of a kind.

It would be rash to suppose that the writers of handbooks, who necessarily sought to present a philosophical system in a concise form, adopted the same approach to the Platonic corpus as those who wrote commentaries, while treatises show a great variety in the ways of demonstrating allegiance to Plato. An author such as Apuleius, who has left us different kinds of works, seems to approach him more as the skilled unfolder of truths in the treatise *On the God of Socrates* and more as an expounder of doctrines in the handbook *On Plato's Doctrines*. The balance between the attention paid to literary and dramatic elements in the dialogues can shift as an author switches to a different genre. While I can offer no clear example of an author who wants now to communicate his own Platonist system (fathering it all on Plato), and now to help Plato to speak for himself, it would not be surprising if this were the case. In any case commentaries were most naturally a vehicle for the latter, helping the reader to get maximum benefit from the reading of Plato by explaining all that needed to be understood in order to appreciate him. The anonymous *Theaetetus* commentator seems to be doing something like this, as does Olympiodorus in a later age. The commentary of Calcidius, however, is more didactic in style, and we get the impression that Atticus for instance must have been similarly didactic. The gaps in our record offer us little hope of understanding the scope of Middle Platonic commentary, and fortunately this is probably not necessary in the case of Proclus, who is widely assumed to be responding only to such material as had already been reported by Porphyry.

The world of Plotinus and Porphyry

From the point of view of the present commentary the next stage comes with certain individuals who appear in Porphyry's *Life of Plotinus*. Since these had at least been identified by a respected Neoplatonist as making a contribution to debate, their treatment seems more even-handed. Among them were the early teacher of Porphyry, Longinus, repeatedly seen as suspect because of his excessively philological approach (*VPlot.* 14), the pagan Origenes (not to be confused with the Christian writer from the same era), and Amelius Gentilianus. Though almost a full member of the Neoplatonic fraternity, and numbered by Proclus among the Bacchic fraternity of Neoplatonism (*Plat. Theol.* 1.5–6), Amelius is peripheral to book 1 of this commentary. Longinus is mentioned

35

Introduction to Book 1

frequently in book 2, but thereafter only once in book 2 (I.322.24 = fr. 19). Origenes is mentioned several times in book 1 only.

Longinus is from the beginning painted as an individual with a facility for commenting on the language of the dialogue's prologue. This is all the more surprising when one considers the evidence of 204.18–24 (= fr. 37). Longinus apparently thought that a little of the prologue was worth attention, but this did not extend to the Atlantis story, which he thought superfluous. Therefore his practice was to move from Socrates' long speech ending at 20c directly to 27a, where Critias asks Socrates whether the planned programme of intellectual entertainment will suffice. That presumably reflects his preferred practice in class, though five fragments refer to his views between 20e and 24c (= frs. 32–6). Clearly somebody, and presumably his one-time pupil Porphyry, had at some time induced him to offer views on matters outside his standard curriculum. These views had passed into the commentary tradition because they filled something of a gap, since up to this point few commentators seem to have included this material. The second hundred Teubner pages make no reference to Middle Platonist exegesis. A mention of Plutarch at I. 112. is in fact a reference to the treatise *De Facie in Orbe Lunae* rather than to anything to do with commentary. Platonist sources are largely confined to Porphyry and Iamblichus, though Panaetius (with other 'Platonists'), Longinus, and Origines are all brought into a discussion of material on the climate of ancient Athens (24c: 162.11–33), and it seems that Panaetius and others were mentioned there because Longinus had found their view incredible, while Longinus and Origenes owe their place to the fact that they in turn had been replied to by Porphyry.

Longinus (*c.* AD 213–72/3) owes his place in the commentary to his blindness to what Porphyry and Proclus would see as the philosophic issues. He finds stylistic devices instead of doctrine. Perhaps his influence diminishes later in the commentary because, when forced to comment upon doctrine and finding nothing of his own to contribute, he lacked anything distinctive enough to ensure the preservation of his name. The single mention of him outside book 1 is about his view that the Ideas are outside the demiurge and *after him* in contrast to Porphyry's early view that they had been outside and *before* him. Porphyry and Longinus are here merely *representatives* of a debate that had presumably flourished in Middle Platonist times, and they have been chosen as such because of the well-known references to the debate on the issues in Porphyry's *Life of Plotinus* (17–20). In a sense, Longinus in Proclus stands for certain types of error, much as Plato does among certain modern analytic philosophers.

His contemporary Origenes was from the opposite spectrum of philosophy. He had studied, perhaps, in the esoteric classes of Ammonius

Interpreting the *Timaeus* in antiquity

Saccas alongside Plotinus, eventually being less meticulous than Plotinus in keeping these teachings secret (Porph. *VPlot*. 3), though not committing them to writing. Longinus is happy to acknowledge that he had attended Origenes' lectures at Athens, and he includes him among those philosophers who wrote very little, mentioning specifically a treatise on *daemones* (ibid. 20), which agrees well with the material that we have in Proclus. Porphyry himself is able to add a work *That the King is the Only Demiurge*, which in all probability argued that the demiurgic power in the *Timaeus* does not, as Numenius had clearly thought (*in Tim*. I. 303.27–9 = fr. 21), conceal more than one Platonic divinity, and that this divinity is to be identified with the 'King' of the *Second Epistle* (312e–313a), something that appears to be equally opposed to the thrust of Numenius.[31] Such views, and a little else that we know of Origenes, would fit a period when the most talked-of exegetical influence was Numenius; and they also suggest that he was somewhat less radical than either Numenius or Plotinus. While there is nothing to say that he did not lecture on Platonic texts such as the *Timaeus*, it would appear that he wrote no commentary, and so we should assume that any material of written origin in Proclus is responding to exegetical elements in the two known treatises. This exegesis involved the hypotheses of the *Parmenides*, where he denied the presence in hypothesis 1 of a transcendent principle above Being.[32] This would make him fit the 'Middle Platonist' mould better than the Neoplatonist one.

This is not the case with Gentilianus Amelius.[33] From the *Life of Plotinus* we learn that he took up the Plotinian cause against a charge (of Athenian origin) that he was dependent on Numenius (17),[34] against certain Gnostics and their texts (16), and against Porphyry's early views

---

[31] The real demiurgic power in Numenius is the *second* god, while he refers to his first god as 'King', distinguishing this figure from the demiurge at fr. 12.12–14. Here too the most plausible origin of the term 'King' is *Ep.* 2, 312e1 and 313a1. It may be that Numenius supported his attribution to Socrates of a triad of gods (fr. 24.51–3) with reference to the same passage of the *Second Epistle* considered in relation to the remark that 'what is now being spoken of belongs to a young and handsome Socrates' (see Dillon (1977), 367). However that may be, it is clear that the thesis that the King is the only demiurge would run directly counter to Numenian theology.

[32] See Proc. *in Parm.* 635–8; Morrow and Dillon (1987), xxvii.

[33] On him see in particular Brisson (1987); Corrigan (1987).

[34] I prefer not to use the loaded term 'plagiarism', which was not considered seriously reprehensible in itself. What the detractors were trying to say was that Plotinus was more dependent than his reputation suggested on the Neopythagorean. What Longinus will later (20) be acknowledging is that Plotinus was more detailed in his treatment of first principles than Neopythagorean predecessors, but with the sting that they were really Pythagorean principles rather than Platonic ones. See on this Menn (2001), especially 115–18.

Introduction to Book 1

(17). Longinus regarded him as being far too keen to write (20), an opinion that was clearly shared by Porphyry (21). Associated with Amelius is an interpretation of the final part of the *Parmenides*, which divided it into eight parts (as opposed to the more usual Neoplatonist nine).[35] I have rashly, but unrepentantly, associated this view with Moderatus before him.[36]

The link between Amelius and the Neopythagorean tradition is clear. Indeed the tendency to associate Plotinus with Numenius and other Neopythagoreans may well have something to do with the proclivities of Amelius, since he wrote much more freely, and people may have assumed that he was Plotinus' mouthpiece. Unsurprisingly the best-attested link with the Neopythagoreans is with Numenius.[37] We are told by Porphyry (*VPlot.* 3.43–8) of his enormous energy in collecting together 'all that belonged to Numenius' (whether writings or doctrines), and committing most of it to memory. He was clearly influenced by Numenius' exegetical tactics. Hence he too can find a plurality of powers behind the much-discussed text at *Timaeus* 39e7–9 (*in Tim.* III. 103.18–32). In his case it is a triad of divine intellects that is discovered there. He is found again in the company of Numenius on the question of whether intelligibles can participate in the Ideas as well as sensibles (III. 33.33–34.3), and in this case Syrianus adds the additional information that Numenius' friend Cronius held this view.[38] One may also mention that they have closely related allegorical views on the interpretation of Atlantis at I. 76.17–77.6. On theology Amelius goes one better than Numenius in that he analyses the Platonic demiurge into three rather than two (1. 303.27–29; 306.1–3). Most tellingly of all, Iamblichus linked the two. He saw fit to criticize Amelius and Numenius together in a single work for a certain type of speculation about the numbers in the world-soul.[39] He attacks their interpretations of 39e jointly at III. 104.8–16.[40] In his work *On Soul* he links the two philosophers (along with Plotinus and Porphyry) in the view that, even in separable soul, the whole intelligible cosmos and the

---

[35] Proc. *in Parm.* 1052–3. The question of whether this interpretation has to come from a commentary (rather than Porphyrian reports) is discussed by Brisson (1987); note, however, that Amelius' love of writing makes it probable that he would have committed his views to some form of detailed exposition.

[36] (1993), 150–61.

[37] See now Bechtle (1999), 257; cf. Brisson (1987), particularly 801–3.

[38] *in Met.* 109.12–14 = Numenius fr. 46b.

[39] *Tim.* 36d; Iambl. at *in Tim.* 2.277.26–31; strangely, this telling passage is not found in des Places' edition of Numenius. It is fr. 57 in Dillon's collection of the fragments of Iamblichus' commentaries. On the relationship between the two see Dillon's commentary, 337–8.

[40] = Iambl. *in Tim.* fr. 72; see Dillon (1973), 359–60.

Interpreting the *Timaeus* in antiquity

whole divine hierarchy is to be found, with Amelius holding this view tentatively.[41]

I think that it is plain from this that Numenius was the single most important interpreter of the second century AD, somebody to whom Origenes responded conservatively, while Amelius tried to outdo him. His influence in the second century itself is more difficult to assess, for while Harpocration and Cronius are clearly deeply influenced by him, others who were probably late enough to show his influence do not obviously do so. While Proclus must have appreciated Numenius' importance, there is little sign that he knew him first hand or that he understood the reasons for his influence. One reason for this may be the reverent silence that generally surrounded the teaching of Ammonius Saccas, though Nemesius at one point expressedly links Numenius with 'Ammonius the teacher of Plotinus'.[42] It may be that Origenes engages with Numenius because of his importance in Ammonius' background. Suspicions of Plotinus' dependence on Numenius may arise from an awareness of the deep influence of some Numenian background assumptions. Such assumptions do not have to be such as to make Plotinus in any sense a Numenian philosopher. They might rather involve ways in which Platonic texts might be interpreted. They share deep interpretation, the belief that Plato can speak in riddles, the notion that x in Plato can stand for y.[43] And I strongly suspect that they share the confidence that certain texts are crucial for the reconstruction of a Platonic or, perhaps, a Pythagorean system. Besides the *Timaeus*, the *Index Auctorum a Numenio Laudatorum* of des Places refers to *Laws* 10 on cosmic souls, the principal myth of the *Phaedrus*, the *Philebus* on *peras* and *apeiron*, and the Idea of the Good from *Republic* 6. In my view the myth of the *Statesman*, the esoteric passage in the *Second Epistle* and the second part of the *Parmenides* are already among texts that need to cohere with these others.[44] Luc Brisson has recently argued in detail for Numenius' dependence on *Epistle* 2, and the *Epistle*'s connection with the metaphysical interpretation of the *Parmenides*.[45] It is noteworthy that Iamblichus seeks to counter the

---

[41] Iambl. in Stob. *Ecl.* 1.49.40 = Numenius fr. 48.

[42] *De Nat. Hom.* 2.8 = Numenius fr. 4b.

[43] The soul's prison of the *Phaedo* (62b) stands for pleasure (fr. 38), Hermes stands for the expression of reason (fr. 57), and Hephaestus for generative fire, i.e. the life-giving warmth of the sun (fr. 58).

[44] *Statesman* at fr. 12.20 (which recalls 272e5; cf. also *aperioptos* at 11.18); *Epistle* 2 at fr. 12.12–14, on which see above n.87; *Parmenides* at fr. 11.11–15.

[45] See Brisson (1999). The article is important for showing their relevance to the Gnostic *Apocalypse of Zostrianos*, a pre-Plotinian text important for its links with Marius Victorinus, and hence with the kind of philosophy that we had been previously unable to trace back beyond Porphyry. The *Apocalypse of Zostrianos* is itself traced to the environment of Numenius, following M. Tardieu (1996).

Introduction to Book 1

tendency of Numenius and Amelius to see multiple divinities behind the mask of the demiurge by appealing to the way Plato establishes different ranks in the *Sophist*, *Philebus*, and *Parmenides*, and does not roll them all into one obscure reference:

> Plato has not made distinctions between divinities of the kind that they suggest in the *Sophist*, *Philebus*, and *Parmenides*, but he offered distinct accounts of each rank there, and distinguished the hypotheses from one another, keeping separate the one about the One and the one about the Whole, and outlining each in turn in the same manner with its appropriate determinants. (III. 104.10–16)

Iamblichus implies, I think, that they too were used to appealing to these works as the basis of their distinctions, and there is no doubt that the *Parmenides* was foremost in his mind. He may of course have Amelius primarily in mind, but he thinks the argument can work against Numenius as well. While steps towards a collection of key texts were already visible in Plutarch and Taurus,[46] it did not yet seem to include any part of the *Parmenides* or any of the *Epistles*.

Numenius, then, is likely to have played a major part in the development of an in-depth interpretation that sees Plato's philosophy, which is for him a fundamentally Pythagorean philosophy, as embedded in such a way in the dialogues that it requires a riddle-solver to extract it. It interprets Plato's words as standing symbolically for something other than their normal referent, so that the soul's prison of the *Phaedo* (62b), for instance, stands for pleasure (fr. 38) or the war between Athens and Atlantis stands for the struggle between good and evil soul-forces (fr. 37: *in Tim.* I.76).

The first phase of Neoplatonism: Plotinus and Porphyry

It may be objected here that I am speaking as if it were not agreed that Plotinus is the founder of Neoplatonism. That is not quite correct. Numenius' doctrine, his avowed Pythagorism, and in particular his dualism, prevents him from being regarded as anything like a founder-figure of Neoplatonism. What we have been talking of is Numenius' *exegetical* legacy. It is no easy matter to speak of Plotinus' approach to exegesis, because what he wrote was a series of meditative treatises. The commentaries that we know were read in his classes were not those of Plotinus himself, but those of respected predecessors (*VPlot.* 14). Plotinus enjoyed thinking things through in minute detail, and, while several of his treatises are closely linked with exegetical problems, a sustained exegetical treatment of a text was not for him. Sentences could be taken

---

[46] Tarrant (2000), 36–7.

Interpreting the *Timaeus* in antiquity

out of their context, aligned with other sentences upon which he had come to rely, so that Plato begins to become a miscellaneous collection of key passages. They are of course the passages that had been vital to the intellectual world in which Plotinus and Origenes had been raised. Iamblichus' later emphasis upon the integrity and unity of purpose of each mature Platonic dialogue had been timely, for it was precisely the unity of the dialogue that we miss in Plotinian exegesis.

A treatise of the *Enneads* may grow out of consideration of a single key Platonic passage. A good example here is I. 2, which is a meditation upon the single most popular passage of the *Theaetetus* in Plotinus and late antiquity (176a),[47] the passage generally thought to offer Plato's *telos*, and a source of great controversy in respect of the identity of the god to which humans should assimilate themselves. Much else in Plato gets brought into discussion, including the virtue-theory of the *Republic*, the purification of the *Phaedo*, the theory of the disembodied soul from the *Phaedrus*. But there is no place for anything else from the *Theaetetus*.

A good example of Plotinus treating a much-debated exegetical issue of his own day is the first chapter (in fact a small, self-contained treatise) of III. 9. The debate is over the alleged necessity for separating divinities, along Numenian or similar lines, at *Timaeus* 39e. Plotinus feels that the stress on the unity or diversity of Plato's *autozoon* (the What-is-Life), his Intellect and his Discursive Power may differ in accordance with the purposes one has in view (26–8). He is attracted to the idea that discursive thought, with the division that this implies, belongs to something other than intellect, at the next level down, something which he would call soul (29–37). However, he has particular difficulty with the idea that life's paradigm should be outside the intellect that contemplates it, for he is committed to the idea that the intelligibles are not outside intellect, and he suspects that the contemplation of an outside paradigm and an outside truth will mean that it is mere images, and not the truth, that exist within that intellect (8–10). This is a contribution to a debate fuelled by Numenius and continued by Amelius (above), but again it has little connection with the rest of the *Timaeus*.

Well-known treatises dealing with his Platonic exegesis are V. 1 and V. 8. The latter treats a comparatively large passage of the *Phaedrus* (246d–7e). While it brings in the *Symposium* (2) and the *Timaeus* (7) it seldom loses its focus. V. 1, on the other hand, expounds Plotinus' theory of the three hypostases, Soul, Intellect, and One. But in chapters 8 and 9 we have what Bréhier (1956), 7, called 'une sorte d' excursus historique et critique' in which the *Parmenides* of Plato, specifically the

---

47 Atkinson (1983), 185, reports that in Plotinus this passage accounts for 76% of references to the *Theaetetus*!

Introduction to Book 1

first three hypostases of the final part (counting according to the Neo-platonic method), are famously employed to suggest that Plato himself had an account of the same hypostases (V. 1.8.23–7). Earlier in V. 1.8 *Epistle* 2, 312e had also been used to suggest a triad of hypostases in Plato, and then a combination of *Epistle* 6, 323d (the Father of the Cause), *Philebus* 26e–30c (demiurgic intellect as cause), and *Timaeus* 41d (demiurge manufactures soul) is used to construct a similar argument for Plato's recognition of the triad One, Intellect, Soul (V. 1.8.1–6). He then recalls how the *Republic* places the Idea of the Good at a higher level than intellect. What follows is worth quoting:

> So Plato knew that Intellect is from the Good, and Soul is from Intellect. And these doctrines are not new, and it is not now but long ago that they have been stated, though not fully unfolded (*mê anapeptamenôs*).[48] Our present arguments have been interpretations of them, proving on the basis of Plato's own writings that these views are ancient. (V. 1.8.9–14)

There is no doubt that Plotinus thought that the basis of his own system was already present in Plato, needing to be teased out. But the teasing out involves no sustained exegesis of any one passage, but long meditation over brief and seemingly esoteric passages, either alone, as in the case of the *Second Epistle*, or in company with other such passages. Though the passage containing the first three hypostases is lengthy (137c–157b), it is clearly not separable from the rest of the final part of the *Parmenides*. Our evidence suggests that Plotinus' associates Amelius and Porphyry were able to give meaning to all eight or nine hypotheses they respectively counted there.[49] One who finds metaphysical levels behind three of the nine hypotheses ought surely either to find nine or to show why nine cannot be expected. Did Plotinus only care about the first three levels? Did he only care about engineering Plato's support for pre-determined Neoplatonic doctrine?

It is well known that, of Plotinus' essays *On the Kinds of Being* (VI. 1–3), the second has a special place for the so-called Greatest Kinds (*megista genê*) of Plato's *Sophist*. But VI. 2.22 considers the findings so far in the context of a variety of texts, *Timaeus* 39e (the same as is involved in III. 9), the second hypothesis of the *Parmenides* (144b), and

---

[48] Atkinson (1983), lxiii, translates this *hapax legomenon* (see 192) 'not explicitly', but I think this fails to capture the somewhat religious tone of a word suggesting that mysteries were not to be wholly revealed. At 191, Atkinson puts it nicely when he says that, for Plotinus, 'Plato did not make everything clear,' and that Plato's remarks (at V. 8.4.51 ff.) 'need interpretation', and he goes on to talk of the religious associations of the vocabulary of riddles, which, as he points out, can be directly linked with *Epistle* 2 312d7–8 (cf. 314a).

[49] Proc. *in Parm.* 1052–4. For the identity of the champions of these interpretations we are reliant on the scholia.

Interpreting the *Timaeus* in antiquity

Philebus 16e.[50] But Plotinus isn't getting what he wants directly from Plato, so the first two of these texts involve Plato's speaking in riddles![51] This will no doubt be controversial, but Plotinus speaks as one who has come to think in terms of a particular metaphysical system, seeing Plato as the vehicle by which he came there. He therefore assumes that Plato, above all in the passages that he has been brought to see as central, is in agreement with this system. But he forgets that it is Plato *as recently interpreted* that has been his vehicle. There had been serious recent work on the Platonic corpus that had highlighted the metaphysical importance of a number of brief passages. But Plotinus himself simply takes over a kind of canon of key passages together with some convenient exegetical tools, whereby Plato can always be found in agreement given sufficient ingenuity. Anybody who wishes to maintain that Plotinus was greatly original in his interpretations needs to grapple with *VPlot.* 3.33–5, where it is remarked that:

> Plotinus went on writing nothing for quite a time, but basing his teaching on the classes of Ammonius; and he went on like that for ten whole years, teaching some people, but writing nothing.

While the emphasis is on Plotinus' lack of enthusiasm for writing, the context is one that concerns the communication of Ammonius' teaching material. This implies a considerable intellectual debt to Ammonius, and while we find his pupils in disagreement over doctrine, we don't find any disagreement over which passages are crucial. It is here then that we can expect the debt to have been considerable.

What then of Plotinus' place in Proclus' work? In book 1 his name occurs only once, in relation to his low opinion of the philosophic value of Longinus. Nothing suggests that he ever paid any attention, even orally, to the prologue of the *Timaeus*. In book 2 his name occurs a number of times in relation to *Enneads* III. 9.1 and once each in relation to six other passages, mostly not directly related to Platonic exegesis. In book 3 there are a couple of references that can be linked with passages in the *Enneads*,[52] and there is a reference to something Amelius attributes to Plotinus' oral teaching. There are two references in book 4 and five in book 5, most of the latter unrelated to specific passages in the *Enneads*. One has to allow for the possibility that Porphyry is ultimately responsible for many of the references to Plotinus having entered the commentary tradition, even though Proclus was of course familiar with

---

[50] On this chapter see Sumi (2006).

[51] For Plotinus' Plato as a riddler see Wallis (1972), 17, Atkinson (1983), 191.

[52] One of these, II. 154.3, is in the context of a large doxography, and the other (II. 11.27) concerns a Plotinian argument against Aristotle.

Introduction to Book 1

the *Enneads*. Rather, it was difficult for Proclus to extract very much of direct exegetical relevance from them, and traditions concerning his oral teaching have not supplied us with very much more. At *Platonic Theology* I. 1.6 Proclus includes Plotinus in his list of 'interpreters of the Platonic higher vision' (*exêgêtai tês Platônikês epopteias*), which captures nicely what Plotinus is doing. It is my contention that he tried to be an exegete of that higher vision without ever having grappled with the earlier task of being an exegete of the texts.[53] His own claims to be an exegete rather than an independent philosopher, which must in any case be seen against the background of widespread reverence for ancient wisdom only, cannot alter the fact that it was his philosophy rather than his exegesis that left its mark on later Neoplatonism.[54]

The scholarship needed for the writing of commentaries is rather to be associated with Porphyry. The extensive fragments of his *Timaeus* commentary were long ago edited – with one exception – by R. Sodano.[55] Porphyry is of special interest to readers of the initial book of Proclus' commentary, since he may well have been the first commentator to try to offer a more or less comprehensive account of the material that precedes the cosmology. Hence he supplies the complete exegesis of the target dialogue in a way that was completely lacking in Plotinus. Porphyry apparently adhered to a similar division of books in his commentary as is used by Iamblichus and Proclus thereafter,[56] another indication of the general conservatism of the genre. Each book was probably introduced by a preface, and for the most part used the same lemmata as are used later by Proclus.[57] One wonders how it was that commentaries were not included in the list of Porphyry's works in the Suda (fr. 2), but the in-house nature of the genre may be the reason. Not only did Porphyry

---

[53] The story of Plotinus' disappointment with all teachers at Alexandria until he found Ammonius (*VPlot.* 14) is clearly the story of a man who wanted to be led directly to the heart of a religious philosophy without the preliminary studies that most would have thought necessary as a first step.

[54] For a discussion of the vexed question of the degree to which Plotinus should be seen as an exegete see Gatti (1996), 17–22. However, her alternatives 'exegete of Plato or innovator?' are not the only ones relevant to our discussion. Rather, with regard to both exegesis and doctrine, there is a considerable question of how original he really was, something that would only be able to be determined if we had adequate knowledge of Numenius and (more especially) Ammonius. It is my position that, although the doctrine was probably original in significant respects, the exegesis, besides being severely limited, was only ever original where it was needed to support new doctrines.

[55] Sodano (1964); one extra fragment is supplied by Smith (1993).

[56] See Dillon (1973), 295.

[57] See Dillon (1973), 54–5; sometimes Proclus has introduced further divisions of his own. It may be advisable to remember that many of Proclus' divisions are dictated by the subject matter.

Interpreting the *Timaeus* in antiquity

write commentaries,[58] he also engaged in debate as to how they should be written, promoting, or perhaps rather reviving,[59] the view that prologues are a treasure house of ethical guidance. This has accounted for the frequency of references to Porphyry in Book 1 (30 in Diehl's index), as opposed to Books 2 (23), 3 (20), 4 (3) and 5 (1).[60] The place of Porphyry will be apparent in the translation that follows, and it will probably be sufficient here to underline the importance for Porphyry's exegesis not only of Plotinus (who provides the philosophic framework within which exegesis needs to occur), but also of Numenius and Cronius, Longinus and Amelius.

One cannot leave Porphyry, however, without mentioning the reasonable theory of P. Hadot (1968) that the fragments of the anonymous *Commentary on the Parmenides* from a Turin palimpsest are actually from Porphyry's own commentary on that work. The authorship will probably never be able to be confirmed, but, in spite of efforts to show that it could have been written earlier,[61] it remains likely that it is a Neoplatonist work dating from before AD 400. If it belongs to this period then the influence of Porphyry is in any case not improbable, and one suspects that there would have been a number of pupils, and pupils of pupils, who had built their own lecture notes on the commentaries of Porphyry. The form of this commentary is certainly very different from the *Theaetetus* commentary, and a few remarks about how it differs would perhaps be in order, regardless of authorship. First, unless we are misled by the one example we have (III. 1–36 = *Parm.* 141a5–d6) the lemmata are long, giving a suspicion that it belongs early in the traditions of *Parmenides*-commentary.[62] Second, the subject matter is much more philosophical

[58] Besides the extant commentaries on Aristotle's *Categories* and Ptolemy's *Harmonics*, this is clear in the case of the commentary on the *Timaeus* which is attested (should any reader of Proclus doubt it!) by both Philoponus and Macrobius. On Porphyry's works see Smith (1987).

[59] See Sedley (1999a), who tries to trace the tactic back to the Old Academy; the use of the introduction to the dialogue within the dialogue for ethical purposes by the earlier anonymous *On the Theaetetus* confirms that Porphyry's position cannot have been entirely original.

[60] We are confronted, then, by the possibility that Porphyry's commentary either stopped shortly after 41e (Dillon (1973), 63), or was lost after that point, or simply faded in importance after that point as far as Proclus was concerned. That his importance is already fading from book 4 on makes this last a possibility, and Proclus might feel that Porphyry had lost sight of anything like the main theological themes as the dialogue progressed.

[61] See for instance Bechtle (1999).

[62] Here one should mention that Aspasius' second-century commentary on the *Nicomachean Ethics* is the closest comparable philosophic commentary, and Wittwer's careful study of its lemmata (1999) makes it plain that there is indeed a fairly close relationship

Introduction to Book 1

and closely argued. However, the commentary is similar to both the anonymous *in Theaetetum* and Proclus *in Parmenidem*, but unlike the *in Timaeum*, insofar as it avoids naming rival interpreters. Whether there were different traditions in commenting on different texts it is hard to tell, and this does make it difficult to argue from the nature of Porphyry's *Commentary on Aristotle's Categories* or *Commentary on Ptolemy's Harmonics* to what his commentary on any Platonic work would have looked like. The Anonymous Turinensis, as it is sometimes called, is unfortunately the only part-extant commentary on Plato, other than the peripheral ones of Galen and Calcidius, between the *Theaetetus* commentary and Proclus, and as such it needs to be compared seriously with what is done later by Proclus.

Unfortunately the excellent research of Hadot has been somewhat undermined in recent times by the work of Tardieu (1996), that has shown that many of the similarities between Victorinus and our commentary, hitherto thought best attributed to Porphyry, are shared by the Gnostic *Zostrianos*.[63] This text, or some version of it, was among many that were fascinating other religious teachers in the time of Plotinus and Porphyry (*VPlot.* 16), and we are given the specific information that Amelius wrote forty books (!) against *Zostrianos*. The interesting point here is that both *Zostrianos* and Amelius can reasonably be associated with Numenius.[64] Amelius may well be taking on this revelationary book in the belief that it is a perversion of the true Neopythagorean philosophy. Amelius is in fact an author who should be reckoned a candidate for having composed this commentary on the *Parmenides*: a work on which he clearly had a very detailed interpretation (see pp. 38, 42 above). If there is something Numenian about the commentary, as Bechtle and Brisson believe, while it is at the same time rich enough in argument to associate with Plotinus' circle, then the hypothesis of Amelian authorship would offer an excellent explanation.

The Iamblichan legacy

As may be seen from the entry in Diehl's index, which is at least half as long again as that of Porphyry, the debt of Proclus to Iamblichus is considerable. It can be observed in a number of areas:

> between the lemmata we have and the lemmata Aspasius used. More importantly, the longer a tradition of commentary lasts, the more detailed the treatment of individual passages, so that we should expect further division of lemmata as time goes on, as seems to have happened in the case of the *Timaeus* (Dillon (1973), 54).

[63] Bechtle (1999), n. 683, gives a list of illuminating parallels between the commentary and Victorinus, also adding in most cases a reference to comparable material in *Zostrianos*.

[64] See Brisson (1999); Bechtle (1999), 257 and 248–9 n. 683.

46

Interpreting the *Timaeus* in antiquity

1. The structure of the commentary;
2. The important principle that everything within a Platonic dialogue aims at a single goal or *skopos*, and requires interpretation *in relation to* that goal;
3. The *canon* of dialogues that constitutes the late Neoplatonist curriculum;
4. A more overt move towards making just about everything contribute in some way to theology, together with the presence of a theurgic element, and enhanced use of theurgic texts such as the Chaldean Oracles.

Significant for structure is a running commentary on the complete text, generally with short lemmata. It involves also the book division and individual prologues to each book that may be traced back to Porphyry (see p. 00 above).[65] On the nature of the *skopos* we shall have cause to comment in relation to the initial few pages of the commentary, and I have dealt with it previously.[66] The most illuminating text on the late Neoplatonic *skopos* is Anon. *Prolegomena* 21–2, though caution needs to be exercised in using it as a source for Iamblichus himself. Some seemingly very strange 'targets' were proposed by persons prior to the likely period of the composition of the *Prolegomena* (perhaps mid-sixth century), with the Demiurge becoming the *skopos* of the *Gorgias*, and the demiurge of the sublunary world becoming that of the *Sophist*. This last is Iamblichus' view according to a scholiast on the *Sophist*, and that should serve to discourage anybody from seeing the word as meaning anything like a 'central topic'. Rather it is what we are expected to get a vision of as a result of the correct reading of the dialogue in question, and while everything was expected to contribute to such a vision, not everything (if anything!) was supposed to be *about* that vision. Divine or transcendent entities seem to have been generally involved. The *skopos* of the *Philebus* was the Good (*in Phlb.* fr. 1); that of the *Phaedrus* was the beautiful at every level, including the Beautiful itself (*in Phdr.* fr. 1); that of the *Timaeus* must have been the total vision of the physical world itself, a god in its own right, but containing other gods within it, since Proclus assumes that there is nothing uncontroversial about this view (I. 1.7–8). Significantly, however, Iamblichus seems to have been less thorough than Proclus in his referring all the content of the *Timaeus* to an ultimately divine vision, for he seems early in book 1 to be regularly associated with what Proclus sees as *physical* explanations

---

[65] See Dillon (1973), 54–5, who makes an exception in the case of books 3 to 4 of Proclus, which he believes were a single book in Iamblichus (see n. 62).

[66] Jackson, Lykos and Tarrant (1998), 23–4; Tarrant (2000), 92–4 etc.

47

Introduction to Book 1

of problems in the text rather than with *theological* ones (such as he and Syrianus preferred).[67] The reason is partly that Iamblichus thought that it was Pythagorean methodology to preface one's in-depth discussion of realities with first likenesses (such as the physical world offers), and then symbols (I. 19.9–20.27 = *in Tim.* fr. 3).

The Iamblichan curriculum involved twelve proper dialogues, i.e. twelve works that had the required unity of *skopos*: *Republic* and *Laws* were not included. There was a decad of dialogues, consisting of *Alcibiades I*, *Gorgias, Phaedo, Cratylus, Theaetetus, Sophist, Statesman, Phaedrus, Symposium*, and *Philebus*. This was followed by the two perfect dialogues, the *Timaeus* (tackling all reality through physics) and the *Parmenides* (doing the same through theology), on which see I. 13.14–19 (= Iambl. *in Tim.* fr. 1). It survived even in the works of Ammonius' successors, when strangely much of the rationale for it would no longer have been accepted.[68]

Iamblichus' interest in theurgy, along with a great deal else that had to do with various theories and practices concerning the gods, has ensured that he is rightly regarded as a turning point in Neoplatonism. While it could have taken a purer and more detached scholarly route associated with Porphyry's *Letter to Anebo*, the movement followed the line taken in Iamblichus' reply, the *De Mysteriis*. In the present commentary the main way that influence is felt is in the large number of quotations from the Chaldean Oracles, that influential second-century text that was itself supposed to be linked intimately with theurgy. Similarly, quotations from late Orphic texts are surprisingly numerous. In Diehl's index the couple of lines of references to Origenes are submerged in two and a half pages of what is otherwise dedicated to the Oracles and Orpheus!

The influence of Iamblichus will to some extent be apparent as we read on. Less apparent is that of the only known pupil of Iamblichus to be mentioned in the current commentary, Theodorus of Asine. In book 1 he is mentioned only once (12.8), tellingly in relation to Amelius, but he receives four mentions in book 2, three each in books 3 and 4, and ten in book 5. Besides Amelius, he is closely associated with Numenius (II. 274.10–14 = Numenius fr. 40). A reader of the present commentary might be surprised to find that Theodorus' name occurs in the Bacchic company of Platonist philosophers in the *Platonic Theology* (I. 1.6). His importance is difficult to determine, and there is little doubt that he represents the later influence of the line passing from Numenius through Amelius rather than that passing from Plotinus through Porphyry.

---

[67] This is most explicit at 117.19 (= Iambl. *in Tim.* fr. 12), but cf. also 16.20–17.9, 19.9–20.27 (= fr. 3), 25.8–14, 27.26–30, 30.2–19.

[68] See Jackson, Lycos and Tarrant (1998), 14.

48

Proclus on questions concerning the *Timaeus*

This brings us to the end of our survey, and to the Athenian School in which Proclus himself was to work. Plutarch of Athens (d. AD 432), important in other ways for understanding Proclus' background, is not mentioned here. He is, however, of vital importance in setting the interpretation of the *Parmenides* on track in Proclus' eyes (1059–61). Syrianus (d. AD 437?), not mentioned by name but often as 'our teacher', is such a pervasive influence that he is difficult to separate from the still youthful Proclus himself. That he wrote a commentary on the present work is attested at various points, and it is a matter of some regret that we do not have a Platonic commentary in his name. His *Commentary on Aristotle's Metaphysics* does however compensate for this, and it is now customary to use the commentary of Hermeias on the *Phaedrus* as more or less direct evidence for Syrianus himself. He is an object of much reverence, and is called at III. 14.19 'the most theological of interpreters'. Whether one should except Proclus is perhaps a question that needs to be asked!

PROCLUS ON GENERAL QUESTIONS CONCERNING THE *TIMAEUS*

There has been much recent attention to the prolegomena of ancient commentaries in general, and to those of this commentary in particular.[69] It seems that in late antiquity there were recognized topics for introductions to Platonic works, some or all of which would be expected to be present, either as distinct strands of the prefatory material, or at least as identifiable elements that could be tracked down. The topics had evolved partly according to the needs of the commentators and partly according to the theory of the rhetoricians. The primary topic, to which all else needed to relate in some way or other, had, since Iamblichus, been the *skopos*, less the 'subject' of the work than its intended focus, the entity or entities that it was designed to illuminate. This would frequently, though not necessarily, be a Neoplatonic divinity. The correct way of identifying the *skopos* had been an important item of discussion in the *Prolegomena to Plato's Philosophy* (21–3) associated with the Olympiodoran school, and in many cases it must have remained the same for generations of post-Iamblichan Platonists. There were, however, important exceptions, as in the case of the *Sophist* and the *Gorgias*.[70] The *skopos* of the *Timaeus* was not controversial, except perhaps in the details of how it was to be expressed,

---

[69] See Mansfeld (1994), particularly 30–7 on Proclus' Plato commentaries. Mansfeld (30) describes Proclan practice as 'less scholastic, or schematic, than that recorded in Anon. *Proleg.*, though not less systematic'. For this commentary see now Cleary (2006), 136–41.

[70] I discuss these in Tarrant (2000), 135–9 and 194–5.

49

Introduction to Book 1

and consequently Proclus can keep his discussion relatively brief. Those seeking a lengthy discussion of the treatment here should refer to Alain Lernould's study.[71] It does, however, commence the discussion, and is followed by several other standard *topoi*.

Festugière identifies the sections dealing with these *topoi* as follows:

- target of the dialogue   1.4–4.5
- treatment of subject[72]   4.6–7.16
- character of the dialogue   7.17–8.29
- background of the dialogue   8.30–9.13
- participants in the dialogue   9.13–24.

This is clearly correct for the most part, though one can quarrel over details. While the first section is marked as tackling the *skopos* by comments at 4.6–7, a large part of this is given over to the allegedly Pythagorean nature of Platonic physics, and the five-cause system that it implies. As in Seneca's *Epistle* 65.7–10 the five causes are the four of Aristotle, plus a paradigmatic cause, but no attempt is made to justify the attribution of such a system to Pythagoras. And while a degree of dependence on 'Timaeus Locrus' *On Nature* (as it is here called, 1.9) is assumed,[73] we are given no reason to associate the five-cause system with that text. In the end it would seem that for Proclus the approach is Pythagorean because, standing in sharp contrast to Ionian physics, it is naturally attached to the western Presocratic tradition from Italy and Sicily.

For Lernould the second section (to 6.16 at least) is the *divisio textus*, dealing with how the work may be split into sections. Anybody wishing to work out precisely how Proclus envisages the breakdown of the text of the *Timaeus* and plans his own commentary is recommended to examine Lernould's treatment.[74] Lernould excludes 6.16–7.16, which is primarily concerned with the agreement between Plato and Aristotle, at least on the more worldly subjects discussed in the later parts of the dialogue. Divisions of the dialogue are included in the proems of the *Alcibiades* commentaries of both Proclus and Olympiodorus, as also of the latter's *Gorgias* commentary. Further, it is debatable here whether there is any real division between background and characters. Separate sections on characters and their symbolism are certainly not mandatory, but they are found in Olympiodorus *On the Gorgias* and Damascius *On the Philebus*. It would be fair to say that Proclus' procedure, like that of Olympiodorus, Damascius, and Hermeias, is not driven by any notion of abstract rules

---

[71] See Lernould (2001), 27–38.

[72] The section is described as being about its *oikonomia* at 9.26.

[73] This was obviously a regular assumption at that time, 7.18–21.

[74] Lernould (2001), 63–79.

Proclus on questions concerning the *Timaeus*

with which he must conform, but is adapted to suit the particular needs of the dialogue at hand.

The section on 'the genre and literary character of the dialogue' does not discuss issues of classification as one might expect from reading Diogenes Laertius' distinction between various 'characters' (3.50–1). Rather, Proclus is concerned to select various qualities that attach to the dialogue because of Plato's debts to Socrates on the one hand and to Pythagoreans on the other. Literary qualities are here treated as having a great deal to do with Plato's methods of communicating with his audience, so that they stem from the educational methods that Plato has inherited from his two major influences, not upon mere aesthetic considerations. The dialogue is depicted as a perfect blend, mixing 'the demonstrational method with the revelational' (8.3–4). This is important, for it is at 8.9–13 that Timaeus is explicit about the dialogue mixing physical and theological content in a way that matches the character of its subject, the cosmos.

The section on the background links the *Timaeus* firmly with the *Republic*, assuming that Socrates narrated the conversation in that dialogue to Timaeus, Critias, Hermocrates, and the unnamed fourth person on the day after it actually happened. This then is the third day of proceedings, but the second dialogue in a series. The number of the participants is then raised as a problem, which is in turn quickly answered with reference to the correspondence of the participants to the Father of Demiurges and the Triad of Demiurges below him.

After these standard *topoi* have been discussed, there is a digression on nature (9.25–12.25), made necessary, Proclus believes, because of the confusion that can occur through the multitude of conceptions of 'nature' used in philosophy. Proclus uses doxographical methods to clarify his own position, or rather the position that he would attribute to Plato: 'a non-bodily substance inseparable from bodies, possessing their formal principles [*logoi*] but unable to see into itself' (12.27–8). The digression then leads into another regular *topos*,[75] that of the work's place in the curriculum, or at least its place in the final stages of Platonic enlightenment, along with the *Parmenides* (12.26–14.3). It is of course important that Proclus' readers are now supposed to have read the group of ten dialogues selected by Iamblichus to precede these two, as well as a great deal of Aristotle, and, as we learn from 1.13–16, the work attributed to 'Timaeus Locrus'.

Before we leave this kind of general question we should consider briefly material at the end of the book that is of a similar type, relating

---

[75] I should perhaps note here that Olympiodorus in his *Commentary on the Gorgias* also treats this topic in the course of his preliminary discussions (*proem* 6–7), and without actually flagging it as a *topos*.

51

Introduction to Book 1

both to the speakers and to the sequence of dialogues. At 198.25–199.11 Proclus embarks on an attempt to show how among the speakers in the (projected) *Timaeus–Critias* Timaeus is both a top and a mean, thus mirroring nature. The order of lengthy speeches is supposed to be:

Socrates–Critias–Timaeus–Critias–Hermocrates

placing Timaeus at the centre, while he is foremost in knowledge. Proclus deals next (199.11–200.3) with the question of what might have been left to Hermocrates, suggesting that he was needed to make the citizens speak. Then he moves on to tackle the problem of why the *Timaeus* was not made to precede the *Republic*. Strangely, while the first two sections of the resumed general discussion had tended to assume the unfinished sequence *Timaeus–Critias–Hermocrates*, this one presumes the complete trilogy *Republic–Timaeus–Critias*! It is the kind of problem that might have occurred ever since sequences of dialogues were taken for granted (following Aristophanes of Byzantium's trilogies, D.L. 3.61–2), and does indeed seem to presume his trilogy rather than Thrasyllus' tetralogy (which placed *Clitophon* at the front). But the problem would have been seen as a greater threat when structure and its ability to mimic the natural order had come to loom so large in interpreters' minds, as they had for Proclus. It is unfortunate that Proclus does not put a name to the objector, but, since he is so ready to name Porphyry, Iamblichus, and others, one wonders whether the objection may be reflecting his own earlier concerns.[76] After several other considerations, Proclus looks to Porphyry for a solution, but makes it clear that Porphyry had not had this problem in mind, strongly suggesting that it is a post-Porphyrian problem. For Porphyry:

Those who are going to get a real hold on the study of the universe must first have been educated in character, so that by assimilation to the object contemplated it [their character] should become properly prepared for the recognition of the truth. (202.5–7)

So the *Republic* comes first so that we may correctly organize our inner constitution, thus being in a more satisfactory condition to appreciate the constitution of the heavens.

---

[76] Note that the Iamblichan curriculum, which treats the *Republic* at best as a side-dish and omits the *Critias* (Anon. *Proleg.* 26), precludes any such solution, and actually makes nonsense of the problem itself.

52

PROCLUS ON THE SUMMARY OF THE CONSTITUTION IN THE *TIMAEUS*

Fidelity to the text and religious interpretation

We come now to matters pertaining to the detailed reading of a text. How one read texts in antiquity was largely bound up with authorial intent. One might show either the message the author hoped to communicate, or the message that some higher power (speaking through the author) had intended for us. Hence interpretation depended on how one thought one's authority was communicating. Usually authors did not broadcast their views on how other authors communicated, which were the most effective methods of communication, or on what principles their own works were to be interpreted in their turn. Plato had left us strong hints, but their enigmatic nature warns us that even these were not intended to supply rules for the would-be definitive interpreter. Proclus was just such a definitive interpreter, with a firm intention to interpret Plato's texts rather than to present an alternative source of Platonist doctrine, like Plotinus for instance. But he was an interpreter with such contempt for purely literal readings that the text became a two-edged sword: many details, when interpreted literally, were an obstacle, though welcomed if treated in the appropriate manner.

It did not escape Proclus that Plato did not think knowledge, as distinct from information, could be transmitted by straightforward didactic processes, whether written or oral. Where Plato's writing seems to adopt a more didactic approach, as in Timaeus' cosmology as well as here in the summary of the constitution, there are sufficient indications to show that even here one may not be hearing the simple truth. Hence Proclus, like Iamblichus before him,[77] is at liberty to select where he will allow a literal reading and where he will not, and to choose where he will resort to his more distinctive and more controversial methods of interpretation. In some cases he will go out of his way to avoid literal readings. In others, as with the Atlantis story, he will not disallow the validity of the literal reading, but will insist that deeper readings are required if Plato is to be properly understood. But for this very case he makes literal use of the statement of Critias that his *logos* is true in every way (20d8).

There has recently been a good deal of discussion of Proclan strategies of interpretation, including the tactics of iconic and symbolic interpretation that appear to give him, as Professor Gonzales has recently

---

[77] See 174.28–32 = Iambl. *in Tim.* fr. 23.

53

Introduction to Book 1

pointed out to me, all the latitude of a Straussian Platonist, if not more.[78] However, most of the attention given to this problem has been focussed on matters that involve the issues on which Proclus also appealed to the inspired poets and religious groups,[79] or at least to his strategies for theological interpretation. In this context we now have two new articles on Proclus' strategies for interpretation which deal with *Platonic Theology* I.4,[80] where Proclus is quite explicit about how his comments apply to Plato's communicative strategies *for theology*: 'the ways in which he teaches to us the mystical ways of conceiving of things divine.' Plato communicates his theology by means of likenesses, symbols, or dialectic, or in the inspired 'entheastic' manner characteristic of the central passages of the *Phaedrus*. It is likenesses and symbols that prove most relevant to Proclus' treatment of the early pages of the *Timaeus*.

Fortunately, not even Proclus believes that Plato is always teaching us theology. How does he approach Platonic interpretation in passages which are not openly theological? What is his interpretation like when he is turning his mind to less exalted texts? We must remember that what survives of Proclus' commentaries is such that it is bound to place a heavy emphasis on theology: the *Parmenides* and the *Timaeus* are the culmination of the Neoplatonic education programme, and together are supposed to reveal its highest secrets. A well-received recent book tackles, among other issues of importance, this interlacing of physics and theology in the *in Timaeum*.[81] The *Republic* commentary is not a running commentary and allows Proclus much scope for concentrating on those parts where theology is an issue, or is at least able to become one for Neoplatonist readers. The commentary on the *Cratylus* seems to be most eloquent when reaching the etymologies of the gods and when treating the secret divine names by which gods refer to things, though it has been subject to reworking in accordance with an editor's seemingly theological tastes. Like the *Commentary on the Alcibiades* it is truncated. This last may more easily be read as a Proclan commentary on a text offering fewer theological opportunities. It is a welcome challenge to be offering the *first* book of the *in Timaeum*, dealing with the early discussion that precedes Timaeus' monologue, because introducing theology would at first sight seem to be a considerable challenge, and yet Syrianus and Proclus, being committed to a unitary interpretation of a dialogue with joint physical and theological implications, must find theological

---

[78] On symbolic interpretation in Proclus and others see Rappe (2000). Note the strong claim 'The language of Neoplatonism is the language of symbols' (117).

[79] Coulter (1976), Sheppard (1980), Kuisma (1996), van den Berg (2001).

[80] Pépin (2000) and Gersh (2000).   [81] See Lernould (2001).

54

significance throughout. I believe that their strategies become rather interesting as a result.

Proclus is offered some scope by the very mysteries that the text confronts us with. From the outset the *Timaeus* itself is *recalling* the discussion between the participants concerning the constitution. This is very different from the way a sequel is made to resume the discussion in the series *Theaetetus–Sophist–Statesman*, or indeed from the way that the *Critias* will follow the *Timaeus* itself. Apart from Socrates, the characters are new to us, and we witness them reassemble after the previous day's exposition of the Socratic constitution. The relation to the content of parts of the *Republic* is evident, but from the beginning there are mysteries about the fourth person present at the gathering, how the constitution was presented, and how the new protagonists came to agree to offer Socrates something in return. Mysteries invite us to think more deeply, and that, if anything, can cause wonder. Proclus frequently finds within the text 'wonderful indications' of what he took to be the higher truths underlying Platonic philosophy – and indeed all inspired philosophy. In fact Jan Opsomer has recently written, concerning Proclus' attention to details of Platonic texts, that 'it may make us call into question our own hermeneutic tools. It should provoke wonder, and hence philosophy.'[82]

The legacy of history

The summary of the *politeia* of the *Republic* is introduced at *Timaeus* 17b5 and continues for less than three pages of OCT to 19b2, at which point Socrates' first long speech commences, in which he reminds the other participants of what he would like to hear from them. The corresponding passage of Proclus' commentary stretches from 26.21 to 55.26, some thirty pages of Teubner text. Plato has represented this summary as a reminder, and reminders are seldom of great interest to anybody who has the original available. The material relates primarily to parts of books two, three, and five of the *Republic*, and should be considered as a summary of a social arrangement or *politeia* rather than of the total dialogue in which it appeared. Opinions will differ as to whether Plato really wants his target audience to remember all features of that *politeia*, or only those to which he chooses to draw attention. The fact that we did not encounter the figures of Timaeus, Critias, and Hermocrates (let alone a mysterious fourth person) as narratees in the extant *Republic* may even suggest a different occasion on which Socrates had communicated his socio-political views, when they had been set out in ways not entirely in

---

[82] See Opsomer (2001b), 68.

Introduction to Book 1

accord with the *Republic*. In fact there is enough here to get the sensitive reader of Plato seriously wondering about the circumstances.

While Proclus was himself such a reader, he already had a tradition to draw on. I very much doubt whether he routinely read commentaries prior to Porphyry, but Porphyry was scholarly enough to have introduced a number of predecessors and contemporaries into his deliberations. The most prominent here are Longinus and Origenes. At that time it may have been novel enough to bother with the prefatory material in a Platonic dialogue at all, and Porphyry searched these pages, and the corresponding parts of other dialogues, for material with some kind of moral content. With Iamblichus comes a significant change. The dialogue has become the unit, just as it has again today. We have now to bear in mind that all material in a dialogue, including the dramatic machinery etc., is now expected to relate to a single overriding *skopos*. Sequences of dialogues cannot operate in such a way as to threaten the integrity of the individual dialogue; if two dialogues are more closely united then they should rather be viewed as one single dialogue, but we know that this did not happen in the case of the *Sophist* and *Politicus* for instance.

The relevance of this for the early pages of the *Timaeus* should be obvious. When Porphyry had interpreted them he could legitimately resort to seeing in them a different sort of material with a primarily ethical and political purpose. After Iamblichus, Neoplatonists were no longer able to do this, for the Timaeus' *skopos* involves, almost inevitably, 'the whole of physical inquiry, rising to the study of the universe, dealing with this from beginning to end'. The summary of the *politeia* must therefore have something to do with this overall purpose, and a moral explanation of a lemma's function can never be the complete explanation. This is the case in spite of Proclus' seeing the *Timaeus* as the close sequel of the *Republic*, to which he takes it to be referring. The sequence does not override the integrity of the dialogue.

Whereas Iamblichus seems to have been content to offer a more strictly physical interpretation of everything in the *Timaeus*, Syrianus insisted also on finding something theological, since at the summit of the natural world were various divinities involved in its direction. The result is that Proclus may approach the text in various ways:

- linguistically (generally in response to considerations adduced by Longinus),
- ethically (generally in response to considerations adduced by Porphyry),
- physically (in the manner of Iamblichus),
- theologically (in response to the requirements of Syrianus).

Proclus on the constitution in the *Timaeus*

It is important that these approaches are not mutually exclusive; rather each successive interpretation is more complete. On occasions ethical, physical, and theological interpretations are presented without any indication that they are specific to given interpreters, and the effect of this is to suggest strongly that Proclus accepts each of the interpretations to some degree. The impression one receives is that he considers Plato to be the kind of writer who is so inspired that the most unpromising snippets of text can yield at least three worthwhile levels of meaning: passages where others had sometimes failed to detect one! In some ways, though, this is not so surprising. The same patterns are always being reflected at different levels of reality in Athenian Neoplatonism, and consequently a pattern that exists among the gods, and can be reflected in the text of Plato, will also be reflected in some way in the physical world. Furthermore, patterns found among the gods provide models for human conduct, and thus can be expected to have ethical implications. While we sometimes become exasperated at what seems to be the proliferation of entities in Neoplatonism, everything is so interlinked that they can concentrate on a comparatively small number of significant patterns. These are seen most clearly and completely among the gods, but they are there nevertheless at lower levels too. This enables Proclus to acknowledge both Porphyry and Iamblichus as inspired interpreters,[83] Porphyry with his more partial moral insights and Iamblichus with his more visionary understanding of the cosmos (cf. 204.24–7).

Some features of Proclus' exposition

We must now be selective, for many of the important themes will actually emerge best as one reads the commentary. I shall begin at the end, as it were, that being the most economical way to discuss this passage. After he has concluded, Proclus says:

Under a limited number of 'main heads' Socrates properly summed up the entire shape of the constitution, thus moving back towards the undivided character of intellect, in order to imitate the god who organized the heavenly constitution in an intelligible way and in the manner of a father. Since everywhere due measures and completion are being determined for the second things by their causes, on this account he himself asks Timaeus to state whether he has included the entire form of the constitution; for all intellect is reliant upon the god that precedes it and determines its own boundaries by looking to it. For to have set forth 'the main heads' (*kephalaia*) is also a symbol of his having organized the primary

---

[83] Note that at *Theol.* I. 1.6.21 he includes even Amelius as inspired (as also Plotinus, who is less relevant here).

Introduction to Book 1

elements of the whole, i.e. its *head*, things which the universal demiurge will arrange more perfectly with an eye on the whole and on the single life of the cosmos. (I.54.28–55.9)

We notice that squeezing the *politeia* into comparatively few words, into five principal points in fact, is seen as an upward movement, a movement towards the intelligible. There is a movement from multiplicity towards unity. Socrates, under the guidance of Timaeus (who has a higher status) rises towards a higher level than had been exhibited in the *Republic*. We notice too the analogy between the various characters of the dialogue and Proclus' four demiurgic figures, the Father of Demiurges and the Demiurgic Triad. This assists Proclus to argue for the theological relevance of the summary, for which his main argument is the analogy that he routinely applies between the constitution applied to the state and the constitution that is laid up like a paradigm in the heaven (*Rep.* 592b), which cannot be separated from the paradigmatic motions of the heavenly soul that humankind should be contemplating in order to set their own souls aright at *Tim.* 90a–d. For the constitution is also imperfectly imitated in the soul of the human being. Soul, state, and heaven are all based on the same constitutional pattern. Furthermore, when we think of the heaven we think also of the gods laid up there, so that the same pattern is present in the visible heavens and in their divine causes.

For Proclus, therefore, the summary of the constitution functions as an image of things of vital importance to the physical and theological subject matter of the dialogue in which the summary occurs. A constitution is the organizing principle that brings about an organic unity in an entity consisting of distinct parts or forces, whether soul, state, heaven, or something else. So this is an image of a pervasive unifying principle, whereas the story of Atlantis functions as an image of a pervasive principle of division and separation. This message occurs already at 4.7–26, and it is reinforced once again in the opening of book 2 (I. 205.4–206.16). The constitution was an image of the 'first creation', the war was an image of the second; the constitution reflected the formal cause, the war the material cause. Between them they prepare the way for a study that shows the imposition of harmony on potentially belligerent contraries. Socrates offered his account in a non-embodied way, offering the intelligible pattern itself, whereas Critias offers an account of material events. Although the constitution penetrates to the lowest levels of reality and the opposition is already present in the heaven, even so the former is more akin to the heaven and the latter to the realm of generation – the former belonging to Zeus and the latter to Poseidon.

So Proclus sees the two main sections of his first book as explaining the significance of the constitution and the war as images of principles that

Proclus on the constitution in the *Timaeus*

pervade the cosmos. His treatment of them is thus 'iconic', images being particularly appropriate to the Pythagorean manner of philosophizing (129.31–130.1),[84] and thus to the dialogue, as well as to the Socratic manner (7.32–8.1), and thus to the constitution. At this point we should perhaps examine Proclus' response to the separation of crafts:

Did we not first of all separate in it the class of farmers and of those with all other crafts from people of the class who were going to go to war for it? (17c6–8)

The discussion on the constitution and the short condensed summary of the classes in it makes a contribution to the entire account of the cosmic creation. For they act like images from which it is possible to re-focus on the universe. Indeed the Pythagoreans were the outstanding exponents of this very method, tracking down the similarities in realities by way of analogies, and passing from images to paradigmatic cases. That is what Plato is doing now too, showing us at the outset things in the universe as seen in human lives, and enabling us to study them. It is not remarkable either, for the constitutions of weighty (*spoudaioi*) persons are moulded on the organization of the heaven. Accordingly we too should relate the present images in words to universal matters, beginning with the matter of the division of the classes. This split of classes, you see, imitates the demiurgic division in the universe . . . (33.1–18)

We note here that it is again the Pythagoreans who are to be associated with the use of such images, tailored to capture the universal via the particular, and that the images concerned are not so much the images within the soul or state, but the images in words that had seemed to apply to these lesser levels. Proclus goes on to develop his comparison in various ways, showing just how versatile his hermeneutic methods can be. In fact one of the most striking correspondences in this lemma is that between the seven 'planets' and the various jobs in society at 34.12–27:

- Moon   farming sector
- Aphrodite   those arranging marriages
- Hermes   those arranging lots
- Sun   educators and judges
- Ares   warfarers
- Zeus   those who lead through intelligence
- Kronos   philosophers who ascend to the first cause

This seems to offer a remarkably detailed comparison between the heavens and the classes of the constitution. But Proclus now has to answer the objection that Plato's lemma had only actually made one division,

---

[84] Compare *Theol.* I. 4.20.8–12 for the Pythagorean nature of this method.

Introduction to Book 1

between the military class and the rest. The text is not as obliging as it might be.

We shall conclude this section with a gem of a miniature lemma from 32.20–9:

And as far as all of us are concerned it was described very much as intelligence requires. (17c4–5)

Narration in accord with intelligence, not in accord with pleasure nor in accord with opinion, indicates his admirable perfection and intellective grasp, and there is a riddling reference to the preceding consensual convergence of all the secondary causes into one intellect and one united creative process. Furthermore the addition of 'very much' signifies the transcendent nature of this unity, through which all the creative causes converge upon the single paternal cause of all things as if upon one single centre.

We have here:

- an ethical dimension, rejecting pleasure
- an epistemological dimension rejecting mere opinion
- a primary reference that is not too obscure
- a riddling (much more obscure) reference to the harmonious agreement of a variety of demiurgic forces
- a linguistic observation
- a link with the single Father to whom all creative causes revert.

Proclus can be ingenious, at times no doubt too ingenious. But let nobody doubt that his comments spring from serious engagement with the details of the text.

PROCLUS AND HIS PREDECESSORS ON ATLANTIS

Introduction

Proclus is the single most important source for the status of Plato's story of the war between ancient Athens and Atlantis. That is because the commentary tradition seldom threw away anything that it considered instructive or interesting, so that Proclus' text preserves what little evidence there is to supplement anything that one can derive from the text of Plato itself. This evidence goes back to the days of the Old Academy, and to the first ever commentary on the *Timaeus*, penned by Crantor and presumably dating from early in the third century BC, or shortly before.[85]

However, the likelihood that Proclus at the age of twenty-eight had immersed himself in all the earlier authors to which he refers, trying

---

[85] Dates for Crantor are variously given. I tend to follow Sedley (1997), 113, who gives 275 as his death, rather than Dillon (2004), 216, who gives 290.

60

Proclus and his predecessors on Atlantis

to understand their work independently and to reassess its import, is slim indeed. Rather one must consider which of those whom Proclus read is likely to have assembled early material and introduced it into the commentary tradition. The only earlier thinkers whom we know to have commented in any detail upon the Atlantis section of the *Timaeus* were Porphyry and Iamblichus (204.25–9). We know for certain that the Middle Platonist Severus did not, and we also know that the excessively 'philological' Longinus made it his practice to omit any detailed treatment of the story (204.17–24). Besides these figures Proclus mentions only Crantor, Amelius, Origenes, and Numenius as interpreters[86] of the story in the course of his exposition between 75.27 and 204.29, and the last three have probably been mentioned because of their importance for the formation of Porphyry's own views (cf. 77.6–7 and 23 on Origenes and Numenius). Porphyry must also be the source of what would appear to be reports of Longinus' *oral* views;[87] indeed, he is the kind of scholar who would be expected to assemble whatever information he could from disparate sources, thereby ensuring a rich tradition in subsequent commentaries.

Perhaps what we can be most sure of is the liveliness of debate concerning the meaning of the Atlantis episode in the time of Plotinus and his friends. Even so, Longinus' habitual reticence on the Atlantis story suggests that it was Porphyry who encouraged that debate, and developed a real interest in producing the first proper commentary on it. So what must hitherto have been skipped over quickly, being regarded as preliminary material that supplied the setting for the serious study,[88] now became a repository of ethical and psychological wisdom that could occupy most of the first book of a multi-volume study of the dialogue (204.27–9).

Early reactions to Atlantis

Literature on Atlantis may speak of a clash about the status of the Atlantis story even among Plato's immediate followers, contrasting the

---

[86] I do not find any strong evidence that Atticus, mentioned at 97.30–98.3, was genuinely interpreting the story, though it may be that he was treating the establishment of Athens prior to Sais at 23d–e, and defending Plato's version. If so, then he was presumably adopting a literal reading. The reference at 112.25–113.3 to Plutarch of Chaeronea, whom I tackle below, is to extant material unrelated to Atlantis.

[87] It seems most unlikely that Longinus wrote much on a story that he could not be bothered to lecture on (204.18–24), and the exchange between Origenes and Longinus reported at 63.24–64.3 clearly derives from an oral encounter witnessed by Porphyry.

[88] With Severus' attitude at 204.17 we should compare anon. *Tht.* IV which declares the conversation between Euclides and Terpsion to be something that requires no interpretation.

61

Introduction to Book 1

view that it is pure fiction, plausibly associated with Aristotle, and the idea that it was verifiable history, associated with Crantor. At 190.4–8 we read as follows:

Hence one should not say that the one who obliterated the evidence [*elenchon*] undermines his subject matter [*hypokeimena*], just like Homer in the case of the Phaeacians or of the wall made by the Greeks. For what has been said has not been invented [*peplastai*], but is true.

This innocuous-sounding sentence takes us straight to the early evidence for Plato's having invented the story of Atlantis. Posidonius (F49.297–303 Kidd), the Stoic from the second and first centuries BC, is being quoted by Strabo 2.3.6. He refers to the second Homeric example used by Proclus, and says of Atlantis 'He who invented it obliterated it, like the poet in the case of his Achaean wall.' The same verbs (*plassô, aphanizô*) are used by Strabo and Proclus for 'invent' and 'obliterate'. These verbs are perfectly tailored to remarks about the status of the story, since Plato himself uses the passive of *aphanizô* for the vanishing of Atlantis beneath the sea (Critias at 25d3), and *plassô* for the invention of such stories (Socrates at 26e4). The first passage is the climax of the story, the second is the battleground over which the status of the story must even today be fought.[89] These passages are thus related, and the original suggestion seemed to be that Plato had followed the best literary precedents by making sure that nobody could ask for the evidence for a story they invented, and actually incorporating the destruction of the evidence in the story. I suspect that both Homeric examples were used when the original remark was made, but one cannot be sure. The key question is that of the relation of the examples to the story of Atlantis' destruction, and it seems that they are indeed well chosen to suggest the elimination of evidence by gods using destructive waters.[90] Somebody then had suggested that Plato had pre-empted doubts about the absence of evidence for Atlantis by writing into the story an account of how it was washed away.

Strabo gives us a strong clue to the identity of this person at XII.1.36. Here the theme of the inventor of a story causing his constructs to disappear in the story, and the example of the Homeric wall, are again used, but here it is to Aristotle rather than Posidonius that the quip is attributed. Aristotle, like other significant pupils of Plato, is likely to have

---

[89] Cf. Johansen (2004), 45–6.

[90] See *Il.* 12.1–33 (cf. 7.433–63), *Od.* 13.149–87. One notes that Poseidon is in both cases involved, after receiving Zeus's consent to the destructive act, which is more or less implied in the curtailed story of Atlantis, where Zeus did indeed speak (*Critias*, 121b7–c5), but the final destructive act through earthquake and flood (tsunami?) bore all the hallmarks of Poseidon (*Tim.* 25c7–d3).

Proclus and his predecessors on Atlantis

had insights into the circumstances of the composition of the *Timaeus* and *Critias*, and it is possible that references go back to either an anecdote concerning him or to a lost work. Somehow that remark was noted by the geographical tradition followed by Posidonius and Strabo, and it could have reached Porphyry either via Posidonius[91] or via Crantor,[92] or perhaps through Ptolemy, geographer of the previous century.[93]

The principal difficulty in having Aristotle make a remark that clearly implied that the story of Atlantis was a fiction is that another seemingly good early authority, Crantor of Soli, has been understood as offering early support for the view that it is simple history. We have already raised difficulties about this view, but it is now time to examine properly what Proclus says.

Some say that all this tale about the Atlantines is [76] straightforward *historia*, like the first of Plato's interpreters, Crantor. He says that [Plato] was actually mocked (*skôptesthai*) by his contemporaries for not having discovered his constitution himself, but having translated the [ideas] of the Egyptians. He took so little notice of what the mockers said that he actually attributed to the Egyptians this *historia* about the Athenians and Atlantines, which says how the Athenians had at one time lived under that constitution. The prophets of the Egyptians, he says, also testify [for him], saying that these things are inscribed on pillars that still survive. (75.30–76.10)

What is not in doubt is that Proclus understood from his source that Crantor took the story of Atlantis as a historical account. So that *historia* is taken roughly as the equivalent of our 'history'. The original sense of the word, 'inquiry', had long since given way to meaning II in LSJ: 'written account of one's inquiries, narrative, history'. In other words it had become more of a name for a written genre, and it was rapidly taken over by the Romans in this sense. A discussion of the failings of Rome in *historia* is found in Cicero, *On Laws* 1.6–7, where Atticus asks Marcus to take up writing history, and what is quite clear is that Atticus' expectation of those who write *historia* is not the truth (which could be provided by mere annals). Rather it is an oratorical style that tells a narrative with dignity. The state that Cicero has saved could be *embellished* by him (*ornata*, 1.6), and his friend Pompey could be *praised* (*laudes inlustrabit*, 1.8). The genre had long accepted the idea that gaps in the historical

---

[91] Quoted at III. 125.14.

[92] Posidonius almost certainly used and responded to Crantor's commentary when offering his own interpretation of parts of the *Timaeus* dealing with the soul, since his position at Plut. *Mor.* 1023c–d clearly responds to Old Academic ideas (1012d–f), as Merlan (1960), 34–58, made clear.

[93] Ptolemy's name is found a number of times in the commentary as a whole, and in the Atlantis section he makes an appearance just before Aristotle at 181.16–20.

Introduction to Book 1

record would be filled, and that fictional speeches would be written for leaders, throwing light on events for sure, but embellishing and even distorting what was actually known to suit one's agenda or that of one's backers.

In these circumstances *historia* is not a word that carries any necessary implication of truth, even though it may perhaps suggest some attempt to find out what may have happened. All of Herodotus was unquestionably *historia*, even if there is a considerable amount of myth, travellers' tales, distortion, and especially magnification involved. The story of Atlantis could similarly be labelled *historia*, even though myth, travellers' tales, distortion, and exaggeration were an integral part of it. That the label could be applied to the particularly disreputable genre of travellers' tales can be seen from the title of Lucian's parody of the genre in which the narrator visits the moon: *Alêthês Historia (True [hi]story)*. What is told by Critias in the *Timaeus* is in fact a traveller's tale from an ancient poet.

For a final proof we should take the story of Phaethon from within the Atlantis episode, which Proclus announces that he will treat in three ways (109.8–9): *historikôs*, *mythikôs* and *philosophikôs* (i.e. as *historia*, as myth and as philosophy).[94] He continues:

> The *historia* asserts that Phaethon, the son of Helios and Clymene daughter of Ocean, veered off course when driving his father's chariot, and Zeus, in fear for the All, struck him with a thunderbolt. Being struck, he fell down upon Eridanus, where the fire coming from him, fuelling itself on the ground, set everything alight. Upon his fall, his sisters, the Heliades, went into mourning. It is a basic requirement that the conflagration should have happened (for that is the reason for the story's being told) . . . (109.9–17)

Nobody would affirm that the outline of the myth of Phaethon given by Proclus was exactly what happened, but it is precisely this outline of putative events that is labelled a *historia*. Proclus correctly sees that such stories are aetiological, i.e. are invented to serve an explanatory purpose. Consequently he does demand that the event requiring explanation, in this case a conflagration, should have happened. Physicists will then be able to treat it as a myth and explain the meaning of the story in their own terms, while philosophers will seek a loftier explanation. But the main point is that the *historia* was the bare narrative, and that nobody is urged to treat that bare narrative as 'history' in the modern sense. In fact, what was for him the *historia* is for us the myth!

Once it is realized that *historia* carries no necessary implication of truth it may easily be seen that the word translated 'straightforward'

---

[94] Festugière marks off the sections as follows: *explication historique* 109.10–16; *explication physique* 109.16–110.22; *explication philosophique* 110.22–114.21.

64

Proclus and his predecessors on Atlantis

which qualifies it, *psilê*, is not present to suggest straightforward *truth*, a meaning that would require something like the *alêthês historia* of Lucian's title above. The adjective's basic meaning is 'bare' or 'unclad', and it may also mean 'light-weight' or 'simple', and it is regularly used in this book to mean 'free of any more weighty meaning' (such as most interpreters from Numenius to Proclus himself attached to it). Hence the phrase as a whole suggests a narrative with no allegorical meaning.

Taking *historia* in its generic sense also throws light upon the first, unnamed group of interpreters to be contrasted with Crantor's group:

Others say that it is a myth and an invention, something that never actually happened but gives an indication of things which have either always been so, or always come to be, in the cosmos.

Now it may be seen that 'myth' is treated as a rival genre, in which a narrative story is consciously composed in such a way as to reflect eternal truths. It seems clear that the position of this group was that the story was 'false on the surface and true in its hidden meaning' (76.15–16). There is a contrast of genre[95] and a contrast between surface and hidden meanings, even without an explicit contrast of true and false. The next group of interpreters, however, seem to agree with Crantor regarding the genre, and with the other group with regard to the presence of an additional and more important meaning. Yet their agreement on the former issue with Crantor does not lead them to affirm the historical truth of the story, but rather to admit that things *might* have happened thus (76.17–18). As Proclus puts it himself 'nothing he said happened was impossible' (190.9). In conformity with this he attempts with reference to Aristotle to make credible the account of the flooding and disappearance of Atlantis (187.21–188.24), and with reference to various geographic sources to make credible the account of Atlantis' size (180.25–182.2). This last extract ends with the words:

We should not be sceptical about it, even if one were to take what is being said as *historia* only.

Here we have yet another indication that *historia* involves no implication of truth, for in that case the statement would be like saying 'we should not disbelieve it, even if one were to take it as true only'.[96]

---

95 This contrast is what is brought out again at 129.10: 'it is neither a myth that is being related nor a straightforward *historia*. While some understand the account only as *historia*, others as a myth . . .'

96 The meaning of *historia* in this debate will be clarified further in relation to Longinus below.

Introduction to Book 1

But let us move on to the real problem.[97] When Crantor's explanation of Plato's tactics is given, nothing is said about Plato remembering an ancient family story and being anxious to have the truth recorded. On the contrary, this is Plato's response to mockery. Public mockery came most often from the comic poets, to whose activity the verb for mocking (*skôptein*) had continued to be particularly appropriate, as one sees from its close conjunction with the verb *kômôidein* itself in Aristophanes' final play (*Plutus* 557). It is thus most likely to be comic poets who are suggesting that the substance of his constitution in the *Republic* was taken over from the Egyptians. Aristophanes' *Assembly-Women*[98] already contained satire at the expense of some philosopher promoting at around 393 BC the community of property and sexual partners, so such ideas were certainly capable of attracting comic attention. What, then, is it about the ideas that had brought Egyptians to mind? Is it that the charge was plagiarism, plagiarism is reprehensible, and the actual origin did not matter? Or was the borrowing of ideas from some quarters acceptable, and from others (including Egypt) ridiculous? I suggest that the parabasis of Aristophanes' *Clouds* (545–59) shows clearly that the poets did not eschew plagiarism, and that nothing was considered wrong about utilizing *good* ideas from other people. There was nothing wrong in imitating whatever it was about the Spartans that gave them an outstanding record in warfare, nor did other cities shrink from introducing the cultural heritage of Athens. Thus the ridiculous thing was that Plato took his ideas from *Egypt*.

Now while Egypt scarcely had the kind of political institutions that a normal Athenian citizen would think worthy of imitation, what was important was the Athenian image of the Egyptians. This has recently been discussed in relation to Atlantis by Johansen, who draws attention to criticism of the Egyptians in Plato's own *Laws*[99] and even at *Republic* 436a. Plato is shown to be building on a stereotype, perhaps present already in Aeschylus (fr. 373), but more visible in comedy,[100] and continuing

---

[97] The difficulties are also felt by Dillon (2003), 219, (2006), 22–3; they are explained away by Cameron (1983).

[98] See 571–82 for the intellectual character of the proposals, 590–610 for the community of property, 614–34 for the community of sexual partners, 635–50 for the recognition of children/parents, 651–4 for the provision of essentials, 655–72 for the novel justice that will prevail under these arrangements, 673–6 for the community of living and eating.

[99] Johansen (2004), 39–40: though Plato admired some aspects of their education, there is a significant reservation at 657a5, and then the charge of knavery and lack of liberality at 747b8–c8.

[100] Johansen (2004), 40, citing Ar. *Thes.* 921–2 (as understood by the scholiast), and Cratinus fr. 378K = 406PCG; tantalizing too is Cratinus Jun. 2, and Antiphanes 147.1–2K = 145 PCG.

66

Proclus and his predecessors on Atlantis

on to Theocritus 15.47–50. Egyptians, it seems, were generally credited with a crafty and untrustworthy nature. Furthermore, discourse on the subject of Egypt was not such as to be trusted, neither the more imaginative parts of Herodotus book 2 where the author's claims of *autopsia* seem particularly dubious, nor Socrates' tales from Egypt such as the Theuth-story at *Phaedrus* 275b3–4.[101] The Athenians would have been well aware that Plato had an interest in certain aspects of Egyptian lore and learning (including geometry), and the comic potential of tracing his precious political ideas back to the devious and illiberal Egyptians was quite considerable.

Mocking ridicule is only successful if there is some element of truth behind it, but it is at first sight implausible to think that the whole account of a Socratic state in the *Republic* could be stolen from Egypt. The Priest of Sais in the *Timaeus* does of course draw attention to the sharp separation of the classes, allowing for a separate priestly caste where knowledge resides, and a separate military class too (24a–b). He also draws attention to unremarkable similarities in weaponry, and to the Egyptian devotion to various kinds of divine learning from which things useful to humans may be found. But this does not add up to an especially close similarity to the state that Socrates has just recalled at 17c–19a, and it leaves out anything to do with community of property and community of wives among the guardians, as well as the arrangements for begetting children and selecting which of them are to be raised. It also makes no reference to most of the educational arrangements. In *Laws*, however, Plato notes things that he likes about the Egyptian rules, including the prohibition of any kind of artistic innovation, resulting in permanent traditions (656d–657a), and of course the importance afforded to mathematical education (747a–c). And to anybody who had studied the *Republic* carefully, the search for a near-permanent social system, inspired by a love for mathematical order and making much of the study of mathematics among its governing class, must have had something of an Egyptian ring about it.

So what response did Plato offer to such ridicule? According to Crantor, we are told, he was so untroubled by it that he actually attributed the story of the Athenians and Atlantines, including no doubt the idea that the Athenians themselves had once lived under Socrates' constitution, to the Egyptians. In fact Plato willingly takes up at 24a–c the idea that the original instantiation of the Socratic state shared *some* of the organization still known in Egypt, as if he were embracing *in part* the alleged charges of his mockers. For the summary of the Socratic constitution shows how limited the similarities are, even as regards education and learning (18a). But in having the Egyptians tell Solon that this sort of

---

[101] Quoted by Johansen (2004), 41.

Introduction to Book 1

constitution, with an emphasis on promoting valour and wisdom, went back to the earliest Athenians, as well as implying that the ideals had captured the imagination of the respected Athenian social architect Solon himself, Plato turns the charges around. He suggests there is nothing foreign about the proposed social structures, and implies that they are a legitimate part of Athenian heritage, lost through the ravages of time. Certainly they can be suspected of belonging elsewhere, but they can be traced back further, if not so much to Athens herself, then to the very goddess of wisdom who is their protector.

What we achieve by following through Crantor's interpretation is to reveal just how unexpectedly well it fits Plato's text, explaining the summary of the *Republic* and the Atlantis story together as part of an investigation into the real model for the Socratic constitution. This model will eventually be supplied by the discourse of Timaeus, when it offers the heavenly motions themselves as the pattern for the human soul to imitate (90a–d),[102] a 'paradigm in heaven' as *Republic* 9, 592b2 would describe it. But in seeing the beauty of Crantor's exegesis we also see that he is attributing to Plato a highly contrived opening dialogue, which excludes any possibility that the story of Atlantis is just an attempt to write plausible history. The more precisely the story is tailored to suit Plato's immediate objective of placing the Socratic state in its true context, the less its contents can be determined by any supposed historical truth. Furthermore, if Plato had been working from within his mockers' assumptions and accepting here the stereotype of the unreliable Egyptian,[103] then he was himself subtly undercutting Critias' story.

Is it really possible, then, that Crantor held *both* that the story of Atlantis was intended to be simple history, and that it was used by Plato as a means of turning the mockers' charges against them?[104] It is theoretically possible that history will coincide with exactly what one needs to make one's point, but it is unlikely that Crantor could at that time have been intentionally contributing to any vibrant debate about whether the story was historically true. Further, too strong a statement from the first

---

[102] It is important here that Crantor, unlike Xenocrates, explains the structure of the world-soul that displays these motions in terms of its cognitive capacities, Plut. *Mor.* 1012d.

[103] One notes that Socrates at 26e, though doing his best to respond positively, fails to make any comment at all about the possible implications of taking such a story from Egyptian sources.

[104] It may be argued that Proclus himself would have had no difficulty in accepting that the story was true in historical details, and yet carefully tailored by Plato to serve a non-historical purpose; but this is due to his assumption that Plato's purpose is to present a recurrent paradigm, for this should be able to be presented through an episode of history in which it is instantiated.

commentator that the tale was factual might have discouraged the development of allegorical interpretations, and indeed it might have been expected to ensure that the early pages of the *Timaeus* did not receive such neglect from early commentators as 204.16–24 may suggest. Yet *something* must have been said to make Porphyry think that Crantor took it as factual.

We now have to employ the distinction so important to those who adopt dramatic interpretations of Plato. We must distinguish, I think, between the view that *Plato* was trying to engage in historical inquiry and the view that Plato represents *Critias* as trying to do so. Commentaries often use the third person singular of verbs of speaking etc. in quite a confusing manner, so that one cannot easily determine whether it is Plato who is meaning something or his character. The problem is at its most acute in the case of characters who can be taken as 'spokesmen' for a Platonic position. Unlike Timaeus, Critias is not listed among Plato's spokesmen by Diogenes Laertius (3.52), but clearly a literal interpretation of Atlantis *as Platonic history* may regard him as such. Crantor did not have to regard him in this way. Now it is strongly suggested by 20d8-e1 that Critias thought he was offering a *logos* in the genre of history, being ultimately based on the same kind of historical inquiries as Herodotus had conducted. That the story had the authority of the respected Solon was enough. It is much less clear that Socrates accepts this because of the relatively obvious irony of his response at 26e4–5.[105] So Crantor could legitimately have been suggesting that *Critias* was offering his story as *historia* rather than as *mythos*, while explaining *Plato's* purpose in offering the story as quite independent of its genre or its truth-status. So far this would make the best sense of Proclus' evidence.

However, the evidence for Crantor then concludes with remarks about the Egyptian priests of his time: 'The prophets of the Egyptians . . . also give evidence, saying that these things have been inscribed on pillars that still survive.' Proclus presents this as evidence used to confirm the truth of the story, but can we be sure that Crantor was doing any more than repeating the element of the story that has the priest affirm that the story is written and preserved in the sanctuaries there (23a4–5)? Let us assume that Crantor was indeed saying that priestly characters in his own day would affirm that the story is recorded. Even this does not guarantee that Crantor accepted it at face value, for there was plenty of scope for irony in such a remark. If the whole discussion had developed from the critics' notion that the Egyptians are unreliable, and from Plato's using their unreliability to explain Critias' convictions about the story's truth, then the commentator's additional note about what present Egyptians

---

[105] See Johansen (2004), 45–6.

Introduction to Book 1

say would be confirming something. However, this would not be the truth of the story, but their own untrustworthy nature. It is easy for those who have listened to the myths preserved by modern tour guides to imagine the Egyptians trying rather too hard to oblige their Greek tourists. Proclus, in his anxiousness to say whatever he could on behalf of the literal as well as the symbolic truth of the Atlantis episode, certainly understood whatever report he received as a confirmation of literal truth, but Crantor's intentions were in all probability different. No commentator since Crantor, we may assume, was ever able to discover the account of Atlantis on the stone pillars of Egypt, and the geographers assumed that it was a fiction.

Our report of Crantor's discussion is of great value, but unfortunately Crantor's purpose in making these remarks could be very far removed from what Proclus wishes to achieve by quoting them. What is certainly interesting is that Crantor offered an account of the connections between the *Republic*, *Timaeus*, and *Critias*, seemingly in the course of offering some interpretation of the preliminary parts of the *Timaeus*, parts which some had refused to address. Whether we can say what type of interpretation he offered, beyond the fact that he did not postulate any deep allegorical meaning and that he stressed Plato's interaction with his own intellectual world,[106] seems to me to be highly doubtful.[107] Yet he has provided for us, in a very different fashion from Iamblichus, a path towards an understanding of the link between the preliminary material and the main dialogue. This was the link between prologue and substance that some figure associated with the Platonic tradition had once felt to be lacking in the dialogues of Theophrastus and Heraclides.[108]

The forerunners of Porphyry

Following discussion of Crantor, Proclus moves on at 76.10–77.6 to discuss several interpreters much closer to Porphyry, whose work was for this reason more likely to have been accurately reported by Proclus.

---

[106] One notes the similarity between this material and reports in authors such as Diogenes Laertius and Aulus Gellius of Plato's relations with figures such as Xenophon and Antisthenes.

[107] Attempts by Sedley (especially 1999a) to trace back the approaches to prologues encountered in Proclus, *in Parm*. 658–9 to Crantor's time seem to me to be reading far too much into Proclus' term 'ancients', which need only go back to the time of the early Neoplatonists. The three approaches listed are those of Severus, Porphyry, and Iamblichus in this book of the *in Tim*. But Sedley's use of the connection with Heraclides and Theophrastus (639) is indeed tantalizing.

[108] Bastianini and Sedley (1995), 489, on the end of Proc. *in Parm*. 659; see also note 118 below.

70

Even here, however, there are problems. It seems at first sight that no spokesman is named for the allegorical interpreters who denied outright that there was any historical truth in the story. This is followed, in an unusual order, by a great many who seem to have postulated a *primarily* allegorical interpretation: Amelius, Origenes, Numenius, Porphyry. Belonging to the middle of the previous century, Numenius is out of place, and his view appears to have been introduced as an afterthought because it is needed to explain the dependent position taken by Porphyry. My inclination is to assume that something is wrong with the way that Proclus has set out his material, and that Numenius had in fact denied the literal truth of the story. I believe this in part because it is much more likely that the first outright allegorical interpretation would have been prompted by the conviction that no alternative was possible. But at 83.25–7 Origenes is said to have followed Numenius' school to the extent that he claimed that the story was concocted. This seems unequivocal, as we shall show in relation to Origenes.

Numenius was typical of his age in respecting the religious traditions of various nations, including the Egyptians (fr. 1a), and his reverence for them would no doubt have made Crantor's explanation of the Atlantis-story very difficult for him to understand. Furthermore, it seems clear that he would not be expecting to find literal truth in such a passage. For he had a particularly strong interest in myth and in allegorical interpretation, which he applies to Homer's Cave of the Nymphs from *Odyssey* 13 (frs. 30–2), to Odysseus himself (fr. 33), to the Myth of Er from the *Republic* (fr. 35), and to the soul's prison (*phroura*) in *Phaedo* 62b.[109] Indeed, his interpretation of Timaeus' monologue discovered much hidden meaning.[110]

Soul and, in particular, a sharp dualism concerning soul are at the heart of Numenius' system. Myth had a history of representing pictorially the experiences of the unseen soul, and a key Platonic text on the interpretation of myths (*Gorgias* 493a–c) explained 'Hades' as 'the unseen realm' (b4) associated with the soul. It is therefore scarcely surprising that the story of Atlantis is taken by Numenius to reflect the conflict that is central to his psychology, the conflict between a finer and an inferior type of soul. The former souls are described as the foster-children or nurslings (*trophimoi*) of Athena, since in Athena's case the Athenians cannot be children but those she has adopted; the latter are generation-workers belonging to the god who has oversight of generation, i.e. to Poseidon. How far Numenius worked out the details of his interpretation is unclear,

---

[109] This is interpreted as pleasure in fr. 38, perhaps influenced by the bond of desire associated with Hades at *Crat.* 403bc.

[110] See now Tarrant (2004).

Introduction to Book 1

for he was not writing commentaries that required smaller matters to be tackled.

The same was presumably true of Origenes, who retained the idea that the war represented a conflict between unseen forces, but sees them rather as *daemones* (76.30–77.3). Once again there should be no surprise here, since one of Origenes' two written works was the treatise *On Daemons* (Porph. *VPlot.* 3), suggesting that the subject was a particular interest of his. Numenius' interpretation was presumably unattractive to anybody who did not recognize two kinds of soul, one intrinsically good and the other intrinsically bad, such that they could be forever in conflict. The study of *daemones* more readily allows for such divisions within its ranks. There is a problem in Origenes similar to the one that I raised regarding Numenius. He seems to be being classed by Proclus among the allegorical interpreters who acknowledge that the story may still be literally true. At 83.25 we read:

Origenes claimed that the narrative had been invented, and to this extent he agreed with Numenius' party, but not that it had been invented in the interests of artificial pleasure, in the manner of Longinus.[111] Yet he did not add a reason for the invention.

The term I translate 'invented', *peplasthai*, is Proclus' usual term for a manufactured story, directly connected with the noun *plasma* which Proclus had used to describe the views of those who denied the literal truth of the Atlantis story (76.10) as well as picking up Plato's *plasthenta mython* at 26e4. That would make Origenes too a holder of the view that the story is without historical foundation. If this is the case, Proclus must be speaking somewhat loosely at 76.21, where 'of these' (*toutôn*) must refer to *both* sub-groups of interpreters who postulate a deeper meaning, both those who deny the literal truth of the story and those prepared to entertain it. Linguistically, the more natural reference would have been solely to the *latter* sub-group, but in fact the latter sub-group may consist *only* of Iamblichus, who at 77.25–7 is the *first* to be credited with the view that the metaphorical meaning of the war does not invalidate its historical meaning, plus Syrianus and Proclus. In that case Numenius, Origenes, Amelius, and Porphyry would all have denied that the story was literally true.

Origenes' tendency to attack Longinus is again in evidence at 86.25–87.6, where Longinus' linguistic observations are scorned as the utterances of somebody who thought Plato's primary purpose here was to

---

[111] As will be shown, this is not intended to credit Longinus with the view that the story is fictitious.

Proclus and his predecessors on Atlantis

devise a feast of artificial pleasures for the readers,[112] turning Plato into a rhetorician rather than a philosopher.[113] Origenes thought that Plato's aim was rather to strive for a spontaneous intuitive rightness, without ornament, capturing with precision the hidden truths to which he alluded. This, I take it, confirms that he did not seriously consider the possibility that the war with Atlantis had ever taken place. Though Origenes was clearly dissatisfied with the linguistic points that Longinus used to raise, this did not stop him from commenting on similar points of his own. We find him at 93.7–15 solving his own puzzle about the use of the term 'most free-spirited' (*eleutheriôtatos*, 21c2) for Solon qua poet. While this proves that he did have some use for philology, in this case the philology seems to have been tailored to the idea that the framework of the story at least was meant, like the regular material of Platonic prologues, to illustrate practical ethics.[114] He also discusses the alleged 'temperance' (*eukrasia*) of the Athenian climate (162.27–30), but in the latter case the philological point relates firmly to the main subject of the *Timaeus*, and in particular to the heavenly motions and through them to soul. It is worth noticing that Origenes says nothing about *daemones* here, even though his own interpretation was supposed to involve a battle between *daemones* rather than heavenly motions (Amelius) or souls (Numenius).

The position of Amelius, who interpreted the story as an image of the struggle between the planets and fixed stars, was clearly an interesting one, but is not mentioned elsewhere. The Athenians represented the fixed stars, the Atlantines the planets, but in the struggle between their motions the overall movement of the universe (and hence that of the fixed stars) was bound to be dominant. We are given a clear indication that Amelius saw some kind of 'map' of the universe in the picture of a central island, surrounded by three 'wheels' of water and two of earth, and finally more land beyond the outside wheel of water (115d–16a, etc.). This does not fit with the seven circles of Proclus' text (176.28), but at least it can represent the earth, the outer circumference with its fixed stars, and *five*

---

[112] Another concept relating to pleasure, *charis*, seems to work itself into the very first sentence of the *Timaeus* according to Longinus (14.19 = fr. 24.14; cf. fr. 14b.2–3, 12), and shortly after at 19b (59.11 = fr. 28.2). Here Origenes agreed to the term *charis*, but still resists the suggestion that the aim is pleasure (160.1–3).

[113] It is no accident that Plotinus' famous remark about Longinus being *philologos* rather than *philosophos* (Porph. *VPlot.* 14, Longinus fr. 7) is recalled immediately between Longinus' observation and Origenes' response, while the idea of Plato aiming at a contrived pleasure recalls the orator and other flatterers in the *Gorgias*.

[114] The conviction that prologues concern themselves with ethics would also quite naturally have led to his attack on Longinus for assuming that Plato aimed here to gratify his readers (60.1–3, 83.27–8, and 86.25–7).

Introduction to Book 1

planetary orbits. It seems to me likely that Amelius had been reminded here of the Spindle of Necessity with its interlocking whorls in *Republic* 10 (616d–617b), which clearly did represent the heavenly motions. It also effectively reduced the number of separate motions between the centre and circumference to five by linking the fifth, sixth, and seventh together.

When one considers Proclus' own interpretative persistence and ingenuity, it is not difficult to understand the assertion that Amelius went to great lengths to justify his interpretation, even though we should not expect to be convinced by it. However, one point is perhaps worth making, and that is the way Amelius did arrive at an understanding of Atlantis that linked it firmly with the subject matter of the *Timaeus*. In particular it linked it with the important circles of the Same and the Other which will determine the heavenly motions and set the standard for the motions of our own souls (36c–d, 90a–d). In that respect he was more successful than either Numenius or Origenes. The main problem with Amelius' ideas is that they do not seem to be explaining anything that cannot be well explained directly, so that it is hard to know why Plato should have needed to tell this story at all. The invisible life of the soul is conveniently conveyed through images, but the motions of the heavens do have their visible indicators.

There is one other important predecessor of Porphyry whom we have yet to tackle, one who is not mentioned in Proclus' introductory remarks on the interpretative history of Atlantis. This is not Plotinus, who evidently felt no need to interpret such passages, but Longinus, who, in spite of his relative lack of interest mentioned at 204.18–24 (=fr.37), is nevertheless mentioned more than the others in the detailed discussion (= frs. 32–6). He is usually present as an object of attack, but his overall view of the story is never openly stated. At 83.25–8, quoted above, Origenes was said to follow Numenius in claiming that the narrative had been invented 'in the interests of artificial pleasure, in the manner of Longinus'. Here 'artificial' translates *memêchanêmenê* (83.27, cf. 86.26), and the point is that, like the word before (*peplasthai*, 'invented') it is suggestive of a kind of Platonic manufacturing. Though Origenes accepts Numenius' kind of manufacture as worthy of Plato, he does not go so far as to accept Longinus' hedonistic kind.[115] So it is important here not to assume that Longinus followed Numenius' view that *the story* is manufactured, for it is doubtful whether Longinus would have felt flattered to be accused of following Numenius in anything.[116]

---

[115] Longinus apparently supported his view that the story was meant to give pleasure with reference to the term *charis* at *Tim.* 21a2.
[116] I judge from fr. 4 and fr. 23.

74

Proclus and his predecessors on Atlantis

Once this is acknowledged, there is no obstacle to crediting Longinus with the view that the story of Atlantis was intended literally, and four arguments against finding deeper meaning in it found at 129.11–23 can readily be attributed to him. They exhibit both signs of his language[117] and his reason for Plato's having included the Atlantis episode: for seducing the reader into persisting with the work, rather like Lucretius' honey on the medicine-cup. The arguments may be summarized as follows:

- Plato's remarks at *Phaedrus* 229d discourage ingenious non-literal interpretations;
- Plato's methods of communicating doctrine are not obscure, like those of Pherecydes, but in most cases direct;
- allegorical interpretation is only necessary if one cannot explain the presence of an episode otherwise, whereas this episode is adequately explained by the need to attract readers into continuing;
- if one tries to offer a non-literal interpretation of everything, one will end up wasting as much time as people who explain every detail of Homer.

Clearly somebody was cautioning against the trend towards allegorical interpretation that had begun with Numenius. Although Proclus represents them as arguments for the story being just *historia* and not *mythos*, there is absolutely nothing here that affirms that the story is true. Rather *historia* is being used for an ordinary narrative exposition, while *mythos* implies the presence of a hidden meaning within the narrative. Since this is the same language as was applied to Crantor's interpretation and its converse at 76.1–10, we may be confident that Crantor was not necessarily taking the story as history in our sense of the word. We can now explain Longinus' absence from the main discussion of the interpretation of the story, for there is no reason to suppose that Longinus was adding substantially to the position espoused by Crantor. In fact Longinus' liking for Crantor may well be the main reason why material about him, and through him about his contemporaries,[118] still found a place

---

[117] I refer to the language of literary seduction (ψυχαγωγία), which had already occurred at 59.28 (Longinus fr. 28.20) and 83.23 (fr. 32.5). For this term's place in literary criticism see Patillon and Brisson (2001), 314–15.

[118] Taking my lead from Sedley's insight into references to the dialogues of Theophrastus and Heraclides at the end of Proc. *in Parm.* 659, e.g. Bastianini and Sedley (1995), 489, and Sedley (1999a), I have thought it right to ask myself how fairly obscure references to intellectuals of the late fourth and early third centuries might best have found their way into the *in Tim.* There seems to be no need to hold Crantor responsible for the use of Timon on the opening page, or to Eratosthenes and Theophrastus on the Nile (120.4–121.12), but when one finds a reference to Praxiphanes, the comrade of Theophrastus, sandwiched between material from Longinus and Porphyry's firm reply

Introduction to Book 1

in Porphyry, and hence in Proclus' commentary seven clear centuries afterwards.

Remarks about his views on the Atlantis story confirm that Longinus was resisting the trends that he detected in Platonic hermeneutics, making much of some details of language and puzzling over others. Interestingly he thinks that Plato is not committed to the remarks about Solon's poetic status offered by the elder Critias at 21c–d (fr. 34 = 90.18–20), and he goes to great length to explain away in particular Plato's seemingly non-factual remark on Athens' climate (fr. 35 = 162.15–27). But Longinus was of course Porphyry's example of how not to do philosophy.

Porphyry on the Atlantis episode

One may assume from the outlines of early interpretations at 76.1–77.24 that the principal influences on Porphyry's interpretation of 20d–27b were the three allegorical interpreters just covered. Proclus actually says that Porphyry thought he was offering a mixture of the positions of Numenius and Origenes, and he is particularly struck by how Numenian his view sounded (77.6–7, 22–4). Longinus, however, was a significant contributor to the exegetical debate, and remained a figure to be reckoned with. Porphyry directly engages with him at 94.7–9 and 162.31–3.

There are a total of seventeen fragments between 77 and 202, nos. X to XXVI in Sodano's collection, and it is not surprising that there are some recurrent themes among these. The majority of fragments contribute to the picture of a man of wide learning, well able to deal with geographical and religious matters, among others. Similarly many deal with, or at least touch on, matters of ethics. Since Porphyry thinks the war between Athens and Atlantis represents the struggle between superior souls and daemons associated with matter, it is inevitable that a number of fragments involve one or both of these. The moon seems virtually to represent Athens, being closely associated with Athena herself (165.16–19), with Asclepius (cf. *Tim.* 24c1) as lunar intellect whose craft is from Athena (159.25–7), and with Hephaestus because Earth and Hephaestus (*Tim.* 23e1), the parents of the Athenians, represent the moon and

---

at 14.20–8, one should ask who has ensured that his contribution to the philological debate was preserved. Theory has it that Crantor's commentary would have included a high proportion of philological material, e.g. Sedley (1997), 113. Again, at 90.21–8, immediately following material from Longinus, and still printed as Longinus fr. 34 by Patillon and Brisson (2001), 174, we have reference made to Heraclides, Callimachus, and Duris (this last a pupil of Theophrastus, ibid. 315). The dates of Crantor's death (possibly 275 BC) and Callimachus' birth (possibly 305 BC) are somewhat in doubt, but, if chronology allows, it would make excellent sense for Longinus to be following Crantor at this point.

76

Proclus and his predecessors on Atlantis

technical expertise respectively – while technically expert souls leaving Athena are sown into the moon (147.7–12). The type of soul sown into the moon then descends with a nature that reflects the terms 'war- and wisdom-loving' applied to Athena at 24d1. They engage with daemonic forces associated with matter, performing great and marvellous deeds (171.17–21). The location of Atlantis is in the west, because this was allegedly the place of badly-behaved daemonic powers (77.20–1).

It is characteristic of Porphyry that he specifies types of *daemones*, and that while the term may be applied to the heroic souls in the retinue of Athena, the daemonic forces whom they fight are described as characters (*tropoi*) embedded in matter, which have the power to affect the character (*êthos*) of souls (171.20–2). These kinds of *daemones* are the lowest two of the three classes posited at 77.9–15, the highest being divine *daemones* whose relevance to the story is not entirely clear. They may be identical with the 'archangels' of 152.12–14, who are turned towards the gods and serve as their messengers. In that case they would be 'divine *daemones*' in the sense of *daemones* belonging to the gods.

A similar tripartition of what are called *daemones* by Plato[119] is found in Calcidius' *Commentary on the Timaeus* (120), which was written well after Porphyry's time but is often thought to be dependent on Numenius for such materials. The three groups are associated with ether, air, and 'humid stuff'. The highest group are called angels,[120] then there are good daemons, and finally contaminated daemons, not specifically called 'evil' (133). Here it seems that as in Porphyry the middle rank of daemons, who differ from the angels only in degree, are actually souls and have a care for bodies (135). But certainly not all daemons can be souls for Calcidius himself, for there are specific denials at 136 that certainly apply to the highest and lowest ranks. The lowest kind, who are defectors from the rank of angels, stand close to matter,[121] which Calcidius reports as having been called 'bad soul' by the ancients.[122] The Calcidian parallels immediately suggest that much of Porphyry's material is as compatible with his Middle Platonic influences (mostly Numenian) as Calcidius' demonology had been. Proclus clearly had good reasons for seeing a close link between Porphyry and Numenius, and it may be that the main differences between Numenius, Origenes, and Porphyry were over which groups were best described as 'souls' and which as 'daemons'.

---

[119] Chapter 119; see Somfai (2003), 133, for discussion.

[120] See Somfai (2003), 137–8.

[121] No doubt the liquidity of the *essentia* with which they are connected symbolizes the flux of matter; cf. Calcidius on Numenius on Pythagoras at chapter 296 (Numenius fr. 52.33–7).

[122] 135; cf. Calcidius on Numenius on Plato at chapter 297 (Numenius fr. 52.64–70).

Introduction to Book 1

When one considers the use of the moon that Plutarch made in his imaginative discussion of souls and daemons in the *De Facie*, *De Iside*, *De Defectu*, and *Eroticus*, the Middle Platonist heritage seems almost overwhelming.

Porphyry does not restrict discussion of souls to his treatment of Atlantis, but also takes the general material about destruction by fire and flood as referring to the destruction of souls by inner forces, the conflagration of the passions and the floods of matter (116.27–117.18). He also uses comparative material from the myth of the war against the Titans (174.24–7). He imports material on the soul's cycle of lives from *Phaedrus* 248–9 into his discussion at 147.18 (cf. 28). And even the extensive scholarly material about children's memories at 194–5 can be seen as further development of psychological subject matter.

The following table, though occasionally requiring subjective judgement, might be useful for giving a general impression of the type of content that Porphyry is known to have included in his commentary.

Diehl	Sodano	General learning	Ethics	Soul	Demons	Moon	Critique*
77	X	Egypt		yes	yes		
94	XI	language					yes
109	XII	comets					
116–17	XIII	Homer & Heraclitus	yes	yes			
119	XIV	Egypt/Nile					
146	XV			yes			
147	XVI	Egypt/rites		yes		yes	
152	XVII	Egypt		??			
156	XVIII		yes	??			
159a	XIX		??				
159b	XX					yes	
162	XXI	geography					yes
165	XXII	rites	yes	yes		yes	
171	XXIII		yes	yes	yes		
174	XXIV	myth		yes	yes		
196	XXV	memory	yes				
200–2	XXVI						possibly
204	XXVII						yes

* usually critique of Longinus
[Note that 200–2 is not from this part of Porphyry's commentary, but does imply an answer to a previous question, while 204 is a general remark of Proclus implying Porphyry's dissatisfaction with Severus and Longinus among others.]

78

Proclus and his predecessors on Atlantis

From this table we have a rough idea of the *coverage* of the Atlantis chapters, and it must be said that we have a clear indication from 204 that his treatment was extensive. There seems little doubt that it was not proposing a particularly original line, but developing the work already done by Numenius and Origenes, perhaps with some attention to Amelius. While his treatment was not polemical in itself, it could not avoid offering firm answers to Longinus, who was at that time the surviving representative of the view that the story was to be read literally. Porphyry therefore must have provided information about a lively debate, extending from the general approach to interpretation to the details of individual passages.

This picture may be extended somewhat if one accepts that Longinus is the source of the literalist arguments at 129.9–23, for that would make it almost certain that the reply on behalf of the non-literalists at 129.23–130.8 is in essence Porphyry's reply. Let us briefly examine this:

> Others, however, base their view on the story of Phaethon, of which Plato says that it 'takes the shape of a myth, whereas its true reference' is to something else, one of the things that happens in the natural world; and they think it right to trace this story back to its connection with nature. For the Egyptians too, whom he makes the fathers of this story, put the secrets of nature into riddles through myths, so that the allegorical unveiling of this narrative would also suit the character who is telling it. Just as Timaeus himself will set forth his arguments in the way that is proper to Pythagorean philosophy, by interpreting nature through numbers and shapes as through images, so too the Egyptian priest would be teaching the truth of things through symbols, the manner that is proper to himself.
>
> In addition to this even Plato himself elsewhere censured those who were saying everything straight off, so that even to the cobblers, as he says, they may make their wisdom obvious. Consequently discourse that communicates truth in riddles is not foreign to Plato. This is what either side says.

There are really three arguments here. First Plato actually states that the story of Phaethon is to be interpreted allegorically; second Egyptian practice is to teach via myths that are devised so that a symbolic interpretation will teach us the nature of things;[123] third Plato thought it crude to reveal everything to the philosophically uninitiated. Now first, Porphyrian material at 116.27–117.18 is in fact talking about the Porphyrian interpretation of the result of Phaethon's journey, which deals with the overheating of quick-tempered souls, so there is no doubt that the story of Phaethon has been given a transferred meaning (somewhat

---

[123] Note that *Theol.* I. 4.20.2–12 agrees with this extract in associating the *Pythagoreans* with the method of teaching through images, and *myths* with teaching through symbols; it mentions only Orphics in connection with myths and symbols, being silent about Egyptian methods.

Introduction to Book 1

further removed from the basic meaning of the story than Plato's text invites). Second the amount of Egyptian material evident in the Porphyrian fragments confirms that he is likely to have related his interpretation to Egyptian interpretative practice if at all possible; and the final argument seems no more difficult to attribute to Porphyry than to other non-literalists. So we are supplied with rather more detail about the underlying rationale for Porphyry's interpretation.

These considerations help to lead us to the conclusion that not only had Porphyry adhered to a non-literal interpretation in which everything was being brought to bear on the unseen experiences of souls, but that he had also actually denied the literal interpretation, like Numenius and Origenes. And that in turn allows us to see the whole debate up to the time of Iamblichus in terms of a dispute over whether the Atlantis story should be read as a straightforward narrative or as an allegory. We are not convinced that there was ever an interpreter who was convinced that the story of the conflict between Athens and Atlantis was historically true in our sense, and hence questions of the detailed truth of the Atlantis story never actually arose. Porphyry had no need to try to compromise by allowing that, though allegorical, it might also have been historical. This would happen only when the terms of the original debate had been misunderstood.

Plutarchean interlude

Before proceeding to Iamblichus we should take a few moments to consider how Plutarch had responded to the story of Atlantis. Since he himself used Crantor and Posidonius in his *De Animae Procreatione*, one would expect the influence of any keen debate about the status of the story to have surfaced in his work. Plutarch does find the occasion to include material on the story in his *Life of Solon* (26.1, 31.6–32.2), and there were three allusions to the *Critias* (though none to the relevant section of the *Timaeus*) in the *Moralia* according to R. M. Jones (1980, 118). One of these is to the universe as conceived by 'Timaeus' (106a at 1017b), while the other two concern the moral values of the ancient Athenian state (109b–c at 483d and 801d). None of these has any implication for the status of the story.

Since he usually favoured a fairly literal reading of Platonic texts, it is not surprising that Plutarch treats the story as a straightforward narrative, and its connection with Solon as a broadly historical one.[124] He does not find it difficult to believe that Solon had heard that story from

---

[124] However, Plutarch does deny Critias' account of why Solon never managed to write his poem on Atlantis, attributing it to old age rather than lack of time (31.6).

80

respected priestly figures in Egypt. However, he seems to have had no interest in finding any historical content in the accounts of prehistoric Athens, Atlantis and their war. The lack of interest is perhaps reflected in 31.6, where he talks of 'the Atlantic account (*logos*) or myth (*mythos*)', a seemingly neutral expression, yet one which clearly calls into question the sincerity of Socrates' assumption that it is a *logos* as opposed to an invented *mythos* (26e4–5). Plutarch was not likely to miss the hints of irony here. Perhaps this perception helped his Academic caution to triumph over his sense of devotion to Plato.

In 32.1 Plutarch ventures to say a little about Plato's plans for the story, but the main motives attributed to him seem to be family obligation and ambition. There is nothing about the preservation of history or any ulterior purpose within a sequence of dialogues. Plato's ambition is supposedly shown in the glorious detail of his picture of Atlantis – the kind that no other *logos* or *mythos* or poetic composition ever had. This seems to indicate that Plutarch thought that, at very least, Critias' account of Atlantis was full of material that was not part of any received story and had been added so as to import an entirely contrived grandeur and magnificence into it. Plutarch, I would claim, viewed the story in its Platonic version as no better than historical fiction. Hence Plutarch does nothing to alter our picture of a scholarly world without any notable advocate of the view that the story of Atlantis was strictly and literally true.

It would be worth adding here that Seneca's *Natural Questions* would be a natural place for some mention to be made of the Atlantis story – if its literal truth had been suspected. The work deals with floods and earthquakes, and mentions well-known examples. The disappearance of Helice and Buris beneath the waves (373 BC) is mentioned at 6.23.4, 6.25.4, 6.26.3, 6.32.8, 7.5.3–4 and 7.16.2, while Atalante's similar fate during the Archidamian War (Thuc. 3.89.3) is reported at 6.24.6. Yet even the last cannot prompt a mention of Atlantis. And in Pliny's *Natural History* (6.199) we do find a mention, in a geographically vague section on islands off Africa, of an existing island called 'Atlantis', again without this prompting any mention of Plato's sunken island. What we do find in this period is the claim in Strabo (2.3.6 = F49.297–303 Kidd), going back to Posidonius, that it is *possible* that such a catastrophe might have occurred. But this occurs in a context with implications for physical science, not for Platonic exegesis.

Iamblichus and Proclus

In its broad outlines the Iamblichan interpretation of Atlantis is also Syrianus', and therefore Proclus' interpretation. This is immediately clear at 77.24–8 (*in Tim.* fr. 7):

Introduction to Book 1

Well, these people at any rate were in my view given a really splendid caning by Iamblichus. Both he and my own teacher prefer to explain this conflict not at [the expense of] setting aside the surface meaning, but on the contrary, in the conviction that these things have happened *in every sense*.

It should be immediately obvious that 'these people' are Amelius, Origenes, Numenius, and Porphyry, and that the thrust of the attack was directed against the view that the surface meaning should be set aside or invalidated. Iamblichus' strategy had been to view the story as a good historical example that could be used to illustrate with considerable precision the rivalry that is fundamentally embedded in the cosmos, appearing at a succession of metaphysical levels in slightly different guises. At the highest level it appears in the juxtaposition of the Dyad with the One (not the supreme One) that is opposed to it. At some levels it is present eternally, at others it appears in a temporary fashion that can be spelled out in a narrative. The ubiquity of the pattern can explain why Plato could take a particular true story and make it mean something on a universal level, so offering a story that accords with Critias' words in being 'true in every way' (20d8). Because earlier thinkers had failed to see the universality of the pattern, and only sought one level at which the narrative would fit some truth, none of them had been in a position to see that a symbolic truth does not exclude a literal truth. This was Iamblichus' invention.

Naturally, an important step towards this interpretation was Iamblichus' conviction that everything within a dialogue must be seen as contributing to its single goal or *skopos*. That meant that the Atlantis story had to be contributing in some fundamental way to the understanding of the natural world. This would require an interpretation rather different from the ethical and psychological approaches adopted by Porphyry and his predecessors. At times he may be found trying to substitute an interpretation that suits a physical study for one better suited to a study of souls and their lives (*in Tim*. frs. 12, 15), though signs of anti-Porphyrian polemic are not limited to such cases. Furthermore, the single-*skopos* idea would entail that not merely the narrative of the war had additional symbolic meaning, but also the frame story about Solon (93.15–30 = *in Tim*. fr. 10) and the passing of the story to Critias (*in Tim*. fr. 24). But occasionally Iamblichus surprises by refusing to postulate a symbolic meaning for some details of the text (*in Tim*. fr. 23), though this may be inspired as much by his dislike of Porphyry's approach as by theoretical considerations.

As will readily be seen, Iamblichus' position involves postulating a column of opposites, whose inspiration was the famous Pythagorean

82

Proclus and his predecessors on Atlantis

column, through which tension or conflict pervades all metaphysical levels below the primal One. This means that the war between Athens and Atlantis symbolizes something that is found everywhere and at every level, being quite as important for the construction of the cosmos as Heraclitus had long ago maintained. So whether Amelius found that conflict in the heavens, or Porphyry found it in a clash between good souls and awkward daemons, they would be unnaturally focussing on a *part* of the meaning that the story needs to have. Its symbolism was of the greatest importance, and, as we have seen in relation to Socrates' constitution, the constitution and the war were images of the unifying and divisive elements in the cosmos respectively. One way in which I feel that Iamblichus differs from Porphyry is in his removal from the Longinus-inspired environment where the text is mined for all that it can yield. An Amelius or a Porphyry can seize upon clues in the text that will support their *specific* understanding of it, but Iamblichus looks rather at 'wholes', relating big episodes to the themes of the whole dialogue, and he needs no clues in Plato's language to narrow his idea of Atlantis' sphere of relevance.

Obviously, given the breadth of Iamblichus' interpretation he had to believe that in human history things like that do happen. If Plato's story accurately reflects a central feature of the cosmos that is instantiated at every level, then it must be instantiated at our level too. Hence we read at 76.17 that 'Some do not rule it out that this could have happened in this way', and this already points forward to Iamblichus. Further, 77.25–8 suggests that the main tenet regarding the outward meaning of the story was that it did not have to be seen as a lie in order for the full allegorical significance to be appreciated. Perhaps he was already keen to claim what we read in Olympiodorus (*in Gorg.* 46.6), that Platonic myths (as opposed to poetic ones) do one no harm if one takes them literally and fails to see an allegorical meaning. What we do not find in Iamblichus is any attempt to prove that the literal meaning is historically true.

Proclus may perhaps have gone one step further in the quest for historical truth. Though much of the argument to support the acceptance of a historical meaning is designed to prove that details given here by Critias are not as impossible as they seem, there are occasions when Proclus seems to demand more than this. While 190.7–8 again stops at cautioning against dismissing the story, his discussion of the less credible details at 177.10–21 and 180.25–182.2 does use material from the geographers that can be seen to support there having been an Atlantis of the general size and type described. Often, however, he speaks as if Plato had been at liberty to alter details, and often he seems to think of

Introduction to Book 1

the demands of history as those of a genre rather than historical accuracy. Some of the tensions here may be due to the particular blend of Iamblichan considerations and what Proclus has updated, but to demand strict accuracy would be superfluous. Neither Iamblichus nor Syrianus nor Proclus ever intended that the historical meaning should get in the way of their metaphysical one.

On the Timaeus *of Plato: Book 1*

*Proclus on the Socratic State
and Atlantis*

Analytical table of contents

Proclus *in Timaeum* 1.1–204

Prefatory remarks, 1.1–14.3

Preliminaries I: the target of the *Timaeus*, 1.1–4.5
  Preliminaries II: the plan of the *Timaeus*, 4.6–7.16
  Preliminaries III: the literary character of the *Timaeus*, 7.17–8.29
  Preliminaries IV: the background of the discussion, 8.30–9.24
  Digression on nature, 9.25–12.25
  Relation to the *Parmenides*, 12.25–14.3

Introductory texts, 14.4–26.20
  The missing person, his sickness, and its consequences, 14.4–26.20

Socrates' constitution, 26.21–75.25
  Remembering the Socratic constitution, 26.21–28.13
  Why recapitulation is appropriate and why it fits here, 28.14–32.29
  The separation of classes, 33.1–36.31
  The role and character of the military class, 37.1–40.13
  Education and upbringing of the guardian class, 40.14–42.8
  Community of property and of lives, 42.9–45.27
  The position of females, 45.28–50.3
  Arranged marriages, 50.4–52.10
  The demotion of children in the universe, 52.11–54.10
  The lessons from the summary of the constitution, 54.11–55.26
  Explaining Socrates' desire, 55.27–59.7
  Socrates' feeling and Plato's beautiful creation, 59.8–61.29
  Point two: Socrates' inadequacies, 62.1–63.12
  Point three: the inadequacies of the poets, 63.13–66.32
  Point four: inadequacies of the itinerant sophists, 67.1–28
  Point five: those capable of such praise, 68.1–69.10
  The qualifications of Socrates' companions, 69.11–72.15
  Transition to the story of Atlantis, 72.16–75.26

Atlantis, 75.27–191.13
  The early debate over the genre of the story of Atlantis, 75.27–77.24
  The Iamblichan view of Atlantis, 77.24–80.8
  Details of the text at *Tim.* 20d7–e1, 80.8–19
  Family trees and their significance, 81.20–83.14
  The appropriateness of the Atlantis story, 83.15–85.30
  Three lemmata in brief, 86.1–88.8

On the *Timaeus* of Plato: Book 1

Athenian religious history, 88.9–89.5
The hidden lessons of the events at the Apaturia, 89.6–90.12
Praising Solon's story and handing down his work, 90.13–93.30
Two brief lemmata, 93.31–94.28
Dynamics of the passage on Sais and Egyptian geography, 94.29–96.2
Individual questions on Egyptian geography and its symbolism, 96.3–97.9
The history and religion of Sais, 97.10–99.26
Ancient and more recent history, 99.27–100.16
Greek and Egyptian antiquities, 100.17–101.24
Was the priest's reply an insult? 102.1–103.6
Seniority and youth as universal symbols, 103.7–104.17
Cyclic processes of generation and destruction, 104.18–108.7
Introduction of, and various approaches to, the myth of Phaethon,
    108.8–114.21
The problem of deviations in the heavens, 114.22–116.1
The temporal spacing of catastrophic events, 116.1–21
Iamblichus criticizes Porphyrian allegorical interpretation, 116.21–117.27
Brief discussion of the theological implications of two more passages,
    117.28–119.6
Geographical interlude: the swelling of the Nile, 119.7–121.26
Temperate climate and continuity of human habitation, 121.27–123.15
The preservation of memory and its universal counterpart, 123.16–124.29
Several lemmata more briefly considered, 125.1–129.8
The question of the status of the story resumed, 129.9–132.30
Solon's request, the priest's response, and what they signify, 132.31–134.22
Digression on the peplos, 134.22–135.15
The symbolism resumed, 135.15–136.8
General digression on cosmic divisions and divine lots, 136.9–139.17
Readiness for the reception of a god, 139.17–140.15
How Athena comes to have Athens and Sais, 140.15–142.10
Hephaestus, 142.11–144.18
The priority of the Athenians, 144.18–145.4
An Iamblichan difficulty and its solution, 145.5–31
The dates of ancient Athens and of Sais, 146.1–148.16
Lexis: details of the text interpreted, 148.17–150.18
The Egyptian class structure compared, 150.19–156.11
Weaponry compared, 156.12–157.23
The wisdom of the goddess and her two cities, 157.24–158.30
Lexis: some details considered, 158.31–160.22
Allotment and selection, 160.23–162.10
Earlier thought on the balance of the seasons, 162.10–30
Proclus on the balance of the seasons, 162.31–164.21
Miscellaneous additions, 164.22–165.5
The dual character of Athena – earlier interpretation, 165.6–30
The dual character of Athena – Proclus' interpretation, 165.30–168.27
Other epithets of Athena, 168.28–169.22

Analytical table of contents

The Athenians and what they stand for on a universal level, 169.22–170.24
The Athenians' greatest deed and its paradigmatic significance,
170.25–171.23
The Athenians' opponents and what their confrontation represents,
171.24–175.2
Lexis: the overall interpretation applied to details of the text, 175.2–177.9
The compatibility of historical and symbolic interpretations, 177.10–178.10
Lexis: principles applied to details of the geography, 178.10–180.4
Symbolism of the confined sea, 180.5–21
The size of Atlantis, 180.22–182.2
The symbolism of the power and influence of Atlantis, 182.2–183.20
The description of Atlantis' power as narrative, 183.20–30
Atlantine power unified within the straits, 184.1–23
What the Athenians stand for, 184.24–185.11
The Athenians and other peoples within the straits, 185.12–186.7
Lexis: details of the text explained, 186.7–187.12
Science, symbolism and the destruction of Atlantis, 187.13–190.30
Summary of interpretation of Atlantis, 190.31–191.13

Closing considerations, 191.13–204.29
The status of Critias and his story, 191.13–192.27
Critias' delayed memory, 192.28–194.9
On the memory of children, 194.10–195.30
The cosmic significance of the agreement with Timaeus and Hermocrates,
196.1–29
Socrates agrees on the story, 197.1–24
Luck, listening, and their cosmic significance, 197.25–198.20
The order of the trilogy: *Republic – Timaeus – Critias*, 198.21–202.10
Lexis: details of this passage and the next considered, 202.11–204.15
Conclusion, 204.16–29

On the Timaeus *of Plato: Book* 1

Prefatory remarks (1.1–14.3)

Preliminaries I: the target of the Timaeus

It seems to me to be glaringly clear to all who are not utterly blind to serious literature that the aim of the Platonic *Timaeus* is firmly fixed upon the whole of physical inquiry, and involves the study of the All, dealing with this from beginning to end. Indeed, the Pythagorean Timaeus' own work has the title *On Nature* in the Pythagorean manner. This was, in the sillographer's words, [the point] 'from which Plato began when he undertook to do *Timaeus*-writing'.[1] We used this work as an introduction to our commentary, so that we should be able to know which of the claims of Plato's *Timaeus* are the same, which are additional, and which are actually in disagreement with the other man's – and make a point of searching for the reason for the disagreement. This whole dialogue, throughout its entire length, has physical inquiry as its aim, examining the same matters simultaneously in images and in paradigms, in wholes and in parts. It has been filled throughout with all the finest rules of physical theory, tackling simples for the sake of complexes, parts for the sake of wholes, and images for the sake of their originals, leaving none of the originative causes of nature outside the scope of the inquiry.

The more sharp-witted of us ought now to go on to observe that the dialogue engages appropriately with an aim like this, and that Plato alone, while preserving the Pythagorean character of the study of nature, has fine-tuned the teaching that he had adopted. For physical inquiry, to put it briefly, is divided into three, one part busying itself with matter and material causes, the next including investigation of the form too and revealing that this is more properly a cause, and the third part demonstrating that these do not even have the role (*logos*) of causes (rather they play the role of supplementary requirements), postulating that the 'causes' in the strict sense of natural occurrences are different: the productive, the paradigmatic, and the final.

---

[1] Timon of Phleious, 54.3 = 828.3 (Lloyd-Jones and Parsons). Timon's story and the question of the Pythagorean background to Plato's work together provide much of the impetus for Siorvanes (2003).

On the *Timaeus* of Plato: Book 1

10   The majority of physicists before Plato have spent time on matter, some affirming that one thing is the substrate, others that something else is. For even Anaxagoras, who seems to have seen that intellect is responsible for occurrences 'while the rest slumbered on',[2] makes no further use of intellect in his explanations, but instead holds various kinds 15 of air and of aether responsible for events, as Socrates says in the *Phaedo* (98c). Those who have led the faction after Plato,[3] not all of them, but at least the more exacting, believed that the physicist should study the form too, alongside matter, tracing back the origins of body to matter and form.[4] For although they may perhaps make mention of the productive

[2] Commentators note that the phrase occurs at *Rep.* 390b6. Though that passage could be quite unrelated, one notices a similar irony, insofar as the very one who exhibits the greatest wakefulness (there Zeus, here Anaxagoras) lapses into forgetfulness. The pioneering (but largely unexploited) causal role of Anaxagoras' intellect was perhaps the best-known feature of his thought, following *Phd.* 97c1–2, Arist. *Metaph.* 984b18–20, 985a18–21 etc.

[3] The term *haeresis*, which sometimes signifies a school in the doctrinal sense, though it does not do so in an institutional sense (Glucker 1978, 166–93), should not here be interpreted as a school, but as an approach to nature that continues to emphasize the part played by matter and material change in a broadly Ionian tradition. It is natural that Proclus should contrast that tradition, which he associates with the *synaitia* or supplementary requirements, with the Pythagorean tradition, linked below with the study of true causes. The germ of this contrast is present in Aristotle, who tackles the Ionian tradition at *Metaph.* 1.3–4, then the Pythagoreans and Plato in 1.5–6; he could be interpreted as seeing the former as his own predecessors (983b1). Hence Festugière errs not only in his interpretation of the word as a formal School (École philosophique), but in the consequent notion that this is the Academic tradition of which Aristotle was seen as a leader. Clearly, for this to be the Platonic tradition, some Platonists or Aristotelians would have to be seen as neglecting form as well as the motive cause.

[4] This is widely assumed to be Aristotle (see *Phys.* 2.1, 192b13–193a2), but the plural suggests that it is not exclusively a reference to Aristotle. I assume that Proclus has post-Platonic materialistic philosophy in general in mind, seeing Aristotelians as offering a version that may at least be *reconciled* with Plato. While one might legitimately ask whether Aristotle's well-known theory of four causes was ever such as to encourage his system to be seen in two-cause terms, one should note that Proclus does not consider Aristotle to be any more than a willing user of *Plato's* system of causes (and then only of four rather than five of them), and that the issue is not one of paying lip-service to a type of cause (as may be seen in the traditional criticism of Anaxagoras), but of actually making use of it. At the universal level it is quite legitimate for Proclus to accuse Aristotle of having no *qualifying* creative power and no purposeful intent. The veiled criticism of Aristotle's theory of causes has its antecedent in Syrianus, e.g. *in Met.* 1080a4, 121.22–31, where the fact that only enmattered form is allowed calls into question the existence of a creative cause motivated by the desire to bring about a form-related end. The absence of the paradigmatic cause effectively excludes the final, which in turn severely limits the concept of the creative cause, so that all three causes in the strict sense of the term are unable to play a significant role in Aristotle. He is therefore left in the company of those who fully utilize only the *synaitiai*.

92

Prefatory remarks

cause as well, as when they affirm that nature is the origin of motion,[5] 20
they still deprive it of any vigorous (*drastêrios*) or strictly productive role,
since they do not agree that this [cause] embraces the structures (*logoi*)
of those things that are created through it, but allow that many things
come about spontaneously too.[6] That is in addition to their failure to
agree on the priority of a productive cause to explain all physical things at
once, only those that are bundled around in generation.[7] For they openly 25
deny that there is any productive [cause] of things everlasting. Here they
fail to notice that they are either attributing the whole complex of the
heavens to spontaneous generation, or claiming that something bodily
can be self-productive.[8]

Plato alone follows [the tactics of] the Pythagoreans: his teaching 30
includes the supplementary requirements of natural things, the recep- **3**
tacle and the enmattered form, that are subservient to what are strictly
'causes' in the process of generation; but prior to this he investigates the
primary causes: the one that creates, the paradigm, and the goal.[9] It is
for this reason that he sets over the All:

demiurgic intellect, 5
an intelligible cause in which the All is pre-established,
and the Good, which stands before the creator in the role of object
of desire.

For because that which is moved by another is dependent upon the power
that moves it, it evidently cannot naturally bring itself forth, nor complete
itself, nor preserve itself. For all these tasks it needs the productive cause 10
and its integrity is maintained by it. That means that the supplementary
requirements for physical things ought to be dependent on the true
causes:

---

[5] On nature as the origin of motion, Festugière refers to *Phys.* 2.1, 192b13ff. and, more
specifically, *Metaph.* 5.4, 1014b16–21.

[6] The absence of the *logoi* in the creative principle (equivalent to Ideas or paradigms to
which the creator can refer) deprives that principle of creative *intent*, and so allows for
unintentional creations. For spontaneous generation in Aristotle see *Phys.* 2.4–6, 195b31
etc.

[7] While it can be seen from the attention afforded to the gods and the heavens in the
present work that the physical world of Proclus extends far beyond generation, he now
has in mind Aristotle's ungenerated and imperishable bodies made of aether.

[8] Though Festugière notes that Epicurus took the first of these alternatives, this is an
unwitting dilemma into which Aristotle is thought to plunge. What Proclus is doing is
deducing the consequences of this denial, based on the true premise that for any x, x
must either be produced by another, or be self-produced, or be un-produced.

[9] Proclus ascribes to Plato the same five causes as had already been found in Seneca *Ep.* 65,
and which are also present in Porphyry fr. 120 Smith (which adds a sixth, the accessory
or *organikon*). See on this Baltes (1987–), IV Bausteine 116–17.

On the *Timaeus* of Plato: Book I

by which a thing is produced,
in relation to which it has been fashioned by the father of All,
and *for the sake of which* it has come into being.[10]

So it is with good reason that Plato investigated and taught in detail about
all these [three], plus the remaining two, form and matter, which are
dependent on these. For this cosmic order is not the same as intelligible
or intellective cosmic orders, which are rooted in pure forms, but there
is in it a part that acts as structure (*logos*) and form, and a part that acts
as substrate. However, this can be investigated another time.

That it was with good reason that Plato attributed the cosmic creation
to all of these causes is evident from this much. [the Good, the intelligible
paradigm, the productive force, the form, the substrate.][11] For if he
were speaking about the intelligible gods, he would only be indicating
that the Good was their cause, as the intelligible number derives from
this cause alone. If it were about the intellective gods, then he would
have posited both the Good and the intelligible as their cause, as the
intellective plurality proceeds from the intelligible Henads and from
the single source of realities. If it were about the hypercosmic level,
then he would be producing them from the intellective and universal
creation, plus the intelligible gods, plus the *overall* cause – for that is, in
a primary, ineffable, and inconceivable manner, the basis of all that the
second things are generative of. Since, however, he is to converse about
immanent things and about the cosmos in its entirety, he will allocate it
both a matter and a form that enters into it from the hypercosmic gods,
he will link it to the whole creative process, he will assimilate it to the
intelligible Animal, and he will declare it a god through participation in
the Good. In this way he will bring the whole cosmos to completion as
an intelligent and ensouled god.[12]

---

[10] At 3.13 editors reject the MSS οὗ ἕνεκα in favour of Kroll's plural; bearing in mind
the singulars in the two lists of 3.3–6, an excellent alternative might be to change the
preceding relatives (ἀφ' ὧν, ἅ) to the singular, for, though the antecedent 'causes' is
plural, that could involve three separate *singular* causes. At the cosmic level there can be
only one final cause (and plausibly one 'father' and one paradigm), but 3.11–13 seems
to be a statement about causes in general, so that the plurals would not be out of place.
Fortunately the question need not affect the translation.

[11] I excise these words as a gloss on 'all of these causes'. They break the natural connection
between τούτων and the reasons that follow.

[12] Note that the five causes are now linked with a fivefold metaphysical hierarchy: (i) a
single final cause, that is a cause of everything, (ii) a limited number of intelligible
gods or henads that function as paradigms of all that comes into being, (iii) intellective
gods responsible for demiurgic creation of all that comes after, (iv) hypercosmic gods
that are a source of form to what lies below within the world, and (v) matter that
is needed as the last of the causes for the physical world that we know. While the

Prefatory remarks

Preliminaries II: the plan of the Timaeus

So we've now identified and described the target [*skopos*], at which, according to us, the *Timaeus* aims. This being so, it's quite appropriate that at the beginning the order of the All is indicated through images, in the middle the total creation is recounted, and towards the end the particulars and final stages of the creation-process are fitted in with the universals. The resumption of the *Republic*'s constitution, you see, and the myth of Atlantis, are instances of the study of the cosmos through images. For if we focus on the unification and the plurality of things within the cosmos, we shall say that the constitution summarized by Socrates is the image of its unification, establishing as its goal the all-pervasive communion of things, while the war between Atlantis and Athens narrated by Critias is the image of their division, particularly of the opposition implied by the two columns.[13] Whereas if [we go] by the distinction between heavenly and sublunary realms, we shall claim that the constitution is assimilated to the heavenly arrangement (for Socrates too says that its paradigm is founded in the heavens),[14] while the Atlantine war is likened to generation, which subsists through opposition and change. So these things precede the universal physical inquiry for the reasons stated.

Following upon this he teaches the demiurgic cause of the All, and the paradigmatic, and the final. With these pre-existing, the All is fashioned both as a whole and in its parts. For its bodily component is constructed with forms,[15] being divided both by demiurgic divisions and by divine numbers, and the soul is produced by the demiurge, and filled

---

passage gives a very economical picture of Proclus' divine hierarchies, it is particularly useful for showing how a complex system of divinities is able to be reconciled with the fairly modest requirements of the *Timaeus*: essentially Good, Paradigm(s) or intelligible Animal, and Demiurge. Given that the five-cause system is itself of much earlier origin, found already in Seneca's *Epistle* 65, it is not surprising that in this economical version the Proclan divine hierarchy seems relatively easily reconciled with some of Middle Platonism, where the pattern Good – Intellect/Ideas – Soul – Body/Forms – Matter recurs (see Tarrant 1985, 136 n.7). Five causes and a five-stage metaphysic are similarly linked in Plutarch of Athens (Proclus *in Parm.* 1059.3–7) and his Rhodian predecessor (1057–8), so the traditional nature of this material is assured.

[13] Referring to a quasi-Pythagorean series of pairs of opposites introduced into the interpretation of the story by Iamblichus, and retained by Proclus; see below 78.1–25 etc. for these *systoichiai*.

[14] A reference to *Rep.* 592b, a passage late in book 9 to which Platonists of antiquity often referred.

[15] I differ from Festugière and Lernould here in taking the first dative with the main verb (is the bodily component *cut* by forms?), the first καὶ as 'both', and the second two participles with the participle.

On the *Timaeus* of Plato: Book 1

with harmonic ratios (*logoi*) and with divine and demiurgic symbols,[16]
5   and the total living creature is bonded together[17] in accordance with the
unified compass[18] of the cosmos in the intelligible realm, while the parts
that are within it[19] are appropriately positioned in the whole – both the
bodily parts and the life-giving ones. For individual souls that are being
settled within it are enlisted in the company of their guiding gods,[20]
5   and become worldly via their own vehicles,[21] imitating their leaders,[22]
and the mortal creatures are fashioned and given life by the gods of the
heavens.

[16] The symbols are, to the reader of the *Timaeus*, the unexpected element of the list.
There is a distinct possibility that its presence here is influenced by *Or. Chald.* fr. 108
(des Places) = Proclus *in Crat.* 21.1–2.

[17] This involves the interweaving of soul and body at 36d–e, where Plato uses a different
verb of weaving (e2).

[18] For comparable meanings of περιοχή cf. I. 73.14, 148.26. Lernould translates 'contenu',
rejecting Festugière's 'plan', and includes considerable discussion at 76 n.34. It seems
clear to me that we have a reference to the paradigmatic living creature at 37c–d to
which the universe is assimilated, and which contains all that is to be contained by the
universe of our experience (39e).

[19] This 'it' is masculine or neuter, and could in theory refer to either the total living
creature (so Festugière and Lernould) or to the intelligible realm (which I feel makes
better sense). Lernould (68) makes the mention of parts a major new step in Proclus'
conception of the plan of the *Timaeus* in spite of the fact that the language does not
suggest any shift, as it certainly does at 4.26 and at 6.7. It seems to me that the place of
the parts *within the whole* is still concerned with the creation *of the whole*.

[20] While the equal allocation of souls to each of the stars at 41d8-e1 is the passage that
Proclus has in mind here, also relevant are the gods of *Phaedrus* 246e4–247c2, in whose
train human souls attempt to follow. Zeus is there spoken of as 'the great *guide* in heaven',
but one can try to follow any one of eleven gods (cf. 250b, 252c–d), so that Proclus'
idea of guiding gods fits this text well. So he argues that the examination of humans
examines the universe through the microcosm (cf. 202.26–8), as well as coupling the
observer with the object under observation.

[21] The doctrine of a *pneuma*-like chariot for each individual soul has a long history, as can be
seen from the relevant appendix in Dodds (1963), 315–21. The Platonic passages that the
doctrine is based on are drawn from the *Phaedo* and *Phaedrus* as well as the *Timaeus*. The
present passage makes it imperative to locate discussion of the chariot in the *Timaeus*,
but the only relevant use of this term for 'chariot' occurs at 41e2. Festugière here denies
that Proclus has in mind the allocation of the souls to stars (or astral souls guiding those
souls), so much as their being mounted in a type of chariot (which Proclus *distinguished*
from the stars themselves in his interpretation of 41d8-e2). That each individual soul
has its own personal chariot is made clear at *in Tim.* III. 265.22–266.14. In this context,
Lernould's reference (69) should read '41d8-e1 et 41e1–42d4'.

[22] It is worth noting that one should not speak of the 'fall of the soul' in Proclus, for
whom the descent is a proper function of soul. See on this Trouillard (1983), who sees
that, just as the process of demiurgic creation necessarily involves a carefully mediated
incursion into generation (with the 'buffer' of the younger gods etc.), so the soul's
descent (mediated by the psychic vehicles) imitates the generosity of god. This analogy
is pursued by Proclus at *in Tim.* III. 324.5–24 (discussed by Trouillard at 188–9).

Prefatory remarks

This is the place where the human being is examined,[23] both the manner of its composition and the reasons for this; and the human being comes prior to all the others, either because its examination is also particularly appropriate to us, as we hold before ourselves the definition of a man and live in accordance with this,[24] or because the human being is a miniature cosmos[25] that contains partially all those things that the cosmos contains divinely[26] and completely. For we are in possession of active intelligence,[27] and rational soul that proceeds from the same father and the same life-giving goddess[28] as the universe, and a

10

15

[23] This refers to the preliminary discussion of human souls from 41d to 47e, which belongs to the works of reason, and is placed before the discussion of the receptacle and the bodily elements. From 5.7 until 6.6 we have in effect an attempt to explain exactly why human beings, though partial, are discussed in relation to the whole.

[24] Proclus is thinking of the widespread *logos* of a human being as a rational animal, rationality allegedly being the area in which humans differ from other animals. The philosopher will try above all to foster that which is most distinctive in him, his reason. Human rationality is particularly important to the Neoplatonists' interpretation of the *Alcibiades*, which is viewed as an essay on the nature of the human being, and as the first step in the process of acquiring a Platonic education.

[25] I.e. a microcosm, embracing all the basic ingredients that constitute the cosmos, particularly body, soul, and intelligence. Proclus finds this in the *Philebus* (29a–30d) as well as in the *Timaeus* (see *in Tim.* I 202.25–8), and it had been a commonplace of Greek philosophy since Democritus B34.

[26] Presumably here 'divinely' = perpetually.

[27] Here Proclus uses the now standard tactic of seeing the active intelligence of Aristotle's *De Anima* 3.4 as a Platonist feature and as part of the human being.

[28] The life-giving goddess, of whom Proclus also speaks at 11.19–20, 2.151.7–10, etc., is identified by Festugière (and those who write on the Chaldean Oracles, e.g. des Places 1996, 133) with Hecate, whose place in the Chaldean Oracles is discussed by Brisson (2003), 118–19. However, this goddess is not mentioned by name in this work except for III. 131.26 (where she and Artemis are said to be residents of the moon) and in the citation of *Or. Chald.* 32 at I. 420.14. If we were to insist on finding a goddess *within this dialogue* to fulfil this function it would have to be Ge, 40b–c, though she would make a strange parent of soul. Rather it is clear that he has in mind the mixing-bowl of 41d, seen from Iamblichus (fr. 82) on as an originative cause of all life, as it is for Syrianus (*in Tim.* III. 247.26–248.5) and Proclus (III. 248.12–13; 249.27–250.8). It would at first sight seem that Proclus' introduction of a mother-goddess for rational soul departs from the authority of *Philebus* 30d, insofar as both soul and intelligence are there seen within the nature of Zeus. However, the situation is more complicated than this, for when we examine his discussion of the mixing-bowl we find that Syrianus had indeed seen the female power as well as the male as belonging (i) to the father and demiurge of all and (ii) his heavenly imitator, and yet thought that the mixing-bowl had been used to give a separate indication of the female life-giving power. *Philebus* 30d is then quoted by Proclus in further discussion (249.3–26) with considerable approval for its suggestion of twin powers in one. This passage would also make *Hera* (cf. III. 251.7–8) the most appropriate additional divine name describing the female generative power. Hera is found to be a generative force alongside Zeus at 46.27 (following Orphic fr. 163; cf. I. 450.21), at 79.5–6 she is the *choregos* of rational animal birth, and at III. 318.6–7 the younger gods

97

On the *Timaeus* of Plato: Book 1

vehicle of aether that has the same role [for us] as the heaven does [for the universe], and an earthly body composed of the four elements – to these it is also *coordinate*.[29] So, granting that it was necessary to observe the All from many perspectives, in both the intelligible and the sensible realms, in paradigmatic and iconic modes, in universal and particular modes, it would be a plus that the account of the human being should also have been fully worked out in the course of the study of the All. Moreover, one could even use the old argument, that, in conformity with Pythagorean custom, he had to link his object of study with an account of the studying subject. Since we are trying to apprehend what the cosmos is, we should presumably add this further question: what ever is it that views these things and comes to apprehend them through reasoning? He showed that he had kept an eye on this too, when he explicitly declares near the end (90d), that whoever would obtain a life of well-being 'must liken that which tries to apprehend to what it is apprehending'. For the totality is always in a state of well-being, and our part too will be well-off when likened to the All. Moreover, in this way it will be returned to its cause. Since the human being here stands in the same relation to the All as the intelligible man does to the Animal itself, while there secondary things always cling fast to primary ones, and the parts do not stray from the wholes and are founded in them, whenever the earthly human being is assimilated to the universe, he will also be imitating his own paradigm in the appropriate fashion, becoming orderly (*kosmios*) through his likeness to the cosmos, and well-off through his being modelled on a god who enjoys well-being.

In addition to what we have mentioned, the final stages of creation have also been elaborated, both their general kinds and specific details,[30]

---

imitate Hera in the creation of life. At III. 190.6–7 Iamblichus is reported as making her cause of power, coherence, fulfilment and life. The situation is complicated by the fact that *in Crat.* 143 (81.2–4) identifies the life-giving power with Rhea, and does so in the context of *Or. Chald.* fr. 56 des Places (p. 30 Kroll), causing commentators (e.g. des Places, p. 134) to speak of Rhea-Hecate. For careful consideration of these issues and discussion of a *triad* of life-giving goddesses (Rhea/Demeter, Hecate, Kore) see van den Berg (2003). However, the moral of this is that simplistic identifications of a given unnamed divinity in Proclus with a related power in *one* of the texts that he sees as inspired are unhelpful. Proclus is assuming that there is a female divine power with a given kind of function; the name that might be given to this power in riddling texts is less of a concern to him.

[29] 'it is likewise coordinated' (Taylor), 'avec lesquels il a affinité' (Festugière). The phrase in fact means that the four elements play the corresponding role for us to the one that the elements play in the universe.

[30] General are the works of necessity, 47e–68d, the receptacle and the four elements, including material on motions within the universe, and also on sensations. Specific are the details of animated physical beings that follow (works of reason working together

Prefatory remarks

those that arise in the skies or on earth or within living creatures – those that are contrary to nature and those that conform with it. Just here the basic principles of medicine are also revealed, this being the point where the natural philosopher leaves off, since he is a student of nature – for what accords with nature goes together with nature, while what is contrary to nature involves passing beyond it. Accordingly, it is the physicist's job to establish in how many ways this deviation occurs, and how one may be restored to balance and to the natural state, but it is for the medical craft to unravel what follows from all this. It is in this [passage] that Plato most closely joins company with the other physicists; for they spent their time on the lowest works of nature that are the most deeply embedded in matter, by-passing the heavens as a whole and the orders of encosmic gods, because they had matter in view, abandoning the forms and the primary causes.

It seems to me that the incredible Aristotle was also pursuing Plato's teaching to the best of his ability when he arranged his whole treatment of physics like this.[31] He saw there were common factors in all things that have come to exist by nature: form, substrate, the original source of motion, motion, time and place – things which Plato too has taught about here, [talking of] distance, time as image of eternity coexisting with the heavens, the various types of motion, and the supplementary causes of natural things[32] – and that other things were peculiar to things divided in substance. The first of these were what belonged to the heaven – in agreement with Plato insofar as he made the heaven ungenerated and composed of the fifth essence; for what is the difference between calling it a fifth element and calling it a fifth cosmos and a fifth shape as Plato did?[33] The second were what was common to all the realm of coming to be, an area where one can admire Plato for the great detail in

with necessity, 68e–90d), including the healthy and diseased states of those beings and how they might best be restored. For a different view see Lernould (71–2).

[31] My division is as follows: *The totality of creation* (Books I–IV): (1) form, substrate, the original source of motion, (2) motion, time and place; *Things peculiar to regions*: (3) Heavens and fifth element, (4) Sublunary world (a) skies (detailed), (b) animals (treated materially). See also Festugière (p. 30).

[32] Distance is spoken of in relation to the world-soul at 36a, where the musical meaning of 'interval' is paramount; time as image of eternity at 37d, types of motion at 40a–b and 43b–c, supplementary causes at 46c–e. Proclus is trying to relate these Aristotelian topics to material in the discussion of the works of reason.

[33] The dodecahedron of 55c and the question of whether there is one world or five at 55d had long been linked, being clearly present in Plutarch *Mor.* 421f. 427a ff. under the acknowledged influence of Theodorus of Soli. The issue of whether Plato acknowledged a fifth element had been hotly debated among Platonists in Middle Platonist times, even within the pages of Plutarch (*Mor.* 422f–423a), with Atticus fr. 5 resisting any such idea. Alcinous (13–15) makes use of it somewhat inconsistently (Dillon 1977, 286).

On the *Timaeus* of Plato: Book 1

5   which he studied both their real natures and their properties, correctly preserving both their harmony and their polarities. As for what concerns coming to be, part belongs to things in the skies, whose principles Plato has accounted for, while Aristotle has extended their teaching beyond 10   what was called for; but part extends to the study of animals, something which Plato has given a detailed explanation of with regard to all their causes, including the final causes and the supplementary requirements, while in Aristotle's work they have only with difficulty and in a few cases been studied in relation to form. For in most cases he stops at the point 15   of matter, and by pinning his explanations of physical things on this he demonstrates to us just how far he falls short of the teaching of his master. So much for these matters.

Preliminaries III: the literary character of the Timaeus

After this let us state the genre (*eidos*) of the dialogue, and its literary character.[34] There is universal agreement that Plato took over the book 20   of the Pythagorean Timaeus, the one that had been composed by him on the subject of the universe, and undertook to 'do Timaeus-writing' in the Pythagorean manner.[35] Moreover, this too is agreed by those who have had a mere fleeting encounter with Plato, that his character is Socratic – both considerate and demonstrative. So if there's anywhere else that he 25   has combined the distinctive features of Pythagorean and Socratic, then he obviously does this in this dialogue too. In the Pythagorean tradition it contains loftiness of mind, intuition (*to noeron*), inspiration, a tendency to link everything with the intelligibles, to depict the Whole in terms of numbers, to give an indication of things in a symbolic and mystical 30   fashion, to lead upwards, to remove one's focus on the particulars, to state with affirmation.[36] From the considerate Socratic [manner] it pos-
8   sesses approachability, gentleness, a tendency towards demonstration, to studying reality through images, to moral content, and so on. Therefore the dialogue is elevated, and derives its conceptions from above, from the very first originative principles. It mixes the demonstrational

---

[34] Note that this is not a reference to the various types of dialogue-character popular in the second century AD, and found in Albinus *Prol.* 3 and D.L. 3.49. That classification had in fact been based more on philosophic criteria, while Proclus here deals with the dialogue's literary character and approach.

[35] An allusion to Timon of Phleious 54.3, as quoted at the opening of our treatise.

[36] The Pythagorean character is crucial for Lernould in his explanation of the way that physics is transformed into theology (2001, 341), but he makes much of the implication already encountered (2.29–3.19) that the Pythagoreans concentrated on the three highest causes rather than form or matter. Note, however, that these causes do not reappear in the discussion of the Pythagorean character of the *Timaeus* here.

Prefatory remarks

method with the revelational, and it prepares us to understand physical things not only from the point of view of physics but also from that of theology.[37] For nature itself, which guides the All, is dependent on the gods and animated by them when it directs the bodily element; though it is not really a god,[38] it is not excluded from the characteristics of the divine because it is illuminated by what are really gods. If then one should actually be making one's words similar to the things 'of which they are interpreters' as Timaeus himself will say (29b), it would be appropriate for this dialogue also to have a theological element too as well as its physical element, in imitation of nature that is the object of its study.

Furthermore, since things are divided into three in conformity with the Pythagorean view, into intelligible things, physical things, and things in between the two, those which they are in the habit of calling mathematicals,[39] and [since] it is possible to observe all of them in all of them in the manner appropriate to each (for the middle and final things are foreshadowed in a primal way in the intelligibles, and both [the other two] are present in the mathematicals, the first things iconically and the third paradigmatically, and there are glimmers of what had preceded them in the physicals), it was surely with good reason that Timaeus, in establishing the soul, gave an indication of[40] its powers, its ratios (*logoi*), and its elements through mathematical terminology, while Plato distinguishes its peculiar characteristics from the geometrical figures,[41] and

---

[37] The theological perspective of Proclus is of central importance to Lernould, who uses such passages as I. 217.25–9, 204.9–15, and 227.2–3, appealing also to Beierwaltes (1969, 131).

[38] I am tempted to read οὔτ᾿ ὄντως for οὔτε ὡς, and Tim Buckley points out to me that a scribe may have deleted what he thought was a dittography, mistaking ν for υ in minuscule.

[39] Diehl compares Iamblichus *VPlot.* 157, but the tripartition would seldom be thought to precede the Academy, and is perhaps most reminiscent of the so-called unwritten doctrines of Plato (see Arist. *Metaph.* 1076a17–22 etc.).

[40] The term *endeiknusthai*, translated 'give an indication', is used in the context of metaphorical, and in particular symbolic, meanings. That is to say that the mathematical terminology does not directly describe what the soul is like. Plato reserves his more straightforward use of mathematics for the construction of the physical bodies.

[41] This translation takes a different view from that of Festugière, who translates 'définisse les propriétés de l'âme à partir des figures'. First, there must here be some kind of *contrast* between 'Timaeus' and 'Plato' which Festugière fails to capture, a contrast indicated by the marked change of subject, and implied by the principal point of this section – that the dialogue blends the Pythagorean approach with the Socratic or Platonic (cf. 9.27 below). Second, this seems to force the meaning of ἀφορίζομαι ἀπό, which would normally indicate separation. Plato, I take it, is thought of as reserving his treatment of geometrical figures proper until the physical elements are explained, while still taking over *from the Pythagorean original* appropriate mathematical terminology for describing

On the *Timaeus* of Plato: Book 1

declares that the causes of all these things pre-exist in an originative way (*archoeidôs*)[42] in the intelligible and demiurgic mind. That suffices on this topic, and our inquiry into the details will be able to give us a better grasp of the dialogue's character.

Preliminaries IV: the background of the discussion

30   The background is roughly as follows: Socrates had come to Piraeus for the festival and procession of the Bendidea, and held a conversation

9   on state organization with Polemarchus the son of Cephalus, Glaucon, Adeimantus, not to mention Thrasymachus the sophist. On the day after this one, in the city, he had told the story of the discussion at Piraeus to Timaeus and Hermocrates and Critias and another unnamed fourth per-

5   son in addition to these, as described in the *Republic*. After this narration he encouraged the others too to repay him with an appropriate banquet of words on the day after that. So they have reassembled on this day to listen and to speak, the second day[43] after the discussion at Piraeus,

10   since the *Republic* said 'I went down to the Piraeus yesterday' (327a), while this dialogue says 'the banqueters of yesterday who are now the entertainers'.

However, they were not all present for this session, as the fourth is missing because of illness. You might perhaps ask why it should be that the listeners for this discussion should be three, when the subject is

15   the entire universe. I shall reply that it's because the father of the *words* should have a position analogous to the father of the *deeds*,[44] because this cosmic creation according to word (*logos*) is an image of the cosmic creation according to intellect. Analogous to the demiurgic triad that take over the one universal creation of the father is the triad of those who

20   receive the words.[45] Of these Socrates is the uppermost, who through the kinship of his life [with the others'] fastens himself directly upon Timaeus, just as the first member of the paradigmatic triad is united

---

the various features of the soul. The 'powers' could be connected with various circular motions (36b–d), the 'ratios' with those of 35b–36b, and the 'elements' with the basics of its construction (35a–b).

[42] The term is confined to Neoplatonist or Neopythagorean authors: Theon, Syrianus, Proclus, and Simplicius.

[43] The Greek says the third, counting inclusively.

[44] For the idea of a father of words, analogous to the Father of Deeds of 41a, see further the note to 95.15 below.

[45] Proclus operates with a Father of Demiurges, lowest member of the triad of Intelligible and Intellective Gods, and a triad of demiurges below this, themselves Intellective Gods.

102

Prefatory remarks

with the one before the triad. These things, if it so please the gods, we shall express more clearly in what follows.[46]

Digression on nature

So now that we have identified and shown the breadth of the dialogue's aim, described its tactics, the literary *character* so admirably blended together within it,[47] the whole background, and also the participants and how they are appropriate to the present discussions,[48] it would be appropriate to pass on to the actual detailed reading[49] and investigate everything as well as we are able. However, bearing in mind that the term 'nature', being applied in different ways by different people, is a source of confusion to people fond of investigating Plato's view – his way of looking at it, and what he wants the essence of nature to be – let us treat this matter first. For presumably this is appropriate for the dialogue, with its inquiry into natural studies, to know what nature is,[50] whence it proceeds, and how far it extends its own productive activity.[51]

This is because some of the ancients (i) used the term 'Nature' for matter, like Antiphon,[52] some (ii) for form, as Aristotle did in many places,[53] and some (iii) for the whole thing, like some of those before Plato of whom he says in the *Laws* (892b5-c7) that they called what arises by nature 'natures',[54] whereas others (iv) equated it with

---

[46] See next 23.31–24.11.   [47] I prefer to delete the first comma of 9.27.

[48] On the preliminary topics see Introduction, pp. 49–52; also Mansfeld 1994, particularly 30–7 on Proclus' Plato commentaries. Mansfeld (30) describes Proclan practice as 'less scholastic, or schematic, than that recorded in Anon. *Proleg.*, though not less systematic'.

[49] The *lexis* is the study of successive lemmata of the text, as opposed to free discussion of longer passages (or of general issues as here).

[50] Festugière compares the proem of Ps.-Plut. *Epitome*.

[51] This is effectively asking at what levels in the hierarchical structure and progression of reality nature belongs.

[52] An unexpected figure to feature in a Neoplatonist doxography, but of course this material is ultimately dependent on Aristotle's *Physics* itself, to which (2.1, 193a9–23) Festugière correctly relates it together with its sequel – even while showing (pp. 35–6) that Antiphon belongs to the Aetian tradition, usually as revealed in Stobaeus only (*Dox.* 1.22.6, 2.20.15, 2.28.4 (both sources), 2.29.3, 3 16.4 (Ps.-Plut.)).

[53] See especially *Phys.* 2.1, 193a30–b12.

[54] Aristotle does not indicate that such a view was seriously held, but rejects it anyhow, *Phys.* 2.1 193a5–6. Diehl and Festugière note that Plato had used the singular, as opposed to Proclus' plural, without observing that the plural is what appears in our MSS at 892b7, corrected by editors from Eusebius (who has a different version of the following six words too), because of a singular relative pronoun that is assumed to refer back to it. But when the Platonic text is in doubt, Proclus' text might perhaps have been used as *evidence* for it. The text of Plato's manuscripts may be defensible (though I prefer to read

103

On the *Timaeus* of Plato: Book 1

10 natural properties – things being heavy or light, and rare or dense – like some of the Peripatetics and of even earlier physicists; others (v) called god's craft 'nature',[55] others (vi) the soul, and yet others (vii) something like this. But as for Plato, he does not believe that the term nature should refer primarily to matter, or the form-in-matter, or the body,

15 or the physical properties, yet he stops short of identifying it outright with soul. He taught us the most accurate approach to it by locating its essence in between the two, i.e. between soul and bodily properties, inferior to the former by its being 'divided about bodies'[56] and by its failing to revert back to itself,[57] yet excelling the things that come after it[58] by

20 its having the formal principles (*logoi*) of all things and generating them all, and bringing them to life. It accords with our common notions that nature and what agrees with or happens by nature should be two different things, just as the product of craft is other than craft itself.[59] And intelli-

25 gent soul and nature are two different things, for nature is what belongs to bodies, deeply embedded in them and existing as something inseparable from them, whereas soul is separable and is rooted within itself,[60] and belongs at the same time to itself and to another – being 'another's' by the participation of others in it, and 'its own' by its not sliding into what participates,[61] just as the father of the soul is only 'his own' by

30 being unparticipated. Moreover, before him, if you like, the intelligible paradigm of the entire world is just 'itself'; for these constitute a

---

ἣν οὐκ ὀρθῶς ὀνομάζωσιν αὐτὸ τοῦτο for the problematic ἣν οὐκ ὀρθῶς ὀνομάζουσιν . . .), the αὐτὸ τοῦτο being included precisely in order to explain, and mitigate the harshness of, the singular relative. These people's use of φύσεις involves an illegitimate meaning of φύσις.

[55] An adaptation of Stoic theory, in which *fire* that operates according to craft is identified with nature, e.g. *SVF* 1.171; 2.774, 1133–4.

[56] The phrase links nature with one of the starting-points of soul at *Tim.* 35a2–3.

[57] The text of Diehl implies that nature fails to revert to soul, but we follow Festugière in preferring αὐτήν to αὐτήν, seeing the typical Neoplatonic concept of self-reflexivity here.

[58] As the text stands this presumably means 'after soul', and it would be necessary to read μεθ' αὑτήν for μετ' αὐτήν to make it clear that 'after nature' is meant. We should thus assume that nature is not seen as something unequivocally 'after soul'.

[59] Refuting view (iii) above, perhaps along lines suggested by *Laws* 892b, where the distinction between craft (b3) and what arises through craft (b8) is similarly present. At b6–7, Plato might not be objecting to the term τὰ φύσει but to the description of such things as φύσεις.

[60] Again we follow Festugière in preferring αὐτῇ το αὑτῇ.

[61] I.e. its identity remains higher than that of a participator, which in this case would be the ensouled creature. My soul will be mine, but insofar as it remains separable it will also be its own.

104

Prefatory remarks

series: itself, its own, its own and another's, another's, other.[62] This [last] is obviously the whole sensible world, in which there is separation and division of every kind, while of the others one was nature that is inseparable from bodies, another the soul that is within itself and gives the light of a secondary life to another, another the demiurgic mind that 'remains within the character of *its own* according to its manner' (*Tim.* 42e5–6),[63] and another the intelligible and paradigmatic cause of all things made by the demiurge, which Plato also saw fit to call 'animal *itself*' for this reason. So nature is the last one of those causes that construct this sensible bodily world and the limit of the plane of bodiless substances, but it is full of formal principles and properties through which it directs immanent things, and while it is a god, it is a god through its having been divinized and does not have its being a god from itself.[64] We also call the divine bodies gods in the sense of images of the gods. Nature gives the lead to the whole cosmos through its own powers, preserving the heaven at its own highest point, governing generation through the heaven, and everywhere securing links between particulars and universals.[65] With a character like this, nature has processed from the life-giving goddess:[66]

Up on the back of the goddess Boundless Nature is hung.[67]

From this goddess all life proceeds, both the intellective [life] and that which is inseparable from things managed.[68] Being attached from that point and suspended from it, it pervades all things unhindered and breathes life into them. On her account even the most lifeless things

---

[62] 'Itself' is the natural translation of the Greek αὐτό, since 'the same' would technically be τὸ αὐτό, yet 'same' would preserve the intended contrast with 'other'. It is tempting to relate this fivefold metaphysic to the system of five causes. In two cases they can be equated: paradigmatic cause = paradigm (itself/same), creative cause = demiurge (its own); a looser connection may perhaps be postulated between final, formal and material causes and (respectively): soul (its own and another's), physical nature (another's), the sensible world (other).

[63] See Festugière's note. It is necessary to read this passage alongside Proclus' treatment of 40e at III. 315.7ff., where ἦθος is taken to indicate the *sameness* of rest, and τρόπος the distinctive manner of the demiurge's rest. Plato's original meaning is unclear.

[64] At 8.5–9 above its status is somewhat less provocatively explained: nature is 'breathed into' by other gods, and given light by them.

[65] Or 'partial entities and wholes', which would include particulars and universals.

[66] Festugière favours Hecate, but see note on 5.15 above. Note Proclus' lack of interest in either naming or explaining this goddess.

[67] *Or. Chald.* p. 29 Kroll = fr. 54 des Places.

[68] I.e. from the things of this world; cf. Festugière who translates 'des êtres administrés par la Providence'.

On the *Timaeus* of Plato: Book 1

partake of a kind of life, and things that perish remain eternally in the cosmos, maintained by the causes of the specific forms within her. As the oracle says:

> Unwearied Nature rules over worlds and over works,
> So that the Heaven may run on, sweeping along his eternal course.[69]

12 And so on. Hence, if one of those who speak of three demiurges chose to relate them to these three principles – the demiurgic mind, the soul, and nature as a whole, he would be quite correct for the reasons stated; whereas if he is postulating three other demiurges of the universe over and above soul, he is not correct. For the demiurge of the whole is one,[70] but particular powers have received from him an allocation from the overall demiurgic task. So whether Amelius wants to establish a hierarchy like this, or Theodorus,[71] we don't accept their account, but we shall remain keen to abide by the theories of Plato and Orpheus. Moreover, all those who have claimed that nature is demiurgic craft[72] are incorrect if they mean the craft that resides in the demiurge himself, but correct if they mean that which proceeds from him. For craft should be conceived as threefold, that which does not venture from the craftsman, that which proceeds from him but reverts back, and that which has already proceeded and comes to exist in another.[73] The craft within the demiurge remains in him and is in fact him; it is by virtue of this craft that he is called 'crafter of works' by the oracle, and 'crafter of a fiery cosmos'.[74] Intellective soul is craft, but craft that stays fixed even while it proceeds; and nature is craft that proceeds alone. On this account it is called 'instrument of the gods', not as something lifeless or deriving motion only from another, but somehow possessing self-motion by operating from

---

[69] *Or. Chald.* p. 36 Kroll = fr. 70.1–2 des Places. Festugière equates the 'worlds' here with stars.

[70] It is worth noting this statement, given the tendency to see Proclus as one who unnecessarily multiplied the machinery passed down by Plato.

[71] For the theory of Amelius, partly influenced by Numenius, see III. 103.18–104.22; for Proclus' interest in exactly what he might mean by them see also I. 361.26–8. Theodorus too stands in the tradition that derived from Numenius (II. 274.10–11), and Proclus associates him with a more sophisticated version of the three-demiurge view at I. 309.14–20. On Amelius and Theodorus see Introduction, pp. 37–40, 48.

[72] Again the Stoics; see on 10.12.

[73] While the triad and its expression are typically Proclan, its relevance is not confined to late Neoplatonist systems; we too can speak of the potter's craft being present in different ways in the master potter, in the apprentice whom he supervises, and in the pot that is produced.

[74] *Or. Chald.* p. 19 Kroll = fr. 33 des Places, parts of which are also encountered at *in Tim.* I. 142.23, 361.30; II. 58.1–2, 87.26.

Prefatory remarks

within itself. For the instruments of the gods have their essence grounded in vigorous principles, and are alive, and keep time with the gods' activities.[75]

Relation to the Parmenides

So now that we have explained what nature is according to Plato, [stating] that it is a non-bodily substance inseparable from bodies, possessing their formal principles [*logoi*] but unable to see into itself,[76] and [now that] it is clear from this how it is that the dialogue is *natural* (*physikos*) when it teaches about the entire cosmic creation, it would be appropriate to add here what follows directly from this. With the whole of philosophy being divided into study of intelligibles and study of immanent things – quite rightly too, as the cosmos too is twofold, intelligible cosmos and sensible cosmos as Plato will go on to say (30c) – the *Parmenides* has embraced the treatment of intelligibles, and the *Timaeus* that of the sensibles. That one, you see, teaches us all the divine orders, and this one all the processions of things in the cosmos. But neither does the former entirely leave aside the study of things within the All, nor does the latter fail to study the intelligibles, because sensibles too are present paradigmatically in the intelligibles, while the intelligibles are present iconically among sensibles.[77] Yet the one spends more time over physics and the other over theology, as befits the gentlemen after whom they are named, because a similar book had been written about the universe by Timaeus, and also by Parmenides about the really real. So it is correct for godlike Iamblichus to say that the whole of Plato's research is contained in these two dialogues, *Timaeus* and *Parmenides*. For the whole of his treatment of encosmic and hypercosmic things has as its goal what's best in them, and no level of reality has been left uninvestigated.[78] It would be obvious to those who don't encounter Plato as dabblers that the *Timaeus'* manner of treating things is very similar to that of the *Parmenides*. For just as the *Timaeus* gives responsibility for all immanent things to the first demiurge, so the *Parmenides* links the procession of all entities with the One. And while the former teaches how they all have a share in the creator's providence, the latter teaches how existent things participate in unitary substantive existence.

[75] *Syndroma* can suggest *either* the following of the same course *or* synchronized operation, but the former here is surely inappropriate, since nature does not return.

[76] For the formal principles of things see 10.19–21. The inability to see into itself is linked with its failure to 'revert' to itself, 12.13–21.

[77] Cf. 8.17–20.

[78] Iamblichus *in Tim.* fr. 1. For commentary see Dillon (1973), 264–5. I have written on the Iamblichan curriculum in Jackson et al. (1998), 13–15.

On the *Timaeus* of Plato: Book 1

Furthermore just as the *Timaeus*, prior to the account of nature, offers the study of immanent things through images, so does the *Parmenides* get the inquiry into immaterial forms under way prior to its theology.[79] This is because one should only be brought to the appreciation of the universe after being trained in the discussion of the best constitution, while only after competing in the demanding problems concerning the forms should one be escorted to the mystical study of the Henads. With this stated, it would be the right time to get to grips with the detailed reading of Plato,[80] and to put each phrase to the test as far as we may.

Introductory texts (14.4–26.20)

The missing person, his sickness, and its consequences

One, two, three – but hello, where, my dear Timaeus, do we have the fourth of yesterday's diners who are now to be hosts of the feast? (17a1–3)

Longinus the expert on criticism,[81] approaching this phrase from the philologist's perspective, says that it is composed of three cola.[82] The first is thin and colloquial on account of the loose expression, and is given a higher-sounding finish by the second through the change of the terminology[83] and the coherence of the terms, but even more added grace and majesty is given to both of these from the third. For the **One, two, three**, being composed of disconnected terms, puts the diction on a low level; what comes next, i.e. **but hello, where, my dear Timaeus, do we have the fourth**, through the term **fourth** which represents a variation on the numbers so far, and which is composed of grander terms, showed more majesty of expression; but **of yesterday's diners who are now to be hosts of the feast**, along with the charm and elegance of the

---

[79] Note that the summary of the *Republic* and the story of Atlantis together are already being treated as the *Timaeus*' equivalent of the whole of the examination of the notion of Ideas that we think of as part one of the *Parmenides*, and therefore as a major part of the investigation.

[80] Cf. 9.30; the *lexis* or detailed reading of the text is usually contrasted with more discursive matters (*theoria*), but this commentary does not persist with *formal* alternation between the two, and hence the term is less technical than in some commentaries.

[81] On Longinus see Introduction, pp. 35–6, 74–6; this text = fr. 24 (Brisson and Patillon).

[82] The colon is a linguistic 'limb' of the sentence, and the term is much used by the grammarians.

[83] Ordinal rather than cardinal number is used.

Introductory texts

language, has also given lift and majesty to the whole period[84] through the figure of speech.[85]

Praxiphanes, however, the friend of Theophrastus,[86] criticizes Plato, saying first of all that this **One, two, three** he attributed to Socrates is obvious and can be recognized by the senses – for why did Socrates need to count for the purpose of ascertaining the numbers of those who had met up for the discussion? Secondly, that he substituted this **fourth**, which does not harmonize with what preceded, for it's 'four' that goes with **One, two, three**, while 'first, second, third' go with **fourth**. That's what he has to say.

The philosopher Porphyry, however, pursues close on his heels.[87] Against the second he argues that this is typical of Greek usage, giving the phrase an aura of beauty.[88] Indeed Homer often spoke like this; for he said that: 'unyielding bronze came parting six layers,' but it was halted 'at the seventh.'[89] He speaks in this way in these exact words,[90] as he does in many other places. But still the substitution has an actual reason here, for Socrates was able to count those present by pointing them out, and the sequence 'one, two, three' has a pointing function; but as for the absent person, because it was not possible to point him out, he indicated him through the term 'fourth', for we use 'fourth' for what is absent as well. In answer to the earlier objection, he said that when the number present corresponds to the number expected to be there, counting is indeed superfluous, but when somebody who is not known by name is missing, then the counting of those present gives an impression of the missing one as if by feeling the need for what's left and by 'missing' a part of the total number. So Plato too was indicating this when he depicted Socrates as *counting* those present and *asking* after the one left behind. If he had been able to identify that person as well and it had been possible to name him, he would perhaps have said that he sees Critias, Timaeus, and Hermocrates, but he doesn't see so-and-so. However, since the absent

---

[84] A rhetorical 'period', here the sentence as a whole.

[85] Rightly identified with the dining-metaphor by Festugière.

[86] For the possibility that such early material was already present in Crantor's commentary see Introduction., pp. 70, 75; Theophrastus also had his views on the *Timaeus*, on which see Baltussen (2003).

[87] Porphyry *in Tim.* fr. I (Sodano); Festugière has 'lui répond point par point', but both ἀπαντάω and κατὰ πόδας are military metaphors, and combine to suggest one warrior drawing closer to, and perhaps catching, another who flees (LSJ s.v. κατά в III. 2, s.v. ποῦς 5 b).

[88] With Festugière and Kroll, I prefer to read ἐργαζόμενον for the MSS ἐργαζομένης.

[89] *Il.* 7.247–8.

[90] Festugière takes τῷ ὀνόματι to refer simply to the term 'seventh', but there is room for doubt.

On the *Timaeus* of Plato: Book 1

20   one was a stranger and unfamiliar to him, it is only through counting that he personally knows that somebody is missing and makes this fact clear to us who have lived so long afterwards.

Well all this is pleasant enough, and as much of this kind of thing that one would wish to take into consideration for the study of the language in front of us. But one should also bear in mind that the dialogue is
25   Pythagorean, and one should make one's interpretative comments in a manner that is appropriate to them. You could surely derive from it Pythagorean moral doctrines[91] of the following kind: those gentlemen made friendship and the life of concord the target of all their philosophy. So Socrates too has adopted this aim above all, calling Timaeus a friend.
30   They believed that the firm agreement that they had made ought to be
16   binding on them. It is this that Socrates too is asking for in desiring the fourth [to be there] too. They welcomed the fellowship involved in the discovery of doctrines, and the writings of one person were the common property of all. Socrates also reaffirms this, encouraging the
5   same people as were feasted to be feasters, the same as were satisfied to be satisfiers, and the same as were learners to be teachers. Other people had written handbooks on duties,[92] through which they expect to improve the habits of those educated by them. Plato, however, gives us an outline impression of our duties through dramatic depiction of the
10   best of men, an impression that has much that is more effective than what is committed to lifeless rules. That is because dramatic imitation informs the lives of the listeners according to its own distinctive character.[93] He is demonstrating through this what the philosopher will most involve himself with, i.e. giving a hearing to serious discourse; and what he
15   considers to be a true feast, i.e. that it's not what most people think (that's just bestial), but that which feeds the human being within us.[94]

[91] There is a good chance that this outline of how the lemma sketches appropriate behaviour (to 16.20) still derives ultimately from Porphyry.

[92] Of those pre-Porphyrian philosophers who had written such handbooks it is natural for us to think of Panaetius, the 'source' of Cicero's extant *De Officiis*, but such handbooks go back at least to the Old Stoa to judge from works entitled 'On Duties' attributed to Zeno, Cleanthes, Sphaerus, and Chrysippus. They are given separate status in the realm of ethical teaching by Philo of Larissa (Stob. *Ecl.* 2.41). It is not surprising that Plato's methods should be found superior in an age when Platonism's triumph over Hellenistic philosophy, particularly Stoicism, was being sealed.

[93] κατὰ τὴν ἑαυτῆς ἰδιότητα is well interpreted by Festugière as meaning the distinctive character of the person actually imitated, and Proclus' comment relates closely to the doctrines of the *Republic*'s earlier treatment of dramatic imitation, 392d–398b, where the influence of persons imitated on the character of the audience is an important factor (395d).

[94] Man and beast within us recall *Republic* 588c–d. For Proclus' vegetarianism, see Introduction, p. 15.

Introductory texts

Hence the metaphor of feasting on discourse is often used by him. 'Or is it obvious that Lysias feasted you on speeches?', and 'You are feasting yourselves alone, and not sharing it with us.'[95]

This, and similar explanations, are ethical; but the following considerations belong to natural philosophy.[96] They [Pythagoreans] said that all physical creation is held together by numbers, that all the products of nature are composed according to numbers, and that these numbers are shared by other things, just as all the forms within the cosmos are shared. It is with good reason, then, that even at the start the discourse proceeds through numbers, and uses the numbers that are there for counting as opposed to those very numbers in which even these participate. For 'monad, dyad, triad' is a different thing from 'one, two, three'. The former are simple, and each is itself, while the latter are participating in those, and Aristotle was not right to say that the gentlemen located numbers in the sensible realm.[97] How could they, when they celebrated number as 'Father of the blessed ones and of men', and the tetractys as 'Source of ever-flowing nature'?[98] So since the dialogue is 'physical', its first line of inquiry begins with the numbers in which it participates, the same kind as all physical numbers. Furthermore the gentlemen affirmed the community of nature, both in the realm of coming-to-be, where all things are rendered rationally expressible and able to be measured against each other, and in the things of the heaven – for they too grant each other a share in their own particular properties. So it is right and appropriate to his purpose that Socrates too is expecting the same people to be givers and recipients of the feast.

On theology,[99] one might discover from these [words] considerations of the following kind. The gentlemen generated everything through the primal and leading numbers, and they explained the foundation of all things in the world as dependent upon the three gods. The monad, dyad, and triad give an indication[100] of these, so that the would-be student of nature should begin from them and keep them in view. Furthermore the subsidiary causes (*synaitiai*) of the things of nature had been studied among other groups too, but the final, paradigmatic, and productive causes were investigated among them in particular.[101] So these causes are shown through the numbers that have been listed. The

---

[95] *Phaedrus* 227b, *Lysis* 211d.

[96] A switch from Porphyrian to Iamblichan material (until 17.9) seems indicated, cf. 19.27.

[97] *Metaph.* 1083b11.   [98] *Carm. Aur.* 47.

[99] Presumably an indication that we now have Syrianus' contribution.

[100] This terminology (*endeixis, endeiknusthai*) regularly implies that the indicator is a symbol of that which is indicated.

[101] This debatable idea is already implied at 2.29–3.4, and presupposes the view of Aristotle (2.15–29) as a crypto-materialist.

On the *Timaeus* of Plato: Book 1

20 final [is shown] through the monad, for it stands at the head of the numbers at the level of the Good. The paradigmatic [is shown] through the dyad, for the otherness between intelligibles[102] is what distinguished the primary causes of the universe, and furthermore the dyad is the starting point of the tetractys of intelligible paradigms. And the productive cause
25 is shown by the triad, for mind is related to the triad, being the third from reality with life as intermediate,[103] or from the father with power as intermediate, or from the intelligible with intelligence as intermediate. For by analogy, as is monad to dyad, so is being to life, father to
30 power, and intelligible to intelligence. And as is dyad to triad, so is life,
18 or power, or intelligence to mind. Moreover all things divine are in all things, and they are unified by one another, so that all are in one and each is in all and they are held together by divine friendship. The Sphere in that realm contains the single conjunction of the gods. So it was with
5 good reason that Socrates too, with the divine in view, makes sharing and agreement his starting point, and urges the others too in this direction. Furthermore both feasting and the banquet are names that pertain to the gods, and not least to the gods within the universe. For they ascend together with the liberated gods to the banquet and dinner, as Socrates
10 says in the *Phaedrus* (247a), and the feast at the birthday celebration of Aphrodite takes place at the residence of great Zeus.[104]

Hence Socrates too thinks that this should apply to himself and his friends by analogy, sharing among themselves their divine intellections. It is in no way remarkable that Timaeus should give a feast to the others,
15 and receive a feast from them, for among the theologians too the sharing out of powers and participation in them is lauded, with divinities enhancing one another and being enhanced by one another. We have heard this from the poets inspired by Apollo, that the gods greet each other with
20 intelligent activities or with provident works towards the universe:

> And they with golden goblets
> Welcome one another, looking upon the city of the Trojans.
> *(Il.* 4.3–4)

But if they recognize one another, they also have intellection:

> For the gods do not pass one another unrecognized.
> *(Od.* 5.79)

---

[102] Diehl suggests νοητῶν for the less attractive ὄντων.
[103] Proclus has the common Neoplatonic triad being–life–mind in view here. There follow two more triads, Father–power–mind, and intelligible–intelligence–mind.
[104] *Symp.* 203b (the myth of the mating of Poverty and Plenty).

Introductory texts

And that which is intelligible is food for the intelligent according to the oracle, evidently because (i) exchanging feasts belongs ultimately with the gods, and (ii) those who are wiser among humans imitate the gods in this respect too,[105] with each ungrudgingly allowing the others a share of his own private intellections.

Some indisposition has befallen him, Socrates; for he would not voluntarily have missed this gathering. (17a4–5)

Porphyry the philosopher asserts that a moral obligation is suggested in these words, namely that (i) this is the only reason for sensible people to miss such gatherings, physical indisposition, and (ii) that one should consider all of this as circumstantial and involuntary; or again (iii) that friends should offer for other friends every available apology whenever they seem to be doing something incorrectly, transgressing a decision taken in common. Consequently this lemma combines an illustration of Timaeus' character with the necessity afflicting the absent person, showing how the former was gentle and truth-loving, while the latter was a hindrance to the life of reason.[106]

The divine Iamblichus, however, using this lemma as an excuse to speak exaltedly of those who are trained in the contemplation of intelligibles, says that such people do not have a proportionate facility for discussion of sensibles. As Socrates himself says somewhere in the *Republic* (516e–518b) those brought up in the pure sunlight squint when they descend into the cave because of the darkness there, just as those who come up from the cave do when they unable as yet to confront the light. And the fourth person is missing for this reason, because he's suited for a different vision, that of the intelligibles, and indeed this indisposition of his is actually a superabundance of power, in which he surpasses the present study. For just as the power of bad people is actually more of an impotence,[107] so weakness in respect of secondary things[108] is a superabundance of power.[109] Hence the passage says that the missing person is absent because he is unsuited to discussion of physics, but that he would wish to join them if they were intending to discuss intelligibles.

In just about everything that precedes the physical theory, the one, Porphyry, offers a more socially-oriented interpretation, relating it to

---

[105] The human goal of assimilation to the divine is of course present.
[106] Porphyry *in Tim.* fr. II. The conflict of reason and necessity prefigures that of the main powers that must come to cooperate in the cosmology (*Tim.* 47e etc.).
[107] This recalls the arguments with Polus in the *Gorgias* 466b–468e.
[108] I.e. in respect of sensibles rather than intelligibles.
[109] Iamblichus *in Tim.* fr. 3. For commentary see Dillon (1973), 265–6.

113

On the *Timaeus* of Plato: Book 1

the virtues and the so-called 'duties', while the other adheres more to physics. For he says that everything must be consistent with the proposed target, whereas the dialogue is on physics, not ethics. These are the different systematic approaches that the philosophers put forward about this section.

I ignore those who harass us with a lot of details with the intention of demonstrating that this fourth person was Theaetetus, because he had become a familiar of those from the Eleatic school,[110] and because he [Plato] had depicted him as sick.[111] So they say he's absent now because of sickness again. That's how Aristocles argues that Theaetetus is the missing person. Yet it was just before the death of Socrates that Theaetetus became an associate of both Socrates and the Eleatic Stranger. But even if he was that person's associate long before, what is Timaeus' connection with him?[112] Ptolemaeus the Platonist[113] thinks that it's Clitophon, because in the dialogue named after him he is not even thought worthy of an answer from Socrates. Dercyllides thinks that it is Plato, because this man had also missed the death of Socrates through sickness.[114] As I said, I am leaving these people aside, since even our predecessors have already rejected them as unsatisfactory, exposing their investigations as unworthy of investigation and their claims as unfounded. All adopt an impoverished approach, and it will be irrelevant to us even if we find what they are after. To say that it is Theaetetus because of his infirmity, or Plato, doesn't even accord with the chronology, as the one was ill at Socrates' trial and the other at his death; while to say that it is Clitophon is utterly strange, as he wasn't even there on the previous day when Socrates was narrating what Clitophon had said the day before that in the discussion at the Piraeus.[115] However, Atticus does make one good point, that this missing person seems to be one of the foreigners with Timaeus, because Socrates asks Timaeus about where this fourth person could possibly be, and he excuses his absence as if he were a friend,

---

[110] Aristocles makes the common assumption that Eleatics are a branch of the Pythagorean school, on which assumption see Mansfeld (1992), 50–2, 243–316. Festugière identifies Aristocles with the Rhodian, mentioned at 85.28, possibly the contemporary of Strabo.

[111] *Tht.* 142b.   [112] I.e. it does not follow that he was Timaeus' friend too.

[113] Festugière had once identified this figure with Ptolemy Chennos, but seems to doubt this following A. Dihle (*RE* XXIII 1859–60), who makes him post-Porphyrian. But Ptolemy's concerns suggest the Middle Platonist period, to which Dercyllides and Aristocles also belonged, and directly or indirectly, Porphyry was surely the source of our knowledge of this debate, since these people had been refuted by 'those before us' at 20.12. Further, these are all included in the generation of Atticus at 20.26.

[114] *Phaedo* 59b, interpreted literally; on these ideas see Dillon (2006), 21–2.

[115] Note that Proclus makes day one that of the conversation at the Piraeus narrated in the *Republic*, day two that of the actual narration involving new friends in the city, and day three that of their reconvening for the contributions of Timaeus and others.

Introductory texts

indicating that it is something forced upon him against his will. That's the contribution of the more ancient critics.

We must now say what my teacher [Syrianus] concluded about this text, as it follows Plato particularly closely. His position was that the more solemn and elevated the lessons become, the more the number of the listeners is reduced, and that the argument moves on to a new degree of religious fervour and secrecy. Consequently at the gathering at the Piraeus on the day before the handing down of the constitution the audience was considerable, while those who received a name were six in all.[116] On the second day those who were privy to the arguments as conveyed by Socrates' narration were four. But on this day the fourth too is missing, and the audience numbers three, and the reduction of the audience is in proportion to the increase in the purity and intellectual nature of the topic.

In all cases the number in charge is a monad. But in some cases its manner is competitive, so that the listeners have both an indeterminate and a determinate element, extending to a plurality in which the odd is interwoven with the even.[117] In other cases it is instructional, though not yet quarrel-free nor purged of dissension of the dialecticians, so that the listeners are four in number, a tetrad having similarity and sameness through its squareness and kinship with the monad and otherness and multiplicity through the influence of the even. <But in still other cases> it is free of all competitive teaching methods, and the lesson is composed in an openly doctrinal and instructive manner, so that the triad is proper to those who are receiving it, as it is in all respects of a similar nature to the monad – in being odd, primary, and complete.[118]

In the case of the virtues some belong among those who are at war, and introduce measure to their struggles, while others separate us from the warring elements but have not yet removed us from them entirely, and still others happen to be entirely separated.[119] Likewise in the case

---

[116] Cephalus, Polemarchus, Thrasymachus, Clitophon, Glaucon, Adeimantus – but Cephalus had soon disappeared.

[117] Six is seen as just such a number, being the product of the first even and the first odd number (when one is not classed as either).

[118] It is interesting to ask how Syrianus would have applied his theories to other dialogues in the Neoplatonic canon. Presumably he would count three listeners again in the *Parmenides*, and four in the *Sophist* and *Politicus*. But there is only one in the *Alcibiades* and the *Phaedrus*, two in the *Cratylus*, *Theaetetus*, and *Philebus*, four in the *Gorgias*, and many at the conversations narrated in the *Symposium* and the *Phaedo* (though only one at the narration).

[119] These are (i) the constitutional virtues that operate within a divided, tripartite soul and are found in book four of the *Republic* and in the *Gorgias*; (ii) the cathartic or purgative virtues supposedly depicted in the *Phaedo*; and finally the theoretic virtues. Plotinus, *Ennead* I.2 is crucial for the establishment of the division.

115

On the *Timaeus* of Plato: Book 1

of discussions some are competitive, some are openly doctrinal, and some a kind of intermediate between the two.[120] Some are appropriate to the intellectual calm and the soul's intellection, others to our opinion-forming activities, and others to the lives that are between these. Moreover, of the listeners some have an affinity for more elevated studies, others for humbler ones. And some of those who listen to grander topics are also capable of confronting the inferior ones, but those who are suited to the lesser ones are ill-equipped for the loftier ones. So too those who have the greater of the virtues also have the lesser ones, whereas he who is graced with the less exacting ones is not entirely in a position to grasp the more accomplished.

Why then is it any longer a surprise that this person who had been listening to the discussion of the constitution has been left out of the study of the universe? Further, how is it not essential in the deeper kind of discussion that the accompanying persons should be fewer? How is it not appropriate to the Pythagoreans that different standards for listeners should be determined, bearing in mind that of those who attended at their auditorium[121] some had a deeper and some a more superficial grasp of the doctrines?[122] How is it not in harmony with Plato that he should blame an indisposition for the absence, bearing in mind that the soul's weakness in respect of the more divine thought-objects separates us from higher studies, in which case there is room for an involuntary element? Everything, you see, that gives us the greater kind of assistance is voluntary, but to fall away[123] in the face of higher perfection is involuntary. Or, more accurately, this [failure] is *not voluntary*,[124] whereas that which not only separates us from the greater goods, but also slips away into the unending sea of vice is involuntary. Hence Timaeus says that the fourth person did **not voluntarily** miss this gathering – he hadn't missed it as one who was entirely shunning study, but as one who was unable to be initiated into the greater mysteries.[125] So to claim that a student of the theory of cosmic creation is also capable of studying

---

[120] There had long been a basic division of Plato's works into a more dialectical (*zetetic*) and a more doctrinal (*hyphegetic*) group, in which 'competitive' is properly a species of the former (D.L. 3.49).

[121] *homoakoeion*: Festugière compares Iambl. *VPyth*. 30, but it occurs more widely, ibid. 6.30, Porph. *VPlot*. 20, Olymp. *in Alc*. 132.

[122] The well-known distinction (cf. Iambl. *VPyth*. 18, Porph. *VPlot*. 37) between the *akousmatics* and the *mathematics*, implying literally that the former merely heard what the latter understood.

[123] *apoptôsis*, cf. *ET* 209.

[124] The distinction between involuntary and not-voluntary occurs in Arist. *EN* 1110b18.

[125] The language that had originally alluded to the Eleusinian Mysteries, as at *Symposium* 209e–210a, is now conventional, and is applied here rather to the two different stages of Pythagorean study.

116

Introductory texts

constitutional theory, whereas somebody who clings to constitutional theory should be missing from studies of the universe because of a 'surpassing of power',[126] is to claim something impossible. Hence the fourth person is missing from the proposed discussions through something he lacks rather than something he surpasses in as some would claim, and his 'indisposition' should not be described as the failure of the others to measure up to him, but as his own falling short (*hyphesis*) of the others.

Let us grant that there is a weakness both among those who descend from the intelligibles and among those being led up from the study of sense-objects, of the kind that Socrates relates in the *Republic*.[127] Even so, he who has become a student of constitutional theory would not through his surpassing ability have gone missing from the study of nature *without his friends knowing*. And the word **befallen** indicates the *inferior* kind of difference from those present, but to my mind[128] it certainly doesn't adequately bring to mind a difference involving the surpassing type. Indeed it is unlikely that his being unnamed signifies for this gathering anything outstanding or beyond description[129] about him, but rather that it indicates his indeterminate and inferior nature. Plato certainly makes a habit of doing this in many places – in the *Phaedo*, for instance, he doesn't even think the author of a trifling objection worthy of consideration (103a); the same with the father of Critobulus, because he was not up to the conversation at that time (59b); and he made a general unspecified reference to many others (59b). That kind of listener would also have had no profit from attending the present discussion, seeing that even among those present here Critias does say a bit but Hermocrates attends in silence. Thus he differs from the missing person only to the extent that he is more fitted to listen, given a lesser role than all the rest through his being left out of the speaking.

Isn't it up to you and these others to fully supply his part for him in his absence?   (17a6–7)

This too agrees with what we have claimed. In things that are always causally more important and divine there is a reduction in quantity and a

---

[126] Festugière correctly associates this phrase with Iamblichus, with whose position Syrianus must have contrasted his own. However, Festugière's translation here betrays a misunderstanding of the Greek.

[127] Referring back to Iamblichus' argument at 19.9–16.

[128] The rare first person singular, because Proclus has reported Syrianus separately.

[129] *aperigraphos*: Festugière translates 'transcendent', and one assumes that Iamblichus had claimed that being unnamed meant that he was indescribable, and that it is primarily what is transcendent that is beyond description.

On the *Timaeus* of Plato: Book 1

lessening of multiplicity, but a surpassing of power. This too is a doctrine of the Pythagoreans, for whom the triad is holier than the tetrad, the tetrad than the decad, and everything within the decad than whatever follows it. To put it simply, the closer a thing is to the principle the more primary it is, and the more primary the more powerful, since all power has been subsumed in advance in the principle and distributed to the rest from the principle. So if the principle were multiplicity, there would be a need for what was more multitudinous to be both more primary and more powerful than what was less so. But since the principle is a monad, the more monad-like is greater and more powerful than what is further removed from the cause. So it is with good reason that Socrates makes the reduction in the number [of participants] a symbol of the higher perfection that has subsumed in advance, as far as possible, all that comes second, and **fully supplied** what is lacking in them.[130] But since, as has been said before,[131] he is the pinnacle of the triad of these listeners, and he connects himself with the monad that organizes the discussions in the image of the demiurgic gods, it is worth seeing how he selects Timaeus from the others and refers to him as to an organizer of the entire discussion, while including the others alongside him as if they fell somewhat short of him in merit. This too sets us on the road to the divine causes, among which the first member of the triad, being unified with the primordial monad, draws the others up towards it, encourages the productive activity of the monad, and awakens the activity of the others directing it towards generation.[132] This is consonant with what has been said before.

Porphyry on the other hand records here a moral lesson,[133] that friends should abide by all agreements on one another's behalf both in words and in deeds, and should turn around any deficiency confronting them until they negate the lack, **fully supplying** their contribution. For this is characteristic of pure, straightforward friendship. Iamblichus, however, having once adopted the position that the unnamed person is greater than those present and a dedicated contemplator of intelligibles, says that Socrates is indicating through this that, although the

---

[130] Festugière explains that ἀποπληρούσης takes up ἀποπληροῦν in the lemma. Timaeus, the healthier, having to supply what is lacking is a symbol for the higher, the more potent, having to supply what is missing from the lower.

[131] 9.20–2 = 3f.

[132] Proclus is utilizing the doctrine of three demiurges, identified with Zeus, Poseidon, and Hades and the Father of Demiurges that stands above this triad. For the triad see *Plat. Theol.* I. 4.18.25–7 etc. and the discussion of divine allocations below. Timaeus is analogous to the monad above the demiurgic triad, Socrates to the highest member of that triad, cf. 9.17–22 above.

[133] *in Tim.* fr. III, in accordance with Porphyry's overall approach to the prologue.

Introductory texts

creations of nature fall short of what is genuinely real, yet they derive from them a certain similarity to them. According to the same principle the study that occupies itself with nature participates in a way in the knowledge of the intelligibles, and this is what the **fully supply** indicates.[134]

Certainly, and to the best of our powers we'll admit no deficiency, because it wouldn't be right after being treated to those handsome[135] gifts of hospitality by you yesterday, for the rest of us not to be eager to give you a full return feast. (17b1–4)

With these words he is indicating the character of Timaeus, which is exalted and prudent, lofty and attuned, friendly and generous. The **certainly** highlights his enthusiasm on the matter of the missing person and the perfection of his knowledge, in accord with which he is ready to fully supply what others have left undone, and also his sincerity. The words **and to the best of our powers we'll admit no deficiency** are sufficient to suggest that there's reliability in his promises and yet a degree of modesty in what he says about himself. These are the *moral* lessons that one can derive from this.

The *physical* lessons are that the repayment of the verbal feast offers an image of the sharing and exchange of powers in the works of nature, in which all things are arranged together and together accomplish the single harmony of the universe. And of the alternation of nature's activities according to time, as different things perform different tasks for different things at different times. This is rather like giving a return feast for yesterday's host.

The *theological* lesson is that the creative cause advances throughout all things, and fully supplies all things, and does away with all deficiency through his own power and the surpassing of his productivity, as a result of which he allows nothing to be devoid of himself. For he is characterized by an overflowing, a sufficiency, and a completeness in everything. Moreover the phrase **give a full return feast** is drawn from the picture of feasting in the divine myths, in which the gods greet each other –

> And they with golden goblets
> Welcome one another. . .
>
> (*Il.* 4.3–4)

– having their fill of nectar from Zeus the greatest one. And Plato didn't just say 'give a return feast' (*anthestian*), but **give . . . a full return feast**

---

[134] Iamblichus *in Tim.* fr. 4. For commentary see Dillon (1973), 267.

[135] I have translated *prepon* ('fair-seeming') as 'handsome' on this occasion, since the aesthetic sense is more important than the moral sense in Proclus' comment.

On the *Timaeus* of Plato: Book 1

(*antaphestian*), for the **full return feast** has incorporated the notion of
complete fulfilment. This is also observable in the universe, because the
visible orders,[136] via their uppermost part, invite the invisible powers,
while they, on account of their surpassing readiness, perfect the former too, and the offer of perfection functions as a repayment for the
invitation.

Furthermore that all this is done in accord with what's **right** introduces an image of Justice who orders all things along with Zeus, the
reference to **handsomeness** an image of the cause that illuminates
the universe with the demiurgic beauty, and the **hospitality gifts** of
the exchange that is determined by the special properties of the divinities (for each of the divinities has its own powers and activities). Just
as Socrates feasted Timaeus on the discussions involved in his own philosophy, so indeed does each of the gods, by activating its own powers,
contribute to the completion of the Demiurge's one overriding providential order of the universe.

Hopefully this has brought out the details of a training lesson[137] in the
study of reality, a lesson that gets reflected like an image in the proem.
Also evident from this passage are the dramatic dates of the dialogues,
of the *Republic* that is and the *Timaeus*, bearing in mind that the former
has its setting at the Bendidea that were being conducted at the Piraeus,
while the latter came on the day after the Bendidea.[138] Those who have
written about festivals agree that the Bendidea at the Piraeus took place
on the nineteenth of Thargelion,so that the *Timaeus* would be set on
the twentieth of the same month. If, as will be said next, it is also set
during the Panathenaea, it is clear that this is the lesser Panathenaea,[139]
as the Greater Panathenaea took place on the third day from the end of
Hecatombaeon, this too being recorded by our predecessors.

---

[136] LSJ associate the term διακόσμησις particularly with texts influenced by Pythagoreanism (beginning with Arist. *Metaph*. 986a6), in later Neoplatonism with the meaning
'order' = 'class' (as here); I usually prefer 'arrangement'.

[137] *Progymnasmata*, a term from the rhetorical schools.

[138] It is strange that Proclus seems now to forget that the narration of the conversations
described in the *Republic* was supposed to have taken place the day after the Bendidea
and in Athens itself (9.2–5).

[139] This is quite wrong, for the Panathenaea took place at the same time each year with the
Greater being celebrated every fourth year, and the Lesser in other years. Festugière
presumes a confusion with the Plynteria on the 25th of Thargelion, judging perhaps
from 84.27: 'around the same time'. However, if he starts from the conviction that
Republic–Timaeus–Critias is a single sequence, and that Timaeus and friends were the
audience for the story narrated in the *Republic*, then Proclus must assume the Lesser
Panathenaea had a different date from the Greater. See Festugière also on 84.27.

Socrates' constitution

Socrates' constitution (26.21–75.25)

Remembering the Socratic constitution

Then don't you remember the sum and subject of what I directed you to say? (17b5–6)

One should first run through the order of the topics. It began with the question of the full number of those participating in the conversation, and then followed the question of fully supplying the role of the absent person. Thirdly he tacks on the question of the rendering of the return speeches for which they had been asked. These questions follow on from one another. Who had to meet relates to the threefold tasks of those assembled, and the fact that they spoke as a threesome relates to who had to speak. Further, in addition to the order, one should ponder the precise choice of the terms.

Remember signifies the *divided* recognition of the discussions among the participants. For there is also memory of all things in the demiurge, the separate and transcendent and *unitary* recognition that accords with the Remembrance (*Mnemosyne*) within him, that being the stable foundation of divine intellection, and among the second gods there is subordinate intellection. Those in attendance are images of the latter. On account of this memory pre-existing in the universe, (i) souls in their entirety are founded in the intelligibles, and (ii) the demiurgic principles (*logoi*) have their inevitable and unchanging character, so that all things that are deprived of it drift away from their own particular causes,[140] like particular souls and the natures of generated things.

The expression **sum and subject** is suggestive of the quantity and quality of realities, which proceed sometimes from the universal creation, but sometimes too from the more particular gods.

The term **directed**, if it were addressed to Critias and Hermocrates, would obviously have to be pointing them upwards towards realities (*ta pragmata*) and to the origins of the creation-process; whereas if it is addressed to Timaeus as well, it is not a token of transcendence, but of the invocation of the intellections within him. In this regard let us look at Timaeus' answer.

Some we remember, and what we do not, you will stand by and remind us of. (17b7)

---

[140] Neoplatonism associates recollection with reversion (see Tarrant 2005, 174–6), so that procession is naturally aligned with forgetfulness.

On the *Timaeus* of Plato: Book 1

In this you can find a moral principle, as Porphyry notes, the mean between false modesty[141] and boastfulness. For he claimed to know neither all nor nothing, but to know some things rather than others. Its lesson in reasoning is that one should provide an excuse for the summing up of one's deliberations (*problêmata*); this is a matter of dialectical procedure. Its lesson in physics is that physical principles are both permanently fixed and in flux, just as the present memory is in a way preserved, but in another way lost. For those things that are said of man should be transferred also to the whole of nature.

The theological lesson is that the one creation, even of its own self, retains the unswerving and immaculate character among its offspring, but that through the secondary and tertiary powers it is supported as it advances and is given an escort by them as it were, as they calm the confusion among generated things in its path;[142] though it is transcendent of itself, it is even further removed on account of its setting secondary powers over the realm that it manages.[143]

Furthermore the recollection-motif introduces an image of the renewal of the principles (*logoi*) in the universe. For whatever flows off from them is recalled back in a circle to the same or a similar point, and the ranks of generation remain unfailing on account of the circular motion of the heaven, and this latter is always accomplished in the same way because of intellect's checking and arranging the whole circular motion by its intellectual powers. Therefore it is reasonable that Socrates should be the one who reminds them of the discussions, the one who tells the story of the constitution for which the paradigm is in the heaven.[144]

Why recapitulation is appropriate and why it fits here

Better still, if it's not a chore for you, go back briefly over it again from the beginning, so that we can be a bit more sure of it. (17b8–9)

While the constitution comes in three phases, the first description of it was genuinely difficult on account of its sophistical struggles, the

---

[141] Or 'irony'; coming from Porphyry (*in Tim.* fr. IV) these words remind us that the Socratic profession of ignorance could become an embarrassment; see Tarrant (2000) 108–11.

[142] Festugière construes the Greek rather differently.

[143] It is here crucial that Timaeus, who stands to be reminded by Socrates, is regarded as analogous to the Father of Demiurges, while Socrates is here (qua the first of the triad of listeners) analogous to the highest member of the demiurgic triad that are to take over the creation from the Father (9.15–24).

[144] See *Rep.* 592b. This passage becomes the basis for Proclus' entire approach to the summary of the constitution.

Socrates' constitution

second was easier than what went before, but the third is the easiest, embracing in a nutshell the entire outline (*eidos*) of the constitution.[145] Recapitulation of this kind suits the things of nature, on account of the rebirth among them and their cyclic return to the same form. This of course is the source of the forms' actually remaining firmly fixed in the world, as the cyclic return recalls them from dispersal and destruction – the return through which the heaven too has eternal motion, and, though tracing many circles, wheels back round[146] to the same life. For what reason then did he make no mention of the present matters in the narration of the constitution, neither of the characters of the dialogue nor of their promises,[147] and yet add this here? It is because in the universe too the exemplars have embraced all the principles of the images, but their copies are not able to embrace all the power of their causes.[148] So just as he mentions at the second gathering those characters assembled at the first, so he makes mention at the third gathering of what had been suppressed at the second. This is because effects may be studied more completely in the context of their causes that lie over and above them.

You might also give a theological explanation: the *Timaeus*,[149] in the position corresponding to the universal creation, has embraced everything, the characters, their promises, their verbal contributions, whereas Socrates in the *Republic*, in a position corresponding to the highest level of the triple creation,[150] spins out only the form of the constitution, which is of heavenly origin. So here everything has been absorbed as if into one total animal, the primary, intermediate, and final stages: the entire unfolding of everything.

---

[145] Festugière relates this to material at 8.30ff., where the actual discussion of the *Timaeus* takes place on day one, the narration of the discussion to Timaeus and others on day two, and now the recapitulation on day three.

[146] On the verb *anakamptô* see note on 126.13.

[147] Proclus means the sequence of conversation which terminated in the promises of Timaeus, Critias, and Hermocrates to present further material for discussion the next day.

[148] Essential here is the theme of the heavenly order being the *paradigm* of the ideal constitution, so that one does not expect a proper outline of the heaven in a work on the constitution.

[149] For reasons given by Festugière we follow him in assuming a reference to the work rather than the character here. The contrast is hence with the *Republic* rather than with Socrates.

[150] Festugière is quite justified in amending ἁπλότητι to ἀκρότητι here; the text will not otherwise accord with Proclan doctrine on the various demiurgic powers. While Festugière correctly draws attention to the fact that 9.17–24 has already aligned Socrates with the highest member of demiurgic triad, and Timaeus with the power set over this, the schema is possibly best studied in *Plat. Theol.*

On the *Timaeus* of Plato: Book 1

Yet how is it that the constitution has been handed down a third time too? For what reason? Is it because the life of soul too is also some triple life? First comes the life that restrains the irrational part,[151] makes it subject to the order of justice, and gives it the appropriate directions. Second is the life that is turned in towards itself, and desires to cóntemplate itself in accordance with the justice that is germane to it. The third is that which ascends towards its causes and implants within them their own proper activities. Even the word **briefly**,[152] you see, introduces an image of the life that is wrapped in concentration upon the one intellect, and of the intellectual embrace of all things; while **go back** offers an admirable indication of the gathering in perfection upon the highest goal,[153] and, if you like, of the more everlasting intellection: for that is what is signified by 'be made **more sure**', being in a more stable and everlasting condition with the same objects in focus.

Well, yesterday the principal question of my discourse on a constitution was which constitutional type and which kind of men would make it turn out best in my eyes. (17c1–3)

Those who explain the return to the constitution[154] more in accordance with ethics say that it is showing us that we should embark upon the study of the universe [only] when we have acquired orderly patterns of behaviour. Others[155] commend the view that it has been placed before the account of all nature as an image of the entire organization of the world, explaining that the Pythagoreans had the habit of placing before their scientific instruction an indication of the topics investigated, by means of similes and analogies. It is after this that they introduce the inexpressible illustration of the same things through their symbols,[156] and then, after the stimulation of the soul's intellection in this way and the purgation of its eye,[157] they apply the total scientific investigation

---

[151] Again read with Festugière τὸ ἄλογον for τὸν λόγον, for otherwise the text makes poor sense. As he shows, the corruption has taken place by a simple palaeographic confusion in uncial script.

[152] Here the Greek says literally 'the speaking briefly', while the lemma had 'go back to them briefly'.

[153] I.e. ἐπάνελθε is here being interpreted as 'go up' as well as 'go back', hence as an indication of the Neoplatonic process of reversion.

[154] The term ἐπάνοδος picks up the ἐπάνελθε from Plato's text in the previous lemma.

[155] Iamblichus *in Tim.* fr. 5 (to 'ways of communication'), answering more Porphyrian theory (*in Tim.* fr. V). For commentary see Dillon (1973), 264–5.

[156] The movement from illustrations to symbols is a movement away from indications grasped primarily by the senses and towards things grasped rather by the mind. Diehl compares here Iamblichus *VPyth.* 66.

[157] τὴν τοῦ ὄμματος διακάθαρσιν. Dillon (109, cf. 268) translates 'the purging of its (= the soul's) vision', correctly. We have been talking here of the purgation that takes

Socrates' constitution

of the topics before them. So here too the epitome of the constitution preceding the account of nature brings us face to face with the universal creation through images, while the narration about the Atlantines does so through symbols. And in general myths have the tendency to give an indication of things through symbols. So the element of natural science is something that pervades the dialogue as a whole, but it does so in one way in one place and in another way elsewhere, differing according to the various ways of communication. This will suffice regarding the target of the discussions before us.

That the summary of the constitution has been included in this investigation with good reason we could deduce from many considerations. The political art first exists in the demiurge of universe, as we have learned in the *Protagoras*,[158] and true virtue shines forth in this cosmos of ours. That's why Timaeus says that it is an acquaintance and friend for itself 'through its virtue'.[159] Furthermore the **constitution** is triple,[160] with the first being consecrated to the universal creation, as we demonstrate elsewhere,[161] so it is reasonable that its form is described in the most concise form here, where the aim is also to study the universal creator as he engenders and organizes the totality of things.

It is possible to work this out to a greater degree, but let us return to the text and to the actual words of Socrates. This is an area of considerable controversy among the interpreters, who write and reply to each other about just one punctuation mark, and who interpret the target of the *Republic* this way or that on the basis of this punctuation mark. Those who punctuate at 'constitution' define its target with a view to the title, appealing to Plato too that it is about a constitution, whereas those who punctuate at 'discourse' say that its target concerns justice, but that what is **about a constitution** is actually this *summary* of what had been said

---

place through the images of mathematics in the *Republic* itself (527d–e, 533d), which is represented as the lifting of the soul above ordinary visual influences. But while 527d–e talks of 'an organ of the soul better than countless eyes', 533d has dialectic, assisted by mathematics, lifting 'the eye of the soul' from impure depths to a non-sensory level.

[158] 321d. As *Plat. Theol.* shows, Proclus does make some use of *Prt.* for theological purposes, even though it is not included in the Iamblichan canon.

[159] 34b7–8; the quotation, referring to the cosmic soul, is incomplete, yet Proclus has done no violence to its meaning.

[160] The language is reminiscent of 28.17; though that seemed to be talking of various constitutional discussions, this seems rather to be talking of types of constitutions that relate to the three phases of creation.

[161] Festugière refers to 29.10 above, and, again, *in Remp.* II.8.15–23, where the key element is that the first constitution is concerned with sharing things in common, the second is concerned with the distribution, and the last is concerned with corrective measures. But surely Proclus is referring to the fact that the 'constitution' is present (i) in the organization of the universe, (ii) in the state, and (iii) in the soul.

125

On the *Timaeus* of Plato: Book 1

with justice in view, that is introduced like a scene on the *ekkyklêma*.[162] However, if we are not to grope in the dark with our claims and counter-claims, we must state that in a sense both views coincide. The discussion about justice is on the inner constitution, for it achieves the correct disposition of the faculties within us; and the discussion about a constitution is in the interests of the justice that arises within the multitude. Hence both amount to the same thing, and justice in the soul, constitution in the state, and orderliness in the cosmos *are* the same thing; one should not make trouble for oneself by dividing from one another things that are joined by nature.

So much for that. Yet Longinus[163] and Origenes begin from a different issue when arguing with each other over the type of constitution that Socrates discusses here, namely whether it is the first or the intermediate constitution. They claim to see the constitution there as involving (iii) a natural life, (ii) a warlike life, and (i) an intellective life.[164] So Longinus thinks that the discussion here has come to concern the middle life, because he calls the assistants 'guardians', and says that it is the guardians who will fight. Origenes however thinks it is about the first; for it is in the context of this that he prescribes the subjects to be learned by the guardians. In answer to these too we shall say that one should not tear apart the one constitution or separate off the continuum of life, one part from another. For there is a single constitution that perfects itself and is increased by the addition of more perfect life-types. This whole constitution has its physical element in the thetes, its warlike element in the assistants, and the intellective element in the guardians. And so the discussion is about the whole constitution, and it is not about these matters one should be disputing; one should rather examine how reasonable it is that one should claim that constitutional study[165]

---

[162] The *ekkyklêma* is a wheeled platform that introduces into the Greek theatre, through the central door into the acting area, a scene representing what had happened within the building behind. For Proclus, therefore, this language introduces us to a separate scene as if through a window, and as Festugière notes, citing also 92.13 and 204.18, the idea of a digression is always present. Theatrical analogy had been particularly popular with some early interpreters, including presumably Aristophanes of Byzantium. See Tarrant (2000), 28–9. Of the different texts, the former would mean 'yesterday the principal point of my discourse was about a constitution, i.e. which constitutional type . . .' etc., while the latter would mean 'of my discourse yesterday on a constitution the principal question was which constitutional type . . .' etc.

[163] Longinus fr. 25; Origenes fr. 8.

[164] Festugière naturally links this threefold life with the three different classes, artisans, soldiers, and philosopher-kings, which emerge as the establishment of the Socratic state proceeds. Proclus seems to be saying that this is a different division from that with which one might begin when discussing three constitutions.

[165] It is tempting to read τὴν πολιτικήν for τὴν πολιτείαν at 32.3–4.

Socrates' constitution

is both inferior and superior to the study of physics. Insofar as it has human affairs as its subject matter and desires to organize them it has a place secondary to physics, but insofar as its foundation is in universal principles and its structure is incorporeal and immaterial it is superior and more universal. For the world-order too is also a kind of constitution and a particular one, since all body is particular, and overall 'constitution' has a prior existence in the intelligible, it is established also in the heaven, and finally it exists in the lives of humans beings too. And so, to the extent that it is superior to physical creation, it is placed with good reason prior to the *Timaeus*, whereas, to the extent that it is inferior, because this had been an ethical order while the other is cosmic and totally perfect, we should arguably need to be ascending from inferior things to more elevated matters. Both points of view are correct for the reasons stated. Accordingly, because as we were saying the form of the constitution (i) is universal, and (ii) has been stamped upon particular matter, Socrates too has taken up the question of **which [constitutional] type** because of the form, and that of **which kind of men** on account of the matter.

And as far as all of us are concerned it was described very much as intelligence requires. (17c4–5)

Narration in accord with **intelligence**, not in accord with their pleasure nor in accord with their vote, indicates his admirable perfection and intellective grasp, and there is a riddling reference to the preceding consensual convergence of all the secondary causes into one intellect and one united creative process. Furthermore the addition of **very much** signifies the transcendent nature of this unity, through which all the creative causes converge upon the single paternal cause of all things as if upon one single centre.

The separation of classes

Did we not first of all separate in it the class of farmers and of those with all other crafts from people of the class who were going to go to war for it? (17c6–8)

The discussion on the constitution and the short condensed summary of the classes in it makes a contribution to the entire account of the cosmic creation. For they act like images from which it is possible to refocus on the universe. Indeed the Pythagoreans were the outstanding exponents of this very method, tracking down the similarities in realities by way of analogies, and passing from images to paradigmatic cases. That is what Plato is doing now too, showing us at the outset things in the

On the *Timaeus* of Plato: Book I

universe as seen in human lives, and enabling us to study them. It is
not remarkable either, for the constitutions of weighty (*spoudaioi*) persons are moulded on the organization of the heaven. Accordingly we too
should relate the present images in words to universal matters, beginning with the matter of the division of the classes. This split of classes,
you see, imitates the demiurgic division in the universe. According to
this it is possible neither for incorporeals to mutate and adopt the nature
of bodies, nor for bodies to secede from their own being in favour of
an incorporeal existence. Again, according to this mortal things stay
mortal and immortal things are fixed and unfailing for eternity. And
the various orders [in the *Republic*] have their paradigmatic causes pre-
established in things universal. You might care to draw a parallel in which
the entire city is analogous to the entire cosmos (for it does not follow
that while a human being is a mini-cosmos, the city would not be a mini-
cosmos), to split it all in two, the upper city and the lower,[166] and to
place the former alongside the heaven and the latter alongside generation. You would then find the analogy plausible in every way. Pursuing
the tripartition, you would get in the city the labouring, warfaring, and
guardian elements; whereas in the soul you would get the appetitive
faculty that looks after the needs of the body, the spirited faculty that
has been given the job of repressing all that is injurious to the animal,
acting as bodyguard to what rules in us, and the rational part, which is
in essence philosophical and lord over all our life. Further, in the totality of souls there is the part that labours over generation, that which
helps out with the providential plans of the gods in the cosmic periph-
ery, and that which returns to the intelligible; and among all the creatures in the cosmos there is the race of things mortal, the family of *daemons*, and the order of gods in heaven. These last are genuine guardians
and saviours of the universe, while the *daemons* provide an escort for
their creation, and check all the error in the cosmos, but there exists
also a kind of natural providence among mortal things, which brings
these into existence and conserves them in accordance with the divine
intelligence.

Moreover, by another division, the farming sector of the state
(i) is analogous to the Moon,[167] which embraces the ordinances of

---

[166] Upper and lower cities are simply description of the warfaring+guardian class and the
artisan class, and the descriptions accurately capture the degree to which these classes
are kept separate. As Festugière points out, the idea will recur, first at 34.30, then at
39.25–6, and 53.8–9.

[167] What follows makes it clear that Proclus is comparing classes with the seven planets,
each conceived as a god (hence the capitals).

Socrates' constitution

generation-producing nature; that which presides over the shared mar- 15
riages (ii) to Aphrodite who is responsible for all harmony and the union
of male with female and form with matter; that which is taking care of
the craftily worked-out lots (iii) to Hermes, both on account of the lots,
over which this god presides, and on account of the element of trickery in them And the educational and judicial section (iv) is analogous 20
to the Sun, in whose domain according to the Theologians are Justice,
the Upward Leader, and the Seven-Rays;[168] the warfaring class (v) to the
rank of Ares that presides over all the rivalry of the cosmos and the difference of the universe; the kingly element (vi) to Zeus who takes the lead
in the wisdom of leadership and intelligence in action and organization; 25
and the philosophic element to Kronos, insofar as it is intellective, and
ascends even as far as the first cause.[169] This is what should be grasped
from analogies in this way.

However, Plato seems to split the state in two, and to posit the farmers
and tradespeople, which he calls the craftsman element, as one class,
while as another he posits the warfaring class as his upper city.[170] This 30
is not, as Longinus claims, because he is now giving a summary of the **35**
warring constitution,[171] but because he has included both the auxiliaries
and the guardians under the heading of the warfaring element, because
the former defend it with their hands, and the latter with their policies.
Similarly, among the Greeks, Ajax fought as the 'defence-wall' of the 5
Achaeans (*Il.* 3.229), but there fought also the 'watcher over' the Greeks,
Nestor, the latter repelling the enemy as a guardian with his counsels, the
former using his hands against them. Perhaps, though, he is also making
special mention of the warfarers here, because he wants to inquire into
the military achievements of such a constitution.

---

[168] On the basis of Julian *Or.* 5.172a–d etc. Festugière tentatively identifies the last two
members of this Chaldean triad with Attis and Mithras respectively.

[169] The detection of a parallel between the tasks fulfilled in the state and the seven planets
seems particularly artificial, and may originate with those of astrological interests.
The division of tasks seems not to be inspired by anything here in the *Timaeus*, nor
does it well reflect anything in the *Republic* itself, separating out philosopher and king,
for example, who are famously supposed to be one in that work. One assumes that
certain interpreters have begun with the notion that Plato's state mirrors the heavenly
paradigm, cf. *Rep.* 592b, and so required that the seven-fold planetary system must be
included among features to be found in the state. Comparison with his view of the
Atlantis myth on 77.17–30 suggests that we could be discussing Amelius' view.

[170] See on 33.26.

[171] Longinus is not only relying on Socrates' professed desire to see his constitution
engaged in armed conflict, 19c, but also using the notion of a triple constitution with
the three lives (natural, warring, and intellective) seen above at 31.18–25.

On the *Timaeus* of Plato: Book 1

10 **And granting according to nature only the one operation that belonged
to each personally, we said of those who should make war above all. . .**
(17c10–d2)[172]

To begin with one should distinguish two readings of the lemma: either
15 'we granted according to nature one activity to each of the citizens,
so that each would have his own proper operation to perform', or 'we
granted to each to perform the operation according to his nature, the
one that belonged to each in accordance with the talent that belongs to
his nature.'[173] Next one should investigate the reason that led Socrates
20 to divide them in that way. Either it is for the reason that he himself
stated,[174] that each operation is rightly performed by one who (i) has
the right nature and (ii) diligently applies himself to the operation; for
neither can diligence achieve anything perfect if suitability is lacking,
nor can cleverness advance into activity without diligence. So the goal
25 is a combination of both. But if that is so, then if somebody were to
perform more tasks he would not be able to be equally adapted to them
all or to be diligent about them all equally, his attention being divided by
his concern for them all. As these concerns are reduced, it is inevitable
that the operations of the citizens should turn out less satisfactory; and
30 if this is not proper, one must distribute one occupation to each of the
citizens, one that he has natural talent in, and instruct him to apply
36 all his diligence to a single thing. For one who is naturally clever in
such and such a life, and approaches his natural task diligently, would
in all probability become excellent at his appropriate job. It is easy to
5 observe this division in the case of our human constitutions, for our
nature is divided, but how can it be true in the case of the gods, seeing
that what is divine is all-powerful and all-perfect? In fact it should be
said to apply to the gods, because, while all are in all, it is according

---

[172] Proclus' text probably lacks the words μίαν ἑκάστῳ τέχνην or anything similar, which
is also absent from Calcidius' Latin translation.

[173] The key words are κατὰ φύσιν, which are taken either as indicating the naturalness of
the general principle of 'one person, one job', or as underlining that each will have a
job to which he or she is naturally suited. To the modern reader it is relevant that each
person's nature is the consideration at *Rep.* 370a7–b2 etc. Proclus seems uninterested
in preferring one reading over the other, and at the end of the discussion he appears
to confirm that he regards both the one-job principle and allocation in accord with
natural abilities as reflecting the cosmic order, and therefore natural.

[174] This seems to relate to *Republic* 369e–370c, where each craftsman must have natural
ability for his own job, and diligence (369e6) in servicing the needs of others for his
product, a diligence that is manifested in his making the most of all opportunities
(370b–c). The twin factors of natural ability and attention to opportunity are best
seen at 370c3–5. That Proclus finds his claims in the *Republic* means that 35.20–2 is an
accusative and infinitive construction, and the infinitive ἐπιτηδεύεσθαι does not require
emendation or an understood δεῖ, as Diehl and Festugière suppose.

Socrates' constitution

to the individuality of each that it is all things and has the cause of all, one in Sun-wise, another Hermes-wise. For, beginning with the Divine Henads, individuality passes through the intellective entities, through the divine souls, and through their bodies. It is on this account that, of these things too, some have received a share of demiurgic power, some of productive, some of cohesive, and some of divisive, and this is the nature of their action upon [the world of] generation.[175]

So *individuality* pre-exists among things divine themselves, distinguishing the henads in accordance with the limitlessness there and the divine dyad.[176] But *otherness* exists among intellects, dividing off both wholes and their parts, allocating the intellective powers, and providing different things with different roles of their own, as a result of which the purity of the intellects is not compromised. And procession and *distinction according to their different lives* occurs among souls,[177] lives that give some a divine subsistence, others an angelic one, others a demonic one, and other a different kind again; and in bodies there is physical separation, giving different properties to different things. It is among these that one finds the final reflections of intelligibles, according to which different things have different effects, and one thing reacts in sympathy to another, while a third has this sympathetic reaction to another still. So, just as in the universe it is natural for each thing to perform that role over which it has been given charge since creation, so in the city too the operations of each class have been distinguished, with each person being given charge of whatever he's naturally suited to. As for the precise jobs of the warfarers, Socrates himself will shortly go on to clarify them.

The role and character of the military class

That they should only be guardians of the state – whether somebody were to come from outside to do it harm or even if one were to come from those within – passing judgement with humanity upon those who were their natural friends and under their control, but getting tough in battle with whichever of their enemies they met. (17d–18a)

In this he wants the guardians and auxiliaries to be judges of those within, should any harm the city, and opponents of those outside, having one way in mind for the auxiliaries, and another for the guardians, as has been said before. That they should *only* be guardians is not a

---

[175] Demiurgic power is associated with the Sun, generative with the Moon (often associated with souls below), cohesive with Aphrodite, and divisive with Ares.

[176] Festugière observes that this is one thing, a single dyad, rather than two.

[177] Procession is not, of course, a description of another means by which x can be distinct from y, but rather it is *in procession* that distinct types of lives can emerge.

On the *Timaeus* of Plato: Book I

diminution of their power. For neither, when we assert of the first principle that it is only One do we diminish it and entirely enclose it within narrow confines; for neither is what has only the best diminished by this, but, quite the contrary, for such a thing as this any accretion would be a diminution.[178] The result is that on these terms *not being alone* would diminish the whole, as opposed to its being alone, and the more you multiply it the more you would diminish whatever has the status of a principle. This applies here.

Again, we must examine how we are to observe what is now being said in the universe. For what is there that is external to the universe? How does the universe not enclose everything? Well surely evil is doubly established within the universe itself, in souls and in bodies, and it is necessary for those who abolish fault and disorder from the universe to extend justice and measure to souls, and to take as their opponent the restlessness of matter. Souls belong naturally to the intelligible, on which account they could be described as **within** and as being from the entire intelligible plain, but those things that are enmattered and far from the gods are alien to them and foreign and external. On this account the administrators of justice treat the former **with humanity** as friends by nature, but with those bodies that travel in a faulty and disorderly fashion they **get tough**, because they are out of sympathy with them and are trying utterly to wipe out their disorder and to eliminate their greed for material supremacy. Some of these do not even abide such an order, but are immediately off and transported into non-being, whereas others that move in a faulty way are held in check by the Justice within the universe and by the irresistible force of the guardian powers of order. That's why he said now that those who wage war for the state are **tough** on whomsoever they meet; for some would not even endure their sight. And in general there are (i) both uplifting and purifying powers for souls themselves, presiding over judgements and justice, and it is clear that the former correspond to the guardians, and the latter to the warfarers; while (ii) for bodies some powers are cohesive while others are divisive, and it is clear that the former correspond to the guardians, and the latter to the warfarers. They reunite with the universe those things that are no longer able to remain in their given order, so that everything may be orderly, and nothing may be indeterminate or faulty.

---

[178] Since the material here relates to the *ethical* treatment of the lemma, with the *physical* treatment to follow, and is thus more likely to relate to Porphyry than to Iamblichus, it is important to note how reminiscent this material is of Anon. *in Parm.* I (often ascribed to Porphyry, see Introduction, p. 45), where Speusippus' minimal One is criticized.

Socrates' constitution

If you were to fix your gaze on the very universal demiurge himself and the unvarying and unyielding nature of the gods,[179] whom the inspired poem too has named guardians of Zeus, you would grasp also the pre-existing cause of these twin kinds (*genos*); all things, you see, have been adorned on account of the Demiurgic Being, while all creation remains eternal on account of the unvarying vigilance within him. You would see there also Justice 'with Zeus' applying correction to all things – for she accompanies him 'as an avenger for the divine law' – [180] and the armed brigade with which he organizes the universe, as those who write about battles against Titans and battles against giants say. But this can wait until another time.

As for the **outside** and **within**, one could also understand them in the following way. The faulty and disorderly flux of bodies at times comes about through the weakness of the principles of order (*logoi*), and at times through matter's greed for supremacy. The principles are closely linked with the productive causes, but matter, because of its own indeterminacy and its extreme subordination, is alien to the powers that bring order to it. The irresistible strength of the gods, with their unvarying order and their vigilance in the creation process that removes its faultiness in every sort of way, renews the principles of order and gives them encouragement in their weakness, while struggling against matter's greed for supremacy; this is not because matter is actively resisting the gods that bring her forth, but because, fleeing order on account of its own indeterminacy, it is mastered by the forms on account of this vigilance in creation, against which nothing is able to make a stand and to which all things must be obedient, so that all things in the world may endure for ever and their demiurge may be the father of things everlasting, because he is unmoved and fixed in transcendence and in eternity.[181]

**We said, I believe, that the nature of the souls of the guardians had
to be at one and the same time outstandingly spirited and philosophic,
so that it could get humane to the one group and tough with the other.**
(18a4–7)

---

[179] For the language Diehl and Festugière refer to *Or. Chald.* 36 (p. 21 Kroll), cf. 166.8–9, 167.6 and 168.15 below.

[180] *Laws* 716a2–3: Plato has 'avenger *of transgressions* of the divine law', while Proclus' 'for' (πρό) implies that she protects that law.

[181] In this final section Proclus discusses the notion that matter can be akin to an external enemy, while the formal principles can on occasion be more like a friend within who is falling short of requirements. As Festugière points out, we have already met the idea of enmattered flaws as an outside enemy at 37.27–8, but it was there opposed to flaws within soul, so that the contrast was between soul and body rather than between form and matter.

On the *Timaeus* of Plato: Book 1

The terms 'philosophic' and 'spirited' apply similarly to both types, to the auxiliaries and to the guardians in the proper sense of the word, just as the term 'appetitive' fits the third type that is known as the 'labouring' one. Because his contrast opposes the upper city to the lower, he has indicated the differences of the orders within it [sc. the upper] using these two names, just as if, in dividing the world into heaven and becoming, somebody were to say there are daemonic and divine orders in the heaven, and to say that both of them were protective of generation and of the universe. For the universe is watched over both by the gods and by the daemons, by the former in a universal and unitary and transcendent fashion, and by the latter in a partial and multiplicitous fashion more in keeping with the things that they watch over. For in the case of each god there is a plurality of daemons that divide up among themselves his single universal providence. So in these circumstances the term 'philosophic' belongs to the gods insofar as they are united [in their focus] on the intelligible and insofar as they are replete with being, while the term 'spirited' belongs to the daemons insofar as they expel all fault from the universe, insofar as they form an escort for the gods in the same way as the heart does for the reason, and insofar as they are the saviours of the divine laws and of the ordinances of Adrasteia.[182] For these reasons they are humane towards those close to them, carefully encouraging them, as if natural relatives, to get over their weaknesses, but tough on outsiders, as if making an exceptional and extreme effort to eliminate their indeterminacy.[183]

Education and upbringing of the guardian class

What about upbringing? Didn't we say they were to have been brought up on gymnastic and music, and on all the disciplines that belonged with these? (18a9–10)

The discussions so far were a kind of blueprint that extended to all in common, distinguishing in accordance with the demiurgic allotment and the otherness within the divine the practices that belonged to each group, and properly allocating the properties to the things that were to receive them.[184] From this point on the life of the citizens is constructed

---

[182] The ordinance of Adrasteia (another name for Nemesis) was well known from *Phaedrus* 248c.

[183] The insiders and outsiders are now once again souls with faults and bodies with faults, and Proclus' concern here remains the universal correction of disorder rather than the preservation of the state.

[184] For the correct punctuation see Festugière.

Socrates' constitution

through their upbringing, their practices, their social interaction, and their child-raising, advancing in the correct way from beginning to end.

So what is their **upbringing**, and how is it an image of the universe? There is an education of the soul in the city, formatting the irrational part through music and gymnastic. Here the former slackens the strings of the spirit and the latter, arousing the desire, renders it perfectly in tune and proportion with the spirit when it has become too relaxed on account of its descent into the material realm and infected with lifelessness from that source. Likewise it formats the reason through the mathematical sciences, which have a drawing power[185] to reacquaint one with reality and which lead the intellective power in us up to the very 'brightest light of being'.[186] This is clear to those who have not entirely sunk into forgetfulness of the things that are set out there.[187]

It is now our task to inquire into what the **upbringing** within the universe is, what its music and gymnastic are, and which are the studies of the guardians of the universe. Suppose we were to say that their upbringing was the perfection that makes each replete with the good qualities that belongs to it and renders it self-sufficient in its intellections and its acts of providence; and that their **music and gymnastic** were respectively what brought their lives to harmonious fulfilment and what fashioned the rhythmical and tuneful divine motions, always unswervingly preserving the same disposition of the chariots of the gods – for this is the reason why he called the divine souls 'Sirens' in another place,[188] and said that the heavenly movement is 'rhythmical', there being 'gymnastic' among them as opposed to 'medicine' in sublunary things, those that are capable also of admitting what's contrary to nature. Suppose we were to say this, we should perhaps be correct. From the intelligibles above, you see, powers reach down to the whole heaven, illuminating their lives with the finest of harmonies and imbuing their chariots with unflinching strength, since even mathematics are intellections of the souls of heavenly beings, in accordance with which they have recourse to the intelligible, following the great Zeus and observing the unitary number and the real heaven and the intelligible shape. Hence you could say that in them is the truest arithmetic, astronomy, and geometry – for they view speed-in-itself and slowness-in-itself, the paradigms of the circuits

---

[185] We are perhaps expecting 'upward drawing power', but the text Proclus has in mind, *Rep.* 521d3–4, has no similar word; it also has ὁλκὸν for ἕλκον.

[186] Cf. *Rep.* 518c9.

[187] I.e. in the *Republic*, according to Festugière. There may also be a suggestion of our forgetting higher truths, such as is postulated by the Platonic theme of recollection.

[188] Proclus refers to *Rep.* 617b5 and c4; cf. the long important passage on Sirens at *in Remp.* II. 237.16ff. Plato refers to the single harmonious sound of the Sirens of the various planetary spheres, but he does not use the terminology of rhythm.

On the *Timaeus* of Plato: Book 1

42 of the heaven, and, summing up, the primary and intelligible circuit and the divine number and the intelligible shapes – and prior to this dialectic, in accordance with which they apprehend the entire intelligible

5 realm and are united upon the single cause of all the henads. And, if one may say it in divided terms, through such mathematical sciences their activity is directed to the primary things, through gymnastic they have unchallenged leadership of the second things, and through music they harmoniously draw together the strings that unite the whole.

Community of property and of lives

Furthermore, it was said surely that those who were raised in this way
10 didn't consider either gold or silver or any other possession as their own private property. (18b9–10)

The requirements laid down for the city with the best laws have an obvious justification, and it was stated by Socrates in those discussions. How, though, are we going to apply these principles to the heaven? Surely

15 we have to notice the reason why humans pursue gold and silver, and what they are thinking of in conceiving this unbounded desire. Clearly [they do so] out of the will to attend to their own needs from whatever source, and out of the desire to provide themselves with what contributes

20 to their pleasure. 'There are many comforts for the rich at least' as Cephalus claims.[189] If this is right then, the perfection of the heavenly gods, which is self-sufficient and directed towards beauty and the good, has no need of this imported and superficial self-sufficiency, nor does

25 it have need as its focus and as its aim, but being situated far from all wants and from material necessity, and being replete with advantages, it has the leading role in the universe. Indeed it does not have anything to do with the partial and divided good, but has fixed its aim upon the

30 common and undivided good that extends to all, and it is with this that it is particularly associated. Hence the words **didn't consider either gold**

43 **or silver or any other possession as their own private property** fit these [heavenly beings] also.

If you prefer, let it also be explained in this manner, in physical fashion. Gold, silver, and all sorts of metals, just like everything else, arise on

5 earth as a result of the heavenly gods and the efflux therefrom. Indeed the theory is[190] that gold is the Sun's, silver the Moon's, lead Saturn's,

---

[189] *Rep.* 329e. The words are actually used by Socrates, and claimed as the opinion of the majority, but Cephalus does express qualified agreement. Obviously the details of the aporetic first book of the *Republic* are not of great concern to Proclus.

[190] Clearly Proclus does not accept this theory, as it would have the heavenly gods somehow dividing property between them; the theory is associated with φιλοθεάμονες at 43.12,

Socrates' constitution

and iron the property of Mars. So these things are generated from there, but they are founded upon the earth and not among those things that release these effluxes, for they (the heavenly bodies) receive nothing from enmattered things. And while all of these metals are from all of them, nevertheless different qualities dominate in different ones, a Saturnian quality in one and a solar one in another; it is with this in mind that the sight-lovers refer one [metal] to one [astral] power and another to another. For they are not the private property of particular gods, being the offspring of them all, nor are they among them, seeing that their makers have no need of them, but they have solidified in this region in a manner dependent upon the effluxes from these [makers].

Why is it then that human enthusiasm for these things is divided? It is because they possess a material life and reach out for what is partial in isolation from the universal. That's why there is a great deal of 'mine' and 'not mine' among them, and why a life of unity and sharing has failed them.

But they should be like assistants receiving whatever wage for their guardianship is reasonable from those who are kept safe by them, the amount reasonable for moderate persons, and should spend money in common and live sharing their lifestyle with one another, having continual concern for virtue and enjoying a respite from all other jobs. (18b3–7)

There would be nothing surprising in the existence of favours and return favours in human life, and in a wage for services rendered. Socrates too had been right (*Rep.* 420b) when he said in that discourse that our goal was to make the whole city happy (*eudaimôn*) rather than one particular class in it, such as the guardian class. If this is right, then one class would need to save the city through forethought and wisdom, while the other class does so through service and labour. This service would fulfil the needs of the saviours of their constitution – just as nature within us provides calm for the thinking part for its own proper activities by attending to the organism's development and integrity. But then what kind of return favour (not to say **wage**!) will the argument say is paid from mortals to the gods in heaven?[191] Perhaps this is a characteristic of

and, when discussing the summary of the *Republic* (cf. 475d etc.), Proclus must be meaning this as a term of criticism, implying an excessive preoccupation with the things of the senses. This is natural, for the property of colour is clearly among those that cause some metals to be associated with some heavenly bodies.

[191] Having applied the analogy between state (upper and lower classes) and individual (highest and lower parts of the soul), Proclus now insists on finding how this analogy is to work on a cosmic level (earthly and heavenly beings). The question recalls the problems raised at the end of the *Euthyphro* (14e–15a), where Euthyphro is unable to give a convincing account of what the gods need from us.

On the *Timaeus* of Plato: Book 1

10 human weakness that it doesn't possess self-sufficiency, but every god is self-sufficient. And in addition to their being self-sufficient, because of the superabundance that accompanies this sufficiency, they fill needier things with benefits while not actually receiving anything from them. Well, even if the divine receives nothing, because it is adequate and self-sufficient, it still needs some sort of **wages** from us and a return for its

15 beneficence, the acknowledgement of the favour and gratefulness for it, through which we revert to them and are filled with even greater goods.[192] This is because, being good, it wants everything to look upon it and be mindful that all exist from it and because of it. For this is what preserves all that follows, the fact that each thing is attached to its divine cause.

20 However, if we interpret these things in this way, resorting to reversions and acknowledgement of the favour as explanations of the **wages**, how will the following continue to be in harmony with us: that the gods lead their lives together and actually spend this **wage**? So it is better to understand this wage more along physical lines: since effluences have

25 come to this world from that, while there are exhalations being set in motion to that world from this, and it is through these that the craftsmanship of the gods concerning mortal things is brought to completion, he called such changes and transfers from earthly things a **wage** being paid from the whole earth to the heaven, so that generation should be

30 unfailing. By the **common** life he meant the integrated life of the divine

45 creation and the like-minded forethought of the gods in heaven.[193] It is on account of this that all that comes in exchange from the earth is spent, while generation is exchanged in a variety of ways through the dance[194] of the heavenly bodies.

It is to this that Timaeus looks when he says (34b) that the whole

5 cosmos is 'a friend to itself' and 'an associate because of its excellence', and that 'it offers as food for itself its own decay', doing everything it does *to itself*, and suffering everything *from itself* (33c–d). What then is the goal of this one common life of the citizens? Excellence is what he says, excellence – clearly divine excellence, as excellence appears first with the

10 gods, and then after them a portion of it comes down to the superior races and to us. So the guardians of the world live in accordance with it and have remission from all other practices (for they do not look to their needs nor

---

[192] Proclus is here seeing prayer and offerings to the gods as a part of that general pattern of things by which all that 'owes' something to a cause 'repays' it by the process of reversion. Compare the account that Proclus gives of prayer beginning at II. 209.13 that turns to reversion at 210.2.

[193] This like-minded forethought matches the guardians' common concern for virtue in the state.

[194] For the dance metaphor see *Tim.* 40c3.

138

Socrates' constitution

to what is outside, since all things are within them), and they preserve all 15
things and fill them with beauty and goodness, serving and assisting the
one father and demiurge of all. Since they determine a measure even for
the changes on earth without stepping outside themselves, but by having
turned inwards towards themselves and being within themselves, on this
account he has also spoken of a **wage** that is **reasonable for moderate
persons**. Being **moderate** through being in control of themselves,[195] 20
they measure out secondary things too, circumscribing their multifarious
changes within the simplicity of their own life.

So much for this path. But according to another we shall claim that it
is above all holiness and reversion to the gods that involve measure and 25
are in the grip of the good, while this [measure] is determined by the
gods themselves, who are able to preserve both themselves and the rest
in accord with their divine wisdom.

The position of females

**Moreover we made additional mention of women, saying that their
characters have to be brought into harmony much the same as the men,** 30
**and they all should be given a share in all the jobs, both in warfare and in
the economy in general.** (18c1–4)

Plato had good reason to approve of men and women having the same **46**
virtues, as he declared that humankind was one species, refusing to hold
that the male was one thing and the female another. Those things that
have a different species of perfection are themselves of a different species, 5
while those that are the same in species have one and the same perfection. Other people,[196] while admitting that there is no difference of
species in this case, have refused to concur,[197] even though Plato has
gone on to prove that this is both possible and advantageous. It is possible, because history gives confirmation of it, as many women turn out
far superior to men after a good upbringing; it is expedient, because it 10
is far better for those who display valour in deeds to be twice the number rather than half.[198] So just as we have perfected guardians with this

---

[195] It seems likely that we should read at 45.20 τῷ ἑαυτῶν <κρείττονες> εἶναι or τῷ ἑαυτῶν
<μείρους> εἶναι.

[196] Proclus has Aristotle in mind, as is clear from *in Remp.* I. 252.24–6. Festugière cites
Arist. *Metaph.* 1058a29ff. as well as *Pol.* 1260a17ff. and 1277b20ff.

[197] I take it that what they deny is the substance of the lemma (differing here slightly from
Festugière and Praechter [1905], but adopting with Festugière the reading of M and
P), and that this is made clear by what follows.

[198] It is characteristic of Greek to think comparatively here, so that one number is double
(that with which it is contrasted), and the other half (that with which it is contrasted).

139

On the *Timaeus* of Plato: Book 1

15 kind of upbringing and education, so, as a result of the same upbringing, we shall bring guardianesses too to perfection – female as well as male warfarers.

However, so that we can admire Plato's plan all the more, we should turn our attention to the wider issues, i.e. to the organization of the universe, where we shall find an amazing integration of the lives of male 20 and female. For among the gods these things are so intertwined, that a single individual can actually be designated male-female (*arsenothêlus*), such as the Sun, Hermes, and certain others.[199] Even where gender had been divided, male and female of the same rank have the same tasks; it is accomplished in an initial way by the male, and in a subordinate way 25 by the female. Hence in mortal creatures too nature has revealed the female to be weaker in all things than the male.[200] Indeed everything that proceeds from the male is also brought to birth by the female, preserving its subordinate role. So Hera processes in company with Zeus, giving birth to all things together with the father, for which reason she is **47** called 'his equal accomplisher';[201] and Rhea processes in company with Kronos, for this goddess is the recess that harbours all the power of Kronos; and Ge processes in company with Uranus, as Ge is mother of all that Uranus has fathered. And if we were to assume, prior to these 5 basic divinities,[202] limit and unlimited, which have been given the status of principle and cause in respect of them, we shall find that everything that proceeds in any fashion into being is generated from both of them.[203]

---

[199] A problematic reference, since Festugière found no reference to a genderless Helios, nor even to a Hermes of this type, even though a male-female supreme principle is to be found in the Hermetic Corpus (*Poimandres* 9). It was of course Hermes' son by Aphrodite, Hermaphroditus, who was of both genders, though Aphrodite herself may also be regarded as *arsenothêlus*, and another god with some gender ambiguity is Dionysus. Present references probably result from an uncritical attempt to collect material on gods of common gender. Various material was available, including (oddly enough) that on the Moon in Plutarch's *On Isis and Osiris* 368c, while one branch of the Pythagorean tradition had made the One *arsenothêlus* (*Theol. Ar.* 5; cf. the pentad at 32).

[200] Cf. *Rep.* 455d8-e2, where nature is again a prominent concept, and it is again greater weakness that is attributed to the female.

[201] *Orph. fr.* 163; the term is *isotelês*, which is somewhat ambiguous and interpreted here according to the requirements of the context.

[202] It would be less appropriate, given the choice of gods discussed, to postulate here the Hellenistic sense of στοιχεῖον as planet (LSJ II. 5, noted by Festugière).

[203] Cf. *Phlb.* 26d7–9, where the huge class of things that is the combined product of limit and unlimited is described as 'generation into being' (γένεσις εἰς οὐσίαν).

140

Socrates' constitution

Here you have the coalition of male and female among intelligible gods,[204] among intellective ones, and among hypercosmic ones. See, then, how the same thing applies to the heaven, since all generation takes its directions from the Sun and Moon, predominantly and in a fatherly way from the former, and secondarily[205] from the latter. Hence she has been described by some as 'a lesser Sun'.[206] [And there are lunar orders corresponding to the male gods in the sun.][207] Then again, if you were to observe the matter in daemons, you will see that the providential assistance of these two kinds is everywhere conjoined, because the godlike daemonesses accomplish everything in unison with the godlike daemons, playing a secondary role to their primary one. The psychic daemonesses [are in unison with] psychic daemons, the natural with the natural, and the corporeal with the corporeal, the females having the same relation as mothers to the males and as dyads to the monads. For they give birth in a derivative way to whatever the others bring forth in their fatherly and unitary way. So if our previous comparison was correct,[208] making the guardians the heavenly gods and the auxiliaries the attendant daemons that serve their providential plans, it is with good reason that Plato welcomes among these types the same conjunction of male with female, granting each sex a share in common virtues and common jobs – just as nature bound these types together with each other and made them bring forth with each other's help. It did not divide the one from the other, but either sex is infertile in isolation, reproduction requiring both. For sure the difference in respect of physical organs is greater than the difference in their lives, but still, even as far as the organs are concerned, nature has made for them a single task. So much the more, then, is it right to approve of their sharing in their jobs and in their life overall.

---

[204] I suspect the omission here of 'and in intellective and intelligible' (καὶ ἐν νοεροῖς τε καὶ νοητοῖς), so that reference is being made to each of the three generations of divine pairs, plus the prior principles of limit and unlimited. For a different view see Festugière p. 76 n.2.

[205] It is tempting to translate 'derivatively' here, since such theory is probably linked to the fact that the moon merely passes on the light that originates with the sun.

[206] Diehl and Festugière cite Arist. *Gen. An.* 777b25; note here that the male gender of the Sun (Helios) is not in question, and contrast 46.21.

[207] The problem here is that it is other male gods, not daemons for instance, who are supposed to be within the Sun. Festugière says 'Mystérieux, et l'on ne peut que conjecturer.' His long note cites Hermetic and astrological texts, but the sentence needs explaining from within Proclus if it is to stand. It adds nothing, and reads like a gloss, and in these circumstances it is legitimate tentatively to excise it.

[208] See 34.8–12.

On the *Timaeus* of Plato: Book 1

What about the business of child-raising? Or was this pretty easy to remember until now on account of the unfamiliarity of what was said? *up to* **This too is easily remembered as you state.** (18c6–d6)[209]

If somebody were to inquire as to why what is unfamiliar is easily remembered, it wouldn't be difficult to answer that it makes more of an impact upon the imagination as being unexpected, and it implants its own outline in greater detail within us. Furthermore it is an easy business to follow Plato in stating how the **community** is meant in the case of wives. He wishes the couplings to take place, along with prayers and sacrifices, on predetermined occasions in accord with the judgement of the magistrates, and that the female in the union should not be the private partner of any one man, but that she should be separated after the coupling and live apart [from the male], and on other occasions she should again be allocated to whatever man the guardians have approved for her. Well, this shows how the study of these things has a bearing on natural philosophy. So let us state how these things pertain to the organization of the universe, for this too is established far earlier among the gods on account of their union. All offspring, you see, are the offspring of all, even though some are characterized by their own special relationships, and all are in all, and all are unified with all with an undefiled purity[210] that befits the gods. It is with an eye on this purity[211] that Socrates welcomed both this **community** [of wives] and the individual one-to-one allocation of the jobs to each person according to his nature. For even the failure to recognize one's own offspring individually is found among the gods: their intellections are shared, and so are their creations. Each assists and preserves what has been born on the assumption that it is the common concern of all. Indeed to regard all one's own rank as brothers, all one's superiors as fathers and ancestors, and all one's inferiors as descendants and children, is a feature that has been transferred from the gods into this constitution [of Plato's]. The similarity of substance, deriving from the same cause, signifies **brotherhood** among them;[212] the procreative cause signifies the **ancestor** element; the

---

[209] Note that the final words here are from Timaeus' reply to Socrates, and the majority of Socrates' present speech has been omitted. For abridged lemmata of this sort, rare in a commentary that deals with minutiae (but not towards the conclusion of the Atlantis section for instance), see Festugière's note.

[210] *amigês*, literally 'unmingled', but, since 'mix' was a common expression for 'have sex' it is unlikely that the sexual sense is meant to be forgotten here.

[211] There are perhaps two points: (i) the community of wives is not proposed as a means of legitimizing impure conduct, as some might think; (ii) there is no adulteration of an individual's own special qualities in the kind of union that is followed by enforced separation.

[212] Festugière here strangely translates ἐν ἐκείνοις as 'chez les êtres d'ici-bas'.

Socrates' constitution

outflow of substance that goes forth into a second or third series (*seira*) signifies the class of descendants. As for the same female being yoked to other males and the same male to a plurality of partners, you could deduce this from the mystical texts and the 'Holy Marriages' that are related in secret texts[213] – marriages with which Plato compared the circumstances of his citizens and their marriages in calling them 'holy marriages' (*Rep.* 458e).

Indeed, in physical theory one can see that one and the same receptacle can come about for different formal principles (*logoi*), and a single formal principle can be reflected in a plurality of receptacles and pervade a multitude of substrates. The forms correspond to the males, and the receptacles to the females. Why ever should it be, then, that this same principle is observed in the universe, but seems paradoxical when applied to human lives? Because, I shall claim, all human soul has been sliced off from the whole and become separate, and it is on this account that it[214] finds doctrines that cling to the principle of sharing to be very hard to accept. But if one were to eliminate this lower standing[215] and raise oneself back to the whole, then one would accept such a sharing, ignoring the divided communal feelings among the multitude. Insofar as each of us is drawn down towards the part and becomes isolated and deserts the unified whole, to that extent he is confined to the corresponding life, a life of ungoverned conditions, of unordered order, and of undivided division.[216]

---

[213] Clearly Proclus has 'Holy Marriages' of Plato's own day in mind, but perhaps also more recent religious texts that he considered indebted to them, one of which Porphyry recalls having read aloud (*VPlot.* 15). Festugière speaks of the 'marriage' of the wife of the King Archon to Dionysus at the Anthesteria, of various celebrations of the union of Zeus with Hera or Demeter, and finally of the marriage of Cybele and Attis. The key thing, however, is the Proclan tendency to seize upon almost any hint of ritualistic language in Plato, though here the original γάμους . . . ποιήσομεν ἱερούς (we shall make marriages . . . holy) involved a predicative rather than an attributive sense of the adjective.

[214] Following the text of Praechter (1905), 516, and Festugière, which delete καί between φαίνεται and αὐτῇ.

[215] For a detailed note on this meaning of κατάταξις and cognates see Festugière, who cites from book 1 also 50.3, 53.30, 89.14.

[216] Festugière admits that he is at pains to understand the last of the three paradoxical expressions (ἄσχετον . . . σχέσιν καὶ κατάταξιν ἀκατάτακτον καὶ ἀδιαίρετον διαίρεσιν) that are applied to the life of maximal separation. It seems to me that one should keep in mind various Platonic notions about the descent into plurality and beyond: (i) *Phlb.* 16d–e, the notion that, after a plurality has been divided as far as it can go, it can then be released into an infinite or indeterminate multiplicity; (ii) *Parm.* 159b–160b (the fifth hypothesis according to the Neoplatonic count, and often linked with matter), where the plurality that is deprived of the one loses all characteristics and all number, and ends up looking rather like a unity as a result; and (iii) Platonic concepts of matter stemming from the receptacle of the *Timaeus* itself.

On the *Timaeus* of Plato: Book 1

Arranged marriages

Moreover, so that they should become, right from birth, of the best character possible *up to* **thinking luck was to blame for their draw.** (18d7–e3)

Plato made a special point of treating geometrical similarity, sameness, and equality along with arithmetical kinds in his *Republic* (524d-527c) in order to preserve in its entirety this comparison between state and heaven (as far as objects of sense are concerned), and between state and intelligibles (as far as hyper-heavenly lives are concerned). It is for this reason that in marriage he joins excellent women to excellent partners, and lower quality women to inferior partners, since among the gods too the primary ones have preferred to become united with other primary ones, and the secondary ones with other secondary ones. And along with their union their purity is undefiled.[217] So even in the second ranks, those coming after the gods, such a distribution according to merit is accomplished as the gods intend. Hence divine daemonesses are paired with divine daemons, psychic ones with psychic daemons, and those with material connections with partners with material connections.[218] Everywhere the analogy proceeds down the ranks until the very last. For even the fact that the rulers should **devise in secret** gives an adequate reflection of how the cause of such coming together is hidden among the gods, a coming together that arises primarily from that [higher] region, and secondarily also from the placement that the lot indicates for each. This lot has a power to bind couples together through the similarity of their lives, which has determined how each is coordinated with one similar, the divine with the divine, the enmattered with the enmattered, the intermediate with the intermediate.

On this account all quarrelling and dissension has been eliminated from things divine, as each cherishes (*stergein*) its own partner in conformity with its own placement, and sees this [placement] as a direct consequence of its own nature, and not as an artificial import. As an image (*eikôn*) of all this he introduces the point about the citizens attributing the pairings to the drawing of lots, and failing to see how ingeniously they are contrived. For in the things of nature too receptacles are

---

[217] This translation requires the repositioning of the definite article in the text of 50.15.

[218] For the tripartition of daemons and daemonesses see above 47.15–18, where the last group are called corporeal (σωματικοί) rather than materially connected (πρόσυλοι). These daemons are not, of course, thought of as consisting of body or matter, but as linked closely with bodily matter.

144

Socrates' constitution

distributed so as to suit the forms,[219] and each of the forms would hold its own standing in relation to the changes it undergoes – even though this too is achieved in accordance with the causes that preside over creation as a whole, which correspond to the guardians. Let that conclude what is said with a view to the study of the universe.

Longinus[220] raises a difficulty here about whether Plato can think that the souls are deposited along with the sperm, bearing in mind that he couples like with like so that the best possible offspring can arise. Porphyry[221] counters this objection, but not forcefully enough. My own teacher thought it right to observe firstly that Plato himself added '**so that they should become of the best character possible**'. For children receive a natural likeness of their fathers and get an allocation of the nobility of their parents in respect of their *natural* good qualities. Next, he thought, one should consider the following, that even if it is true that souls are not deposited along with the sperm, the distribution of physical organisms [to them] nevertheless occurs according to their merits: i.e. it is not the case that all souls settle in any organism they encounter, but each settles in the one that suits it. As Homer says 'the good man puts on what is good, but to the inferior inferior is given.'[222] Furthermore, just as the initiate, by decorating the statues with certain symbols, makes them readier[223] for the reception of higher powers, so too universal nature, by using natural formulae to fashion bodies as outward images of souls, implants a different suitability in different bodies for the reception of one kind of soul or another, better ones and worse ones. The politician, having a correct understanding of this, takes a great deal of account of the seeds and of natural suitability in its entirety, so that he also gets the best souls to arise in the bodies with the best natures. This is also what must be said in answer to Longinus' difficulty. Why, though, did Plato suppose it to be better that the citizens think chance to be the reason for such a distribution? Presumably because while it is beneficial, in the case of what we consider to be goods, to be aware of the reason for them too – for we admire that still more – in the case of what are supposed by us to be evils, it is better to believe that their presence is without a cause than to put the blame on some cause that distributes these things for the better. This tends to stir us into looking down on the giver, or

---

[219] It is important that female and male are now being related, as often, to receptacle and form.

[220] Longinus fr. 27.   [221] Porphyry *in Tim.* fr. VI.

[222] *Il.* 14.382. The quotation concerns the putting on of armour.

[223] The concept of readiness is related to theurgic theory, and will appear again at 139.20–140.15.

On the *Timaeus* of Plato: Book 1

10 rather into hating him, seeing that every creature must shun that which does it harm.

The demotion of children in the universe

Indeed, that we claim that the offspring of the good are to be raised, while those of the bad are to be secretly passed on to the rest of the city.[224] (19a1–2)

This too is among things determined there, but its occurrence in the uni-
15 verse is prior by far. Of the things that are produced by the gods and daemons, you see, some remain among them, pure in race and far removed
from generation, which are also called immaculate on this account; but
some descend into generation, being unable to remain in the heaven
20 without slipping. Some are from good stock, and others from inferior –
for **bad** signifies inferior here. The 'horses and charioteers of the gods
are all good',[225] and from good stock, but the corresponding attributes
of individual souls are mixed.[226] Hence there is among them a 'turn of
the scales', a 'falling away', and a 'loss of feathers',[227] and they get sent
into generation by the <gods> in the heaven and by the daemons in
25 charge of the descent of souls. Further, the classes of soul that are heavenly and immaculate receive nourishment as they are carried round 'in
the company of the gods' 'to a feast and banquet',[228] as it is said in the
Phaedrus, while the generation-producing classes are sent from there to
associate with generation.

53 The lemma says **secretly**, indicating the invisible and secret cause
among the gods of the descent of souls, <while **passed on to the rest of
the city** indicates>[229] how the souls that descend from there are placed
under a different providential power and under different overseers, those
in charge of generation.

---

[224] Cf. *Rep.* 460c, which is rather less specific than is the *Timaeus*, though it does appear to
entail it. Festugière corrects the view that these children are being given *to a different
polis*, which besides misunderstanding the Greek would make nonsense if the analogy
of the universe is to work for Proclus.

[225] Quoting *Phaedrus* 246a7–8 with slight variation.

[226] Proclus is presumably thinking of the tripartite soul as illustrated again in the *Phaedrus*,
where the horse that stands for the appetitive part is an inferior beast, while the other
horse is better and obedient to the charioteer, 253d1-e5.

[227] The first and third terms are inspired largely by the *Phaedrus* 247b4, 246c2, 248c8;
the second is already part of the same vocabulary (indicating the fall of the soul) by
Plotinus' time.

[228] The second phrase was well known from *Phdr.* 247a8, the first is an allusion to 248a2.
In both cases there is variation in the direction of a less poetic style.

[229] Festugière is clearly right in postulating some such supplement as this to fill the lacuna
marked in Diehl.

Socrates' constitution

And as they grow up, they should continually be on the lookout for 5
worthy ones and bring them [back] up again, while transferring unworthy
ones in their own number back to the place the others were being
upgraded from. (19a3–5)

In the *Republic* he advocates the transferral not only of those being distributed from the higher ranks to the lower city,[230] but also of those 10
born [down] there with a golden streak, whereas here [in the *Timaeus*]
he advocates the return of those who had been sent down.[231] So how
could these two passages be reconciled with each other? Perhaps it is
possible to make this lemma too agree with his determinations there if
you take **as they grow up** to refer not to those who have been sent down
from above alone, but rather to all those being reared below. Whether 15
they are simply born below or have got down there from on high, <one
must> investigate their natures, determining their types, and accordingly bring back the ones who deserve it. But if you want to take it as
we said in the beginning, one has to say that Socrates took up now as
much as accorded with the purpose before them. For it is the souls who 20
have descended who go up again, without all those who have their initial
foundation in generation and in the material realm – the type of soul
belonging to most non-reasoning creatures. So much concerning the
lemma.

Observe how the same arrangements apply in the universe as Socrates 25
had laid down in his constitution.[232] Certain things always have the same
place in the heaven, remaining divine and unshifting, others have sunk
for ever into the material realm, but intermediate things belong to both in
a sense, sometimes dependent on those divine things, and at other times
mingling with those that welcome generation. So one cannot identify the 30
race of daemons with what is being given a [new] station above or below,
nor are the various lives or deaths concerned with daemons, but they are **54**
concerned with individual souls, which at one moment commune with
generation, and at another transfer to the portion of daemons or gods.
Knowing this, Socrates has legislated for corresponding arrangements
in the *Republic*, because heavenly Zeus had earlier arranged for gods in 5

---

[230] I am tempted to read at 53.9: οὐ μόνον <τῶν> ἀπὸ τῶν ἄνωθεν.

[231] Proclus draws attention to the slight difference between the two works, insofar as *Rep.*
415c3–4 talks solely or primarily of the promotion of those *born* to the lower ranks, not
of those who had previously been demoted. In the *Timaeus* it looks as if he is concerned
with restoring previously demoted individuals back to guardianship (which would in
effect be admitting that a mistake had been made). There is a slight ambiguity in that
the word used in the lemma for 'bring up' (ἀνάγειν) may also mean to 'recall' an exile,
but the πάλιν strongly suggests that Proclus is not misunderstanding this text.

[232] I decline to take this as the title *Republic* as others appear to have done; the work is
Plato's, but the proposed constitution is that of (Plato's) Socrates.

147

On the *Timaeus* of Plato: Book 1

heaven and daemons to bring individual souls back up, and others to send them down into generation, so that the descent and ascent of souls should never entirely desert the universe; for you would see this soul returning to square one,

But another the father sends in to be numbered among them

10 according to the inspired teaching on these things.[233]

The lessons from the summary of the constitution

Then have we now covered it as we did yesterday, to go back over the main heads again, or do we still desire something that's been left out from what was said, Timaeus my friend? (19a7–9)

15 The résumé of the constitution taught us through images how the universe has been made replete with the finest principles (*logoi*). For things generated have been kept separate in it, and each operates according to its own distinctive character in its association with the rest. The first things have been separated from the second, and they employ activities of the
20 latter as something necessary for the completion of the All. The second things are organized by the first, and the best of them are harnessed symbiotically with the best of encosmic things, the middle ones with middle things, and the last with the last. The same principles penetrate several
25 substrates, and the same receptacles participate in several principles. At various times living creatures exchange their various allotted portions in accordance with their personal deserts. All this was enough to focus our attention on the organization of the universe.

Under a limited number of **main heads** Socrates properly summed up the entire shape of the constitution, thus moving back towards the undi-
30 vided character of intellect,[234] in order to imitate the god who organized the heavenly constitution in an intelligible way and in the manner of a
55 father. Since everywhere due measures and completion are being determined for the second things by their causes, on this account he himself asks Timaeus to state whether he has included the entire form of the constitution; for all intellect is reliant upon the god that precedes it and
5 determines its own boundaries by looking to it.[235] For to have set forth **the main heads** (*kephalaia*) is also a symbol of his having organized the primary elements of the whole, i.e. its *head*, things which the universal demiurge will arrange more perfectly with an eye on the whole and on

---

[233] *Od.* 12.65 is used in normal late-Platonic fashion.
[234] For the undivided character of intellect (ἡ νοερὰ ἀμέρεια) see Festugière's note.
[235] Socrates is analogous to the highest member of the demiurgic triad, Timaeus to the Father of Demiurges who precedes that triad: see especially 9.15–24.

148

Socrates' constitution

the single life of the cosmos.[236] So much for the analogy between parts and the whole.

It is not particularly problematic for us to inquire whether this lemma is stating that he has now gone through **the main heads** of the constitution that he went through yesterday, or that he had included it all under main heads both yesterday and again today.[237] That's because, whether he sketched it in greater detail yesterday and under main heads today, or whether he outlined the main heads in both cases, the divine Iamblichus is satisfied,[238] and it makes no difference to us. Perhaps, though, it is rather the latter that agrees better. 'To go back over the main heads *again*' signifies that it had been stated 'under the main heads' yesterday too. It would not be at all surprising that its summary nature should not be mentioned in the *Republic*, because many other things that are stated here as if they had been said the day before are not mentioned there. On the other hand it may be that here too the **again** should not be taken with **the main heads** but with **go back over**, because he who narrates the previous conversation **goes back**, while he who summarizes the long account under main heads **goes back again**.[239] However things are, it is not a problematic matter.

Explaining Socrates' desire

Now then, about this constitution that we've run through, kindly listen next to the kind of feeling that I happen to have experienced about it. (19b3–4)

There are five points here, to list the main heads, that the forthcoming speech of Socrates has incorporated. *First*, what it is that he yearns for as a supplement to what has been said, after the exposition of the constitution. *Second*, that he himself is not capable of supplying this. *Third*, that neither does any of the poets have the capability for this. *Fourth*, that neither should one entrust such a task to the sophists. *Fifth*, that only those who've been listening could give a worthwhile account of what Socrates is keen for.

---

[236] I.e. the upper member of the triad of demiurges arranges only the highest level of the universe, which must be integrated with the lower levels by the universal demiurge; cf. 57.31–58.2.

[237] Though the puzzle is not attributed to any particular pre-Iamblichan commentator, its philological character strongly suggests Longinus.

[238] Iamblichus *in Tim.* fr. 6. For commentary see Dillon (1973), 268.

[239] One must bear in mind that Proclus views the *Republic* as going back over a conversation, whereas this summary can be seen as going back again.

On the *Timaeus* of Plato: Book 1

What then is this thing that Socrates yearns for after this constitution, as we must necessarily say something about that first of all? It is to view this city in motion, as he says, in struggles, in competitions, and in warfare, so that after its life in peacetime, which he himself recounted, he should inquire into its behaviour under outside pressure. So that is what he's looking for.

One might here raise the puzzle[240] of what this desire of Socrates has in view, and for what reason he yearns for this to occur. Porphyry offers a solution to this puzzle, saying that it is activities that bring states-of-being (*hexeis*) to completion, not only those prior to the states-of-being but also those that proceed from them. For that which is complete in its state-of-being comes after activity; otherwise, it slumbers in a kind of potential existence, if deprived of its activity. Therefore, so that Socrates may genuinely observe the constitution in completion, he asks also for an animated picture in words of its deeds in warfare, and of its struggling against the others. It is likely, [Porphyry] says, that [Plato] is proposing that the condition of virtue is not *by itself* sufficient for happiness, but *when in activity*.[241]

Well if the goal were war-related, one might say to him, he ought indeed to be saying that war perfects the constitution, but if it is peace-related, what need is there to drag in Peripatetic doctrines to solve puzzles in Plato? Surely, even if the goal is not war-related war still shows up the extent of one's virtue more clearly than peace, just as 'triple-waves',[242] a strong swell, and external pressures in general, show the qualities of the helmsman, as the Stoics too are accustomed to say: 'Add external pressure, and find the real man.'[243] For to be undefeated by pressures that enslave others shows up comprehensively the quality of one's life.

Perhaps, though, it is odd to make this the only reason, even if it does offer a *political* explanation,[244] and not to keep in view the overall

---

[240] Another puzzle that one might naturally attribute to Longinus, given that Porphyry is answering it.

[241] Aristotle had not only made wide use of his distinction between potency (δύναμις) and act(ivity) (ἐνέργεια), but had also placed some emphasis on happiness as *activity* in accordance with the best of the virtues, e.g. *EN* 10.7, and it is clear that Porphyry (*in Tim.* fr. VII) is taking a broadly Aristotelian approach to Plato's text at this time.

[242] Practically a proverbial expression for a mighty wave or group of waves, first appearing in its literal sense in Euripides (*Hipp.* 1213), but used prominently by Plato in a metaphorical sense (*Rep.* 472a, *Euthd.* 293a), thus inviting further use among his commentators.

[243] = *SVF* 3.206, p. 49.33.

[244] Here I consider Festugière to have missed the point, misled perhaps by the rather odd phrasing; the point is that this explanation of the difficulty appeals only to the world of public conduct, and takes no account of physics or theology. That of course is typical

target of Plato, [and see] how the god who arranged the constitution of the heaven wishes (i) that generation too should be directed by the heavenly gods and (ii) that the warfare between the forms and enmattered things should be established, in order that the cycle of generation should mirror the heavenly cycle.[245] And this is what it is to view the city actively engaged in deeds of war, to view generation being marshalled alongside the heavenly, and united in taking its lead from there. This seems analogous to what will very shortly be said about the universal demiurge: 'And when the father who brought it into being saw it in motion and transformed into a living image of eternal things, he was pleased and delighted.'[246] Presumably this is what Socrates wants too:[247] to see his own city in motion and activity in the same way as the mainstay of the heavenly constitution[248] wants to behold the things of this world actively at work in organizing the generation-producing conflict. That will be how we explain the correspondence between these things for now.

Don't be surprised that we earlier linked the lower city with generation, and now link it with war. It is a sound practice to correlate the same things with different ones according to a variety of analogies, since, though generation resembles the lower city in its plurality of inseparable lives, it resembles war and hostilities in its conflicts and its material disturbance.

Then again, so that we may link all these claims with the study of cosmic wholes before the separate examination of each, consider how the second claim[249] is in harmony with this. Because Socrates corresponds to the first of the Three Fathers, the one who organized the first stages, he declares that he is not capable of fashioning the next stages too – for the founder of all is different from the founder of the middle or third things.

---

of Porphyry's exegesis of Plato's prefatory material, and already outdated by the time of Iamblichus. The objection to Porphyry, then, may be designed as an *ad hominem* objection that remains within Porphyry's interpretative strategy, probably either devised or reported by Iamblichus before demanding a *skopos*-related interpretation.

[245] On the superiority of the text of MP to that of C (printed by Diehl) see Festugière's note, which explains well the way in which the heavenly cycle must be reflected in the cyclic changes within the realm of matter.

[246] The quotation seems to have been from memory, as there are several variations from the text (37c6–7).

[247] It may be significant that Proclus has replaced terminology of desiring with a verb indicating rather a rational wish.

[248] Presumably the overall Demiurge, to which Socrates somehow corresponds; see 9.15–24.

[249] We have returned to points two to four enumerated above at 56.2–5.

On the *Timaeus* of Plato: Book 1

[Consider] the third claim, that the poets are not capable either, and
the fourth, that neither are the sophists. These [agree] because the one
group imitate those things in the midst of which they were brought
up,[250] and the other group are wanderers who fail to combine philosophy with community politics.[251] See once again how these claims follow from what has been said, for the powers that are going to master
generation must not be inseparable from it while operating within it –
these, you see, are analogous to myth-weaving poets and imitators,
for they too spend their time on images, admiring only those things
that they are also familiar with, enmattered and particular things, and
unable to rise up above matter. Nor yet must they be separated, while
being subject to frequent change and ascending or descending to other
levels at different times – that is a property of individual souls, that are
likened to sophists because they too have beautiful reasoning devices,[252]
but they wander to different sectors of the cosmos at different times.
It is consequently imperative that the powers that control generation,
which is steered from the heaven, should be philosophically *and* communally minded, so that, being separable from what they govern on
account of the philosophic element and providential on account of
the communal one, they may manage their own domains intelligently.
The natural power, being 'poetic', is inseparable from matter, while
the class of individual souls, being 'sophistic', is nomadic. But before
things in motion must come the eternally stable providential plans of
the gods, and before the domains of change must come the changeless
realms.

After these, as his fifth claim, he identifies the ones who are capable
of doing this – for this too should be transferred from the verbal sphere
into deeds – the universal and transcendent demiurge of the whole, and
the remaining Fathers, of which one is the founder of the middle things,
and the other of the final things; to these are analogous Timaeus, Critias,
and Hermocrates. Of these the first has been marvellously praised (with
Socrates adding 'in my opinion' (20a5)), the second moderately so in

[250] Since the Platonic view of a poet, especially in *Republic* 10, is that they are inevitably
imitators of life rather than ideals, they cannot depict what lies outside their
experience.

[251] The emphasis would appear to be on their inability to really become part of a *polis* and
be communally minded because of their travelling lifestyle. Proclus has in mind the
Republic's ideal of the philosopher-politician, and would not be worried about Plato's
lack of enthusiasm for those who occupy the middle ground between philosophy and
politics at *Euthd.* 305c–306d.

[252] I have tried to preserve the idea that the sophist's reasoned speech is akin to the principles of reason (*logoi*) in the soul.

152

Socrates' constitution

accordance with the rank <given> him by his own <people> (a6),[253] and the third in the most basic fashion in accord with the evidence of others (a8).

Socrates' feeling and Plato's beautiful creation

My feeling is actually rather like this *up to* **and participating competitively in one of the challenges thought to be the province of the body.** (195b5–c1)

At this point Longinus[254] says that Plato employs a decorative style, on account of the bold similes and the graceful vocabulary that adorns the diction, making a point against certain Platonists who claim that the style of this passage is spontaneous, and not something contrived by the philosopher. He says that the selection of terms has been carefully pondered by Plato, and that he doesn't adopt the first words that occur [to him] for everything. Well, one could say that it's because of the mode of expression customary at the time that this ability has come to him too, but (says Longinus) he also puts a great deal of forethought into their composition. For the atoms of Epicurus could more readily come together to make a cosmos than a random combination of nouns and verbs could make the perfect sentence. Certain people found fault with Plato for his choice of words because he used metaphors, but everybody admires him for the way he put them together. Nevertheless, not even from this alone could one establish his meticulousness over expression, but rather from his habit of doing this kind of thing, the kind he displays here. For Socrates doesn't simply state the treatment he is longing to receive from Timaeus' group, but he is like someone who uses beautification to win the listener over: **My feeling is actually rather like this, as if somebody who was watching beautiful animals either reproduced by drawing etc**. That's what Longinus says.

Origenes agreed that Plato is taking care over the grace of his writing, not however because he is aiming at pleasure, but in the course of using this comparison for the presentation of what he felt. Similarly, we should claim that this comparison has also been adopted because the constitution has been written up in such a way as to resemble things divine; that the grace of the language mirrors the grace that has been instilled into

---

[253] It is obvious that Proclus must be commenting here on the *source* of this estimation of Critias, and I read κατὰ τὴν <τῶν> ἑαυτοῦ τάξιν, ὁ δὲ ἐσχάτως κατὰ τὴν [τῶν] ἄλλων . . ., postulating the misplacement of this article by a scribe who was an educated but hasty reader. It is also tempting, if unnecessary, to read ἀξίωσιν for τάξιν.

[254] Longinus fr. 28; Origenes fr. 9.

On the *Timaeus* of Plato: Book 1

heavenly things by the demiurge; and that the scientific contrivance (*technikon*) of his communication blended with some spontaneity mirrors the divine creation, which has both a self-derived element of control and a factor that proceeds from being (*einai*) and essence (*ousia*).[255]

If one were to undertake an examination of the analogy itself, the phrase **beautiful animals** would signify those bodies that outshine others in beauty, and **reproduced by drawing or even really living** [signifies] that they display both bodily images and actual lives that precede them; for the outward shape of the gods is a representation (*agalma*) of the lives within them. The phrase **keeping still** [signifies] that they are replete with intelligible order and with smooth, continuous life, while **moving** [indicates] their proceeding to another level of arrangement and a second creation. The [phrase] **participating competitively in one of the challenges thought to be the province of the body** signifies the things that give a share of their own effluences and powers to things less complete, and that act upon other things with their own powers. So much for the image. As for the phrase **whether reproduced by drawing or even really living**, both its parts are correctly applied to divine bodies, for they are both **reproduced by drawing** in the dodecahedron,[256] and by living vigorous and craftsmanlike lives. And if it were understood as a disjunction it would be signifying that the stated constitution had been fashioned by reason and assimilated to the heaven, and that it exists among true or daemonic lives though not among humans. Furthermore the desire to see the state in motion corresponds to where it is said: 'and when the Father saw it in motion, he was delighted, and still more' did he wish 'to liken it to its paradigm' (37c–d). That

---

[255] 'Très mystérieux' says Festugière. 'Element of control' translates ὅρον, but 'a factor' represents only the neuter of the article, which therefore suggests that the masculine ὅρον cannot be understood with it. To begin with it should be clear that this is particularly concerned with *heavenly* creation; second, that 'creation' here means 'totality created', and not the creation process; thirdly, I think, unlike Festugière, that the key here is that the term 'spontaneity' (τὸ αὐτοφυές) can likewise signify 'sprung from itself', and is therefore analogous to the 'self-derived element of control', which is to be identified with the extent to which heavenly souls have control over their own motion. In spite of the fact that they are self-moved, there are limits imposed upon this motion by factors akin to the scientific standards of which Plato's writing has to take account. It seems clear that these technical requirements for heavenly motion must derive from the intelligible patterns by which it functions, and we should perhaps think of the various abstract elements that are used for the construction and organization of the soul at 35a ff.; these are what makes it be what it is, and indeed one of these elements is a new intermediate essence described at 35a. Heavenly soul at least cannot engage in motions that contravene the requirements of intelligent psychical motion.

[256] Proclus is perhaps excessively reliant on the fact that Plato at 55c says the creator has used the dodecahedron for the whole *diazôgraphôn* (sketching it out?).

154

Socrates' constitution

is how the arranger of the heaven too wants to see it moving, and [to see it] guiding along the war of generation through this motion. He used the phrase **in one of the challenges thought to be the province of the body** because some of them belong to souls, some to bodies. For instance running, wrestling, and gymnastics are called challenges of the body.

I too felt the same way about the city that we described *up to* **in respect of their verbal communications with each of the cities.** (19c1–8)

Here you have a concise defence of Socrates' having associated with Alcibiades and Plato's visit to Dionysius. Both expected that they would become manufacturers of a decent constitution, and that they would see constitutional life in action, because it is for this that Socrates yearns here too: [he yearns] for some praise to be spoken of such a *polis* as it triumphs in war; and it has been stated why [he wants it] and to what sort of paradigm he is looking.[257] Now cities use both words and works against their adversaries: words in embassies, in compacts, in challenges to battle, and all things of this sort; works in pitching camp, ambushes, skirmishes. Because of this he wants such a city to be praised in both areas, for its sensible, secure, high-minded, and firm use of words, and for its bravery, exertion, and discipline in works. In both of these ways he would be imitating his paradigm, a paradigm which controls the entire 'war' of generation as it shines through in both physical and intellectual creations.[258]

Point two: Socrates' inadequacies

This is the charge, Critias and Hermocrates, that I've accused myself of, that I should never have been capable of delivering an adequate encomium of the city myself. (19c8–d2)

This is the second of the main points before us. The reason for it we have already stated, but now we have to examine it again in a different fashion. For among earlier interpreters (*presbuteroi*) the point has already been made (i) that the genre of the encomium is fulsome, solemn, and grand, while the Socratic manner is lean, precise, and dialectical, i.e. it is diametrically opposed to the other. Hence Socrates too avoids using encomia, being well aware of what his inner abilities are suited to. Besides directly

---

[257] Referring back to 60.30–61.2.

[258] These 'physical and intellectual creations' (ταῖς τε φυσικαῖς ποιήσεσι καὶ ταῖς νοεραῖς) correspond to the works and words referred to above.

On the *Timaeus* of Plato: Book 1

questioning the authenticity of the *Menexenus*,[259] those who make this claim seem to me to be insensitive even to the grandiloquence of Socrates in the *Phaedrus*. There are others (ii) who claim that those who craft such encomia ought to have had some experience of the deeds of war too, and hence that many of the historians slip up in how they describe things[260] through inexperience of battle strategy. However, Socrates at least had been on campaign at Delium and Potidaea, and was not inexperienced in any of these things. Others (iii) claim that it is in irony that he asserts here that he is unable to praise this city adequately – just as he professes not to know various other things too. However, this irony of Socrates was directed towards sophists and young men, not towards gentlemen of such wisdom and knowledge.[261] Rather than these [explanations] it is preferable to say that he is avoiding becoming 'third from the truth',[262] because the deeds of the correctly constituted state are third from the paradigm of the constitution. So wishing to remain at the second level he says that he is not able to endure the descent to the third type of life. And such a 'lack of power' is a superabundance of power.[263] For to remain as far as possible among paradigms occurs through excess of power.

63 Observe how this too is consonant with what we have said before about the analogy between these things and the universe. For the second creation had been made a likeness of the previous one, and on this account it is directly linked with it. Indeed all the demiurgic series is one, possessing unification as well along with division. So in all likelihood Socrates deliberately appeals to Critias and Hermocrates, and

---

[259] 'Authenticity' refers not to the attribution of authorship to Plato, but rather to the assumption that the work accurately depicts Socrates himself. Confusions over whether the authorship or Socraticity of a work are questioned are natural among Socratic dialogues, and Panaetius (fr. 126) seems to have sought for truly Socratic works among the followers of Socrates; it may be this that gave rise to the later belief that he had rejected the *Phaedo*, meaning that he had rejected its Platonic authorship (frs. 127–9). See Tarrant (2000), 56–7.

[260] 'How they describe things' translates ἐν ταῖς διαθέσεσιν, and I presume that the original interpreters had historical descriptions of battle arrangements in mind, but Proclus' response seems either to presume that it was in encomia that the performance of these historians was criticized, or to assume that such descriptions will be part of the encomium that Socrates prefers to avoid.

[261] On this passage see Tarrant (2000), 110. It is interesting that young men (many no doubt Socrates' friends) are considered an appropriate target for irony just as sophists are, but the division reflects the two species of investigative or 'zetetic' dialogue, one that is competitive and the other that is used for training.

[262] Appropriately the allusion is to the final book of the *Republic*, 599d2 etc.

[263] Cf. 19.19 above, where Iamblichus is explaining the 'weakness' of the fourth person in the same terms.

Socrates' constitution

thinks it right that they should weave on[264] what comes next. Timaeus, you see, is going to hand down this teaching in a *more* universal and *more* elevated way, and not through images, directly preserving his position analogous to the universal demiurge, mapping out the heaven with the dodecahedron and generation with the shapes appropriate to it.

Point three: the inadequacies of the poets

My own condition is in no way surprising, but I have come to the same conclusion about the poets too, both those who lived long ago and those who live now. [This is] not out of any disrespect for the poetic race; rather it is clear to anybody that the imitative tribe will imitate most easily and most excellently the things that one's brought up with. For any group to give a good imitation of what is beyond their native experience is hard in deeds and harder still in words. (19d2–e2)

This is the third of the main points recorded earlier. Here he shows that poetic ability also cannot extend of itself to the praise of such men, because they have been put by fortune in position for deeds of war. Difficulties for the account are raised by Longinus[265] and Origenes, who don't believe that he could have included Homer too among the poets when he says that he has come to the same conclusion not only about the present poets (that's nothing peculiar) but also about those who had lived long ago. And so, says Porphyry, Origenes spent three whole days shouting and going red in the face, and getting into quite a sweat, saying that the claim (*hypothesis*) was important and problematic, and very keen to demonstrate that the imitation in [the works of] Homer adequately depicts actions of excellence. Who, after all, is more grandiloquent than Homer, who, even when he brings gods into strife and battle, does not fall short of capturing their likeness, but matches the nature of their deeds in his majestic language. This is the argument that confronts us.

In answer to it Porphyry says that Homer is quite capable of dressing their passions in intensity and majesty and lifting their deeds to an imposing magnificence,[266] but he is not able to convey a *dispassionate* intellective state or the activities of the philosophic life. Personally I wonder whether Homer could be incapable of these things while Critias is capable or Hermocrates is worthy to speak on the subject.[267] My view

---

[264] *prosyphainein* here recalls *Timaeus* 41d1, where the lesser gods must weave on the mortal parts of living creatures. Once more there is an analogy between the events of the dramatic setting and the cosmology presented by *Timaeus*.

[265] Longinus fr. 29; Origenes fr. 10.

[266] Porphyry *in Tim.* fr. VIII; on the meaning of φανταστικός here see Festugière.

[267] Or 'while Critias or Hermocrates is worthy . . .', if one deletes the second ἱκανὸς in 64.12 as a gloss.

157

On the *Timaeus* of Plato: Book 1

is that Plato distinguishes god-given poetic ability from poetic skills, a division that makes the gods responsible for inspired grandiloquence and majesty. It is oracles above all that have this fulsome and grand style, and [Plato] is making the point that the [poetry] derived from human skills does not have the required capacity for praise when compared with the valour of this city and the achievements of men raised in it. Even if there is some majesty due to skill in the works of any of the poets, its artificial and bombastic character is considerable, relying for the most part on metaphors, like the work of Antimachus.[268] What Socrates needs is an encomiast who displays a spontaneous majesty and possesses an unforced and refined grandiloquence, in the same way that the achievements too don't acquire their grandeur from chance, but as something that is intrinsic to the upbringing and education of the men. Socrates himself, I believe, has shown that he does not reject either the divinely inspired poet or the whole of the poetic art, only the skilled kind, when he actually states himself that he isn't showing disrespect for poetry – 'Certainly the poetic race too is divine', as [Plato][269] himself said elsewhere – just the imitative kind, and not even this in its entirety, only the part raised on poor laws and character. Because this has an inclination towards things inferior, it is not of a nature to imitate a more elevated character.

This much should be said in answer to the difficulty, so let's give due clarification to the end of the lemma, which is in a way rather problematic. Here it is: **For any group to give a good imitation of what is beyond their native experience is hard in deeds and harder still in words**. It seems easier, you see, to imitate their words than their deeds, and certainly there is no shortage of persons who set themselves up as sophistic teachers,[270] whose display of excellence extends to their words, while in practice they are totally divorced from it. So perhaps it is better to interpret these statements like this: understand what's **beyond their native experience** as what's most excellent, and take **in deeds** and **in words** as the equivalent of 'in respect of their deeds' and 'in respect of their words', and [substitute] for **give a good imitation** 'get well imitated'. Putting [the threads] together from all this, 'For the most excellent to be well imitated is hard in respect of deeds, and harder still in respect of its words, though it is imitated *verbally* – this is

---

[268] An epic poet of the late fifth century BC.

[269] Technically, perhaps, one should understand 'Socrates' here, but it is the 'Athenian Stranger' who speaks these words in *Laws* 3, 682a, which suggests that Proclus here conflates 'Socrates' and Plato.

[270] One thinks of rhetoricians of the age, though Proclus may have a range of educators in mind.

158

Socrates' constitution

basic to poetry.[271] And you see how this is in agreement with the facts: somebody who relates in a verbal account the deeds of excellent persons is composing history, while somebody who composes their speeches, if he is to preserve the character of the speaker, must himself adopt a disposition that matches the character of the speaker.[272] That's because inner dispositions obviously make a difference to speeches. Accordingly we ridicule those who have written defence-speeches of Socrates – most of them apart from Plato – because they haven't preserved the character of Socrates. Yet when they are recording this basic story, how Socrates was accused and defended himself and met with such and such a verdict, they wouldn't deserve of ridicule; rather it is the failure to capture a likeness in their imitation of words that shows up the imitators as ridiculous. Even in the case of Achilles, it is not difficult to say that he came out armed in some such fashion as this, and did some such deeds as this, but to supplement this with an explanation of what words he might say if caught in the river (*Il.* 21.273–83) is no longer easy – this is the work of one who is able to assume the character of the hero and to speak forth his words while rooted in that character. A further indication of the difficulty of imitating speeches is given by Socrates in the *Republic* (386c–98b).[273] Most of his rebukes[274] to Homer there concern his imitation of speeches.

In the case of the gods, however, they say that it is easier to imitate in words the words of the gods than their deeds. For who could craft a worthy description of their productive acts? Or maybe the imitation of words and of deeds is just the same in their case, for because their words are their intellections, and these in turn are their acts of creation,

---

[271] Proclus' strategy here is difficult to understand. Festugière is concerned to answer Taylor's belief that Proclus was taking Plato's μιμεῖσθαι as a passive. My translation is slightly different from Festugière's, and it is based on the view that there is a sharp contrast between the 'in deeds [=in one's actions]' – 'in words [=via a verbal medium]' distinction and the distinction between deeds and words as objects, and that Proclus thinks that imitation through the medium of words is a lot easier than 'in deeds' imitation, while 'in deeds' imitation of words is nevertheless harder than 'in deeds' imitation of deeds. So presumably Proclus' rhetorical opponents are imitating *in their words* rather than in their deeds, in which domain they are no more successfully imitating the words of true virtue than its deeds.

[272] Proclus has in mind the theory of speech-imitation present at *Republic* 3, 393c.

[273] In the passage Socrates distinguishes narrative compositions from dramatic and mixed ones, and assumes in the case of dramatic content (where characters deliver speeches in direct discourse and so *in character*) that the assimilation of the artist to the character imitated is involved (393c), contrary to the rule that we should imitate only good character. The specific criticisms of Homer, however, mostly precede the general complaints about the use of direct discourse.

[274] The verb chosen by Proclus, ἐπιπλήσσω, though not foreign to Attic prose, has an archaic ring, and is itself used by Homer.

159

On the *Timaeus* of Plato: Book 1

the imitator of their words is also an imitator of their deeds: to whatever extent he falls short of the one, to that extent he will be failing in the imitation of the other.

15 Longinus used to puzzle over the phrase before us.[275] Presuming this to be the reason that the poets are not worthy imitators of the deeds and words that belong to such a city, that they have not been raised according to the city's standards, then neither could Critias and his sort achieve the business before them. They had not lived among people who
20 conducted themselves like that either. Whereas if it is because they don't have knowledge, but are merely imitators,[276] why will they not be able to take the outlines from us[277] and imitate them, seeing that the ability that they have is mimetic? We should say in answer to these problems, that the imitation of such a constitution proceeds through a life that
25 is in agreement with the paradigms, for somebody who doesn't live in accordance with virtue is unable to express the words that befit persons of moral stature. Accordingly it is not sufficient for its imitation that one should merely hear what type of life exists under the constitution, as implied by the sceptical argument of Longinus. Porphyry[278] adds that
30 just as for painters not everything is imitable, like the midday light, so neither is the life of the best constitution [imitable] for the poets, for it transcends their power.

Point four: inadequacies of the itinerant sophists

67 **Again, as for the race of the sophists, I consider them very experienced in many fine [types of] speech** *up to* **they might act and speak.** (19e2–8)

5 Sophists often used to be involved in the practice of astronomy, or of geometry, or of politics, or of division, and because of this they are now said to have **many fine [types of] speech**. But, since they did not have scientific speech, they were called **experienced**. The term **experienced** implies a non-rational routine applied in insignificant debates without
10 the knowledgeable cause.[279] Because they not only reaped a living in different cities at different times, but were also full of deceit, false wisdom, and unscientific error, they have justly been termed **wanderers**.

---

[275] Longinus fr. 30.   [276] As suggested by *Republic* 10, 595c–599d.

[277] Festugière's translation fleshes out the Greek to offer more explanation: 'why, after we have taken over the models, could they not imitate them . . .'. There is no indication that he proposes to alter the text.

[278] Porphyry *in Tim.* fr. IX.

[279] Proclus' description is closely linked to Socrates' treatment of rhetoric in the *Gorgias*, 462c ff. That dialogue (e.g. 465a, 501a) does not so easily explain the notion of 'the knowledgeable cause' (ἡ ἔμφρονος αἰτία), to which *Phlb.* 23d ff. may be relevant.

Because they led a disorderly and uneducated life, operating according to the passions, it is quite reasonably said that they had not occupied their own proper dwellings, when each should have put himself in order ahead of the rest – for everything that applies in the household and the city applies also to the realm of character, and this should be corrected ahead of what is outside one.

So who then are the fitting imitators of the deeds and words of the best constitution, if neither poets nor sophists are? These are surely those of political and philosophical character, as he himself says. One needs both, so that one is able to survey their deeds through statesmanship, and their words through philosophy, with a prior insight into their lives as something within one, and so that one may comprehend their practical wisdom through the former and the intellective activity of the rulers through the latter. From these images one should cross to the demiurgic causes as well, [and observe] that these too must be intellective and concerned with the entire universe[280] if the universe is to be brought to fulfilment, and if generation is to possess as images all that the heaven has in a primary way.

Point five: those capable of such praise

Then there remains the type in your own condition, [the type] that through nature and through nurture shares in both together. (19e8–20a1)

Longinus,[281] who does not disdain to examine the diction, says that the phrase 'as for the race of sophists, I am afraid that because it is nomadic' is characteristic of one who is beginning[282] to change the expression out of a desire for grandeur; that the next [phrase] 'the quantity and nature of their deeds in war and battles' and what follows is characteristic of one who distorts the natural expression; and thirdly that '**then there remains the type in your own condition**' is altogether grating. For [he says] it's not at all unlike 'the force of Heracles' and 'the holy might of Telemachus' and so on. Origenes took the mode of address in the phrases at issue as being characteristic of historical writing, because

---

[280] I translate *holikas* here in this way, since it is clear that in order for the analogy to work the demiurges must be acting like universal statesmen. While one might have been tempted to read instead *politikas*, one should note that the received text is supported by 69.8–9.

[281] Longinus fr. 31; Origenes fr. 11.

[282] Festugière postulates a lacuna, and his supplement would yield <and trying> at this point. However, there must be some doubt as to whether the lacuna must be postulated, for it would be bold to believe that ἄρχομαι ('I begin') cannot take an infinitive in late Greek in a context like this (as in Homeric Greek).

On the *Timaeus* of Plato: Book 1

15   such periphrases are suited to such diction, just as it is to poetic style.
Our position, however, is that Plato everywhere alters his communicative strategy to suit his subject matter and pursues changes in mode of
address for changes in topics. Still, we deny that the phrase before us is a
20   periphrasis. It doesn't indicate the same as 'you' like 'the force of Heracles' indicates the same as 'Heracles', but indicates the actual **type** in the
best **condition**; when they began from this [condition] they alone could
give a fitting return [of a favour] by imitating the best constitution. They
do this by operating in accordance with this condition of theirs, a condition that differs from the poetic and sophistic conditions. So much for
25   the details of the text. With our attention fixed on the *intentions* (*ennoiai*)
behind these words, we shall say that Socrates is motivating Critias and
Hermocrates to [discuss] what remained to be said of the constitution,
but he is exhorting Timaeus too to apply himself to what he requires.
For this is the fifth of the main heads that we had proposed to exam-
30   ine.[283] And see how respectful he has been towards the gentlemen right
from his introductory words, referring to their [stable][284] **condition**, so
69   that you eliminate all sophistic straying;[285] speaking of them as **sharing**
in political art '**by nature and by nurture**'[286], so that you draw a contrast with the political imitation that is nurtured under inferior laws; and
defining their final state[287] in terms of their nature and nurture, so that
5   you do not make their *nature* defective by depriving it of nurture or think
that their nurture had been set aside for an unsuitable or incompatible
recipient (*hypodochê*). This much has been said *in general* about the *men*.
And if you would like to move on to discuss the paradigms, we are left
the lesson that the demiurgic type, that is concerned with the entire universe and intellective,[288] should be assigned to the providential care of
10   the universe. But we also have to inspect what is being said about each
individually.

The qualifications of Socrates' companions

**Timaeus here is from Locris in Italy, a city with the best of laws, and in
property and family he is second to none of those there. He has turned
his hand to the highest magistracies and roles of honour available in his**

---

[283] Cf. 55.30–56.7, and for the fifth 58.27–59,6.

[284] It is characteristic of a *hexis* that it is stable; see Lee (1997).

[285] πλάνη is a word for error that literally means 'wandering'.

[286] Cf. 20a7 (Hermocrates).

[287] Festugière translates 'perfection', and indeed the implication is that the final state is
one of perfection in certain respects, but such a translation seems to pre-empt the
possibilities for misjudging them that are then suggested.

[288] Cf. note to 67.26 above.

Socrates' constitution

city, yet as regards philosophy in its entirety, in my judgement he has also got to its summit. (20a1–5)

What testimony could be more full of admiration than this? What praise could be greater? Has he not first of all testified to Timaeus' political skill, and then to his intellective insight, saying that he has **got to the summit** of **philosophy in its entirety**, and adding **in my judgement**, which has put the coping stone on all his praises? What other [testimony] among men could better assimilate him to the one [universal] Demiurge than this picture? To begin with, by his being a man of politics and a philosopher he is Zeus-like, and next by his being from **a city with the best of laws** he imitates the god brought up in the intelligible realm by Adrasteia,[289] and that god's universal, intellective, and unitary nature is mirrored in *his* excellence of family – for he has all these [qualities] by participation in the Fathers that precede him. [Mirrored in Timaeus'] having **turned his hand to the highest magistracies** is his kingly nature and power over the whole universe, seeing that his sceptre according to the theologians is of four and twenty measures,[290] while his surpassing transcendence of all things 'in seniority and power' (*Rep.* 509b) [is mirrored in] his enjoying the **highest roles of honour**. Indeed, it is he who distributes the roles of honour to other things besides him. And you could say that his stamp has been completely reproduced by [Timaeus'] having **got to the summit** of **philosophy** with respect to his having all knowledge together within himself. Consequently you could grasp from all the things that have been said, as if from images, the identity of the universal Demiurge – that he is an intellect embracing many intellects, ranked among the intellective gods, and filled with the very first intelligibles, deserving royal honours, and enthroned above the other demiurgic gods in seniority. It is not at all surprising that [Plato] called the city of Timaeus Locris, when the Greeks are accustomed to call it not that, but merely 'Locrians', to distinguish it from the Locris that is set opposite Euboea. For he makes many changes in order to signify more clearly what he's aiming at. It is obvious that the Locrians had good laws, because Zaleucus was their law-giver.

[289] As Festugière notes, this should be understood in the light of *in Tim.* III. 274.17ff., where Proclus reports that in Orphic cosmology the Demiurge is nourished by Adrasteia, consorts with Necessity, and engenders Fate. The universal demiurge is of course rooted in the triad *above* the triad of demiurges, in a realm that is intelligible as well as intellective. Adrasteia is seen as akin to an intelligible law at this point.

[290] This Orphic theme also appears below at I. 451.1ff., and at *in Crat.* 101, p. 52.26–30, where Zeus is thought of as ruling hypercosmic and cosmic worlds, each of which is somehow seen as twelvefold.

On the *Timaeus* of Plato: Book 1

20   **And surely all of us here know that Critias is not an amateur in any part of our subject!**   (20a6–7)

Critias was of a stout (*hadros*) and noble nature, and he was taking part in philosophical gatherings as well. He was called 'an amateur among philosophers, but a philosopher among amateurs', as history says.[291] He **25** was personally involved in tyranny, after becoming one of the Thirty, but it is not fair to blame Socrates just because he held him worthy of some praise at this point. In the first place one should pay attention to the manner of his praise: he **is not an amateur in any part of our subject** because of his nature and his spending time in philosophic gatherings. Next, note that the tyrannical element itself is also evidence of natural **71** gifts, as the myth in the *Republic*[292] teaches us when it shows those souls 'who come down from the heaven' specially drawn towards the tyrannical life. That's because, after becoming used to 'spinning about with the gods [up] there',[293] and managing the universe with them, they rush off to what appear to be roles of power here too – just as it is those who **5** have a memory of the intelligible beauty who welcome the appearance of beauty.[294] That he is linked by analogy with the middle creation you may infer firstly from his taking over the discourse of Socrates, then from **10** his narration of the story of Atlantis, and thirdly from his personal life: for the leadership role, and extended influence over many, and power in general are among the *middle* things – hence it also has the middle position in [Socrates'] praise. That he has been called **no amateur**, while still not sharing in Timaeus' outstanding qualities, signifies his lower rank **15** as compared with the first, while the fact that he does not entirely lack them signifies his close relation to him.

---

[291] This material is also present in the Platonic scholia to 20a, but since it is reproduced virtually word for word, with the omission of 'as history says', it seems clear that the scholia are indebted to Proclus. Whether the Critias of *Tim.* and *Critias* is to be identified with the tyrant himself or his grandfather has been a matter of controversy (the case for the grandfather being based on the assumption that the chronology is otherwise too difficult), but Proclus assumes the obvious identification.

[292] 619b7–d3: the man who is unfortunate enough to choose the life of a tyrant, with its many concealed misfortunes, has been sent on the better path in the other world as a result of an orderly life beforehand – a life governed by virtues of habit without the guidance of philosophy. Such people were said to be 'not in the minority' to be caught making reckless choices.

[293] Now Proclus uses *Phdr.* 248a concerning the best human souls (cf. 246b7 and *Tim.* 41a3 for the verb περιπολέω).

[294] Now alluding to *Phdr.* 250c–251c, a passage explaining homoerotic attraction to beautiful youths. It may be a point against Proclus that the tyrannical life comes ninth and last after the visions of the world above at *Phdr.* 248e3.

Socrates' constitution

Furthermore, concerning the nature and nurture of Hermogenes, given that many testify that it is sufficient in all these areas, one has to believe it. (20a7–b1)

Hermogenes is a Syracusan general with a desire to live lawfully. Hence he participates in a way in both politics and philosophy. He too has a role in the analogy, having a resemblance to the *third* creation. Generalship is appropriate to the one who orders the last and most disorderly parts of the cosmic composition; **that many testify** belongs to one who advances the creation to total multiplicity and the ultimate partition. So that is how we rank him in our scheme, so that the men may stand in analogy with the subject matter too.

Others,[295] however, rank Critias lower than Hermocrates. Still, if the missing person is fit neither to speak nor to listen, then of those present the one who listens but does not make a speech himself ought also to come second to the one who speaks as well, who, in so doing, imitates people like Socrates and Timaeus. Next one should also consider this point, that Socrates has given Critias pride of place in his speech by praising him after Timaeus.

There are some also[296] who distribute the following kind of ranking to these characters, and who rank Timaeus with the paradigmatic cause, Socrates with the productive, Critias with the formal, and Hermocrates with the material. It is for this reason that he is fit to listen but not to speak, because matter too receives its instructions (*logoi*) from elsewhere, but is unable to generate any. Such a distribution of rank would make considerable sense, quite apart from its not conflicting with our previous approach.

---

[295] Who are these others? The fact that the prologue is being extensively discussed, but that the characters and their order (as implied by the previous sentence) have no symbolic significance, suggests Porphyry, who sought for ethical lessons in the prologue. This rank would naturally be accompanied by a lower view of Critias than the one that Proclus is inclined to take at 70.21–71.15, and concentration on moral issues would lead to such a view. Note how Proclus has already felt the need to defend the tyrannical element in Critias' character at 70.25–30.

[296] Clearly this is a position that Proclus feels an affinity with, but one wonders how the omission of the final cause has occurred. This would normally be placed at a very high level among the causes, and indeed occurs first at 17.18–27 where it is correlated with the monad, followed by paradigmatic (and dyad), and creative (and triad). If it is indeed viewed as the highest of the causes then it would naturally be correlated with a character even higher than Timaeus, and only Iamblichus, with his view that the missing person is too elevated for physical inquiry (19.9–29), has somebody with whom to associate that final cause.

On the *Timaeus* of Plato: Book 1

Transition to the story of Atlantis

This was what I had in mind yesterday also when you requested me to run through the discussion on the constitution *up to* and most ready of all to receive it. (20b1-c3)

20 The summary of the constitution, as Socrates now says, appears to have taken place with a view to the narration of the wartime struggles of the city with the correct constitution. In fact both [parts] are directed towards the single creation of the cosmos, both the brief overview of the constitution and the story of Atlantis. For prior to the universal creation

25 and the whole scheme of cosmic ordering, it is better to begin one's study, as was said before,[297] with its parts and its images. So it is reasonable that Socrates should resume the constitution in rough outlines, and, after first imitating the universe through this, take his own place

30 in [the realm of] being as it were,[298] and stimulate others too to [take

73 up] the argument, people who can laud the power of such a city and imitate those who arrange the All according to the intermediate type of creative activity and who make the rivalries within it and its multi-

5 faceted movements cohere. So as Homer's Zeus, sitting upon the top fold of Olympus,[299] and remaining in his own accustomed oneness,[300] sends the gods in charge of cosmic rivalry to the Greek war, so too does Socrates, taking up a position of purity in the intelligible kind of

10 constitution, prepare those that follow him, who are able to laud the movement and power of this constitution – summoning the science of Timaeus to a general study of the universe, and preparing the others for a general and concise summation of the parts. Just as he gave a gen-

15 eral description of the whole constitution, so he wants its power to be hymned by the others; but, since all these accounts bear an image of the creative tasks and the whole encounter is [an image] of cosmic creation, it is quite reasonable that Socrates said that he had arranged himself in

20 order and was ready to receive the accounts, having equipped himself for the discourse with the appropriate form of excellence, i.e. *orderliness* (*kosmiotês*).

And indeed, as Timaeus here said, Socrates, *up to* we were examining this very matter on our journey. (20c4–8)

---

[297] 30.2–18; Festugière announces that this is Iamblichus' doctrine, and indeed this had been the only alternative offered to the ethically-based view of Porphyry (29.31–30.2).

[298] Festugière aptly compares 73.8 below for the idea that Socrates' interest is not situated firmly in the *intelligible* constitution.

[299] An allusion to *Il*. 20.22.

[300] Festugière compares *Tim*. 42e: 'remaining in his own accustomed character'.

166

Socrates' constitution

Hermocrates had to say something too, and not be there in silence like the characters in comedy who stand idly by. Hence he too has been depicted as saying something to Socrates. That was a compositional matter, whereas there is another point that pertains to the subject itself. That the final powers of creation follow the one father of the universe, and on account of their likeness to him consent to the one providential plan for the cosmos, <you could deduce>[301] from what is now being said, as if from images. For Hermocrates, taking the lead from Timaeus,[302] says that they are in no way lacking in either the enthusiasm or power for the accounts sought by Socrates; for these two things are particularly inclined to hinder us in our cooperative activities, our own lack of interest and any external obstacle that may pertain. So he eliminated both of these in saying that they neither lacked enthusiasm nor had any excuse to prevent them from fulfilling the requirement of Socrates. So it was reasonable that he (Hermocrates) called upon Critias too for the narration of the ancient works of the city of Athens, deeds in which the request of Socrates finds its fulfilment (much as Socrates called upon Timaeus), and that he makes himself an associate in Critias' account. For he says that on the previous day they[303] had examined the question along with him, just as in the universe the third demiurge participates in the creation of the second. For the whole of generation requires also return contributions from the entire[304] subterranean world.

[If this is how that is, it seems appropriate that the Atlantis story has occupied third place in the telling. They say that the dyad and the triad are numbers that belong to the intermediate creation, the former through its power and the latter through its creative providence that is perfective of encosmic things. Hence, whether you assign to it the second or third telling, you are able to work back from either of these numbers to the notion of the median position.][305]

---

[301] These three words are a translation of Diehl's supplement to the manuscript text.

[302] Timaeus demonstrated enthusiasm and affirmed their ability to deliver at 17b.

[303] Or perhaps 'he' (αὐτός for αὐτούς); that would suit the analogy with third and second demiurges better, but fit less well with the original text.

[304] Reading παντός for the MS πάντως; the position of the adverb here, within the noun-phrase and well separated from the verb, would be hard to explain, but the emendation produces a parallel between universal generation and universal underworld.

[305] This is at best an afterthought, fitting only loosely into the structure, and with no special application to the lemma. Unless there is some way of relating it to wider themes of Proclus, it is tempting to regard it as a gloss. The identity of the subject of 'they say' is far from clear. It is obscure how the remarks are to be reconciled with those expressed earlier (4.7–26 above), where it is the relation between the summary of the constitution and the preview of Atlantis that interests Proclus; these remarks seem rather to pertain to the order of the dialogues *Republic–Timaeus–Critias*, whose main speakers do not in any sense correspond to the three creators and their creations.

On the *Timaeus* of Plato: Book 1

So this man related to us a story from ancient oral tradition. Tell it again now, Critias, for him, so that he may test whether it suits his request or not. – This should be done if our third participant, Timaeus, also agrees. – Indeed I agree. (20d1–6)

75

Treating these words too as images, you could find in them a wonderful indication of matters divine. As among them the second rank call forward the generative powers of the first and direct them to the providential care of things they manage, so among the persons here Hermocrates calls Critias forward to speak and to fulfil the request of Socrates.[306] Further, as among them the things that are caused revert to clinging closely to their causes, so among these persons Hermocrates strives [to attach himself] to Critias, while Critias looks toward the request of Socrates. Again, as among them the creative causes depend upon the one father and steer everything according to his will, in the same way here too they all seek refuge in Timaeus, and in Timaeus' nod, assent, or will, so that, by making that the root they start from, they may handle the argument as intended by him. That is how what is going to be said would make a contribution to the overall depiction of the cosmos. Moreover the phrase **from ancient oral tradition** signifies temporal age if the story is of a historical kind, while if it is an allegorical indication of things that go on taking place in the cosmos it could be hinting at the principles that have existed within souls from eternity. If again it is offering an image of the divine causes, it shows that these divine causes, themselves receiving fullness from the most senior gods above, give a share of their own providential care to their subordinates too.

Atlantis (75.26–191.11)

The early debate over the genre of the story of Atlantis

Hear then, Socrates, an account that is very unusual, yet certainly true in all respects, as Solon, the wisest of the Seven, once used to claim. (20d)

76

Some say that all this tale about the Atlantines is straightforward narrative, like the first of Plato's interpreters, Crantor.[307] He also says that

---

[306] Reading πληροῦν with Festugière's note.

[307] An extremely important testimony, though its source is not clear. While it is unlikely that much information on Crantor had survived until Proclus' day, Plutarch may indeed have had access to an exegetical text of Crantor's when writing his *On the Procreation of the Soul in the Timaeus*. However, Plutarch does not give us reason to believe that there is a substantial difference between the form of exegesis coming from Crantor and the form that had already come from Xenocrates. I deal with Crantor's contribution at Tarrant (2000), 53–6, and in the introduction to the Atlantis section, but see also Cameron (1983), Clay (1999).

168

Atlantis

[Plato] was mocked by his contemporaries for not having discovered his constitution himself, but having translated Egyptian originals.[308] He took so little notice of what the mockers said that he actually attributed to the Egyptians this narrative about the Athenians and Atlantines, saying that the Athenians had at one time lived under that constitution. He says[309] that the prophets of the Egyptians also give evidence, saying that these things are inscribed on pillars that still survive.

Others say that it is a myth and an invention, something that never actually happened but gives an indication of things which have either always been so, or always come to be, in the cosmos. These people pay no attention to Plato when he exclaims that the account **is very unusual, yet certainly true in all respects**. For what is **true in all respects** is not true in one way and untrue in another, nor false on the surface and true in its hidden meaning. No such thing could be **true in all respects**.

Some do not rule it out that this could have happened in this way, but think that it is now adopted as [a series of] images of pre-existing rivalry in the universe. For [they say that] 'War is the father of all' as Heraclitus puts it (B53 DK). Of these[310] some look upwards for the solution to the fixed stars and planets, supposing the Athenians to be analogous to the fixed stars and the Atlantines to the planets, with the conflict arising from the counter-revolution, and the one side winning because of the single turning-motion of the cosmos. The goodly Amelius is certainly of this opinion putting up such a fight to support its being so, because of the island of Atlantis being clearly divided into seven circles in the *Critias*,[311] that I know of nobody else [who fought as much] in support of their personal doctrines.

---

[308] By 'translated' I do not necessarily mean 'rewrote in a different language', but little more than 'transferred to a different culture'. Nor does the Greek make it clear that the Egyptian ideas had ever been committed to writing.

[309] This appears again to be what Crantor says, because of the indicative mood of the verb. Cameron (1983) takes it rather as what *Plato* says, but the earlier parenthetic 'he says' at 76.1 counts against this.

[310] A problematic reference most naturally taken to refer to the last group mentioned, but in fact embracing all non-literal interpreters. See Introduction, pp. 60–84, on the Atlantis story.

[311] How Amelius manages to argue this is not obvious, and Festugière refers to 113e where the island is divided into *ten* parts, a figure that is repeated elsewhere, making it unlikely that Amelius' interpretation could be explained by a different reading. What has a greater claim to stand for the heaven is the arrangement of land and canals around the central royal island of the kingdom, involving three circuits of water and two of land, of varying widths (115d–16a). Five circuits could equally be interpreted as representative of the heaven, since the motions of the Sun, Mercury and Venus were interlinked (cf. *Tim.* 38d). If one then counts the inner island and the land beyond the circuits, one does get *seven areas*, but surely not seven areas that could be directly linked

169

On the Timaeus of Plato: Book 1

77 Others interpret it as a conflict of *daemons*, with some being better and others worse, the one side superior in numbers, the other in power, with the one being victorious and the other vanquished, as Origenes supposed.[312] Others interpret it as a dispute between the finer souls – the foster-children of Athena – and others who work at generation and

5 who belong to the god presiding over generation.[313] Others combine (or so they believe)[314] the views of Origenes and of Numenius and say that it is a conflict between souls and *daemons*, with the *daemons* being a down-dragging force and the souls trying to come upwards. Their view is that

10 there are three kinds of *daemons*, a divine type of *daemon*, a type now in that condition (*kata schesin*) which is made up of individual souls who have received a daemonic lot, and the other corrupt kind – the soul polluters. So *daemons* of the final type strike up this war with souls on their descent

15 into generation. And they claim that, just as the ancient theologians refer this to Osiris and Typhon or to Dionysus and the Titans, Plato attributes it to Athenians and Atlantines out of reverence. For he hands down the tradition that, before they come into three-dimensional bodies, there is

20 rivalry between souls and the enmattered *daemons* that he assigned[315] to the west;[316] for the west, as the Egyptians say, is the region of harmful souls.[317] The philosopher Porphyry is of this view,[318] and one would be surprised if he is saying anything different from the view authorized by Numenius.

The Iamblichan view of Atlantis

Well, these people at any rate were in my view given a really splen-

25 did caning by Iamblichus.[319] Both he and my own teacher preferred to

---

with the seven planets. The probability is that Proclus has misinterpreted an account of Amelius that he read in Porphyry or a similar source.

[312] Origenes fr. 12 in Weber (1962).

[313] Clearly the latter are the Atlantines, who are the descendents of Poseidon, who is in this context the god of generation.

[314] Proclus thinks they are in fact indistinguishable from Numenius; see below, 77.22–4.

[315] It seems that προσοικειόω may here be an astrological term for influences that reside in the same heavenly parts; see LSJ II 3.

[316] As Festugière points out, this is Atlantis' location.

[317] Festugière's note draws attention to Lact. *Div. Inst.* 2.9.5–6 and Porph. *Antr. Nymph.* 29. For Porphyry's attention to the moon in his interpretation see the Introduction, pp. 76–7, and table on p. 78.

[318] Porphyry *in Tim.* fr. X. Bearing in mind that Porphyry thinks the position combines the best of Origenes and Numenius it is clear that Proclus would have been able to deduce their positions from reading Porphyry alone.

[319] Iamblichus *in Tim.* fr. 7. For commentary see Dillon (1973), 268–70, who assumes that the wording is largely post-Iamblichan.

Atlantis

explain this conflict not [at the expense of] setting aside of the surface meaning, but on the contrary, in the conviction that these things have happened *in every sense*. However, as we are accustomed to refer what precedes the primary discussions to the same target as the discussions, so we prefer to take this rivalry also from the human realm and to distribute it, in this same way and according to a similar pattern, across the whole cosmos and particularly among generated things, so giving it widespread meaning to all things, and studying how they partake of this rivalry in accordance with their variety of powers. I mean that since everything is from the One and the Dyad that comes after the One, and they are somehow brought into unity with each other and have acquired opposing natures, just as there is also an opposition among the Kinds of being,[320] of Same against Other and of Motion and against Rest, and everything in the cosmos participates in these Kinds, it would make sense to study the rivalry that runs through everything.

Moreover, assuming that we have observed the analogue of the constitution in the entire cosmos, we must surely also take note of this 'war' that is embedded in the whole of nature. For the constitution is analogous to being and the substances, while the war is analogous to their powers and their unvarying motions. And one should say that the former, the constitution that makes all things in common, is assimilated to the total unification, while the latter is assimilated to the ascendancy of strife.[321] So if you bisect the whole into incorporeal and corporeal, and then the incorporeal into the more intellective and the more enmattered parts, and the corporeal into heaven and generation, and the heaven into the opposing revolutions but generation into the contrasting properties – or however you understand this contrasting life either among gods or among *daemons* or among souls or among bodies – you would in every case be able to bring analogies that begin with humans to bear upon things.

For the divine Homer develops oppositions,[322] setting Apollo against Poseidon, Ares against Athena, the River against Hephaestus, Hermes against Leto, and Hera against Artemis.[323] It is necessary, you see, to

---

[320] See Dillon (1973), 270, for the meaning the phrase will have for Iamblichus and the noetic nature of the Kinds, themselves of course relating to *Sophist* 254d.

[321] Festugière suspects the influence here of Empedocles' cosmic cycle, hence I have chosen to translate δυναστεία by a term suggesting temporary domination. However, its derivation from δύναμις must here be of significance.

[322] *Il.* 20.67–74; the River is Xanthus, the divine name for Scamander at Troy. See also *Crat.* 391e–392a.

[323] The first three pairs put the pro-Trojan god first, but the remaining two put the pro-Greek god first. Zeus and Aphrodite are not considered here, though the latter will be mentioned at 79.17.

On the *Timaeus* of Plato: Book 1

view generation in incorporeals, bodies and combinations of the two, and to posit Poseidon and Apollo as demiurges of all of becoming, the former universally and the latter partially; to make Hera and Artemis as the leaders of animal birth, the former of rational life and the latter of physical life; to make Athena and Ares responsible for the rivalry that runs through both, through being and through life, her for the [rivalry] determined by intellect, him for the more material and more impassioned kind, and to make Hermes and Leto the chiefs of the double perfection of the soul, the former of the one [achieved] through cognitive powers and the offering[324] of reasoned arguments, the other through the smooth and willing and assenting elevation of the vital forces; to make Hephaestus and Xanthus the chiefs of all bodily composition and of the properties within it, the former of the more active properties, and the latter of the more passive and more material so to speak.[325]

As for Aphrodite he leaves her all by herself so that she may be the light behind all unification and harmony, fighting as an ally of the weaker powers, because in the things of this world the one is weaker than plurality. For all rivalry is properly studied along with the one, for it (the one) is either prior to it, or naturally implanted in it, or somehow supervenient upon it.[326] It is this that Plato like the theologians[327] has noticed when before the single cosmology he rightly hands down the multiple one, and before the whole the parts. And discovering all this in images before their paradigms, he studies in the human realm this rivalry that exists also in a corresponding form within the universe, requiring no battles with Titans or Giants.[328] How [in that case] was he to say anything acceptable to the Socrates who had yesterday criticized the poets for inventing these stories? Rather, he took his subject matter from history to avoid setting in the divine realm his account of mutual hostilities. Rather, by introducing events in the human realm, through the cautious use of analogy he tries to bring it to bear upon the gods as well. Such wars are traditionally

---

[324] While it is tempting read προσβολῆς for προβολῆς (this would give the sense of 'application'), one must remember the special connection of Hermes with the delivery of speeches.

[325] There seems to be an acceptance of the Stoic idea that body is either active or passive, and the association of fire with the former.

[326] One wonders here about a possible relationship, perhaps indirect, with the hypotheses (specifically two, four, and five) of the *Parmenides*, in which the one is now the source of subsequent opposition, or such that the opposition participates in it, or arises afterwards since privation of unity removes all differentiation that could establish a genuine plurality (*Parm.* 142d–143a, 157c, 159d–160b).

[327] Festugière assumes simply that Proclus refers to Homer here.

[328] These conflicts from Hesiod are themselves explained by the Neoplatonist allegorists in terms of the natural oppositions within the universe, as we see in what follows.

172

Atlantis

placed by the inspired poets too before the single order, but that is their proper manner, whereas this is Plato's. His, with its political context, is more prudent, while theirs, with its priestly context, is more inspired.[329] So much for the account as a whole. 5

Details of the text at 20d7–e1

Of the diction under examination the word **hear** has a proem-like character, and is being used in the circumstances where one wishes to appeal for attention on the part of the reader. It is the equivalent of saying 'take note of things worth hearing'.[330] The word **unusual** indicates what's illogical, as when it's said in the *Gorgias* (473a1) 'Certainly unusual, Socrates'; or what's unexpected as in the *Crito* (44b3) when he uses the expression 'What an unusual dream, Socrates!'; or what's wondrous,[331] as when he says in the *Theaetetus* (142b9-c1) 'Actually it's nothing unusual, but it would be a great deal more wondrous if he were not like this.' [The term] has been adopted here as indicating 'worthy of wonder'. He shows this straight away while continuing with the same subject, saying that the ancient deeds of this city were 'great and wondrous'.[332] The term **account** makes plain the truth of what is about to be said, for that was how myth was said to differ from an account in the *Gorgias*.[333] That Solon should have been called **the wisest of the** 10 15 20

---

[329] Festugière, following Trouillard, draws attention to material on Homeric myth in *in Remp.* I. 69–86; one might add 159–63, and material in post-Proclan commentaries. *In Crat.* 70 treats 'Homer and the other poets' as similarly inspired (ἔνθεος), a lesson that Proclus has derived from *Crat.* 391d and a good deal of the next fifteen or so pages until our version of his commentary fails. It appears from *in Parm.* 646.21–34 that Proclus considers the link between such inspiration and mythical language to be important. This creates difficulties, since *Plat. Theol.* I. 4 links symbolic rather than inspirational communication with myth, but Gersh in Steel and Segonds (2000), 18, interestingly observes that '(a) when Proclus considers Plato alone as theologian, he ranks the entheastic mode of exposition above the symbolic; and (b) when he considers Plato and Homer together as theologians, he allows the entheastic and symbolic modes of exposition to coincide.'

[330] Compare the comment of Olymp. *in Gorg.* 47.1 on the opening of the *Gorgias'* myth.

[331] Proclus here (as opposed to 80.17–20 below) uses θαυμαστός (wondrous) in the sense of 'surprising' rather than 'admirable', but Plato himself uses this sense in the passage cited as well as at *Tht.* 154b6 and probably 151a3. He may be trying to tell us something about the experience of wonder here, for that is the beginning of philosophy (155d), but he is also prone to using non-'admirable' senses of this word elsewhere.

[332] Notice how Proclus now assumes that Plato uses θαυμαστός in the sense of 'admirable'.

[333] 523a1–3, where the story's alleged truth is precisely what justifies the term *logos* rather than *mythos*. Olympiodorus does not make anything of the role of truth at *Gorg.* 523a1–3, which he takes to be a symbolic truth rather than a literal one. The best to be said for the literal meaning in his eyes is that it is harmless (Olymp. *In Gorg.* 46.6–47.1).

173

On the *Timaeus* of Plato: Book 1

Seven was entirely reasonable, given that it was said (i) by a relative,[334]
(ii) to another Athenian, (iii) at the Panathenaea, and (iv) to demonstrate
that what will be said is aiming at complete wisdom. And one shouldn't be
surprised that he is described as **wisest** of them all, nor be over-desirous
for a way that he could be being called wisest of the *other* men, but *one* of
the sages, all of whom were wisest.[335] What would be strange even in one
of those ranked with him being called 'wisest man'? Anyway as testimony
to his wisdom there is (i) his lawgiving, (ii) his feigned madness is in
defence of Salamis, (iii) his armed[336] opposition to Pisistratus the tyrant,
when he declared himself cleverer than those who did not see through
him and braver than those who understood, (iv) his conversation with
Croesus, and (v) his response to the man who said he'd instituted the
finest laws: for he said that he hadn't made the finest, but those that were
possible – though he knew better ones.[337] Furthermore (vi) the story
about the tripod trawled up by some youths, even though not everybody
records it, relates that, when the god proclaimed that it should be given
to the wisest, it was first given to Thales, but he sent it to another of the
Seven, he to another, and finally it came to Solon, when everybody else

---

[334] Proclus adheres to the view, probably false, that Solon was the brother of Dropides (81.28–82.1), and so related to both Critias and Plato.

[335] This piece of philological ingenuity would have the phrase mean rather 'he from the Seven, wisest Solon'. The subject matter, and the excessive puzzling over such details, is suggestive of Longinus.

[336] This is clearly an encounter firstly *through public speaking* and then *through poetry* as can be seen at Plut. *Solon* 30, where, in addition to some words delivered on leaving the Assembly, his poetry (fr. 11 West) is held to criticize the stupidity of those who trusted Pisistratus, and the cowardice of those who didn't. Straightforward 'armed' opposition to Pisistratus would have been something other than an indication of wisdom at the age of seventy-five or eighty! One might suspect therefore that ἔνοπλος should be emended to ἐνόπλιος, a regular term for martial poetic rhythm (the *enoplion* is in fact encountered in the last three and a half feet of lines 1, 3, 5, and 7 of fr. 11). However, Plutarch is not Proclus' immediate source here, and the story told at D.L. 1.49 does have Solon donning his arms to denounce Pisistratus publicly for *aiming* at tyranny. Here too (D.L. 1.52) fr. 11 is seen as criticism of the people *after* the tyranny is in place.

[337] While Plutarch's lives are often a significant source for Greek biographical materials in Neoplatonist writings (see particularly Olymp. *in Gorg.* and the index loc. of Jackson-Lycos-Tarrant 1998), Diehl and Festugière give an exaggerated picture of Proclus' likely dependence here. The story behind (ii) is told at Plut. *Solon* 8 (Solon cannot openly revive the Athenian claim to Salamis because it was banned by law, so feigns madness and recites the poem of which fr. 1 is the beginning), and the very famous material behind (iv) is found at 27. Variant stories are told at 30 (iii), of Solon's opposition to the rising Pisistratus, and (v) has a weak parallel at 15. However, story (vi) is not told about Solon himself in Plutarch, whereas (ii) is also found at D.L. 1.48, (iii) at 1.49, and (iv) at 1.50. Clearly there would have been a range of possible sources for Proclus to draw on for very similar information.

Atlantis

had deferred to him, but he returned it to the god from himself saying that it was he who was really wisest.[338] It is also to Solon's credit (vii) that the lunar month is not of thirty days, and hence he was the first to refer to the 'Old and New',[339] and the backward count of the days [of the month] from the twentieth on is also attributed to him. Some people claim (viii) that he also declared that intellect is in charge of the universe before Anaxagoras did so. From these considerations it is obvious that he participated in some kind of wisdom.

Family trees and their significance

He was close to us and a special friend of Dropides my great-grandfather, as he mentions at several points in his poetry. He [Dropides] said to Critias my grandfather, as the old man related to us in turn, that there had been great and admirable deeds of our city in ancient times, which had vanished through the passage of time and mortal catastrophes. (20e1–6)

The history that deals with the family of Solon and Plato's kinship with him goes like this.[340] The children of Exekestides were Solon and Dropides, and Dropides' son was Critias, whom Solon mentions in his poetry, saying:

> Tell Critias with the golden hair to listen to his father;
> For he will not be obeying a leader with an errant mind.

From Critias there came Callaeschrus and Glaucon, and then from Callaeschrus came this Critias. The 'Critias' in the *Charmides* identifies Glaucon, the father of Charmides, calling him his uncle.[341] From Glaucon came Charmides and Perictione, and so from Perictione came

---

[338] The story has a parallel at Plut. *Solon* 4, but in Plutarch's alternative versions it is Thales or Bias who finally receives the tripod a second time and so dedicates it to Apollo of Ismenus or of Delphi.

[339] Besides Plut. *Solon* 25, Proclus would have known this from Ar. *Clouds* 1134, 1190. Material about the count-down to days after the twentieth is closely connected with his other reforms of the lunar month in the account of Plutarch.

[340] The identity of the Critias who speaks in the *Timaeus* and *Critias* is one point of controversy in what follows. Some favour identifying him with the tyrant's *grandfather*. If this latter path is rejected, on the grounds that Plato's audience would certainly have seen the tyrant here in the absence of indications to the contrary, then Plato appears to have omitted two generations. For literature see Morgan (1998), 101 n.3. Davies (1971), 322–33 includes useful discussion, but the main point on which he differs from Proclus is in refusing to infer from *Tim.* 20e1–2 that Dropides and Solon were brothers; in fact Plato's expression seems to exclude this.

[341] The relevant passage is 154a8–b2.

On the *Timaeus* of Plato: Book 1

Plato. So Glaucon was the uncle of Critias, Charmides was his cousin and the uncle of Plato, while Solon was the brother of the great-grandfather of Critias.[342] The real position was like this. The divine Iamblichus, however, hands down rather a different account of the family history. He makes Glaucon an immediate son of Dropides.[343] Others say that Critias and Glaucon were sons of Callaeschrus, as does Theon the Platonist.[344] And yet 'Critias' says in the *Charmides* that Charmides is the son of 'Glaucon our uncle', using these exact terms, 'and my cousin'. So Glaucon was neither the son of Dropides, nor the younger brother of Critias. But enough of this. The truth of these matters is of no significance to the man whose concern is with realities.[345]

If you proceed to realities, you could grasp from this as if from images that the whole mapping of the cosmos and the columns of coordinate pairs within it[346] are not only joined to contiguous demiurgic causes but also are related to other more intellective and more senior causes, and that the causal factors behind this motion [in our world] are contiguous and unified and stemming from one point.[347] And [you could also learn] that the higher ones are senior in their intellective activity, and that the second [generation] take over the creation of the first, and while differing from them still have a family connection with them. In addition

[342] Here is a family tree according to Proclus:

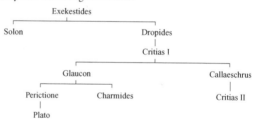

[343] Iamblichus *in Tim.* fr. 8 Dillon. The error is a puzzle to Dillon (1973, 270–1), but such matters may be complicated by the duplication of names that tends to occur every two generations.

[344] Presumably Theon of Smyrna, whose introduction to the reading of Plato was used later in the Arab world (al-Nadîm, *Fihrist*, trans. Dodge p. 614). On him see Dillon (1977), 397–9. Proclus utilized him at *in Remp.* II. 218–19.

[345] After Proclus has shown sufficient concern to enter the debate over Critias' family history, demonstrating his ability to compete on matters of prosopography, it comes as a shock to read such a strong disclaimer, but cf. 'Socrates' at *Prt.* 347b–348a. One wonders whether the 'errors' of Theon and Iamblichus were due to information unavailable to us, to a misunderstanding of what they had said, or to the lack of any desire to get the historical truth correct.

[346] The term is συστοιχία. We have here the Neoplatonic successor of the Pythagorean columns of opposites; cf. 4.18 above, a preview of the current interpretation of the Atlantis story. See further 84.1, 97.1, and regularly from 130 to 190.

[347] Here perhaps we see why it is thought that Solon and Dropides were brothers.

Atlantis

to this [you could also learn] that a double forgetting arises in souls   30
of things universal and of their study of universal things that are mag-   **83**
nificent and wondrous, either through their being far removed in time
from such a life or through their falling too steeply into generation –
this being the death of the real human being.[348] But the souls with recent
experience[349] and a memory of things there easily remember the truth   5
because they do not become immersed in matter.[350] This is how one
should deal with this.

One should not be surprised that he called Solon simply by the term
close. For it was not only one's acquaintances but also one's relatives that
they called 'close'.[351] By the addition of **and a special friend** he shows   10
that the family relationship among the ancestors of Plato was no light
matter, but a sameness or similarity of life. He called the elder Critias
an **old man** to indicate his good sense, his intellect, and his aptitude for
grey-haired lessons.[352]

The appropriateness of the Atlantis story

There was one single greatest thing of all, which it would now be   15
appropriate for us to tell you of, and so repay you while also fairly and
truly, in a kind of hymn, singing the praises of the goddess at her
gathering. (20e6–21a3)

Longinus[353] raises the difficulty of what the presentation of this narrative
means for Plato. For it hasn't been composed for the relaxation of the   20
audience nor because he requires them to remember it. He solved this,
as he thought, with the observation that he had taken it up prior to the
physical theory to charm the listener on and to make the presentation

---

[348] See Festugière's note, and consider also *Gorg.* 492e, with its use of Euripides to suggest
that real life is other than this embodied life. If I understand Proclus correctly, it is
not embodiment as such that Proclus sees as the destruction of what is really human,
but rather the sudden embodiment that results in the obliteration of our connection
through memory with the higher world.

[349] The term νεοτελής suggests the recent initiation in some rite, as at *Phdr.* 250e1 (cf.
ἀρτιτελής 251a2). Festugière cites many parallel Proclan passages, but overlooks their
Platonic original.

[350] Compare *Phdr.* 250e–251a, where the notion of immersion in matter is absent; this
might rather be sought from 248c5–8 (which is also related to the theme of forgetfulness) with *Phd.* 81c–d and similar passages.

[351] Proclus is forced to comment because of linguistic change. In classical times the adjec
tive οἰκεῖος, originally 'of one's household' and hence 'one's own', could be used as a
noun, meaning either a close acquaintance or a relative. It is ironic that Plato had only
meant that Solon was a close friend!

[352] As Festugière points out, the phrase is reminiscent of *Tim.* 22b8, and refers there to
ancient history.

[353] Longinus fr. 32; Origenes fr. 13.

177

On the *Timaeus* of Plato: Book 1

25 an early antidote to the dryness of its style. Origenes claimed that the narrative had been invented, and to this extent he agreed with Numenius' party, but not that it had been invented in the interests of artificial pleasure, like Longinus.[354] He didn't add the reason for the invention.

30 As for us, we have repeatedly said that it is helping to complete the entire study of nature, and moreover we claim in the case of these words that he is labelling as the greatest and most wondrous of deeds the single common principle of the twin columns of opposites in the cos-

84 mos, and the single conflict that extends through the universe, on the grounds that it holds in an unbreakable unity the entire creation that is founded upon opposites, upon Limiters and Unlimiteds as Philolaus

5 (fr. B1 DK) says – and as he says himself in the *Philebus* (30c) when he says that there's much limit in the cosmos, much unlimited also, the two being opposites that combine to make up this All.[355]

Since everything that helps complete the creation is said to show

10 gratitude to the universal causes, it is with good reason that Critias too is saying that it's appropriate for him to repay the favour to Socrates, after he [Socrates] has set in motion the second and third powers.[356] This much you can grasp straight away.

But what about the gathering in honour of Athena? Would you not say that this too involves an indication of works of creation? For this

15 goddess holds together the whole cosmic organization and holds intelligent lives within herself which she uses to weave together the whole, and unificatory powers which she uses to manage all the cosmic oppositions. The gathering in honour of Athena indicates the gift from the goddess that pervades all things and fills all things with itself, and the

20 union that traverses all complexity. For it is particularly at such gatherings[357] that we welcome a shared life in concord. And if we have got this right, it is possible to transport ourselves from this too to the varied and single life of the cosmos and to observe the difference between

25 the *Parmenides* and this dialogue. For both have their setting at the Panathenaea, the former at the greater [Panathenaea] and the latter at

---

354 Festugière draws attention to the earlier passage, at 60.1–4 above, where Origenes (fr. 9) resists Longinus' belief (fr. 28) that Plato's aesthetic concerns aim at artificially contrived pleasure, and also to the comparable passage at 86.19–30 below. By talking of artificial pleasure Origenes hints that such pleasure is in a sense unnatural, and so to be avoided even in Epicurean philosophy.

355 This is paraphrase, and clearly shows Proclus' tendency to quote from memory, as well as being designed to exaggerate the degree to which Plato's principles are parallel ingredients in reality.

356 Socrates, Critias, and Hermocrates correspond to the first, second, and third members of the demiurgic triad (9.17–24).

357 The *panegyris* is technically a gathering, usually religious, of the whole people.

Atlantis

the Lesser, for the Lesser Panathenaea was celebrated at about the same time as the Bendidea.[358] Reasonably so, for while the creation associated with Athena is twofold, universal and particular, hypercosmic and cosmic, intelligible and sensible, the former [dialogue] partners her transcendent creations, unveiling the intelligible series of the gods, while the latter deals with her lower ones, communicating the powers of the gods in the cosmic area. It is likely that the festival of the Bendidea signifies the conflict that comes upon the whole from the barbarian surge outside,[359] that is brought under control by the gods presiding over the festival. Hence word is handed down that it was being held in the Piraeus, that being most akin to the remotest and closest parts of the universe to matter. But the Panathenaea signifies the orderliness that comes down into the cosmos from intellect and the unblending separation of the opposing cosmic powers; for this goddess is 'a lover of wisdom and of war' (24d1). So this is being dedicated to the goddess as a different kind of *peplos*,[360] in which the foster-children of Athena are victorious, just as that *peplos* at the Panathenaea has the Giants being vanquished by the Olympians. It is a fair and true hymn (cf. 21a2–3) being offered up to the god: fair because it is fair that all that proceeds should revert to its own origin, and true because the hymn has been drawn from the real world via actual happenings. Bearing in mind that some hymns praise the substance of the gods, some their providential care, and some their works, this last kind being the final type of laudation – reverent accounts of their substance are the most outstanding type of all, as Socrates tells us in the *Symposium*[361] – it was reasonable that he added **a kind of** hymn, because it is from the *works* of the Athenians that he is going to praise the goddess. The commentators affirm that the Panathenaea followed the Bendidea, and Aristocles of Rhodes relates that the Bendidea at the Piraeus are conducted on the twentieth of Thargelion, followed by the festival of Athena.[362]

---

[358] On the erroneous chronology (which might be anticipated from the vagueness of the reporting) see 26.10–20, and Festugière's notes on both passages.

[359] Bendis being a Thracian goddess first celebrated in Athens at the beginning of the *Republic*, while the 'surge' is meant to recall the floods that will finally destroy Atlantis (25c7).

[360] The new robe that was woven for the cult statue of Athena at each celebration of the Greater Panathenaea, and which contained martial representations, well known from the description at *Euthph.* 6c.

[361] In fact Agathon at 195a; to refer to 198d3 etc. with Festugière and Diehl seems to me to overlook the only clear statement of the principle that Proclus wants to espouse.

[362] Aristocles has appeared at 20.2 above in relation to the 'missing person', while Proclus has earlier given the date as the nineteenth of Thargelion (26.14). As this is an all-night festival there may be no conflict.

On the *Timaeus* of Plato: Book 1

Three lemmata in brief

86   **Well then, what deed was this that Critias was relating as unreported, but actually performed by this city of old?**   (21a4–6)

5   Socrates, inciting Critias to take up the story, demands the telling of this greatest of deeds, which Critias the elder heard from Solon, one not circulated at all but that still happened. Here this is the first point worth examining, that many things go unnoticed by the masses in the
10   universe too (this being how the elite differ from the rest, that they see things of this kind too and observe them happening), and next that the more perfect of causes delight in simplicity and proceed from composite things to principles, while debased things on the other hand descend from simples to composites. This is the way that Socrates here too has
15   hastened back up to Solon from below, while Critias on the contrary began with Solon and came down to his own memory (20d–e).

I shall set forth an ancient account, heard from a man not young. (21a7–8)

20   Longinus[363] points out here too that Plato worries about the freshness and variety of his diction, pronouncing the same things in different ways. The deed he called 'ancient', but the man he called 'not young', yet he is making the same point throughout and able to call everything by the
25   same term. But he was 'a philologist', as Plotinus says of him,[364] and 'not a philosopher'. Origenes would not agree that he was aiming at artificial pleasure and various embellishments,[365] but [said] that he was concerned about a spontaneous and unembellished plausibility and accuracy in his character-portrayal, and moreover that this kind of commu-
30   nication comes spontaneously, as becomes an educated man. He thinks
87   Aristoxenus the musical writer was right in saying that the dispositions of the philosophers extended to their voices, exhibiting an orderly quality in everything they say[366] – as, I presume, this heaven of ours also offers
5   clear images of the splendour of its intellections, images that move in time with their invisible circuits.

---

[363] Longinus fr. 33; Origenes fr. 14.
[364] Porph. *VPlot.* 14.19–20, the best-remembered feature of Longinus, and one repeatedly brought out in this commentary.
[365] See above on 83.27.
[366] Aristoxenus fr. 75 Wehrli; it seems to me that a polemical context is likely, obliquely criticizing the discordant remarks of those who would be regarded as philosophers. Origenes seems to be saying that the philosopher does *not* vary his voice (and hence his written style) from speaker to speaker, an idea associated in the *Republic* (396c–397c) with the principle that it is only the best that one should be imitating.

180

Atlantis

The great Iamblichus deems rather that we should refer the variety of terms to realities, and see how in nature too the opposites are blended into the one unity and how the one is varied, and how great an interchangeability the same principles demonstrate, existing in one way in the intellect of the universe, in another in soul, in another in nature, and finally coming to be in matter and in the realm of matter showing the great multiplicity of otherness that exists alongside similarity. It's this that's worthy of Plato's intellect, and not a preoccupation with diction.

Critias was then already nearly ninety years old as he claimed, and I was about ten. (21a8–b1)

There are these three characters who have preserved this story, whether history or myth: Solon, Critias the elder, and the present younger Critias, because the causes of the creation that render perfect the things under their control are themselves perfect.[367] Now Critias heard the story from Solon, one to one; two heard it from him, Critias and Amynander, and from this Critias three hear it; for via the dyad the monad proceeds to the providence that brings the universe to completion. And their ages, taken as numbers, have considerable relevance to reality, the decad exhibiting the reversion of all encosmic things to the one, and the number ninety a return to square one in the monad after procession.[368] Both numbers bear a symbol of the cosmos. So if you wished to put it like this, Solon is analogous to the cause of stability, Critias the elder to the one that leads the progression, and this Critias to the cause that turns back what has proceeded and joins it to its origins. And the first preserves the *logos* of the leading cause,[369] the second of the cause that touches without involvement[370] on the cosmic creation, and the third of the cause that already takes care of the universe and manages the war within it.

Athenian religious history

It happened to be Koureotis at the Apaturia *up to* many of us children sang. (21b1–7)

The Apaturia is a festival of Dionysus celebrating the single combat of Melanthus against the Boeotian Xanthus, and Melanthus' victory by

---

[367] I.e. they constitute a complete triad.

[368] For the significance of ninety, see II. 215.20.

[369] Here *logos* is the correspondence within the *analogy*.

[370] On ἀπολύτως see Festugière's note.

181

On the *Timaeus* of Plato: Book 1

deceit during the war between Athens and the Boeotians over Oenoe.[371] It was celebrated over three days. The first was called Anarrhysis because many sacrifices are made on it, and the sacrificial victims are called *anarrhymata* because they are sacrificed by drawing [their heads] back, and dragging upwards (*anô erhyomena*).[372] The second day was called Dorpia, as there were many feasts and banquets on it.[373] The third was Koureotis, because on this day they enrolled the boys (*kouroi*) in their phratries at the age of three or four. [374] On this day too the brightest boys of the phratry sang certain poems, and some won victories over the others – those who remembered more of them in fact, as they were giving rhapsodic performances of the works of the ancients.

There is a certain amount that one should be aware of about the phratry-members. There had been four tribes after Ion, ten after Cleisthenes, and twelve after this.[375] Each tribe was divided into three, and the third portion of the tribe was known as the trittys, and then *patria* (fatherhoods) and *phatria* (brotherhoods).[376] Those enrolled in the same tribe or phratry were called Brothers, as being of the same kin, and it is into these [lists of] Brothers that the enrolment of boys took place. And the day took its name Koureotis from this – from the enrolment of boys, as we've said. So much for history.

[371] The legend goes that the war concerned the border villages of Oenoe and Eleutherae, they resorted to single combat to settle it, Melanthus sent a man dressed in a black goatskin behind Xanthus, and he then complained about the latter's bringing an assistant. Thus distracting his opponent, he is able to kill him by trickery. See Festugière's note.

[372] The drawing back of the neck and slitting the throat while it is held on high is not an unusual procedure in sacrifices to the Olympians.

[373] *Dorpon* was an Homeric word for the evening meal. According to the scholia on Ar. *Ach.* 146, Dorpia is the first day and Anarrhysis the second, but, while this is the accepted view, it seems counter-intuitive that the main feasting should precede the sacrifices. Nevertheless nothing precludes the carrying out of sacrifices at the Dorpia also, for sacrifices did also take place at the Koureotis; see Zaidman and Pantel (1992), 66.

[374] The phratry (brotherhood) was a traditional religious and family unit, the kinship aspect being important as part of its function related to the cult of ancestors. Admission of boys to the phratry was thus admission to the extended family.

[375] The ten tribe system of Cleisthenes was clearly going to be a landmark in any history of the number of tribes. This system makes careful use of trittyes that are composed of demes from different areas. The phratry seems not to have been an essential unit of the Cleisthenian system, which was part of a political rather than a religious system. See Festugière's note.

[376] We seem to be dealing now with the pre-Cleisthenic division in which phratry and trittys may have meant the same thing (Arist. *Ath. Pol.* frs. 3–5 with Festugière's note). It is of course the pre-Cleisthenic state of affairs that is pertinent to the story. I find no good explanation of the addition of *patria*, which though used for such an entity (πάτρα LSJ II. 2) seems not to have been an Athenian form. Proclus may be including it for regions linked with etymological speculation.

Atlantis

The hidden lessons of the events at the Apaturia

The Festival of the Apaturia, then, for which the rationale is a victory of the Athenians, is consistent with the overall plan, according to which the Athenian victory parallels the triumph of all intelligibles over what is enmattered. The aspect of deceit is naturally associated with the encosmic forms, which leave the undivided and immaterial principles (*logoi*), and become apparent rather than really real. The enrolment of boys represents the enlisting of individual souls into their own allotted roles and their descent into a variety of births, and the festival element represents the everlasting orderliness in the cosmos. In for ever being filled with gods it celebrates an eternal festival.

The **competitions for recitation** are analogous to the challenges that souls confront as they weave their own lives together with the universe. This recitation resembles the interlinked and interwoven life of the universe, for <the latter> involves the imitation of the intellective forms, just as the former involves the imitation of heroic actions and characters along with the preservation of this connecting thread.[377] The phrase **many poems from many poets** reflects the many natures and many cosmic <principles>, and in sum the diversity of nature's imitations, while the **youthful** poems mirror the forms that are for ever in their prime – ever complete, fertile, and able to act on other things. So much for that.

It is not with regard to popular poetry-composition that mention has been made of Solon's poems, but it is because he blended philosophy with composition. For intellect is in charge of both encosmic works and the composition of the whole. Praise [of Solon] is attributed to another person, Amynander,[378] because the judging role is separate from that of creating and fathering, as we have learned from the *Phaedrus*.[379]

Through the entirety of what has been said, referring it to the All as if from images, the entire account makes a further point, that individual souls, individual natures, divided forms, and above all those which are ever youthful and vigorous, contribute something to the war that goes

---

[377] The translation of *mimêsis* as 'imitation' is not ideal (Halliwell 2002, 13), but to preserve the Greek in non-poetic contexts would sound strange. Narrative poetry's constructing a continuous narrative out of episodes seems crucial for the comparison here (though Festugière fails to see this in trying to divorce the 'preservation of the connecting thread' from poetry and attach it to the universe), and Proclus preserves the priority of plot over character that is found in the tragedy of Aristotle's *Poetics*, for Homer is of course 'the first of the tragic poets' (*Rep.* 607a3).

[378] He is just 'somebody' at 21b7, but is identified by a vocative at c4. Note that this material belongs more properly to the next lemma (21b7–d3).

[379] This is a reference to 274e, where the Egyptian Pharaoh is critical of the clever inventor Theuth.

183

On the *Timaeus* of Plato: Book 1

10   on in the cosmos, and all these things are coordinated by the gods that
preside over creation with a view to a single cosmos, a single harmony,
and a single complete life overall.

Praising Solon's poetry and handing down his work

15   **So one of the phratry-members said, whether because he really
thought that then, or whether he had the ulterior motive of giving
Critias cause for gratitude *up to* would have become more famous than
he.** (21b7–d3)

At this point once again the dedicated observers of detailed diction point
out to their devotees that, when Plato praises the poetry of Solon, he
is safely attributing the praise to an amateur and suiting the tastes of
others, but not speaking his mind or his reasoning.[380] For if anybody
20   else is a good judge of poets, Plato too is an excellent one as Longinus
argues.[381] Certainly Heraclides of Pontus says that, though Choirilus'
poems were then highly regarded, Plato preferred those of Antimachus,
and persuaded Heraclides to go to Colophon to make a collection of the
25   man's poems.[382] So the burbling of Callimachus and Duris is pointless,
when they claim that Plato is not an adequate judge of poets.[383] One
might regard this discussion as too historical.

    The person who investigates facts will require us to say that all the
91   causes of cosmic arrangement, which keep the rivalry intact, reach back
towards a single principle, and the final things cling to the first things
via what is between them. In this way those who received the story from
Critias the elder look back towards him, while he looks to Solon. And
5   while this latter admires the poetic power of Solon, the former are taken
back to Solon's poetry through Critias' intermediate role – in gratifying
him they are also praising [the other's poetry].

    But what is it that Critias says about Solon? [He claims] that he is
10   second to the divinely inspired poets for two reasons, because he took

---

[380] Though there appears to be a little satire at the expense of the Longinus-type, he is
nevertheless treated here as a potential ally in divorcing what is said from the true
opinions of Plato. One assumes that Longinus would have pointed to Plato's own
suggestion that Amynander could not be relied on to speak his mind. For Proclus' own
view Festugière quotes at length *in Remp.* I. 65.2ff., where Proclus can give some kind
of defence of the views expressed, if not according to standard aesthetic criteria.

[381] Longinus fr. 35.

[382] For Antimachus see above, on 64.23; Choerilus is presumably not the tragedian of
the late sixth and early fifth centuries, but an epicist (like Antimachus) of the fourth
century, who wrote *Persica*.

[383] In the Introduction (pp. 75–6), I raise some issues concerning Proclus' source for
Heraclides, Callimachus, and Duris. The material may go back to Crantor.

184

Atlantis

up poetry as a diversion, and because he found the city of Athens in a state of civil strife when he returned from Egypt, and out of concern for his fatherland he wasn't able to compose the story properly that he's brought back from there. What that story was he will go on to tell. From this as from images he makes clear that everything that is foremost in its creative and productive role[384] does have other activities as its primary concern, while its production directed towards secondary entities is a secondary concern. Further [he makes clear] that the discordant and unstable aspect of matter often does not accept the order that comes from more divine causes, but it is in too unbalanced a state for the gift that they offer, on which account secondary or tertiary powers have processed, which are the immediate source of arrangement for its formlessness.

Solon, then, because he was the **most free-spirited**,[385] and in imitation of the transcendent causes, did not hand down the story of the war with Atlantis in poetry, while Critias and his successors relate it to others as well, in imitation of the secondary and tertiary causes, which bring forth for all to see the variety of the formative principles (*logoi*) and the arrangement involving the harmonization of opposites. Furthermore, that Solon was **extremely wise** highlights a correspondence with the primary principles, while his being **most free-spirited** reflects the power of the <cause>[386] that is transcendent, founded in itself, and fills all things without becoming involved.[387] Such an attribute in a way goes hand in hand with wisdom, as it is immaterial, independent, and of itself.

That Critias here, Critias the elder that is, should have been called an **old man** symbolizes the remoteness from becoming and the intellective nature of the cause. For wisdom and true opinions, [Plato] says,[388] are welcome to whomsoever they come to, even in old age. Further, that this Critias should have **vividly remembered** reflects the secure preservation of the everlasting formal principles and the constantly active attention of the second causes to the first.

That poetry should have been a diversion for Solon [reflects] the fact that among the first [causes] also productive activities directed

---

[384] Like Solon himself.

[385] Festugière includes a long note on the exact sense of this word, in which he approves this translation of Cornford's.

[386] A feminine noun is missing, with οὐσία added in Diehl and Festugière. I prefer αἰτία.

[387] Compare 88.6 for the term ἀπολύτως, with Festugière's note at that point.

[388] At *Laws* 653a; Proclus' memory of this passage is imperfect, for Plato says that its presence is *eutychês* (a difficult word, only roughly translated as 'fortunate'), not 'welcome' (*agapêtos*); he also requires that true opinions should be 'secure'.

185

On the *Timaeus* of Plato: Book 1

10 towards the second take second place, because their first activities are intellective, involving their unification by the principles that precede them.[389]

If somebody, on hearing this from us and ignoring [deeper] realities, were to investigate what reason Plato had for introducing these apparent digressions, he would probably find everything in accord with the overall 15 purpose. Plato's target had been to tell the story of the war with Atlantis, and it was important that the reporter of this narrative should neither deceive nor be deceived. Hence Solon was said to be both **extremely wise** and related to Critias' family, his wisdom making him impossible to deceive, and his family links making him free of deceit. However, the 20 recipient of the tale needed to be neither [yet] in his prime, to enhance the impression of the story's antiquity, nor so youthful as to be forgetful. Consequently, Critias is depicted as a youngster, but well able to remember, so as to be able to contend with the others in giving recitations – for which a great deal of memory is required. Furthermore, Critias the 25 elder needed to pass on such stories as this not just to the youth, so that they should not seem easily dismissed. So it was with good reason that one of the phratry-members is represented as inquiring about Solon and hearing the story. Yet this person too needed to be connected with Solon in some way, so that the old man, given the opportunity, would relate 30 the entire story as he [Solon] had told it. Hence the praise of his poetry, that was offered by Amynander to please Critias, precedes the narrative. So much for the handling of the story.

93 It is clear that Solon did not travel to Egypt simply to research history, but also so that the Athenians might live according to his laws for a certain time, a time during which they had promised him that they would not dissolve any of the laws that he had established.[390] It was during this time 5 that he visited Croesus[391] as well as sailing to Egypt. On turning back he found the city in confusion because of the Pisistratids.[392] That will do for the historical inquiry.

Origenes, raising a difficulty about how Solon was called **most free-spirited** (for he claimed that it wasn't the right sort of praise for a 10 poet), solves his problem by claiming that he is so described either as

---

[389] Cf. 91.8–16. The current comment is more *lexis*-like (as all material since 91.27), the former more typical of the *theoria*.

[390] This story concerning Solon's departure was well known in antiquity, being disseminated through Herodotus (1.29–30) and Plutarch (*Solon* 25.4–28.4).

[391] The famous king of Lydia, with whom Solon converses according to the same passages of Herodotus and Plutarch .

[392] The city had been taken over by Pisistratus himself.

Atlantis

somebody who is resourceful in the use of vocabulary (from those who are financially generous), or as one who is very free of speech, and consequently **most free-spirited** with no holds barred in his poetry, an employer of 'abundant free speech',[393] or as one who is relaxed and unforced in his verses.[394]

Iamblichus,[395] though, says none of these explanations is right, but that this is hinting at Solon's detachment of intellect, his independence in virtue, and his seriousness and excellence in all else. And indeed the same interpreter affirms that Critias' **smiling** is an indication of the perfection of the causes' generative activity, [generative activity] that delights in its own products, while his vivid memory symbolizes the preservation of the productive principles within the cosmos.

So why then would Solon have been so serious about passing down [the tale of] the war with Atlantis in poems? Because, he claims, all works of nature and the cosmic rivalry are established through imitation. And he [Solon] corresponds to the productive and primary causes, just as Critias corresponds to secondary ones that come next. And why was he prevented by the civil conflict? Because enmattered motions and enmattered disturbance gets in the way of the productive principles of encosmic things, as was said earlier.[396]

Two brief lemmata

About an achievement that was tremendous, he said, and that would have rightly [been (thought)] the most famed of all, which this city did achieve, though on account of the passing of the time and the death of the perpetrators the story has not endured to this time.   (21d4–7)

Longinus believes that the language here is elliptical, because **would have rightly** requires 'been thought', this being demanded by what

---

393 An allusion to *Phdr.* 240e6: strangely part of a description of the lover in Socrates' speech that argues he should not be gratified, a speech whose authority is immediately undermined thereafter.

394 The meaning of the Greek is not clear; for a different view see Festugière.

395 Iamblichus *in Tim.* fr. 10 Dillon. In his commentary (273–4) Dillon claims that the language follows Iamblichus very closely, and that the exposition follows Iamblichus' own principle of fr. 5 (30.4–18), requiring the expression of truths first through images (*eikones*), then through symbols. This principle is in fact attributed to the Pythagoreans, and the Atlantis story itself was regarded there as symbolic, though Iamblichan exegesis in this passage is clearly iconic.

396 At 91.16–21. Note here that the term *logoi* serves both for cosmic principles and literary accounts, while the term *poiêtikos* serves both for 'creative' and 'poetic'.

On the *Timaeus* of Plato: Book 1

follows, not just 'been'.[397] However, Porphyry[398] claims that he did not
understand that Plato added **that would have rightly [been] the most
famed** on account of its being a **tremendous achievement**, though *not
yet* famous. But let us adhere to the [higher] realities, and state that he
called the achievement **tremendous** because it offers an all-pervading
image of universal rivalry, but **most famed** because it contributes to the
completion of the visible creation. Similarly, in Orpheus too the works
of nature are described as 'glorious':

Both the glorious works of nature endure, and boundless Eternity.[399]

**Tell me from the beginning, said he, what and how and from whom
Solon claimed he'd heard the truth.** (21d7–8)

What refers to the wondrous deed itself; **how** refers either to the manner
in which it was done or the manner in which it was known to Solon; **from
whom** refers to those who preserved it for Solon to hear. It seems that
through these words he is going on to ask for the very form of universal
rivalry, how it is accomplished or recognized, and upon which causes
of those invisible to us it depends. Previously he had worked back to
Solon's account through his[400] relatives, but now he is seeking a glimpse
of higher causes for the story than this, or, to speak more plainly, for
the beginnings of this creation process.[401] In the investigation of those
questions you will be investigating all causes right up to the very first
through symbols as if in images.[402]

---

[397] The observation of Longinus seems excessively pedantic, for *onomastos* can mean something like 'famous' or 'of note'. Whereas a difference might be claimed between being
of note and being thought of note, it is scarcely conceivable that being famous can ever
be separated from being thought famous. What is remarkable is the extent to which
Proclus feels obliged to record the debates about matters which he would have found
trivial. Lightweight philological comment is of course what Plotinus had associated
with Longinus long before.

[398] Porphyry *in Tim.* fr. XI.   [399] *Orph.fr.* 83.

[400] The younger Critias' relatives are also those of Plato.

[401] Because Solon corresponds to the primary productive causes, and Solon is only the
primary source for the story *in the Greek world*, a question that seeks to go back to
Solon's sources in a different world must be concerned with causes of being rather
than of production and becoming. Hence Proclus assumes that these new questions
correspond to questions that the scientists ask about the intelligible and archetypal
world.

[402] The phrase ὡς ἐν εἰκόσι διά τινων συμβόλων shows the difficulties of trying to distinguish
too sharply between iconic and symbolic methods of investigation. As Festugière shows,
the text here is sound.

Atlantis

Dynamics of the passage on Sais and Egyptian geography

There is in the region of Egypt, he said, at the Delta around whose   **95**
head the flow of the Nile is split, an administrative region called
'Saitic'. (21e1–3)

Here is the first worthwhile point, to notice how the account constantly
sets forth the more confined areas [by approaching] from the more
embracing ones, from Egypt the river, from this the Delta, from this   5
the Saitic region, and from this Sais, the holy city of Athena. Next, with
this in view, to be transported back through the analogy of these things to
the first and most all-embracing causes of the creation process. For you
could see that a given cause here too is embraced from above by more   10
universal causes, and so on until the final ones, and that everywhere
those that embrace are immediately prior to those that are embraced by
them, and the more universal [immediately prior] to the more partial.
[You could see] the undivided creation of divided things, called the 'new'
creation,[403] to which the present account will transport the 'father of the   15
discussions',[404] being filled thanks to them[405] and receiving from Athena
in particular a share in their immaculate power, while filling all the vast
array of things in the cosmos with itself.

    Overall, since we have associated this war, for the sake of which the
entire narration has been set in motion, with cosmic rivalry, it is a good   20
tactic to continue 'along the same track'[406] and liken the complete knowledge of the priests in Egypt to the more ancient creation process that
holds in a fixed embrace the creative principles in the universe, but to
liken Solon's ever new and changeable narrative to the still newer one,
which governs the varied cycles of encosmic things, and to see how the   25
difference in the creation processes is reflected in images that pertain to
human affairs. Further, just as in these words Solon summons the priest
to the revelation of deeds of old, while he knows also all that is thought
ancient among the Greeks and, before that, the really ancient deeds,   30
so in that area too the new creation has reverted back to the older one
and is brought to completion from it, while that [older one] has a prior
grasp of the causes of this one, and is founded higher than it, through   **96**

---

[403] A recurrent phrase used to distinguish the creation of all that is subject to change in
the world. See Festugière's note as well as the continuation of the text above.

[404] The phrase is otherwise introduced only at 9.15 above. At 41a the demiurge calls
himself a 'father of works' (*erga*), inviting the natural comparison with the notion of a
'fathers of words' (*logoi*); Timaeus, of course, in some way is analogous to the universal
demiurge. Reference to a father of the debate (*logos*) is made at *Symp.* 177d5 and at
Phdr. 257b2 (referring to Phaedrus and Lysias respectively).

[405] I.e. the more universal causes.   [406] An allusion to *Republic* 420b3.

On the *Timaeus* of Plato: Book 1

intellections and powers that are greater and more complete. So much for the overall tale.

Individual questions on Egyptian geography and its symbolism

We must also deal with the individual questions.[407] As for Egypt, some regard it as an image of matter, others of the earth as a whole on the grounds that it is divided in a manner analogous to [the earth],[408] some of the intelligible or the intelligible substance. Our view is that it is being assimilated here to the whole invisible order, the source of things visible. For the Delta arises as the Nile is split in the region of the Saitic province, turning from its one straight course to the right and to the left, and passing out to the sea, so that the hypotenuse of the triangle is the seashore. This is what Plato meant in describing the Saitic province at the point as something **around whose head the flow of the Nile is split**. It corresponds to the single life-generating source of the divine life as a whole, and in visible things to the heavenly triangle that causes all generative force to cohere.[409] It neighbours on the Ram, which those people[410] especially admired, both because Ammon was constituted with a ram's head, and because the Ram is the starting-point of generative force[411] and most fast-moving of all, because it is positioned in the heaven at the equator. Hence his mention at this point of the Delta was appropriate, since the triangle is also the first principle of the construction of the elements of the cosmos, as we shall hear in what follows.[412]

They give the Nile a place analogous to the zodiac, as something placed beneath it,[413] similarly inclined, and imitating by its branches

---

[407] A clear indication of the passing from *theoria* material to *lexis* material.

[408] Festugière has an extensive note on what the intended correspondence of division might be. More important, if I am correct in supposing that these views are about what Egypt symbolizes here in the *Timaeus*, might be the identity of these interpreters, and their approach to the Atlantis story as a whole, for it seems that they sought for a deeper meaning behind these details without wishing to make them refer to anything properly transcendent.

[409] Festugière quotes passages from Prolemy, *Tetr.*, 1.19.1 and 2.3.3, that speak of a triangle (one of four) of Aries, Leo, and Sagittarius, associated specially with the Sun and with Jupiter.

[410] We now move on to what Proclus sees as Egyptian doctrine, with a strong astrological element.

[411] Festugière cites passages of Nigidius Figulus, Ptolemy, and Lydus that corroborate this statement to the extent that the Ram is the starting-point of an annual cycle. This occurs in spring, making the connection with generation natural.

[412] Simply a reference to the material elements as explained in the *Timaeus* 53c–55c.

[413] In the sense of placed under its control; see Festugière's note.

Atlantis

both the [zodiac's] obliquity and its being divided in the region of the equinox.[414] It introduces a symbol for the life that pours out into the entire cosmos. And indeed the two flanks of the Nile that are carried to the sea from a single head, in a way resemble the two correlated columns of opposites that proceed from the same root as far as generation, and for which generation is the receptacle – with a triangle emerging from the two of them and their common receptacle that they flow into.

The Saitic region is a large portion of the Delta, and has correspondence with a large sector of the heaven. Certainly Sais for them has reference, in priestly terms, to the Great Bear, not because it lies beneath it nor because of its cold, but in the belief that it participates in some efflux from this divinity, a fact that makes it stable in earthquakes because it receives a secure foundation from its situation towards the pole.[415]

The history and religion of Sais

Of this administrative region the largest city is Sais, the very place from where Amasis their ruler came. For them the founder-divinity of their city is one called in Egyptian Neith, but in Greek (according to their account) Athena. They are very pro-Athenian, and claim to be in some way close to those here. (21e3–7)

The term for **administrative region** (nome, *nomos*) gets its name from the way their land has been distributed (*nemesthai*). Thus the Egyptians called the large-scale divisions of Egypt **nomes**. The entire **nome** is called 'Saitic' from the name of this city, just like Sebennytic from Sebennytos and Canobic from Canobus. Reference to Amasis has been brought in now as one analogous to Solon, as he too cultivated justice and temperance as compared with kings as a whole. He is therefore a partner of Solon, and has the same relation to him as that of the one city to the other.[416] So from one monad, the goddess, you will see that both the cities and the people have been ordered, and from what is more complete [you will see] secondary things always being completed.

Callisthenes and Phanodemus record that the Athenians were fathers of the Saitic people, but Theopompus to the contrary says that they were colonists from them. Atticus the Platonist says that Theopompus changed the record out of hostile jealousy, because in his time certain people came from Sais in order to revive their kinship with the

---

[414] Manilius 2.218–20.

[415] The geography is looked at from the perspective of Egypt alone, giving Sais an extreme northerly position.

[416] Sais to Athens.

On the *Timaeus* of Plato: Book 1

Athenians.[417] Plato, however, only says this much, that the people of Sais
5 were **pro-Athenian**, and **in some way related**. And he is able to say this
because they have a single 'city-holding' goddess.[418]

Concerning the overseer of these cities there is this to be aware of,
that as she processes from the intelligible and intellective causes through
the hyper-heavenly orders down to the heavenly portions and allotments
upon earth,[419] she has drawn as her lot places that naturally belong to
10 her. She doesn't receive her leadership as something that is incidental to the place, but [she gets it] because she has already got within
herself its substance and its form, and in this way she has drawn this
lot as something that belongs to her. That the control of this goddess
stretches to the very last things is shown by the Greeks when they say
15 that she was born from the head of Zeus, and by the Egyptians when
they relate that the following epigram is carved upon the goddess's inner
sanctuary:

I am the present, the future, and the past. Nobody has removed the covering of
my cloak. The fruit that I have brought forth the Sun has generated.[420]

20 Hence the goddess is involved in creation processes, invisible and at the
same time visible, possessing an allocated portion in the heaven while
illuminating generation below by means of the forms. For not only is
the Ram, from the signs of the zodiac, dedicated to the goddess, but
also the equatorial circle itself – the region in which the power that
moves the whole is specially seated. So it is with good reason that Plato
25 will call her 'both war- and wisdom-loving',[421] and now describes her
as **founder-divinity** of these portions of hers upon earth. [This is so]
firstly because he honours the goddess through his native language,
for the Athenians called their guardian 'founder-divinity', in celebration of her <power> as eponymous and founding divinity; and secondly
30 to give an indication of her manifold embrace, that is pre-established

---

[417] Callisthenes of Olynthus, Phanodemus the Atthidographer of Athens, and 'Theopompus' the falsely-named author of the *Tricaranos* of Anaximenes of Lampsacus. This is
Atticus fr. 17 (des Places), whose notes refer back to Festugière.

[418] 'City-holding' (*poliouchos*) was a conventional epithet of Athena, as protecting divinity
of Athens, and is occasionally used of other divinities.

[419] For the range of areas in which Athena functions see also *in Crat.* 53, 22.19–25.

[420] On this passage, similar in formula to Isiac aretologies, see Festugière's note. Plut. *Mor.*
354c has a slightly different version, and stops before the last sentence. Proclus finds
in the fragment evidence of the goddess's concealment, but at the same time of her
involvement with visible life-forms.

[421] At 24c7-d1; this influential description appears in discussion of Athena at *in Crat.* 185,
112.4–5.

Atlantis

within her under a single form, of the allocations that she governs, and in addition to present us with an explicit statement that it is possible **99** for the same entities to be signified by a plurality of names, since the sounds are images of the thing signified by them.[422] For many statues could be made of a single individual out of materials that are different. Consequently both the Egyptians will offer an explanation of why they **5** call her by this name of theirs, and so will the Athenians. It is not at all remarkable that both should name her correctly, because they apply their names in accordance with a single science.

If, then, there is one overseer of the two cities, Sais and Athens, it is with good reason that the inhabitants of Sais are a **pro-Athenian** people, because they are **in some way close to** them. The closeness is not **10** absolute; for in the same providence some would be able to participate more and some less, some in one of its powers, some in another. For one should also realize this, that variations occur in various races according to the different areas in which each lives, according to the make-up of **15** the air, to the position in relation to the heaven, and still more specific, if you like, in accordance with the seminal formal principles. You might say that they differed most of all in relation to the herd-tending management of the gods and the differences among their overseers,[423] thanks to which you will detect variations in colouring, stature, language **20** and movements in different places. The result is that even colonists often undergo change in the colouring and the dialect of the settlers when they come to different places, just as plants change together with the quality of the soil if they happen to be transplanted into different **25** ground.

Ancient and more recent history

Solon said that he had travelled there and became particularly renowned among them, *up to* **he found out . . . about such matters.** (21e7–22a4)

Because of his wisdom in political matters and because of the merit of **30** his city it was with good reason that he was shown respect by the priests of Sais. Yet as far as concerns their communal memory and their history, **100** he found that neither he nor any other of the Greeks knew anything of antiquity. But the memory of ancient things contributes to political excellence, and it also contributes to the observation of the cycles of the

---

[422] Festugière aptly refers to 204.10–12.

[423] Herd-tending is an art that appears in the *Statesman* (275e5), but this language is clearly ingrained, as shown by *in Tim*. III. 279.11–13.

193

On the *Timaeus* of Plato: Book 1

5 cosmos. Solon was striving for this,[424] and as a result of inquiring from the priests he discovered that he was utterly deficient.

Here too are symbols of things divine. For among the theologians[425] a 'young creation-process' is spoken of, and this received special honour from the universal Father and from the intelligible gods,
10 among whom there are transcendent and more elevated[426] intellections, while those among the secondary gods are more partial and weaker. Hence there is this difference among the creative principles, that some are more able to get an overall grasp of the more universal forms, and others a more partial one, and some excel 'in seniority and
15 power',[427] while others are young compared with them, and with lowlier power.

Greek and Egyptian antiquities

And once, when he wanted to draw them into open discussion about ancient times, *up to* **to count up the periods of time.** (22a4–b3)

20 That is what all divine causes are like, invoking the more complete powers, and through this invocation being filled with more divine and more universal intellections from them. That is just what Solon is doing here. Using the more ancient things known to the Greeks as an inducement to the priests, he seduces them, as it were, into discussion of
25 antiquity as *they* knew it. This was a subject the Egyptians have an outstanding grasp of, since they observe the heaven unhindered on account of the purity of the air, and they preserve things of old in their memory on account of their being destroyed neither by flood nor by fire.[428]

30 Iamblichus says that the Assyrians did not merely make observations
101 over twenty-seven thousand years, as Hipparchus records, but have also

---

[424] The reference to his attempts at calculation at 22b2–3 are supposed to indicate his interest in cycles, though the actual cyclicity of nature is introduced by the priests at 22c.

[425] This would usually signify an Orphic reference, but it does not seem to be verse and is not given in Kern.

[426] Tentatively accepting Festugière's ἀνωτέρων for the meaningless MS readings αἰωτέρων or βιωτέρων. One might also consider ἁγιωτέρων.

[427] *Republic* 509c9 is quoted.

[428] While it seems strange that the Egyptians, whose floods were famed far and wide, are thought immune from the kind of floods that can wipe out peoples elsewhere, this is to be found at *Timaeus* 22e, and credited to the absence of precipitation.

Atlantis

handed down by memory the total times for return to square one[429]
and for the revolutions of the seven planets that control the cosmos.
One is very far from being able to compare this with the much-vaunted
'archaeology' of the Greeks. From this it is clear that the narration that
we are dealing with ought not to be looking to minor matters, but to the   5
universal and the whole.

Different Greeks have different versions of ancient history. Whereas
for the Athenians it goes back to Erichthonius the 'autochthonous',
for the Argives it reaches to Phoroneus and Niobe, because these are
the most ancient among the Greeks, Argus being from Niobe, and
from him Iasus and Pelasgus, while Argos is called 'Pelasgian' from   10
this latter. The stories about Deucalion and Pyrrha, that they were
saved on Parnassus when there was a flood, and that they relocated
and established the human race, are common knowledge – as is the
fact that the Thessalians trace their ancestry to them. In some versions the Argive race begins with Inachus, and the Athenian with   15
Cecrops, both of whom precede Deucalion.[430] So Solon, by recount-
ing this kind of story, induced the Egyptian priests to narrate what
they see as ancient history. We shall observe[431] what one of the
elderly priests said in response, and that will become clear through   20
what follows. Solon met at Sais a priest called Pateneït, at Heliopolis Ochaäpi, and in Sebennytos Ethemon, according to the records of
the Egyptians.[432] Perhaps that was this Saitic priest who told him what
follows.

Was the priest's reply an insult?

O Solon, Solon, you Greeks are always children; there is no such thing   102
as an elderly Greek.   (22b4–5)

---

[429] The *apokatastasis* in which all planets return to a starting point, fundamental to the
theory of a 'great year'.

[430] No Dorian race is included since the Dorian arrival was later. Festugière points out
that neither Erichthonius nor Phoroneus, being born from the seed of Hephaestus and
from the river Inachus respectively (Paus. 2.15), had human ancestors, and thus they
mark points beyond which the history of the Athenians and Argives cannot be traced.
Likewise Deucalion is the son of the Titan Prometheus, Pyrrha the daughter of his
brother Epimetheus. Since the genealogy of the Greek ancestors had been a popular
subject amongst Greek writers, Proclus would have had no shortage of possible sources
with which to flesh out the Platonic text. What may be of interest is his decision to
include the Athenian material to which Plato does not allude.

[431] Reading θεασόμεθα for θεασώμεθα at 101.18.

[432] Seemingly dependent upon Plut. *Solon* 26.

195

On the *Timaeus* of Plato: Book 1

The priest is **elderly**,[433] so that he may avoid being rude in his criticisms, and so that he may have reasonable grounds[434] for expounding ancient history. He does not employ repetition of the name of the addressee solely to strive to give extra force to what he is going to say, but also to give an indication of revolution back to the same point of origin. This is grasped in a stable and intellective manner through their indelible cognition by the more general causes of what arises in the universe, causes to which the priest corresponds. He accuses the Greeks of being **always children**, because, instead of pursuing the multi-faceted wisdom of the Egyptians, the majority of them 'carried the slavish cut in their souls'.[435] Alternatively, because of the continuity of the cycle of mass destruction that afflicts them, and before the present generation can become old they become young again through mass destruction. Or again, because [the memory of] ancient deeds is not preserved among them, whereas their cognition is always of the present and of as much as sensation sets before them. By contrast, the past too is always fresh in the memory of the Egyptians, and memory is preserved through historical inquiry, while this latter is preserved as a result of the pillars on which they record unexpected and remarkable things, whether in achievements or in discoveries.

'But why', people say, 'did this priest rudely rebuke him? What is so wonderful about the knowledge of the past? "Much learning does not breed intelligence", as the noble Heraclitus says. Even if what Eudoxus says is true, that the Egyptians called the month a "year", the counting of this many years would not involve anything remarkable. So the Egyptian's pride in these things is superfluous.' Indeed it is impossible

[433] Part of a few words (22b3–4) that do not feature in the lemma. It is almost as if Proclus had forgotten these when he speaks at 101.18–19 as if going straight on to the content of the speech, and then checks himself, and remembers to include comment on the identity of the unnamed elderly priest.

[434] Proclus interestingly uses the phrase εἰκὼς λόγος that usually applies to the account of the world given by Timaeus. This passage, in explaining a peripheral feature of the story in accordance with what is morally appropriate, accords with the standard tactic of Porphyry in the prologue, though Porphyry does of course give a deeper explanation of the Atlantis story itself.

[435] The reference is to *Alcibiades I*, 120b2–3, where in my view it is implied that this is a saying that was a popular one among women. However, Denyer (2001), 168–9, speculates that the reference to women is related to the fact that a woman's accent is to be imitated at this point, referring to the notion of a hair-cut in the soul as 'bizarre', and comparing the plumage of the soul at *Phdr.* 246c. Yet it would make good sense that women, always ready to criticize cowardice etc., should have referred to alleged slavish traits of character in males as the equivalent of the short haircut which was normally the mark of a slave, but could be more quickly outgrown. The metaphor is used in the *Alcibiades* to indicate the lack of subtlety found in people who turn to politics with no skills for the job.

Atlantis

that either memories or sensations should be productive of knowledge, 30
as Aristotle asserts, but one should grant that they nevertheless contribute to the recollection of universals.[436] For when we tell more and
more similar stories, we display the single form that covers them, and **103**
when in lots of cases we discover from history how their paths back
to square one are in accord, we are on the path back to their single
cause. Philip's observations of atmospheric phenomena[437] were consol-
idated in the same way, as were the discoveries of the heavenly motions 5
through astronomy. Let that be the reply from us too to that person's
difficulty.[438]

Seniority and youth as universal symbols

We should retrace our steps to the study of the universe, and consider in
that context the new creation that is controlled by Athena and brought
to fullness by the older and first-born causes. It is from there that this 10
[creation-process] has its stability and transcendence, and contributes to
the cosmic rivalry. For everything belonging to *this* creational procession
that becomes divided and multiplied proceeds as a result of *that* cause.
Given that there are [two sets of] causes in the cosmos, one that is pro- 15
ductive of cyclic rebirth, and another that is protective of the constant

---

[436] The theory of recollection from Plato's *Phaedo* is now grafted onto an essentially Aristotelian theory about the centrality of such empirically discovered universals to all
science, for which see *Metaph.* 1003a13ff., 1059b24ff., 1060b19ff. While the place of
empirically formed universals had long been acknowledged in Platonism, the interesting thing about this passage (and 123.29–124.4 below) is how 'recollection' takes one
simply to an empirical concept, but this discovery nevertheless sets one on the road to
the discovery of a transcendent cause. Hence there remains a parallel with the *Phaedo*,
where 'recollection' is linked with the Ideas (75c–d, 76d–e), and the Ideas are seen as
causes of related particulars being such as they are (100b ff.).

[437] Philip of Opus, usually seen as the author of the *Epinomis*, is otherwise known to have
been engaged in studies of such topics as lightning and the rainbow (Dillon 2003, 181
with n.11), this latter phenomenon being mentioned in Alex. Aphr. *in Mete.* 151.31 ff.

[438] This indicates that the objection given at 102.22ff. came from another interpreter, who
had assumed that the prologue ought to be offering paradigms of ethical behaviour.
The difficulty exists only if there is some obligation on Plato's part to idealize the
Egyptians. The solution also would itself seem to be concerned to give the Egyptians
a *legitimate* pride in their pursuits; hence it may be that this is presenting what had
once been Porphyry's response to Longinus (hence Proclus' 'from us too'). Longinus
is associated with such difficulties (*aporiai*) at 51.9, 63.24, 66.15, and 83.19 above (frs.
27, 29, 30, and 32; cf. below at 162.16 = fr. 36). The problem in that case would be that
Longinus is known to have habitually declined to tackle the whole passage from 20c4
until 27a2, regarding the Atlantis story as superfluous. Even so fragments 32–36 all
come from this passage. Perhaps Porphyry himself had encouraged Longinus to give
his views on elements of the Atlantis story. Hence 204.20 below (= fr. 37) specifically
points to Longinus' *usual* practice.

On the *Timaeus* of Plato: Book 1

integrity of the creative principles, the priest has been adopted as analogous to these latter causes, and Solon to the former. Hence too the one gives evidence that exceptional memory of antiquity exists in his people, while the other is said to relate various stories of change, generation, and destruction. That the elder should be given priority over the younger also seems to me[439] to have been adopted in a manner that fits the organization of the universe. That is the relation to each other that things have in the creation-cycle of Zeus: those who are said to live under the cycle of Kronos are said to travel from older, as the Eleatic Stranger says, to younger, while those under [the cycle of] Zeus go in the opposite direction.[440] Here too (34bc) Timaeus will say about the soul that the Demiurge introduced soul to be older than the body, and on this account gave it greater seniority. So in this case the priest who is protector of the divine laws[441] lays claim to precedence in virtue of antiquity, even though the younger comes from a higher rank, insofar as Solon has also come from a city more closely connected with Athena. On the cosmic level the older works have great import.

104   **'You are young in your souls', he said; 'for you have in them no old opinion stemming from ancient oral tradition, nor any learning grey-haired with time.'** (22b6–8)

These things also have their analogue in that [higher] realm. The youth of their souls is analogous to the rejuvenation of life and the more partial causes, while the **ancient oral tradition** is analogous to stable intellection and the older causes. The **grey-haired learning** is analogous to the unified and ever-identical content of the nature and constitution of all things in the cosmos, thanks to which the primary and most divine encosmic things embrace in a universal and transcendent manner the causes of all that comes to be, and have a prior grasp of things in time, while the things closer to the totality do so in a partial and less exalted fashion because they fall short of the unitary intellection of wholes. Hence to some of the gods the **grey-haired** quality has been deemed appropriate, and youthfulness to others. That is because the grey hair is a symbol of intellection and of a life that is immaculate and far from generation, while youth is a symbol of a more partial cognition that already involves contact with things generated.

---

[439] On the first person singular see on 108.20 below.

[440] A reference to the popular myth of the *Statesman*, that accounts for the majority of uses of that dialogue in late antiquity; see 270c–272d.

[441] There is a correspondence with the causes that are 'protective of the constant integrity of the creative principles' at 103.15–16.

198

Atlantis

Cyclic processes of generation and destruction

The reason for this is as follows: there have been, and will continue to be, many losses of people's lives in many circumstances, the greatest by fire and water, though other slower losses occur by countless other means.[442] **(22b8-c3)**

The discourse is asking why the Greeks are **always children**, and there is no **learning grey-haired with time** among them. Or, if you prefer, it is studying[443] the paradigms of these things, the reason why the new creation-process controls the variety of things that come to be, as things that grow old are for ever coming to be and getting renewed. But before it discovers the cause behind these problems, it first runs through the matter of the cycles in the totality, and demonstrates their variety – a variety that the first orders of the gods have a prior grasp of in secure and united fashion, while the second [orders] do so partially and in the course of touching the nature of the things that they manage. For this latter [process] is cognition of what's present at any given moment, while the former is the apprehension through memory of what is absent too.

What then are the cycles of things in the cosmos? One must indeed postulate that there is always generation and always destruction in the totality. For that which is perceptible is 'coming to be and passing away, but never really real'.[444] But this generation and destruction must be postulated[445] in one way for the heaven and in another for material things. In the former realm the motion and the change of figure is fixed beforehand, and it is because of those changes that generation is governed and turns back upon its proper cycle. But in the latter cycle now some elements and now others gain the upper hand.

And wholes preserve the same or a similar order in conformity with nature, whereas in various parts the natural and the unnatural arise at various times. For it is necessary[446] that either both wholes and parts are constantly in a natural state, or both are sometimes contrary to nature, or the one group is contrary and the other in accord: and this last in one of

---

[442] Note that this is the first lemma to generate extensive discussion without involving earlier interpreters.

[443] Reading θεωρεῖ rather than θεώρει. I do not see why the sequence of third person singulars should be broken by an imperative.

[444] See 28a, perhaps the best known of all passages from the *Timaeus* in antiquity.

[445] Reading θετέον (C) with Festugière (as also at 105.5) rather than θεατέον (NP) with Diehl.

[446] At 105.15, I follow Festugière, who favours Praechter's neat correction δέοντος over Diehl's δεόντως <ὡς>.

On the *Timaeus* of Plato: Book 1

two ways.[447] If everything is in its natural state, the variety of generation is lost, and eternal things are the last of realities to arise and the first things are last of all.[448] If everything is arranged contrary to nature, there will be nothing stable enough to provide for any constancy in things that change, and the cycle of generation will not be preserved. That wholes should be contrary to nature, and parts in accord, is problematic, since the parts take their lead from the wholes, and wholes are such as to embrace the parts. Hence if the former were contrary to nature it would be impossible for the latter to remain in the natural state. For neither[449] is it possible, if this living animal of our own is totally altered and loses its own order, that any of its parts could still be in the natural state. It remains therefore that, while the wholes are firmly fixed in the natural state, the parts are at one time in the natural condition, following the wholes, and at another time tend towards an unnatural state.

Just as, of the partial living things, each is always being subjected to generation and destruction[450] on account of the outflow of material substances, or rather the one is more in generation than another, and one is more in destruction than another, and one is readier for being and another for destruction, so, while each of the regions of the earth admit both, some are more able to stay in the natural state, while others variously endure deviations away from the natural state. This may be (i) because of their different climate; and then again (ii) because of their location being different from the others; and further (iii) because of their relation to the heaven, with different parts being in conjunction with different parts of the heaven and being preserved by the different figures;[451] and besides all that's been said (iv) because of the power of

---

[447] Presumably (with Festugière) either wholes accord and parts are contrary, or vice versa.

[448] Since passing away involves a *movement away* from the natural state, the absence of deviation from that state will entail the eternity of all that exists, so that you will have no further orders of things beyond the imperishable ones.

[449] I follow Praechter's correction οὐδὲ for Diehl's οὐδέν.

[450] The view that movements towards and away from the natural state can be seen in terms of generation and *destruction* appears explicitly in Plato's *Philebus* 54a–55a (cf. Aristotle *EN* 7.11 and 10.3), though Plato distances himself somewhat from this view. However, the replacement of *what is lost* by new generation in both living bodies and souls is a prominent theme at the climax of the *Symposium* (207d–208b), and it may be that which Proclus has in mind here.

[451] The term σχῆμα is here translated in its basic sense, though it is important to realise that these figure are patterns of cyclic motion, and that the word can mean 'phases' in the context of astronomy (LSJ 8b); there may also be a hint of the resemblance to dance figures (LSJ 7).

Atlantis

their overseers[452] and of the gods in control of climate who have as their lot this or that characteristic, some delighting more in motion, some in rest, some in sameness, and some in difference.[453]

Well, while total and partial cases of destruction occur in this place or that, the species in the whole universe continue undiminished. There will always be humans, always earth, and always each of the elements. Since destruction and birth occur as a result of the heavenly figures, and these are enactments (*mimêmata*) of the divine intellections, while these intellections are dependent upon the intellective forms, so[454] it is from there that the stability has come, that the security of the species within the cosmos arises, and that the visible heavenly figures are able to preserve the species while destroying their parts – for destruction too must come around to those things that are born in time.[455] The All does not begrudge the preservation of as many things as are able to coexist with the All, but it is impossible that what is unable to conform with the constitution of the All should endure within the All. The law of Zeus banishes everything like that from being as if it had lost its civic rights.[456] For while remaining without rights it is altogether unable to exist, and what is altogether deprived of order is without rights.

The reason for both total and partial cases of destruction occurring in this or that locality has been stated, but we should now say why the greatest instances of destruction occur through the ambitions[457] of fire or water, but not of the other elements. Fire, you see, has a vigorous and productive role among the elements, it has the capacity to pass through all the others, and is of such a nature as to divide the others.

---

452 Such as Athena and Hephaestus in the case of ancient Athens (*Critias* 109c), and Poseidon in the case of Atlantis (113c).

453 The two pairs of opposites involved in the construction of soul at 35a.

454 Read δή with Schneider and Festugière rather than δε with Diehl and the MSS at 106.19.

455 The principle that everything created is destructible is clearly to be found in the text of the *Timaeus* itself (41a, cf. 38c), though the continued will of the creator for the preservation of what is well constituted explains the ongoing nature of the world itself and its gods. Obviously Aristotle had difficulties with the notion that anything could be subject to generation and destruction, yet in fact never destroyed, for which reason he criticizes the notion of a created universe in the *Timaeus* (see Introduction p. 26). The majority of ancient Platonists, who deny that creation is taken seriously in the *Timaeus*, escape his criticism. On 38b–c Archer-Hind (1888), 122–3, quotes *in Tim.* 3.30.1–20, where Proclus holds that Plato is demonstrating clearly that the heaven is ungenerated and indestructible.

456 The metaphors of city life continue to be applied to the life of the universe.

457 The word is the moral term *pleonexia*, often translated 'greed' elsewhere. The use of it suggests that elements too are able to indulge in hubristic conduct by exceeding their measures – cf. Heraclitus B94 etc.

On the *Timaeus* of Plato: Book 1

Water is easier to move than earth, but less easily affected than air. By its ease of movement it is able to act, and by its resistance to affection it can avoid succumbing to duress or weakening by dissipation like air.

Consequently it is to be expected from this that violent and extreme cases of destruction bring about inundations and conflagrations. You could also claim that the remaining two elements belong more naturally to ourselves. The fact that we are pedestrians links us naturally with earth, while our being surrounded on all sides by air, and living in air and breathing it, demonstrates the natural affinity of our own bodies to it. So these things, being somehow more natural to us, are less destructive for us, while the others, having the opposite properties to those, bring on more violent cases of destruction.

Furthermore these elements, earth and air, seem in another way too to be operating upon us in conjunction with their being themselves affected before we are. It is when air undergoes putrefaction that it causes plagues,[458] and when earth is split that it causes widespread entombments.[459] But (i) the plague is an affection of air, and (ii) earthquakes and [the formations of] chasms are affections of earth. Yet fire and water are able to act upon us without themselves experiencing prior affection, the one by submerging us, and the other by exerting pressure from the outside. Hence these two work more widespread destruction, because they are stronger than those – as they are unaffected in the destruction-process. So these are the greatest [forces of] destruction, inundations and conflagrations, while famines, plagues, earthquakes, wars, and other comparable partial affections[460] could come about for other reasons too.

Of all of these things you could say that the cause is the motion of the heavenly bodies and the general order of the All, and prior to this the new creation that is always making something new, and brings on the occurrence of different things at different times. That is what the myths of the Greeks say, and it is also what the tradition of the Egyptians

---

[458] Cf., with Festugière, Theophr. at Diels, *Dox.Gr.* 487.20. The link between air quality and health is of course important in ancient medicine, including the Hippocratic tract *Airs, Waters, Places*.

[459] Festugière gives 'des goulets serrés l'un contre l'autre', then gives the Greek below as if to indicate uncertainty. Literally the phrase means 'closely connected swallowings' or similar, but *in this context* it must be concerned with multiple human deaths (on a similar scale to fire, flood, and plague) for which the element of earth can be held responsible. That kind of death would most naturally occur by earthquake in Greece. And it would not be unnatural to think of many earthquake deaths, whether involving the opening of ravines or landslides, as the earth swallowing up people.

[460] I.e. they occur locally.

202

Atlantis

indicates when it says of the sun in mystical fashion that it undergoes **108**
various changes of shape in the signs of the zodiac.

Thus it is nothing remarkable that, while many cases of destruction
occur in many places, there is always a human race and always every
other species, because of the unerring procession of the divine forms.
It is on account of them that the formal principles in the universe are 5
always fixed in the same condition – for everything that arises from an
unmoved cause is constantly linked with its own particular cause.[461]

Introduction of, and various approaches to, the myth of Phaethon

Take the story that's told in your country, that once upon a time
Phaethon, the son of Helios, yoked up his father's chariot, and then, 10
because of his inability to steer his father's course, burnt up things on
earth and perished himself in a bolt of fire. The telling of this takes the
shape of a myth . . . (22c3–7)

It is quite obvious that the very first principles of existent things embrace
things moving in static fashion, things multiplied in singular fashion, 15
things partial in total fashion, and things divided in time in eternal fashion. And it is a familiar fact that the theologians trace back the causes
of the cycles, of the descent and ascent of souls, and of all pluralized
and divided life, to the [forces] positioned immediately above the world.
Hence the account (*logos*) seems to me[462] now too to be tracing the myth 20
of Phaethon back to the Greeks and to Solon's recognition that[463] all
such generations and destructions are accomplished as a result of the
new creation – the creation from which is accomplished *both* the cycle
of words (*logoi*) *and* the variety of physical and psychical cycles.[464] For 25

[461] Though 'dependent on' rather than 'linked with' would be the normal translation, that
does not capture the everlasting nature of what has one eternal cause. Editors point
out that Proclan doctrine here conforms closely with *ET.* 76.

[462] Proclus uses the first person singular sparingly, generally with the intention of express-
ing a strong personal feeling. Since the prologue (1.8, 6.21, 9.15), where personal views
might be expected, this has occurred at 20.11–12, 23.4, 49.23, 62.14, 64.11–27, 76.29,
77.24, 87.3 and 103.20. Its use here accords with the general impression that there had
been very little detailed discussion of these parts of the dialogue before Proclus.

[463] Festugière interprets the ὅτι as 'because' rather than 'that'; I assume this to be a reference to the latent recollectable knowledge referred to at 108.29.

[464] I offer this translation with some hesitation. Festugière takes the reference to *logoi* at
108.24 to be referring to the seminal principles so often referred to by that word in this
treatise. But with a lemma that concerns myths, which were also thought of as cycles
(LSJ s.v. κύκλος II.11, cf. s.v. κυκλέω II.4, κυκλικός II) it seems to me necessary to take
the word here in a verbal sense, contrasting this with the physical and psychical cycles
(on which Festugière aptly compares 95.23–7 and 104.24–6). Given the reference to
'constant integrity of the creative principles' at 103.15–16, as well as the statement that

203

On the *Timaeus* of Plato: Book 1

just as, while they remain among things divine, perfection reaches the second from the first, so too the Egyptian, preserving the story as told among Greeks, uses this to teach Solon of things he has prior knowledge of.[465]

30 So what riddling message does this account offer? It [signifies] that both psychical life and the nature of bodies involve a variety of changes, and that they are controlled by the hypercosmic powers,[466] while being

109 conserved also by the intelligible orders of gods. That the phenomenon is related among the Greeks is a symbol of the former, but that the priest tracks down the meaning of the story, and unveils for Solon what is

5 revealed by it, is a symbol of the latter. Let this be what we say for the sake of our study-passage (*theôria*)[467] as a whole, as this too would not be out of tune with the overall purpose.

The myth of Phaethon, however, involves detailed study of various kinds, for one should first of all treat it from the historical point of view, secondly from the physical one, then from the philosophic one.[468]

10 The narrative asserts that Phaethon, the son of Helios[469] and Clymene daughter of Ocean, veered off course when driving his father's chariot, and Zeus, in fear for the All, struck him with a thunderbolt. Being struck, he fell down upon Eridanus, where the fire coming from him, fuelling

15 itself on the ground, set everything alight. Upon his fall, his sisters, the Heliades, went into mourning. Such is the account from the historical perspective. It is a basic requirement that the conflagration should have happened (for that is the reason for the story's being told), and that the reason given for it should be neither impossible nor anything that could easily occur. It will be a case of the impossible if anybody should

20 think that Helios sometimes drives the chariot that belongs to him, and at other times changes his tune,[470] stands aside, and entrusts his own proper task to another. It will be a case of what could easily arise if somebody postulated that this 'Phaethon' was a comet, which produced

---

'the formal principles in the universe are always fixed in the same condition' at 108.5–6, I have problems with the idea that there can be an *anakyklêsis* of such *logoi* here.

[465] Festugière notes that Solon is analogous to the second, and the Egyptian to the first. Note the passing application here of the Platonic theory of recollection.

[466] Presumably this should be connected with 'the [forces] . . . immediately above the world' (108.17).

[467] This seems not to be a *theôria* as opposed to a *lexis*, for the *theoria* will continue. Rather it is a general approach to the lemma that precedes material specific to individual approaches.

[468] Note that 'philosophic' here is virtually the equivalent of 'theological'.

[469] The divinity Helios is simply a personification of the Sun, which is itself called by the same name.

[470] It is of course the notion that a god can change that is thought impossible.

204

Atlantis

an unbearable heat when breaking up. At any rate, Porphyry[471] says that people used to take the movement of comets for signs, of storms if it occurred toward the south, of heat to the north, of plague to the east, and of prosperity to the west (and they called the disappearance of the comet a thunderbolt): as if the concurrence of these things was quite familiar. A great deal has been said by the physicists about comets.

If one should be giving the myth more of a physical solution, it is better to follow my companion Domninus' approach to interpretation.[472] [He says] that such a compilation of dry exhalation arises at times[473] that it can easily be ignited by the heat of the sun, and, when this is ignited, it is not at all surprising that it sets alight all the underlying region of the earth. By setting it alight it produces just the kind of conflagration that the myth speaks of, and after doing so it is quenched and becomes undetectable. That the igniting force comes from the sun is the reason for Phaethon being called the son of Helios by the myth-makers, and he is male on account of the vigorous nature of the power of fire. For they habitually call fire itself male too, just as earth is female, this latter being matter, and the former form.[474] The fact that this exhalation did not occur on the same latitude as the sun is why they say that he did not drive the chariot along the course of his father. The dissolution of the cloud near the earth [accounts for] the fall of Phaethon, and its being extinguished [accounts for] the thunderbolt from Zeus, while a barrage of rain upon it – for this too happens after great conflagrations – [accounts for] the mourning of his sisters (who are wet exhalations),[475] in as much as mourners pour forth moisture. And the exhalations, both the dry and the wet, have in the sun a single cause, but one belongs to the male and the other to the female. So these ways of explaining things are more physical.

But the myth could be saying something loftier. Individual souls have proceeded from the father of the universe, and have been sown in the region of the encosmic gods, so that they should not be intellective alone, keeping in contact with the intelligibles and rising above bodies.

---

[471] = in Tim. fr. XII Sodano.

[472] Domninus is known also from 1.122.18, from Marinus VProc. 26, and from the Suda (see Damasc. Philos. Hist. 89–90, Athanassiadi (1999)).

[473] It seems to me that Festugière's attempt to have Domninus say this happened only once is mistaken. This present infinitive (and ἐξάπτεσθαι 110.3) should not be ignored, and the closely connected aorist infinitives are aorist for aspectual reasons, indications of definite events within a sequence. The key factor is that Domninus is clearly interested in all sequences of events of this type, as can be seen from 110.17–18 below.

[474] Neither the term for fire nor that for form is masculine in gender in Greek, though the Stoics had of course seen fire as the manifestation of Zeus.

[475] While Diehl deletes the words τῶν ὑγρῶν ἀναθυμιάσεων, I prefer to alter τῶν to οὐσῶν.

On the *Timaeus* of Plato: Book 1

They should also have an encosmic basis, just as the divine and daemonic souls were enlisted under secondary leaders, some beneath the divinity of Earth, others under the Moon, others under Helios, others under Zeus, and other under the leadership of Ares. And [note that] what is sown always acquires something extra from the nature of what it's been sown in, seeds sown in earth from the earth, seeds sown in an animal from that animal's natural characteristics. Consequently with offspring too some take on the special character of the locality and others the likeness of the mother. Because of this, souls too, when they are sown in the region of their associated stars, receive a special type of life from their leaders themselves, so that each is not only soul, but a given kind of soul, for example Areic, Jovian,[476] or Lunar. Whether the god is unresponsive [to the world of generation], or a demiurge or a life-generator,[477] some reflection of the special character of the one they have been allocated to extends to all the souls ranked beneath it. That is hardly surprising, when the special character of the presiding gods has reached down even as far as types of grass and stone – and there is grass and stone dependent on the power of the sun, whether you care to call them 'heliotrope' or by any other name.[478] It's much the same in the case of other gods.

Of these souls, then, some remain immaculate, always linked with their special gods and assisting their governance of the All; others do descend into generation, but they are workers of greatness who remain undamaged; others descend and are filled with the vice of producing generation, and take on something of the character of things governed. For this is the final type of life. So the first are genuine children of the gods, because of their <purity and> their inseparability from their fathers, as if they had been born within them and remained inside, children who escort their gods, with the rank of bodyguards or possibly of attendants. The middle rank are *called* children of the gods, but they take on the second life in addition and become children of human beings

---

[476] As this deals with planets, I have thought it best to preserve something of the Latin names that we use of the planets.

[477] Festugière translates the first as simply 'transcendent', but that is not specific enough. Whereas demiurgic and generative activity must at some stage be directed downwards to this world of ours, the highest divinities never turn towards us. A demiurge may, like that of Numenius (fr. 12.20; cf. also *aperioptos* at 11.18), turn now one way now another, which recalls the helmsman of *Statesman* 272e5. This figure is of course seen in Proclus too as another Platonic depiction of the demiurge; see 288.14–16 (where his phases are important), 315.23–4 etc.

[478] This is a reference to the plant heliotrope (which follows the sun) and bloodstone, a stone which has a red streak and was thought to have special powers (LSJ I.1 and III).

Atlantis

too. The <third> are called children of the gods, but not legitimate ones, on the grounds that they have not preserved the form of their special god; they have inclined to earth and experience forgetfulness of their proper fathers. So whether the myth-makers say that Tityus is the son of Earth or that Phaethon is the son of Helios, or that Musaeus is the son of the Moon or some other god, they are calling them children in this sense – while they call others [children] in a different sense for the reasons stated.

With the others we deal elsewhere; Phaethon, however, is the son of Helios in the sense that he belongs to the Helian chain – hence his Helian name.[479] As long as he stayed on high, went circling round with his father, and shared with him the management of the All, he has been said to drive the chariot of his father. Indeed that is because the vehicle[480] of Phaethon is one of the Helian chariots. For that too is entirely Sun-like. But when he veered towards generation (for he was not one of the first souls) he is said to have been struck by the thunderbolt of Zeus. That's because the thunderbolt is a symbol of creation, because, without touching them, it passes through all things and preserves them all – not because it is the cause of the destruction of the breath that carries the soul.[481] There are many transfers of souls from one environment to another, and from some elements to others, some coming from earth into the sphere of fire, others from fire to earth, and some in a disciplined way, others suddenly, with a great deal of disturbance and disorderly motion. That's the kind of thing they say happened to Phaethon. After being carried down suddenly from above dragging with him fiery tunics, when he got close to earth, by moving erratically through them[482] he set light to certain parts of the earth. For in their descent souls clothe themselves in many tunics, of air or water, though some have fiery ones. For these [souls] the part derived from fire that some have is quite faint, while it is for others intense and with a powerful impact. Some shed it while they are in the air and take on thicker [tunics], others keep

---

[479] The name suggests shining or blazing.

[480] The Neoplatonic doctrine of a soul's vehicle, connected ultimately with 41e, considered in relation to the myth of the *Phaedrus* (248a etc.) which is critical for the doctrine of gods and their followers found in our present passage.

[481] Presumably an earlier theory about the meaning of the Phaethon myth.

[482] The text is highly dubious. MSS read διὰ τούτων Ἀτλαντικῶς κινούμενος, and Festugière keeps the first three words, changing the last to βαρούμενος, translating 'alourdi par ces vêtements à la manière d'un Atlas'. But the adverb is very difficult, and the genitive with the preposition perhaps unexpected. I prefer to assume that the demonstrative points forwards to the parts (μέρη) of the earth, and that the adverb should be πλανητικῶς, formed from a well-attested adjective.

On the *Timaeus* of Plato: Book 1

them in use all the way to earth. I know that Plutarch of Chaeronea[483] tells the story that, on one of the little islands around Britain – one that is reputed to be holy and inviolate, and has for this reason been left alone by those in power – there often occur disturbances of the air and the unleashing of either downpours or thunderbolts. Further [he says that] the inhabitants who are used to such happenings say that one of the superior powers has passed on, meaning by 'superior ones' souls that are experiencing a change of bodies and are leaving one life-form. All the same one should not dismiss the idea that such things occur also when souls descend into bodies, especially in the case of those who are workers of greatness and have received a daemonic lot, such as this myth riddlingly suggests was the case with Phaethon's soul.

It would not be at all surprising that souls in descent should be more involved in the affections of those elements that correspond to the gods that preside over them, and attract and clothe themselves in more tunics of those elements. So the result would be that Saturnian souls rejoice more in the humid and damp ones, while the Helian ones rejoice in the fiery ones, each type preferring bodies with weight and matter to immaterial ones. And that the gods should use these souls, as they also use matter-bound daemons, as tools for their operations on earth, and that through these they should effect conflagrations or plague or various other sufferings for those who deserve to suffer them. And that they should use those souls that are related to the heavenly causes of generation as assistants in whatever tasks they undertake. That there should be many causes of the same events is not surprising, when some are acting in one capacity, others in another.[484]

So when Phaethon was carried close to earth and, in some daemonic way, ignited by his fiery trail those regions to which he drew near (for individual souls also do many things when outside the body, as tools of the avenging or purifying daemons), he was mourned by the Heliades, a group of Helian souls, as a result of which they were also called the sisters of Phaethon. They mourn him not simply because they feel pity at his descent to generation, but also out of concern for how he might keep immaculate his care for things that come to be and pass away. For the River Eridanus and his fall to that region give an indication of the transport of the soul to the sea of generation. When it is there, it depends on the forethought of families who are related to him and the

---

[483] *De Defectu* 419e ff., as opposed to the passage of the *De Facie* (941 ff.) referred to by Diehl, where islands off Britain are also mentioned.

[484] I assume that this appeals to the distinction between types of cause, and in particular between true causes and auxiliary causes.

Atlantis

assistance of souls who have stayed behind. The theologians also signify
the concern of Helios through the tears:

Your tears are the much-enduring race of men.[485]   5

Therefore it is probable that the myth about the Helian souls signalled
their concern towards Phaethon through their tears. So again a supplementary lesson[486] should be drawn from this myth too, that the descent
of souls is accomplished through a lack of power – for Phaethon too   10
wants to drive the chariot of Helios, but he is unable to do so and falls
on account of this lack of power. And that it is not only the souls but
also their vehicles that come to share in the distinctive character of their
leading gods, with the result that it is also from them that they get their
names, some Helian, some Areic, and the rest from one of the other   15
gods. And that even destructions are accomplished in accordance with
the providence of the gods – for it is actually Zeus who is responsible for
the conflagration, because he hurled his thunderbolt at Phaethon. And
that the descents of the souls are [all] linked to the one creation-process,
for which reason Timaeus too will not inform us only about their substance (*ousia*), but about their ascents and descents, and their lives and   20
choices of all kinds.[487]

The problem of deviations in the heavens

**Whereas its true reference is the deviation from their course of the
bodies that circle the earth in the heaven and the destruction of things
upon the earth in a huge fire that takes place after long intervals of
time.** (22c7–d3)   25

The Egyptian has explained only as much of the myth as contributes to
his present purpose, [mentioning] that there occur cases of widespread
destruction of things on earth through fire on account of the deviation
of the bodies encircling the earth in the heaven. What does he mean
by **deviation**? Possibly the lack of alignment, on the part of earthly
things, with those in heaven. For if everything is aligned with the influ-   30
ences emanating from the heaven it can endure, but out of alignment

---

[485] Orphic material = fr. 354 Kern. The 'your' is now singular, indicating a single addressee,
not a plurality of Helian souls.
[486] Or 'corollary': a geometrical term. The corollary is in four parts.
[487] Festugière explains that a single providence connects all the arrangements made for the
soul, including the cycle of incarnation and the possibility for their choosing inferior
lives; this is not a secondary happening that comes about from powers in conflict with
the creator's will.

209

On the *Timaeus* of Plato: Book 1

115 it is destroyed. For those things able to survive the divisive power of Ares are saved, while those things too weak to withstand its operation are easily dissolved. It is like the case of our eyes being blinded and unable to withstand the rays of the sun, even though something else's eye could look directly at them without trouble. A similar situation applies to the other gods and their configurations. For the world is one living creature, and, because its parts mutually interact, it preserves some of these through these ones, and others through those. And none of the things that occur in it are contrary to nature for the All, for what occurs within it occurs through it, and the cosmos itself is what acts, and the object of its action is itself. So either one should say that this is what the **deviation** is, rather as a good father, who, though always concerned for his son, would sometimes actually strike him for his own good, would seem to deviate somewhat from his normal behaviour, or it is the variations in the configuration of the heavenly ones. These are those [beings][488] **that circle the earth in the heaven**, exhibiting different figures at different times on account of variations in the intellections of their souls. For their figures are their writings, or a kind of imprint that operates because of them.[489]

But then again both of these [reasons] are true – both the deviation of those [higher] things and the lack of alignment of things in earthly regions brings on this kind of destruction. If one must also describe the fall of Phaethon from the heaven to the earth a **deviation of the bodies that circle in the heaven**, that's nothing surprising. For the deviation of the heavenly gods themselves is one thing, a change of figure that is immune to influence, while that of the souls that revolve in their company is another, their coming-into-relation with earthly things after life free of relations, and that affecting earthly places[490] is another, a basically destructive change. In this sense neither do souls deviate nor, far less, do the gods that are leaders of souls. So such cases of destruction to earthly things arise both through partial souls and through isolated daemons. Just as, through the latter, a type of destruction appropriate to their series results, so also does it in the case of souls. For those which rejoice

116 above in shedding light in an immaterial fashion rush into conflagrations here.

---

[488] Proclus makes the phrase from *Timaeus* 22d1 masculine, suggesting heavenly gods rather than heavenly bodies.

[489] 'Because of them' could be referring to either the souls or their intellections. Perhaps we should think of the writer in the soul which represents the decision-making power at *Philebus* 39a, and imagine that Proclus is positing a similar function, visible to all, in the souls of the heavenly gods.

[490] The text here, marked as corrupt by Diehl, is defended by Festugière.

210

Atlantis

The temporal spacing of catastrophic events

But why do cases of widespread destruction occur **after long intervals of time**? Is it because many things must coincide so that such a case of destruction may occur? [These include] the condition of things being affected, both individually and generally; the united tendency[491] of the active causes (for what if something destructive of one thing were salutary for another?); the suitability of the matter; the preparation of the instruments; and appropriate timing. This is so even in limited cases of destruction, but occurs more rarely in general cases, and with good reason. For nature must necessarily progress from the indestructible to the easily destructible via what is hard to destroy. So if the universe is ever indestructible, while more partial things are easily destroyed, it is with good reason that what lies between the two should be ranked among things hard to destroy, waiting to undergo their destruction **after long intervals of time**. Those things that endure for the entire cosmic cycle are indestructible and imperishable, for there is no configuration able to destroy them, since all have been brought on in the course of an entire cycle of the universe, while partial and particular things[492] easily admit of dissolution. But those partial things that are concentrated are dissolved only **after long intervals of time**, but are dissolved nevertheless. For just as an individual man has a life, so does a given species or city or tribe, and cycles too:[493] in some cases over a longer span, in others over a shorter one as Aristotle says.[494]

Iamblichus criticizes Porphyrian allegorical interpretation

So at those times all those living among the mountains and in high or dry locations are more subject to destruction than those living beside rivers or the sea. (22d3–5)

[491] Either the term σύμπνοια, usually translated here as co-animation and implying a unity of breath or spirit, has lost its full force, or else we should read συμποιῒαν. I have opted for a bland translation.
[492] The term is *atomos*, but this cannot in this case mean 'impossible to split' as in Epicureanism, where 'atoms' are indestructible precisely because of their indivisible nature. Even in Plato, *Phaedo* 78–80, what is indivisible has an indestructible nature. Hence *atomos* here might be thought to be the smallest portion into which a species can be divided, and yet even that does not seem to be quite what Proclus intends, for the overall division is of physical things, not the tripartition genus–species–particular. Perhaps one should think in terms of everything that cannot be split *without destroying the nature of that thing*.
[493] On the text here see Festugière, who argues convincingly against Diehl's exclusion of καί, comparing 124.7–9.
[494] The reference is apparently to *Long.* 465a9–10, where the neuter plurals of Proclus' text are better explained. The terms *brachyporôteros* and *makroporôteros* also figure in later books of *in Tim.*, II. 289.18,III. 23.25, 29.26, 93.30.

211

On the *Timaeus* of Plato: Book 1

25   This is likely to happen in cases of observable destruction by fire, for
those living close to water are protected from damage arising from fire.
However, Porphyry the philosopher transfers the story so that it applies
to souls, and he claims that in these as well the spirited element sometimes
117   overheats, and that such 'conflagration' is the destruction of the person
within us.[495] Homer[496] says of Agamemnon in a temper:

His eyes were like blazing fire.

5   But when the appetitive element is weakened when flooded by the
generation-producing moisture[497] and is submerged[498] in the rivers of
matter, this too is another sort of 'death' for intellective souls, 'becoming damp' as Heraclitus says. If these matters have been properly distinguished, all those people remain untested[499] by the affections that
10   go with temper who have their spirited part relaxed and commensu-
rate with their oversight over secondary things. This is what the hollow
places close to water signify. On the other hand, those people [remain
untested by the affections] that go with appetite who have their appetitive part fitter and more alert in the face of matter. This is what the
15   high places indicate.[500] For the spirited element has a fast-moving and
vigorous character, while the character of desire is slack and feeble. But

[495] = *in Tim.* fr. XIII Sodano. For Porphyry's overall stance on Atlantis, in which he interprets it as an allegory involving souls and daemons, see 77.6–24 above. I have preserved
the translation 'conflagration' for the term *ekpyrôsis* here in spite of its sounding too
strong (because it is usually applied to cosmic events), but have avoided taking *hyperzeô*
as 'overboil', since there is no implication of any liquid element in the soul. The phrase
'the person within us' has already been encountered in a Porphyrian context at 16.16,
but does not recur after this. I am unsure whether the phrase 'the real human being'
at 83.3, cited by Festugière, is exactly comparable.

[496] The reference is to *Il.* 1.104, and the reference to Heraclitus below is to B77; it seems
clear that Porphyry is responsible for the citation of these texts.

[497] See note on 77.4 for the association of generation-production with Poseidon, otherwise
god of the sea and of fresh waters. The term 'generation-producing' (*genesiourgos*) is
there associated with Numenius, probably again reported by Porphyry.

[498] For *baptizesthai* in such contexts see also 179.3, where Diehl and Festugière compare
Or. Chald. 114. But such images are natural to Platonism, particularly where the flux of
matter is highlighted, and Plutarch has an extended image of the better soul's rational
part (or intellect or *daemon*) sitting like a float above the waves, supporting the other
faculties that are submerged beneath, while inferior souls have even this part dragged
down beneath the surface (*Mor.* 591d–e).

[499] The meaning of *apeiratos*, found only here and at 156.3, needs to be determined
in the context of this text. The variation on *apeiros* (A) would seem to be quite
deliberate.

[500] It seems that the locations are thought to signify the psychical environment that the
rational soul (117.7: *psychôn tôn noerôn*) finds itself in.

212

Atlantis

it is the way of the 'musical' man to relax the strong tension of spirit, and to tighten up the poor tuning of the desire.[501]

The philosopher Iamblichus, however, thinks it right to interpret these words in relation to natural, not moral philosophy.[502] So he says that when a conflagration occurs those who live in the high mountains are more liable to be destroyed because they are furthest from the exhalations from water, since these do not rise far up because of the weight of their damp nature. Hence the air that surrounds them is not moisture-laden, but dry, and it provides fuel for the fire as it rises naturally upwards. But when inundations occur, on the other hand, those who live in the hollows are more liable to destruction, since all heavy things are naturally carried downwards.

Brief discussion of the theological implications of two more passages[503]

But in our case the Nile, our saviour in other respects, saves us then too by its release from this difficulty. (22d5–6)

The observable fact is that the Nile is responsible for a great variety of blessings for the Egyptians. It is responsible for geometry, arithmetic, physical inquiry, the growing of fruit of course, and their escaping conflagrations. Not only is its water able to preserve their bodies, but the divinity that maintains it is able to lift up their souls. You may grasp from this that the primary causes, which are also full of life and of generative power, not only maintain themselves and endure eternally, but also grant to those other things that are scattered in flux a right to that maintenance [that derives] from themselves. It seems to me also that the name of **Saviour** reflects divine and transcendent providence, from which even among the gods the gift of maintenance shines out upon all the intellective and demiurgic causes.

---

[501] Still printed as Porphyry (fr. XIII) by Sodano. The influence of *Republic* 410c–412a, where there is much talk of achieving the correct 'musical' balance in the soul, particularly with regard to its spirited part, is obvious; one may suspect also the influence of *Symp.* 187a–c, which provides a link with Heraclitus once more.

[502] Iamblichus *in Tim.* fr. 12 Dillon. The appeal to Porphyry's habit of mining prologues for moral messages seems misplaced here, since any ethics in Porphyry's explanation seems subordinate to his cosmic psychology.

[503] Full discussion of the term 'release' in the present lemma is delayed until 199.20; I have sought a translation of the participle λυόμενος that preserves some of the ambiguity that the differing interpretations of Porphyry and Proclus reflect. The participle may be passive ('getting released'), middle in a reflexive sense ('releasing itself'), or middle in a transitive sense ('releasing us from the difficulty').

213

On the *Timaeus* of Plato: Book 1

15   **Yet whenever the gods submerge the earth and purge it with water, those who live in the mountains, cowherds or shepherds, survive, while the cities in your country are carried out to sea by the rivers.**   (22d6–e2)

20   In these cases[504] he explicitly connects the efficient cause with the gods, making it legitimate to say the same thing in the case of the conflagrations too. The one [type of] purgation arises through water, the other through fire, and in every case purity comes to the second things thanks to the first. Hence in Orpheus' work too[505] Zeus is required to bring the

25   purgatives from Crete, as the theologians usually make Crete stand for the intelligible. He connects the flux of matter with that of water, for he makes each of these to be carried unthinkingly by its own natural inclination. Therefore there needs to be something pre-existing that uses them well and acts for the sake of the good, [a function] that the story

30   rightly attributes to the gods. Then, if there are certain purifications on a universal scale too, there are surely those who preside over these purifica-

119   tions, acting upon the All as purifiers who precede the partial purifiers – and divine rites, moreover, where some initiate, others are initiated. And these things never fail the Whole. Realizing this, the priest also has called

5   the cases of destruction by water or fire by the hieratic name 'purifications', but not 'destructions', as he would have said if he were only doing natural philosophy.

Geographical interlude: the swelling of the Nile

In this country water has never fallen on the fields from above either then or at any other time; on the contrary, it is all disposed to rise up from

10   **below. Wherefore, and for which reasons, stories preserved here are the most ancient to be told.**   (22e2–5)

Even if occasional showers should fall across Egypt, they would still not be across the whole of it, but are inclined to occur only in Lower Egypt, and this region is evidently the work of the river according to

15   Aristotle.[506] Upper Egypt receives no rainfall of this kind. So where is it that the Nile rises from?[507] Porphyry[508] declares that there was

---

[504] Or possibly 'In this passage'.   [505] *Orph. fr.* 156 Kern.

[506] *Mete.* 351b29–352a8, where Aristotle makes the river responsible for the silting which led to the building up of marshes around the Delta. Proclus' idea here is simply that the Delta is not really part of Egypt proper, but an addition that is subject to slightly different conditions.

[507] Festugière's note on this long-debated topic of natural philosophy is particularly full. Increasing knowledge of these regions in later antiquity meant that the debate had continued to develop.

[508] = *in Tim.* fr. XIV Sodano.

214

Atlantis

an ancient doctrine of the Egyptians that the water spouted up[509] from below at the rising of the Nile, for which reason they called the Nile 'the sweat of the earth'. That it should **rise up from below** for Egypt and 'save us by its release' (22d6) does not signify that the release of snow makes the quantity of water, but that it is released from its own source and proceeds into full view when it was previously contained. We, however, shall understand the term 'release' as relating to the difficulty. For the statement that the Nile 'releases' us from the difficulty is in Attic. It is neither true that the Nile expands because snows are 'released' (for where in the tropics, from which it flows, will snow congeal?), nor that the parts beneath the earth rise up as [the ground] is rarefied (for the rarefaction of the ground does not bestow on water the property of rising upward, but there must in any case be something to push it out of the caverns into the air above). So much for the Egyptian theory. Others say that the Nile expands as a result of certain rains that flow off into it, something explicitly stated by Eratosthenes. So this is not what **rising up** signifies here, its spouting up from somewhere underneath, but rather that the water is increased from another source and flows above [the level of] the ground as water dashes down into it from other places.

Iamblichus[510] says that one should not look for any such meaning, but that one should understand the water's **rising up** from below in a more straightforward manner, in the same sense as we use 'swelling'.[511] However, when he offers a reason why the Egyptians escape both droughts and floods, it is clear that he endorses the [theory of] expansion owing to rain. He states that the primary cause[512] of the salvation of the Egyptians is the will of the gods who have been allocated them and creation's original determination, while the secondary cause is the climate. For the seasons are opposite among those who dwell on the opposite side (of the tropics),[513] from whose land the Nile flows into our part of the

---

509 We meet here the particularly rare form *anablusthainô* that also occurs at 120.7 below; it is found also in a scholion on this lemma. Other versions of this verb are similarly scarce.

510 Fr. 13 Dillon, concluding at 120.21.

511 I.e. as flooding; since the term *anabasis* is little more explicit than *epanodos*, and still captures the notion of upward movement, I am reluctant to use any term as explicit as Festugière's *crue*.

512 We have here a different version of the distinction between primary causes and auxiliary causes encountered already at 2.29–3.4, with the first cause here including a final element, and the secondary cause a material element.

513 See Festugière's long note. These are separate from the antipodeans, who not only have the seasons reversed, but also night and day, living diagonally opposite to the world around the Mediterranean, rather than due south of it.

215

On the *Timaeus* of Plato: Book I

world, and the times at which drought and rainfall occur among them are reversed.

If somebody[514] criticizes this doctrine on the grounds that expanding waters that are swollen by rain are without any regular order, we should mention that though fluctuations[515] in [the level of] the Nile often do occur too, nevertheless the *continuity* of the rains is the cause of the *unrelenting* expansion of its waters, together with the magnitude of the mountain range where the sources of the Nile are located. When these mountains receive the rains from the clouds that are squeezed upon them by the etesian winds, they cause a flow over all their slopes into the headwaters, and they fill up the river and cause its expansion. For Theophrastus says that this too is one of the causes of rain, the compression of the clouds against some of the mountains. Moreover, it is still not at all remarkable that clouds should not be seen in the region of the Catadupa,[516] because it is not from these that the Nile first comes, but from the Mountains of the Moon, so-called because of their height, and from the clouds that are gathered upon them, which bypass the Catadupa but cling to those [mountains] as they are higher. This much is our reply to the *Egyptian Discourse* of Aristides.[517]

Eratosthenes, though, says that one should no longer even inquire into the expansion of the Nile, for certain people are actually known to have come to the sources of the Nile and seen the rains that occur; and so Aristotle's theory is confirmed. So we give this brief overview of this topic, and it is on this basis that the story of the Egyptians claims that neither conflagration nor [total] inundation happens to them.

All the same, it would not be surprising for this to fail,[518] if Aristotle[519] is right to say that in the infinity of time every part of the earth is turned to sea, and that the same place happens to be dry land at one time and sea at another. Hence even in the case of the Nile he did not rule out that the water should fail, having regard for the infinity of time. For what if, because the etesian winds were to blow more gently, they did

[514] Aristides, as we see at 121.7; the doctrine is therefore that of Eratosthenes rather than of Iamblichus.

[515] *Apobasis*; I resist Festugière's explanation here, when he translates 'baisses de niveau' (falls in level) on the grounds that the key term in Iamblichus' explanation is *anabasis*, applied to the rising level of the Nile, so that this term ought to signify something to do with its rising also. It makes sense that Proclus should be answering Aristides partly with the counter-claim that the level of the Nile is not quite as regular as is claimed.

[516] The First Cataract of the Nile.

[517] Aelius Aristides 36.23–6, quoted by Festugière on p. 163 n.1.

[518] It is remarkable here that Festugière is content to have Proclus again return to Aristides' objection, and to translate *ekleipein* with 'il y a manque de l' eau'. The reference is to the immunity from fire or flood that the Egyptians boast of.

[519] Pseudo-Aristotle in the *De Mundo* 400a6.

216

Atlantis

not push the clouds into that region? What if the mountains against which the clouds gather were to collapse, with that wind, by which the Oracle says cities too are destroyed men and all, ripping them from their ground-level locations? Without that wind the river will constantly diminish and come to a halt,[520] as it is absorbed by the ground owing to its aridity.

Temperate climate and continuity of human occupation

Yet in fact, in all places where a violent winter or summer does not prevent it, there is constantly a race of humans, sometimes greater sometimes less. (22e5–23c1)

Mention has already been made of the cosmic cycles,[521] and of the various deviations,[522] [noting] that salvation is possible for the Egyptians as a result of the position of the land and the Nile's providential care.[523] So now he draws a general inference of the following kind about the places of the earth. Every place that is not flooded or consumed by fire always has **a race of humans**, greater or smaller, left to survive.[524] For the greatest cases of destruction are through fire and water, as stated earlier (22c2). Yet someone might claim that **a race of humans** could peter out in other ways too, [arguing that] the inhabitants of particular areas of Attica no longer exist, even though there has been neither inundation nor conflagration – rather some terrible act of impiety that has completely obliterated human life.[525] Perhaps one should interpret **places** as 'climatic region', so that he is claiming that every climatic region has **a race of humans** unless inundation or conflagration occurs, sometimes more, **sometimes less**. But some people could be saved even during an inundation, as Deucalion [was saved] from the climatic region across Greece that was inundated. At least, that is the tale that certain people tell.

But as my companion[526] noticed, Plato could claim that every climatic region of the earth that is neither too icy nor too oppressively

---

520 Reading the future μενεῖ in place of the present of Diehl and Festugière.

521 For Plato see 22c1–d3, and for the commentary 105.3–12 as well as 116.1–21 (with Festugière).

522 See now 22d1–3 and 114.25–115.28.

523 For the particular conditions that save the Egyptians see 22d5–6, with Proclus' comments at 118.1–13, where the term 'providence' is used in this context at 118.11.

524 The verb *perileipomai*, occurring in Plato at 23c1.

525 Festugière is surely right to think in terms of Christian atrocities against pagans, though we do not have to follow him in understanding *tousde* to be referring to the whole of Attica!

526 Domninus was so described at 109.31.

217

On the *Timaeus* of Plato: Book 1

hot always has people, in greater or lesser numbers. For the mathematicians[527] also say that some places are uninhabited on account of an excess of heat or cold. So every place and every climatic region suitable for human habitation has a greater or lesser number of people, and this too is arguable and in accord with the details of our text, for **where a violent winter or summer does not prevent it** appears to signify 'where an excess of one or the other of the opposites does not prevent it'. And overall, since he first said that the tales of the Egyptians are the oldest (22e5), he had good reason to add that in fact, every climatic region compatible with human habitation constantly has humans, either more or less. Indeed not only the mathematicians speak about not every climatic region of the earth having humans, but also Orpheus, when he makes this distinction:

> But for men he determined that they
> Should inhabit a seat far removed from the gods, where the Sun's
> Axle turns on a moderate approach, and is neither too sharp
> With its overhead frost, nor with fire, but between these extremes.[528]

This is what Plato now said, that **where a violent winter or summer** is not [found] there is a greater or lesser **race of humans**. But that a loss of memory occurs among other ancient peoples, not because humans die out, but because, as continual destructive events occur, a variety of illiterate and uncultured people are left behind. With us,[529] however, many very ancient tales are told because of everything being recorded in the temples.

The preservation of memory and its universal counterpart

Whatever happens in your country or here or in another place that we hear about, at least if it's something noble or grand that took place, or with something special about it, has all been written down from antiquity here in the temples, and kept safe. (23a1–5)

Just as both the position of the country and the god who has been allocated it provided preservation for the Egyptians, so too, with regard to the preservation of history, firstly they achieve it through their own diligent study, through which they control the forgetfulness that

---

[527] The term now generally referred to astrologers, though we are expecting this to be an aspect of geographical theory, but as Festugière notes, the two could be easily combined, as they had been in Claudius Ptolemaeus.

[528] = *Orph. fr.* 94 Kern.

[529] Proclus is paraphrasing the words of the Egyptian priests.

218

Atlantis

comes with time; and secondly they are well assisted by the temples in their midst, upon which they inscribe all great and remarkable deeds, whether their own or belonging to others, and the unexplained results of their undertakings – for this is the meaning of **or with something special about it**. The historical study of these things contributes to their recognition of similar patterns, as a result of which the recollection of universals occurs,[530] and towards the prediction of the future. For it is through such watchful investigation that they discover the powers productive of heavenly figures, because, when they grasp what has occurred in which circumstances, they are able to calculate the causes of what will come to be from the same signs.

It seems to me also that the discourse (*logos*) of the Pythagoreans, which prepares souls to recollect their former lives as well, imitates this historical study of the Egyptians. For just as in the case of one man – or one soul rather – duty requires that he grasp his different lives, so too in the case of one race it requires that they grasp their different cycles. So as among the former[531] the recollection of their previous existences is perfective of their souls, so too among the latter the historical study of earlier cycles contributes very greatly to their perfection in wisdom. Furthermore such watchful investigation also assimilates them to the arrangement of the All, since they are imitating the established formal principles of nature, through whose changeless permanence order falls to changing things too.

If then the most sacred of temples is the cosmos, in which the formal principles that conserve the All are eternally fixed, the recording of ancient deeds in their temples would involve an image of the conservation of this world. What the story of the Egyptians would be saying is that whereas everything in the sensible world that is stable, strong, and ever in the same state originates from the intelligible gods, everything that moves in different ways at different times, coming into being and passing away, derives from the new creation. What is more, their priestly caste that retains the memory of ancient deeds involves an image of the permanent divine order that conserves the Whole and guards all within the divine memory. Deriving fullness from this [memory],[532] the new creation also sheds the light of sameness, coherence, and stability upon unstable things.

---

[530] Festugière aptly compares 102.31–3.

[531] The contrast remains one between individual men and races.

[532] Festugière takes the feminine noun to be understood here to be the order (*taxis*), but the section, dealing as it does with the preservation of memory, is rounded off better if it is memory (*mnêmê*) which must be tapped by the new creation.

On the *Timaeus* of Plato: Book 1

Several lemmata more briefly considered (Tim. 23a5–d1)

30

> **But your [business] and that of the others has always recently**
> **come to be furnished with writings and everything else that cities need.**
> **(23a5–7)**

125

This 'furnishing'[533] is a symbol for the cause that is always fashioning things new, producing what does not yet exist, and harmonizing all things with a view to the united perfection of the cosmos. In households too,

5   you see, we call the provision of all things necessary their 'furnishings'. In cities writings fall into this category, and skills, markets, baths and all such things, but in the universe it is everything admitting a temporal and partial composition. So just as the temples[534] signify the receptacles of the eternal formal principles and the powers that maintain and protect,

10 so these **cities** indicate the foundations of the ever-changing, composed of many dissimilar perishable components. The histories of those who have written about discoveries, by attributing the acts of discovery to certain people born not long ago, show that the establishment of such things (I mean writings and skills) is more recent.

15

> **And again, after the customary number of years the torrent from heaven**
> **comes rushing upon them <like> a plague.**   (23a7–8)

This also is clear as far as humans are concerned. For it is inundations that destroy races, set in motion by the circuits of the heaven, with water as

20 their matter. Hence this whole [class of events] is called a **torrent from heaven** and **like a plague**, because that is something else destructive (what is 'destructive' is bad for the part, but good for the whole).[535] [He says] **after the customary number of years**, because even such cases of destruction are accomplished in accordance with certain cycles, cycles

25 that also have some correspondence with the entire cycle of the divinity that came to be.[536] This further point also seems to be indicated through these words, that all those things that come about only from universal [causes] are necessarily accomplished according to cosmic cycles determined by the same number, whereas all those that happen as a result of

30 partial causes do not turn out the same in all respects, though the same cyclical patterns take place.

---

[533] Proclus' *kataskeuê* picks up 'furnished' (*kateskeuasmena*) in the lemma.

[534] *Tim.* 23a5, cf. 124.16–19.

[535] Proclus is anticipating the observation that one phrase implies a heavenly origin of the floods, while the other implies that these same events are an evil, and cautiously clarifying the extent to which it can be evil. In so doing he refers to the doctrine of *Laws* 903b–e that local evils are for the preservation of the whole.

[536] I.e. the universe, cf. *Tim.* 92c.

220

Atlantis

As far as the All is concerned, you could observe the same lesson by bearing in mind that all things that come to be are destroyed and succumb to cosmic cycles and to the revolutions of life as a whole, and that the cycles join up with one another and accomplish a single continuous life.

126

And it has left only the illiterate and uncultured of you, *up to* **all the things there had been in ancient times.** (23a8–b3)

He stated that following the inundation cowherds and shepherds are left, while those in the cities perish. So those left behind are **illiterate** and **uncultured**, and because of the former they do not have the ability to hand down the events of the previous cycle to memory[537] through writing, while because of the latter they happen to be incapable of preserving what they had previously lived through in hymns and poetry. Hence it is reasonable that they should come to be in a state of forgetfulness about everything, and in their forgetfulness wheel back round[538] to the life of children. For Aristotle claims that in respect of their life 'one immature in age in no way differs' from them.[539] A rather similar thing happens to those souls that are descending into generation.[540] As they exchange their previous intellective cycle for a second generation-producing one, they experience forgetfulness of the intelligibles on account of the inundation produced by matter, and any impressions of them they have as a result of their observation of them they lose as time goes on. In this way all things within the cosmos wheel back round through rebirth from old age to youthfulness, being carried on a

5

10

15

20

---

[537] I.e. the collective memory.

[538] The distinctive verb *anakamptô*, found here at 126.13 and just below at 126.22, owes something to *Phd.* 72b3–4 (along with the noun *kampê*), the only point of the Platonic corpus where it occurs; this might suggest that the commentary tradition is here drawing on an ultimate source that discusses Plato's ideas on the soul, possibly (as we see below) Numenius and/or Porphyry. The verb, not found in Diehl's index, is also found in a Porphyrian context at *in Tim.* II. 309.21 (= Porph. *in Tim.* fr. lxxvi.17 Sodano), though I find it elsewhere in Porphyry only once, at *Harm.* 31.10. It is notable for its presence in Damasc. *in Phd.* (six times, but is also found in his *Parmenides* commentary (5 times), as also in that of Proclus (5 times between 1122 and 1189). Total occurrences in Proclus number fourteen, several of these having a geometrical context; the total in *in Tim.* is only five. We have already met 28.26, we find two cases here, there is the Porphyrian passage, and a final passage at III. 92.11.

[539] Following Festugière, one could clarify Proclus' meaning and translate what Aristotle writes at *EN* 1095a6–7 (that one immature in character in no way differs from one young in age) rather than the elliptical Greek of the Proclan MSS, but there is no need to do so.

[540] This is surely a comment deriving from that part of the tradition that connected the Atlantis myth with the descent of souls, i.e. with Numenius (77.3–6) or Porphyry (77.6–24); the term 'generation-producing' (*genesiourgos*) in the next sentence was already associated with Numenius at 77.4.

On the *Timaeus* of Plato: Book 1

variety of paths at different times because their nature is to have the form
25 in motion. Moreover, the fact that when changes occur **the illiterate
and uncultured** should be left behind gives an indication, examined
from the perspective of physics,[541] that it is right down to the formless
and shapeless condition that the dissolution and the destruction of the
elements occur (something indicated by the term **illiterate**).[542] Also that
a breakdown of the harmony[543] takes place, something that the gods who
30 preside over the rejuvenation will easily heal and restore to its natural
state.

127 **Certainly the genealogies presently on offer, which you told us about
your people, are scarcely any different from children's stories.** (23b3–5)

The Egyptian compares the solemn and ancient narratives of Solon with
5 childish stories. For the stories of the wise concern eternal happenings,
while those of children concern minor temporal matters; and the former have a hidden truth that is intellective, while the latter have one
that is down to earth and gives no indication of anything elevated.[544]
So Solon's historical accounts correspond to myths of this latter kind,
10 those of the Egyptians to those of the wise, since the former histories
have a very limited field of view, and the latter have a very extensive
one; the former are simply histories, the latter contribute to scientific
knowledge.

Beginning with these [two kinds] we should consider their paradigms,
15 [noting] that things proceeding from the new creation are called 'play-
things of the gods'[545] and resemble myths. For they are images of realities

[541] This suggests a switch to Iamblichan material, since Iamblichus insists on relating all
material in the introduction to the target inquiry, i.e. to the study of the natural world
(e.g. 117.18–20 = *in Tim*. fr. 12 Dillon; cf. especially 19.27–9, the sequel to fr. 3). It is
usual for material on Iamblichus' physical interpretations to follow an ethical account
from Porphyry, often with a focus on souls, as 116.27–9 and 171.17–23 (= Iambl. *in
Tim*. fr. 22 Dillon).

[542] It is important that the term for the elements (*stoicheia*) is identical with the term for
the letters of the alphabet.

[543] Proclus has now moved on to comment on the term translated 'uncultured' , which
means literally 'muse-less', and can thus be interpreted as 'unmusical'. Festugière's
translation becomes contorted because of his failure to see this distinction between
Iamblichus' comments on the two separate words.

[544] It is important that Proclus' remarks here are not mistakenly applied to *Greek* myths in
general, which are usually taken as offering a deep meaning as well as a superficial one.
The Neoplatonic view of myth is well summed up at Olymp. *in Gorg*. 46.2–6, which
has parallels in Proclus *On the Republic*. The *literary* myths from Homer and elsewhere
would here be viewed as myths of the wise.

[545] The image derives from *Laws* 803c (cf. 644d), where humans are such a plaything.
Proclus extends Plato's image to apply to all products of the new creation; cf. 334.7–10
where the same idea is dressed in slightly different terms.

222

Atlantis

and participate in the forms at the final stage. But things that owe their initial foundation to the intelligibles are intellective and eternal and static, and have their being hidden away.

You who firstly remember a single inundation of the earth, though there have been many before. (23b5–6) 20

The Greeks talked incessantly of Deucalion's flood though many others had taken place before, as the Egyptian says. Correspondingly, among wholes, the new creation brings wholes to completion in a partial and reduplicated manner, and by means of regeneration sets the present situation aright, whereas in the intelligibles the causes of the first foundation and cyclic return of specific forms are already assumed in a unitary fashion.[546] 25

Moreover, of the finest and most excellent race among humans in your own land, *up to* **died without a voice in writing.** (23b6–c3) 30

He wants the second cycle to link up with the former, and [he wants] there to be a single continuous life of the Athenians, the first ones and those now, through the **slender seed** of which he speaks. For in the cosmos too the final stages of the former cycle link up with the beginnings of the[547] one after it on account of the substantive existence (*ousia*) of the causes, the unceasing motion of the all, and 'the unchanging change', as someone puts it.[548] **128** 5

Let us not be surprised that while he himself says at this point that Solon is a *descendant* of those **excellent** men, we relate him to the *cause* of the whole cosmic rivalry.[549] For as a living creature he owes his origins to them, but as a particular intellect, receiving the tales (*logoi*) of the war, he corresponds to the divine being that conveys[550] the principles (*logoi*) of cosmic conflict from the intelligibles to the sensible world. Further, one should not be confused by objections of this kind, but recognize the nature of analogies – that in analogies the same things are used as the first, last, and middle terms. 10

---

[546] In this difficult sentence 'wholes' would appear to be species, which are restored periodically in the new creation as many duplicated parts of the whole, but the paradigms of each and patterns of its regeneration have a single existence in the intelligible world.

[547] Festugière corrects the dative plural of the article to the genitive singular, giving natural Greek.

[548] We do not know who, as Festugière is able to dismiss Diehl's alleged parallel.

[549] For earlier discussion of what Solon symbolizes see 88.1–8, 91.27–92.11; the objection is that Solon is seen by Plato as a descendant, but Proclus' interpretation requires him to be viewed as an ancestor.

[550] The verb *diaporthmeuô* recurs in relation to Solon and to the 'intermediate orders' at 133.23–4.

On the *Timaeus* of Plato: Book 1

15   Indeed, Solon, back beyond the greatest destruction by water, the city that is now the Athenians' was once the most excellent in war and in all things exceptionally lawful. To that city were said to belong the finest
20   deeds and finest constitutions of any beneath the heaven that we have received word of. (23c3–d1)

By **greatest destruction** he means not the one in Deucalion's time, but presumably one of the inundations that had occurred previously. He described the city of the Athenians as very warlike and **excep-**
25   tionally lawful as one that takes after its presiding goddess, whom he will shortly describe (24d1) as philosophic and war-loving. They get their warlike quality from her love of war, and their lawfulness from her philosophic quality. By **finest deeds** is meant the victory against the Atlantines, while [he uses the plural] **finest constitutions** not
30   because it had several in succession, but because one could call the single
129   system the sum of several systems of government, in the same way as one would say that the single cosmic arrangement embraces many arrange-ments. For if the life of each man is a kind of constitution, while the combined life is an association of many particular living creatures, it would be a unification of many constitutions according to one principle: the fine.

5   [He says] of any under the heaven that we have received word of, because it is the first imitation of the constitution of the cosmos, so that one could say that it is the best of those under the heaven. For its paradigm is in the heaven. That's what we have to say about the separate phrases.

The question of the status of the story resumed

But we should again remind ourselves about this entire business con-
10   cerning the Athenians, that it is neither a myth that is being related nor a straightforward historical study.[551] Some understand the account only

---

[551] Proclus takes up material from 75.30–76.21, giving more fully argued positions than he had given there, and in a different order. In this case the argument for a literal interpretation is clearly offered in opposition to an already popular allegorical inter-pretation, and bears no resemblance to anything earlier attributed to Crantor. Of those post-Numenian figures used by Proclus, it is clearly Longinus who took the most lit-eral approach to the Platonic text, and that this applies to the Atlantis story is evident from 162.15–27 (= Longinus fr. 36). That we should trace these arguments to him is confirmed by the language of seduction (ψυχαγωγία) in relation to Proclus' third point (129.19–20), for this had already occurred at 59.28 (Longinus fr. 28.20) and 83.23 (fr. 32.5), which directly concerns the purpose of the Atlantis story. Cf. also Longinus fr. 48.22.

224

Atlantis

as history, others as a myth. And some say that, firstly, the allegorical unveiling[552] of these and similar tales appears to Plato to be 'for a hard-working person who is somewhat wide of the mark'.[553] Secondly, Plato's communicative method is not of the same riddling sort as Pherecydes',[554] but gives clear teaching on very many points of doctrine – so one should not be forced into explaining it away when the man is proposing to teach us directly. Thirdly, that an allegorical unveiling of the story is not necessary in the present circumstances, since there is an acknowledged reason for the presentation of this narrative – the seduction of the listeners.[555] And further, fourthly, if we explain away everything, then we shall suffer the same fate as those who waste time with tricky minutiae of Homer.

Others,[556] however, base their view on the story of Phaethon, of which Plato says that it 'takes the shape of a myth, whereas its true reference' is to something else, one of the things that happens in the natural world; and they think it right to trace this story back to its connection with nature. For the Egyptians too, whom he makes the fathers of this story, put the secrets of nature into riddles through myths, so that the allegorical unveiling of this narrative would also suit the character who is telling it. Just as Timaeus himself will set forth his arguments in the way that is proper to Pythagorean philosophy, by interpreting nature through numbers and shapes as if through images, so too the Egyptian priest would be teaching the truth of things through symbols, the manner that is proper to himself.

---

[552] An ἀνάπτυξις is literally an 'opening up', and sometimes an 'explanation'. In 'allegorical unveiling' I seek to combine both notions, at the same time as capturing the rarity of this term, found only here (129.15, 19, 30) and at III. 29.13. Interestingly, while Proclus does more often use the verb ἀναπτύσσω, the verb that corresponds here is ἀναλύω, 129.18, 22.

[553] Quoting *Phaedrus* 229d4, where Socrates himself discusses attempts to explain away myths in an allegorical manner.

[554] Diehl refers to Pherecydes fr. 4.6, and this fragment had seemed to be a text Porphyry had in mind at 77.15 above, hence this may be Longinus' attempt to dampen Porphyry's enthusiasm for allegorical interpretation. Only here and at II. 54.28 does Proclus refer to Pherecydes by name.

[555] Clearly Longinus' view of the story, see 83.23 (fr. 32.5).

[556] It is difficult to say whether Proclus has in mind Amelius, Numenius, or Porphyry (76.17–77.24), though the first point would suit Numenius' approach to Plato in *On the Good*, which proceeds via Pythagoras and respected beliefs in other cultures including Egypt (fr. 1a); while the second point better fits those who give pride of place to Plato, interpreting Plato through Plato, and hence perhaps comes from Porphyry. Certainly Porphyry is often the source of the last view considered before that of Iamblichus, whom we know from 77.24–80.7 to have taken this general line.

On the *Timaeus* of Plato: Book 1

In addition to this even Plato himself elsewhere[557] censured those who were saying everything straight off, so that even to the cobblers, as he says, they may make their wisdom obvious. Consequently discourse that communicates truth in riddles is not foreign to Plato. This is what either side says.

Let us say that all this is both a historical study and an indication of the cosmic rivalry and the universal order, relating things that have happened among humans, but symbolically including within it the revolutions[558] in the All and the cosmic rivalry. For from the first intelligibles at the top level[559] came the procession by juxtaposition, and it divided the cosmos according to opposing powers. If you wish, let us divide the All also in the theological manner according to the divine orders in turn, and let us see the coordinated ranks in Pythagorean fashion. At the level of the two principles, then, there is a division into Limit and Unlimited, or rather into things akin to Limit and Unlimited, because of composite things some are on the former side, some on the latter. At the level after that, which has a threefold aspect, there is a division into things unified and things multiplied, for it is at that point first of all that there is multiplicity, in a unified way. At the level of the next triad there is a division into things eternal and things perishable, since for all things the measure of their existence comes from there. At the level of the third [triad] there is a division into male and female, for it is in this triad that they appear for the first time. At the level of the first triad of intermediates there is a division into odd and even, for that is where unitary number appears. At the level of the second there is a division into whole and partial, and at the third into straight and circular. Again, of intellective things at the first level there is a division into

---

[557] The reference is to *Tht.* 180d3–5, where 'Socrates' contrasts the new Heraclitean simplicity with the cautious concealment of the ancient poets who, according to them, were embracing the same doctrines. This fairly obscure passage of Plato, alluded to only here in this commentary, would have become of interest as soon as the poets were treated as in some sense 'Orphic', providing a text that shows Plato's approval for the ancient manner in which Orphic theology had been presented. The passage is easily associated with the Heraclitean etymologies of Ocean and Tethys at *Cratylus* 402b-d, where Orphic verses are actually cited in support. Note that Proclus introduces *Crat.* 402 and other Orphic texts into a discussion of Tethys (*Tim.* 40e) at III. 179.8–30.

[558] I suspect that the text is corrupt at this point, and that a verb indicating cyclic motion such as περιιόντα is to be supplied for περιέχοντα. As things stands the second, seemingly unrelated occurrence of the same participle gives rise to suspicion, as well as defying a reasonable translation. Festugière is clearly puzzled at this point, and the vulgate tradition had already provided its own tradition by reading the middle περιεχόμενα.

[559] See 78.6–8 above (= Iamblichus fr. 7 Dillon); the opposition is traced particularly to the Dyad that follows the One.

226

Atlantis

things in themselves and things in others, at the second level into things animate and inanimate, standing still and moving, and at the third level into things same and other. At the level of hegemonic principles there is a division into things delighting in similarity and things akin to dissimilarity, at the level of independent principles into separated and unseparated, <at the level of encosmic things into things equal and unequal>.[560]

Well, these things have been set out in order elsewhere, and may this now be the 'historical account', as it were, that we give of them.[561] For at every division the goodness of the better, in its desire to fill the inferior level and to remove its imperfections, brings about the war, while the desire of the worse to draw to itself a share of the better provokes manifest opposition. For in [human] wars too those who struggle against one another want to subdue their enemies' [forces] and get them entirely out of their way. That much is clear. Yet one should conceive the opposition of universal powers in the following way, employing a division into things arranging and things arranged. First of all [divide] into super-substantial things and substances, for the whole race of the gods is super-substantial. Next [divide] substances also into eternal lives and those that operate in time, and of those that operate in time [make a division] into souls and bodies, and of bodies into those in the heaven and those in generation, and of the latter into wholes and parts. For division goes on to the last levels.

Furthermore, of the super-substantial things [make a division] into the divine attributes, like male and female, odd and even, unifying and dividing, static and moving.[562]

And of eternal things [make a division] into whole and partial substances, and of wholes into divine and angelic ones, and again of souls into divine ones and their attendants, and of the divine ones into heavenly ones and those that make provision for generation, and of those that are in attendance on the gods into those that are eternally ranked alongside them and those that are constantly seceding, and those that

---

[560] The text at this point has been supplemented by Diehl in accordance with Proclus' other discussions of the metaphysical levels, particularly in *Plat. Theol.*, with some help from scholia. The necessity that encosmic principles should appear may be seen from 167 13 and 269.28–30.

[561] It is clearly intended that the sort of account that Proclus gives should be analogous to the quasi-historical account of cosmic opposition supposedly given by the priest, and there is no need for Festugière's surprise or Kroll's emendation. For the reconstruction of Proclus' metaphysical hierarchy see now Opsomer (2000, 2001b).

[562] As Festugière notes, this might more correctly have been inserted at 131.18; as in its present position it interrupts the progressive division of substances.

On the *Timaeus* of Plato: Book 1

secede into those that stand immaculate in the face of generation and those that are corrupted. The descent continues to this point.

5 Of the heavenly bodies [make a division] into inerrant ones and planets, of these latter into those that move on a simple path and those that [move] on a complex path, and of those on a complex path into [divisions reflecting] the distinctive characters of their powers. Universal features of all the divisions mentioned are that which arranges, that which is arranged, that which fills and that which is filled. And if the task is not to look at a part, but to get a firm hold on an understanding of the Whole, one should postulate this rivalry everywhere – as it is in gods, intellects, souls, and bodies. At that [first] level it is limit and unlimited, in intellects it is sameness and otherness, in soul it is same and different, and in bodies heaven and generation. The second ones are always drawn up in dependence on the better ones.

That is why we say that this myth is useful also for the total study of nature, as, from the activities and movements [depicted], it gives an indication of the cosmic rivalry. For all those who have taught about nature begin with opposites and make these principles. As Plato knew this, he conveys to us the rivalry and the races in the All through symbols and riddles, [saying] what it is and how in accordance with the intellective activity of Athena the corresponding inferior things are placed below the better. So it was with good reason that Plato referred to both the **deeds** and the **constitutions** as the Athenians', because he knew that the same kind of proportionate relation (*analogia*) ran through all things. This relation was maintained by the new creation too, but also, far earlier, by the universal powers. Brought to fullness by these, it establishes the encosmic minds, souls, and bodies according to its own distinctive character.

Solon's request, the priest's response, and what they signify

So when he heard it, he said he was amazed and very keen indeed, requesting the priests to narrate to him next in detail all about the ancient citizens. (23d1–4)

In reality this too is peculiar to things divine, that secondary things cling fast to the first and are founded in their immaculate intellections, while the first, in their ungrudging power and goodness, cast the fullness that comes from themselves like a light upon the second. So amazement comes first, because in us too it is the origin of the cognition of the whole,[563] while among things divine it joins the subject of amazement

---

[563] Presumably an allusion to *Tht.* 155d2–5, rather than to Arist. *Metaph.* 982b12 and 983a13 to which Festugière refers us.

228

Atlantis

with its object. Hence those wise in divinity praise Thaumas too as a very great god,[564] who uses amazement to make the second things subject to the first. And there follows the insistent request, making ready what needs to participate in the more perfect goods.

So the priest said, 'This is not something we begrudge, Solon, but for your sake I shall tell you, and for that of your city, and above all as a favour for the goddess. (23d4–6)

Even through the language the story gives sufficient indication of the divine causes of the phenomena. Solon, as an Athenian, introduces reflective glimpses of the city's official goddess, insofar as he also holds out for a more complete intellection, while the priest, as if making a pronouncement from some inner sanctuary – for he is actually teaching what is inscribed upon the temples – also offers a representation of the orders intermediate between the new creation and the paternal cause of the whole. These orders transport the gift of the higher causes to the one below, filling the second in rank with the former as if from a kind of spring. And everything is being agreeably fulfilled by the speaker. For Solon is being perfected, the city is being commended, and the goddess is being hymned – and the upward path leads from Solon through the city as intermediary to the goddess, in imitation of the goddess's own power of reversion. It is true that even this has something good about it, to engage in one's activities for the perfection of things secondary, since it imitates[565] the providential care and overflowing power of the divine. More significant still is [acting] for the sake of the city, because it extends the activity wider and harnesses a greater power. But still more divine than this is to reach out and direct the entire narrative to the goddess, and to bring the whole narrative to a conclusion in her.[566] All these things suggest the ungrudging nature of the priest, not merely indicating the absence of envy, but also the readiness of the divine to bring forth good things.

Here again, however, let us not be secretly worried by these claims, that at one moment it is the priest, as the one who shapes the story, who is said to be reflecting a greater and more divine cause, while at another it is the Athenians, the ancestors of Solon more ancient than the people

---

[564] It is clear from 183.12–14 that we are dealing with an Orphic text (= fr. 118 Kern); cf. III. 186.23, 189.8.

[565] Accepting the μιμεῖται of Taylor, followed by Festugière, for the manuscript ποιεῖται which is unsatisfactory. The verb is prominent in this passage, appearing just before at 133.29 as well as at 135.16 and 136.6 as noted by Festugière

[566] Reading συντείνειν and καταλήγειν as active with Festugière

229

On the *Timaeus* of Plato: Book 1

of Sais:[567] the ones whom we rank at the level of the organizing causes of
15   universal rivalry. For, as far as their place *in the narrative* goes, that is the
rank they have, but as far as *the natural procession* is concerned, they bear
a likeness to certain higher and divine orders. And if you like, since the
whole creation and cosmic rivalry are subsumed within the father of the
20   universe, both the organizers and the organized, you could by analogy
find there too the paradigmatic cause of the Athenians in intellective
lives.

Digression on the peplos

Furthermore, the *peplos* too is a final image of universal rivalry. There
precedes it the actual deeds of the gods[568] both in the All and in their
25   productive and primary causes: where indeed they affirm that Athena
was made manifest along with her arms. Or rather the *peplos*, the work
of weaving which the goddess weaves along with her father,[569] is the
final stage, introducing an image of the cosmic war and of the creative
30   order coming from the goddess that proceeds into the All. But superior
to this is the [*peplos*] offered by Plato in words and in riddles about the
universal rivalry and Athenaic deeds,[570] which makes its own contribution to the total picture of creation, in the same way that the former
135   contributed to the procession of the goddess and the festival as a whole.
For the Panathenaea is an image of Athena's productive activity upon
the All. Higher than both of these is the [*peplos*] woven in the All by
the intellective light of Athena, for the rivalry underlies the single life
5   of the All, and part of the creation is the war that Athena's generalship
directs in a proper fashion. Before all of these things is the [*peplos*] that is

---

[567] Festugière's long note shows how the ancient Athenians are regularly held superior to
the people of Sais.

[568] Proclus knew that the *peplos* represented the battle of the gods with the giants, 85.14–
16; his path back from the representations on the *peplos* to the deeds of the gods is
perhaps inspired by *Euthphr.* 6b–c, where discussion of the deeds of the mythical gods
prompts mention of the images embroidered on the *peplos* at the Great Panathenaea;
Proclus would no doubt have taken Euthyphro's acceptance of all stories told about the
gods with rather more seriousness than we should today, making him inclined towards a
'dramatic' reading in which everything said is potentially the source of serious messages.

[569] A strange inclusion from the point of view of mythology, but her father is of course a
demiurgic power.

[570] Festugière takes the adjective *Athenaikos* at this point to mean Athena's, the deeds of
the goddess rather than the inhabitants, but Plato's words have both a *riddling lesson* and
a *straightforward meaning*, so that it is both about one war and one victorious nation,
and at the same time about cosmic rivalry and the exploits of the entire Athenaic *seira*
('series').

Atlantis

pre-established among the paradigmatic causes in the intelligible world, which is contained within the single intellection of Athena.[571]

'For she is the most accomplished of all immortals at working on a loom', as Orpheus says.[572] So it is there that weaving initially appears and the web of this goddess's substance, which, in intelligible fashion, is all of the things that the All is in encosmic fashion. For when she presides over the universal war she focuses nowhere else but upon herself. 10

The symbolism resumed

But so that we may get back to our main purpose, the Egyptian is directly imitating the ungrudging and providential care of the Demiurge, concerning whom it will shortly be said (29e) that 'He was good, and for one that is good no envy ever arises in respect of anything.' For also the orders that come immediately after him get their ungrudging share of good things supplied from him and because of him. And it is because of this liberality that he brings Solon's idea to fullness, praises the city, and hymns the city's official divinity, joining things partial with things whole, uniting things maintained with their maintainers, and joining all things belonging to the goddess with a single bond in a single series. 15 20 25

Who drew as her lot both your land and this one, and nourished and educated them. (23d6–7)

It is amazing how the Egyptian makes everything revert to the goddess, to proceed from her, and to revert to her once again. For by working back from the citizen, through the city, to the official civic goddess, he was carrying out a kind of reversion here, while by moving from the goddess to the things that have both primary and secondary participation in her, he imitates the procession from her. But further, by postulating that participants are both **nourished and educated** by the goddess he made them revert again to her.[573] Surely this is an amazing imitation of the 30

136

5

---

[571] We have here five levels of rivalry's being manifested in some kind of *peplos*:

1. An intelligible *peplos* within the intellection of Athena
2. Rivalry on the intellective plain woven by Athena's own creative power
3. The Panathenaic Festival that physically re-enacts the rivalry in (2)
4. Plato's account of rivalry on earth that alludes to (2) in riddles
5. The pictures on the physical *peplos* depicting rivalry within the natural world.

The five might be said to belong to thought, craft, deeds, *logoi*, and images.

[572] *Orph. fr.* 178 Kern, quoted more fully at *in Crat.* 53, 21.25–6.
[573] We had in the previous lemma the sequence (1) citizen, city, goddess (d5–d6), and in this one (2) goddess, Athenians, Egyptians and (3) this further twofold process.

231

On the *Timaeus* of Plato: Book 1

creative powers, which are themselves founded in the things that precede them, and, regarding what comes after them, both engender them and get them to revert to their own causes.[574]

General digression on cosmic divisions and divine lots[575]

While that will do for these matters, whatever is meant by **drew as her lot**? And how are the gods said to divide up the All?[576] Of lots then, some belong to individual souls, others to the immaculate races, others are demonic, others angelic, while some belong to the gods themselves. For if there were just one single father of all, one providence, and one law, then there would be no need for lots or for a distribution between

[574] The engendering is thought of as a procession away from their causes.

[575] Regardless of the overall importance to Proclus, and to other Neoplatonists interested in theurgy and astrology, of the notions that particular gods, identifiable with those of the ancient Pantheon, had special connections with regions of the heavens and the earth alike, it is clearly difficult to postulate a literal as well as a metaphorical meaning of the Atlantis story without taking for granted the connection of gods like Athena and Poseidon with particular cities or peoples. Also relevant is the connection of individual persons with individual divine leaders in the myth of the *Phaedrus* (248a–c, 250b, 252c–d, 253a–c), along with other passages of Plato and relevant authors that postulate a divine influence or presence within any part of the sublunary world. Hence we have a digression lasting until 142.10, designed to explain the everlasting presence of the heavenly within the changing world of our experience.

[576] The notion of an allocation by the drawing of lots naturally causes Proclus to think of the myth according to which Zeus, Poseidon, and Hades *divide* between them the heaven, the sea, and the underworld, retaining Olympus and earth as common property, a myth best known from Homer, *Iliad* 15.187–99 (quoted in part by Proclus below). But there are other reasons why, for him, the idea of divine lots comes naturally. We shall see below various divisions that could in Proclus' time be said to concern the allotted spheres of influence belonging to various divine powers. The allocation of a divinity to the heaven in particular could apply even to Proclus' Christian and Jewish opponents, and this leads to the *twin* lots below; the Homeric division is *triple*; in Empedocles, seen by Proclus and others as a Pythagorean (e.g. Olymp. *in Gorg.* proem 9 (with Jackson, Lycos and Tarrant (1998), 63 n.44), 30.5; several Neoplatonic passages are discussed by Mansfeld 1992, 245–62; cf. below 136.29–30). The gods' names were readily used for the *four* elements (DK 31B6), and a Platonist might find it natural to extend this to the *five* regular solids (*Tim.* 55d). Gods' names were also used as today to distinguish the planets Mercury, Venus, Mars, Jupiter and Saturn, and Sun and Moon, being likewise divine, made *seven*. The twelve signs of the zodiac invited speculation about a correspondence with the traditional number of the Olympians, endorsed by Plato in the myth of the *Phaedrus* (246e–247a), the text most important for the establishment of the Neoplatonist theory of various divine series, each dependent on a different god. So we should think of the 'lots' of the gods as their allocated spheres of influence, within the heaven or below it. There is no hint in Proclus that such an allocation could involve chance, as would normally be the case with the terminology of lotteries.

Atlantis

gods. But since after the one [father] there is a triad,[577] and after the uniform providence a varied one, and after the one law the multitude of laws of fate,[578] there must also be a division of things governed, and a different providential power and different duty for different groups. So it is for this reason that the All has been divided by the creational numbers: dyad, triad, tetrad, pentad, hebdomad, dodecad. For after the single creation the division of the whole into TWO, heaven and generation, established twin lots, heavenly and generation-producing. After this that triad divided the All – the triad of which even Homer's Poseidon speaks the lines:

> Nay I drew as my lot the grey salt sea,
> And Zeus drew as his the broad heaven,
> While Hades took over the misty gloom.[579]

And after the triple cosmic arrangement is the fourfold distribution, making a fourfold disposition of the elements in the All, as the Pythagoreans say,[580] one in the heaven, one in the 'ether', one over the earth and one below it. After this comes the five-part [division], for the cosmos is one, established out of five parts, and divided up both by shapes and by their own gods in charge of them: heavenly, fiery, airborne, water-dwelling, and terrestrial. After this allotment comes the seven-part one. Starting up above with the inerrant sphere, the heptad wanders through all the components.[581] In addition to them all is the allocation of the universe along the lines of the dodecad.[582]

Linked with the divine lots are those of angels and daemons, with a more varied distribution, since a single divine lot is inclusive of several angelic lots, and of even more daemonic ones – as each angel also governs more daemons, and every angelic lot has more daemonic lots relating to it. For what the *monad* is among gods, this *a number* is among angels, and what *each* [*number*] is among the latter, this among daemons is a *tribe* corresponding to each. So instead of a triad we shall get three companies, and instead of the tetrad or dodecad four numbers and twelve choruses, each group following their own leader. In this way we shall always preserve a greater unity in the higher allotments. For, as in the case of substances, as in that of powers, as in that of activities,

---

[577] See on 9.15–22.
[578] As referred to at *Tim* 1.262–3.   [579] Homer, *Iliad* 15.190–2.
[580] Thinking presumably of Empedocles, who uses the term 'aether' rather than 'air' (B100.5), as Festugière notes, is the earliest extant exponent of four-element theory, and is known to Proclus as a Pythagorean (see n. on 136.10).
[581] 'Components' here = *stoicheia* in the astrological sense which relates to the seven planets.
[582] The twelve signs of the zodiac are referred to.

On the *Timaeus* of Plato: Book 1

processions engender a plurality, so too in the case of lots the very first [orders], while outstripped in quantity, are pre-eminent in power, because they are closer to the one father of all, and to the one overall providence. But the second [orders] are allocated both a reduction in power and an increase in the quantity. These are the general questions to be studied concerning lots.

However, since in the course of the division into two we divided lots into heavenly ones and sublunary ones, no account would have doubts concerning what the former are and whether they remain in the same condition forever, whereas it is right to be puzzled about the sublunary ones, whether one were to call them eternal or not. For if they happen to be eternal, how is this possible? For how, given that things in generation all change and are in flux, could the lots of those with concern for us be called eternal? For things in generation are not eternal. But if they are not eternal, how is the machinery of divine control not subject to conditions that change in time? The [drawing of the] lot is not some activity separate from the gods, so that we should say that this is an exception to these changing things, and that it remains unchanged. It is not just something under management – in which case it would be nothing odd that the lot should be in flux and subject to all sorts of change; but it is a god's business, his area of providential care over earthly things, and his unchecked [area of] control. Further, because of its being managed it does not conform to the definition of something eternal, whereas because of its being in charge[583] it defies destruction – so that we do not transfer the experiences of individual souls to the gods by giving them different lots at different times!

So what account that preserved the unchanging nature of the gods and the change of things in generation could interpret the **lot**, and explain how we should take it? Perhaps if we pursue that manner of investigation which we have often endorsed elsewhere too, our explanatory task will be easier – where we say that one should not believe that all things in generation and generation itself are solely derived from things in change that disappear in flux, but that there is something unchanging in these things too, and of a nature to remain ever in the same state. For the space that receives all the sectors of the cosmos and embraces them within it, and is stretched throughout everything bodily, is immobile, so that by being among things moved it should not

---

[583] Festugière is content to interpret ἐφεστώς as 'stable' (à cause de sa stabilité),, but the theme of divine control over the sublunary world runs throughout the discussion of this problem; see also ἐπιστασία at 138.4 and 10, as well as the terminology of management at 138.7 and 10.

Atlantis

itself require yet another place, with an unnoticed regress to infinity. 25
Moreover, the vehicles of ether belonging to divine bodies, in which
they have been clad, by imitation of the lives in heaven get a substance
that is eternal, and is everlastingly dependent on the divine souls, being
full of fertile power and engaging in a circular motion conforming to 30
a secondary circle of heavenly things.[584] Thirdly, moreover, the totality
of our four elements here remains the same, even though the parts are
destroyed in all sorts of ways. For it is necessary that each form should **139**
be unable to be lost from the whole, so that the All may be complete
and so that what derives from an unmoved cause should be unmoved
in its substance. Every totality is a form, or rather[585] it is that thing
which it is called by participation as a whole in one form. Observe how
the nature of the physical things has proceeded in an order. For the 5
first is free from all motion; the next has received locomotion alone –
this being the furthest removed from change in substance; the next admits
the other [motions] too within its parts, but as a whole remains entirely
unchanging.[586] The heavenly lots, involving the immediate division of 10
space, divided up the heaven too along with it. By way of contrast, the
sublunary lots partitioned those shares that are within space, secondly
carried out the distribution relating to the distinctive vehicles of souls,
and thirdly remain ever in the same condition qua entire parts of generation.[587] Hence the lots of the gods do not change, nor do they vary in 15
condition over time. That is because they do not have their foundation
directly among changing things.

Readiness for the reception of a god

So how is it that the luminary influence of the gods is found among
things here too? How does their residence in temples come about? How
is the same place occupied at different times by different spirits? Per- 20
haps it is the case that, while the gods have eternal lots and divide
up the earth according to divine numbers in the same manner as the
heavens are partitioned, things here too are illuminated to the extent
that they share the *readiness*. This readiness is brought about both by

---

[584] Festugière finds an allusion here to the circuit of the Other at *Tim.* 40b1–2, and, though
not convinced, I have no better solution to offer.

[585] Festugière notes that Proclus must avoid confusion between an entire class composed
of all instances, and the intelligible form that unites that class.

[586] In isolation the meaning of this tripartition seems unclear, but I believe that it is a
reference to the order of examples of stability in the natural world just given by Proclus:
(1) space, (2) the vehicle of the soul, and (3) each of the four elements taken as a whole.

[587] This shows that all three of the types of 'stability in generation' apply to sublunary lots,
and explains how these types must come in a certain natural order.

235

On the *Timaeus* of Plato: Book 1

25   the revolution of the heaven, which through given configurations provides given things with a power greater than their present nature, and also by nature in its entirety as it puts divine codes into each of the illuminated things, through which they participate through their very own nature in the gods; for because [nature] is linked to the gods it places different images of them in different things. It is also brought about by

30
140 opportune times, according to which the composition of other things too is managed, and by temperate climatic conditions. And in general all that concerns us contributes to an increase or a decrease in their readiness.

  So whenever, in accordance with the conjunction of these many causes, readiness for participation in the gods arises in something with

5   a natural disposition to change, the divine shines out in these things too where it had previously been concealed by the unreadiness of its future recipients. It has the same lot eternally and is offering participation in itself, but participation is not taken up by these unready things. Rather, just as when particular souls are choosing different lives at dif-

10   ferent times, some choose those appropriate to their own gods, while others choose different sorts and forget what belongs to them, so too with holy places some have been adapted to the [god] which drew the lot for that place, while others are linked up with some other order, and on this account some 'travel a more prosperous course'[588] and others less

15   so, as the Athenian Stranger says.

How Athena comes to have Athens and Sais

Whether it is the ritual or the legislative art that is responsible for dedicating a given city to a particular god who has received this share in accordance with the original and everlasting allotment, life there is assimilated more closely to its presiding divinity, and its deeds, which are great

20   and wondrous, are more sure-footed than for one who does not embark upon his actions from such a starting point. Furthermore, the one who has chosen the life of his allotted divinity is more sure-footed than one who has transferred his allegiance to another god.

  It is in this way then that the Egyptian says that Athena drew as her

25   lot both the city named after her and his own city, Sais, possibly using as evidence the considerable resemblance of the life of its citizens to her, or possibly by becoming conscious of this allotment through the ritual art or his priestly functions. For just as in the case of the other gods, so

---

[588] The phrase in particular alludes to *Laws* 771b8, a passage talking about the distribution of 5,040 lots within Magnesia, which brings in both gods and numbers in a manner that must have seemed tantalizing to Proclus.

Atlantis

there is a lot for Athena too as she proceeds from the intellective causes to the earthly region. Certainly she belongs in the first instance in the father; at the second level she is among the hegemonic gods; thirdly she embarks on a procession among the twelve rulers; and after this she reveals her independent authority in the heaven. [She reveals herself] in one way in the inerrant region, since even there a lot for this goddess has been unfolded, either the region around the Ram, or that around the Virgin, or one of the Bear-stars, as some say the moon there is;[589] in another way at the sun, since there too, along with the sun, an amazing power and Athena-given order is fashioning the whole according to the theologians;[590] in another way at the moon, as the monad of the triad there; in another way on the earth, according to the likeness of allotments on earth to her heavenly allocations, and around the earth in different ways in different places, in accordance with their peculiarities [determined by] her foresight. So there is nothing surprising that it should be said that one goddess has drawn as her lot both Athens and Sais. For we should not think of the gods too in this way – the way that particular souls are not of a nature to inhabit two bodies, because their exercise of providential care comes with a passing relation. Rather there is participation in the same power in widespread places, in the one power there is a many, and participation occurs in one way at such and such a place and in other ways in others – sameness predominating in some, difference in others. So if what we are saying is true, then (i) the lots of the gods are eternally established in the All, and (ii), this being the case, there are also manifestations of them in time, different in different places.

Ancient theology also shows the eternal being of the lots, as when it is said in Homer:

> Nay I drew as my lot to dwell forever the grey salt sea . . .[591]

'Forever' here is signifying its eternal nature. And in general, since before there can be things temporally participating in the gods there must be things for ever participating in them, it is necessary that the eternal lots should also pre-exist temporal lots. For just as daemons also follow gods

---

[589] It is conceivable that one of the stars of the Great Bear was known as its 'moon', though there may be something wrong the text here. The likeliest emendation of Σελήνη would seem to be Ἀθήνη, and it is also possible that a star of this important constellation was given that name. But Porphyry is said below (165.16–17) to have placed Athena in the moon itself.

[590] No references are given in Diehl or Festugière, and this passage is not listed as an Orphic fragment by Kern.

[591] Here the full line of *Iliad* 15.190, truncated at 136.26, is quoted.

237

On the *Timaeus* of Plato: Book 1

in advance of particular souls, so too the allocations are linked eternally
to the gods prior to their particular illumination by them. Encosmic gods
conserve their allocations, earth-gods the ones on earth, water-gods the
watery ones, air-gods those in the air, and prior to these familiar bodies
they ride on chariots of ether.[592] As to whether one should also posit
further sublunary lots that proceed from above together with the divine
light, this has been examined elsewhere.[593] This suffices for the present.

Hephaestus

**For she [took over] yours a thousand years earlier, after receiving your
seed from the earth and Hephaestus, and this land later.** (23d7–e2)

Concerning the creative activity of Hephaestus, how could one spell
it out in order without totally missing the god's power? What is said
about him by ordinary people belongs to the totally discredited kind of
story,[594] whereas what more recent people to tackle it are saying may
indeed be true, but needs quite a bit of establishing. So let us start
from the beginning with the theologians and apply our proofs about
him to the tradition we have received. That he belongs to the creative series, and not to the life-giving[595] or conserving ones, or to some
other, the theologians show by leaving a tradition of him in the role
of a blacksmith who applies the bellows, and basically as a 'worker of
crafts'.[596] These same people also show that he is a fashioner of sensible
things, not of psychical or intellectual deeds. For his manufacture of the
mirror, his bronze, his being lame, and all such things, are symbols of

[592] Rather than following Diehl's conjecture, with Festugière, I prefer to take the accusative
τοὺς ἐν οὐρανῷ θεούς as a gloss. What the earthly allocations require here, as elsewhere
in this digression, is a heavenly link to explain permanence, not to be completely
contrasted with what belongs in the heavens. Hence the gods that maintain them
should in turn have such a link.

[593] Diehl and Festugière refer only to *in Remp.* I. 178.6ff. and II. 94.26ff.

[594] Myth sometimes treats Hephaestus as a rather ridiculous figure, lame and ugly enough
to have provoked his mother Hera into throwing him down from heaven to the island
of Lemnos (alluded to at 142.29–30 etc.); making the gods laugh at himself by trapping
his unfaithful wife Aphrodite in bed with Ares (*Od.* 8.266–359); and ejaculating upon
the ground as a result of his desire for the newly-born Athena (144.6–10).

[595] Numenius identified Hephaestus with 'the life-generating heat of the sun', a 'generative' fire (fr. 58). Numenius' explanation of the lameness of Hephaestus (that fire cannot
continue without fuel) is also something that Proclus will reject.

[596] As Festugière points out, this term has already been used at 12.18, and apparently
derives from the Chaldean Oracles (fr. 33.1 des Places = p. 19 Kroll), at least as a term
for the demiurge to whom it is there applied. Although 'theologians' are mentioned here,
there is no certain implication that the term goes back that far.

Atlantis

his productivity in the sensible realm. Moreover, that he is a maker of all sensible things is clear from the same sources, who say that he was carried from Olympus above all the way to earth, and who make all the receptacles of the encosmic gods 'Hephaestus-wrought'.

So if we claim that this is so, then this god would be the overall fashioner of the entire bodily construction. He gets the gods' visible dwelling-places ready for them in advance, contributes everything required for the single harmony of the cosmos, provides all the creations of bodily life, and uses forms to give coherence to the intractable and dense nature of matter. That is the reason why he is also said by the theologians to be a smith, as being a worker of solid and resistant materials, and because the heaven is brazen insofar as it is an imitation of the intelligible, and the maker of the heaven is a smith. He is said to be lame in both legs, because he is the demiurge of the final phase of the procession of reality – that being bodies – and because he is no longer able to advance to another stage. Also because he is the maker of the All, which is 'legless', as Timaeus will say (34a5–6). He is cast from above to the earth, because he extends his creative activity through the whole of sensible substance. Whether people speak of 'natural' or of 'spermatic principles' one should attribute the cause of all of them to this god.[597] For what nature produces by sinking down into bodies, is also shaped in a divine and transcendent manner by this god, setting nature in motion and using it as a tool for his own creative activity. For innate warmth is Hephaestan, introduced by him for the making of bodies. So our account traces the universal cause of things that come to be back to this god.

Since, however, there is also a need of matter for things that come to be – for even the gods in heaven 'borrow parts from the whole as something to be given back again' for the generation of mortal animals[598] – [Plato] has quite remarkably conveyed this too with his reference to earth. For even in the very seed there are formal principles and a substrate, and the one comes from Hephaestus' craft and the other from the earth. For at this point one should understand by earth all the

---

[597] One may think here of the Stoics, for whom *logoi* of a spermatic type were embedded in the fiery active principle, occasionally called 'Hephaestus' (Chrys. *SFV* 2.1076, p. 315.14), and who resorted to much allegory to explain away the gods in later antiquity (as in the case of Cornutus). Stoics, however, do not need to go beyond Zeus himself as a source for such *logoi*, and in Cornutus (*De Nat. Deorum* 33.12–16) Zeus is connected with pure shining ether, while Hephaestus involves impurities through an admixture *of air*. In fact the term 'spermatic' has more to do with the *sperma* (seed) of the lemma.

[598] A slightly modified or misremembered quotation of 42e9–43a1, where the younger gods borrow earth, air, fire, and water from the whole.

On the *Timaeus* of Plato: Book 1

144 material cause, not because the Athenians are 'autochthonous',[599] but because they are in the habit of calling all generation 'earth' and all that is embodied in matter 'earthy'. So of necessity the seeds are from the earth.

Hephaestus' tool is fire, but his material is earth that is set in motion
5 by fire and generates life,[600] though cold and lifeless in itself. Consequently in this text too it has been introduced as something that fulfils this material role for Hephaestus, and accordingly it is said that the seed of Hephaestus founded the Athenian race together with earth. For according to the myth too Hephaestus in his desire for Athena spilt his
10 seed upon the earth, and it is from this source that the Athenian race sprang up. So Hephaestus on the one hand is eternally and completely in love with Athena, imitating her intellective character in sensible works. But 'Athenaic' souls on the other hand, in conformity with this activity of Hephaestus, receive their vehicles from him, and are housed in bodies
15 based on the formal principles of Hephaestus and on earth,[601] principles that have received Athenaic codes. For this god is the one who gives bodies their pre-natural perfection, imposing on different ones different symbols of the divine.

The priority of the Athenians

But what is this figure of **a thousand years**,[602] by which the Athenians precede the people of Sais? While we may assume that this too has
20 a historical sense, it appears to signify also the seniority of the life of the Athenians insofar as they maintained a life that was in its overall character superior to that of the Saitians. For just as in the invisible orders several races are linked with the same leader, some more closely and others at a lower level, in the same way, among Athenaic souls that
25 descend into generation, some are assimilated to the goddess to the highest extremity, and others come next in line after these. So it is this extremity that the figure of a thousand years signifies, since it is a measure of a complete generation-producing cycle because of its being a cubic

---

[599] I.e. 'straight from the land', as legend stated, Erechtheus (or Erichthonius, above 101.7) having been descended from Earth and Hephaestus.

[600] Note the resistance to making Hephaestus a fire-principle; for Apollo, Helios, and Hephaestus as separate possible symbols of fire see Betegh (2004), 203.

[601] It is not directly clear from the Greek whether one should understand '[the formal principles] of earth' with Festugière, or regard earth as giving a matter-like contribution, but the latter accords best with 143.30–2 and 144.3–6, which suggest that Hephaestus is the sole source of the formal principles.

[602] LSJ s.v. χιλιάς, under II.

Atlantis

number.[603] Hence in all likelihood it fits in with the superior kind of life in generation, life better assimilated to the presiding divinity. 30

If you would like to give these [words a meaning] transferred to the All, you will see that there too all the visible arrangement is Hephaestan, both arrangers and things arranged, and of arrangers some are more **145** universal and some more particular, the former corresponding to the Athenians and the latter to the Saitians. For nothing prevents one in studying the same things, by analogy, among the creative causes, and in the All, and in the historical account.

An Iamblichan difficulty and its solution

Iamblichus,[604] though, raises the difficulty of how the gods are said to get 5 certain places as their lot for determinate periods of time, as for instance Athena gets Athens first and Sais later. For if they commence occupation of their allocation at a given time, they could also end it at a given time, everything measured out in time being of that kind. Further, [he asks] whether whatever lot that they receive is vacant when they receive it, or 10 presided over by some other god. If it is vacant, how could any part of the All be entirely deprived of a god, and how could any place endure when totally unguarded by the superior powers? And if it is self-sufficient enough to preserve itself, how could it later become the lot of some god? 15 On the other hand, if it belongs[605] under one leader and another god gets it, that situation too is unreasonable. For it can neither be the case that the second misappropriates the control and the allotment of the former, nor that they keep swapping places with one another, for not even daemons engage in an exchange of lots.

So, after raising these difficulties, he offers a solution, saying that the 20 allocations of the gods are eternal, but things that participate in them at one time enjoy the presence of their leaders, and at another are deprived of them. And these are the cases of participation measured in time, which the holy ordinances often call 'birthdays' of the gods.[606]

---

[603] Festugière cites passages from Iambl. *in Nicom. Arithm.*, but they explain little; given the prominent role afforded this cubic number here, it is perhaps worrying that nothing helpful can be quoted from the rest of this commentary.

[604] *In Tim.* fr. 14 Dillon, who compares Sallustius *De Deis* 18, pp. 32–4 Nock; note that we have not heard anything of Iamblichus by name since 120.9, but we shall now do so regularly until 174.28.

[605] Literally 'pays taxes', meaning is reckoned as subject to; see LSJ s.v. II.3.

[606] The meaning of this birthday is discussed in Festugière's long note. More circumspect is Dillon's note. Since gods were often thought to take up residence at a shrine on a given day of the year, the celebration of a birthday of sorts would have been natural enough; but if we could be sure of the identity of the holy ordinances we might better appreciate the reference.

On the *Timaeus* of Plato: Book 1

25   But we have said[607] that it is like what happens in the case of souls.
While every soul also has a presiding god in any case, some choose lives
that really belong to other gods. Accordingly, while every place is a lot of
some particular god, there are times when it becomes another's lot, either
because of the passing of certain cycles which make it ready, or because
30   of some rite established by humans, when the allotment is double, one
according to essential nature, the other according to temporal condition.
But let us proceed to the next passage.

The dates of ancient Athens and of Sais

146   The date of arrangements made in this place is written among us in our
sacred writings as amounting to eight thousand years ago.   (23e2–4)

5   To the Athenians he attributed the number of nine thousand, getting
this too from historical inquiry, but to the Saitians that of eight thousand according to the writings in their temples, measuring out the lives
of cities in millennia. For daemons too are said to measure time in
this way, as the philosopher Porphyry says.[608] Furthermore, by basing
10   this narration upon the sacred writings, he[609] signifies the permanent
watchfulness of the cosmic divine forms, as Iamblichus would say.[610]
The numbers also relate to kinds of life, this in accordance with the
'likely account'.[611] Eight thousand is a cube times a cube, and the other

---

[607] See 140.9–15.

[608] *in Tim.* fr. XV; Porphyry of course linked his whole interpretation of the Atlantis story
with daemons and/or souls (77.6–24).

[609] The subject of 'he attributed' and hence of 'he signifies' is the priest; I have deleted the
article ὁ here, which I believe gives a slight improvement in the sense. The participle
ποιούμενος was otherwise dependent upon the verb 'attributed' two sentences earlier.
There is also a possibility that this sentence is a gloss, since it interrupts the discussion
of numbers, intervening between an historical explanation of them and an explanation
in terms of what they are an image of (*kata ton eikota logon*, 146.12).

[610] Festugière admits to uncertainty about the meaning of this permanent watchfulness of
divine forms, but Dillon (1973, 279) refers us to the watchful role of encosmic gods.
Though printng this as fr. 14A, Dillon declines to believe that this is a true fragment
of Iamblichus as opposed to something offered by Proclus in Iamblichan vein. While
the mention of Iamblichus immediately after Porphyry is very much a part of Proclus'
methods this sentence interrupts the flow (see last note).

[611] We now meet the key notion of *eikotologia*, going back to the status of Timaeus' cosmology as an *eikôs mythos* or *eikôs logos*, 29c–d etc. The phrase *kata ton eikota logon* derives
from *Tim.* 55d5 and in modified form at 53d5–6, and it offers something of a guiding
principle of this part of the dialogue (cf. 48d6, 56a1, 68b7); in Proclus the phrase occurs
in full also at *Plat. Theol.* 5.43.11. This is more than reference to the probability of the
account since likeliness includes the notion of resemblance, and one of Plato's methods
of inquiry (according to Proclus) is the iconic method that involves studying images
and paradigms together (see 1.22 above), associated in the *Platonic Theology* (I. 1.6) with

242

Atlantis

is a two-dimensional square times a cube. The one gives depth to the square, doing so through the indeterminate dyad, while the other, keeping the square character for itself in the likeness and perfection deriving from the triad, does not allow the cube to remain outside its grasp, but has embraced that too.[612] That which remains in itself and *arranges* secondary things is the symbol of a better life, while what *comes down into* those things, assimilates to them, and is infected with a kind of indefiniteness, is more imperfect. But since even the second is not entirely removed from similarity to god, the descent for those things sharing a resemblance to the triad takes place by cubes. But it would be better to imitate what is better through a simpler rather than a more complex life, and the square is simpler than the cube. Yet if you were to say that the figure of nine thousand is also appropriate for those derived from the earth and Hephaestus – for *qua* cube the number one thousand is associated with earth, while nine belongs to Hephaestus as he says himself:

> Close to these I forged many skilled works for nine years.[613]

– you would not be far from the mark.

In general the cube is fitting for the earthly works of Athena, as people attribute the decad to the heaven, while the procession of the decad stops finally at the 'solid' number one thousand – for gods have processed from the heavenly lots to stop finally at the earthly ones. That is what we have to say.

But the philosopher Porphyry,[614] when he interprets this, hypothesizes that Hephaestus is technical expertise, and earth is the lunar sphere, since [the moon] is called 'the earth of ether' by the Egyptians.[615] So the souls that have received their existence from god[616] but participate in

---

the Pythagoreans. So the numbers, besides being historically correct, are also offered as an image of something higher.

[612] I delete the words 'through the ennead' here, as a probable gloss, written on the mistaken supposition that Proclus wants to say nine contains eight by being greater; in fact Proclus sees the superiority of 9,000 over 8,000 in terms of the superiority of the two dimensional (more form-like) over the three-dimensional ('solid' and hence body-like), and with the superiority of the triad (inclusive) over the dyad (ever divisive and more like matter). Festugière corrects to 'through the chiliad' (1,000), since that contains the *notion* of the cube, which seems reasonable if that is what Proclus wants to say.

[613] *Iliad* 18.400: the reference of the initial 'these' is to Eurynome and Thetis.

[614] = *in Tim*. fr. XVI Sodano.

[615] Festugière refers to II. 48.17 for the attribution of this view to Orpheus, though in reality Orphic lines (fr. 81 Kern) that make no mention of ether are merely used there to support the description, which is associated if anything with 'Pythagoreans'.

[616] Referring to the process mentioned at *Tim*. 41d–e.

On the *Timaeus* of Plato: Book 1

technical expertise are sown into the body of the moon, he says, because that is where the technically expert sort of soul belongs, and they have bodies that are effluences of the bodies of ether. The nine thousand years are suited to these souls in the following way. Ten thousand years, he claims, is the period of the soul's ascent and descent through the five planets, so that each [planet] could have it for two millennia. However, it is not a continuous succession, though the time[617] [is reckoned] continuously by contiguity. That is because it is not[618] contiguous with itself.[619] Hence the total number of lives is nine,[620] which he riddlingly refers to by the nine thousand years – and people carry out nine-day rites to the dead, and similarly some people give names to the new-born on the ninth day, using periods of time as symbols of coming into and passing out of life. So he did not adopt the period of ten-thousand-years at this point, but took the figure of nine thousand so that they should still be in the region of the earth drawing near to the [completion of the] ten thousand year cycle.[621]

This entire line of interpretation is something the divine Iamblichus[622] refuses to endorse, saying that the account at this point concerns not lives but different degrees of participation in the heritage

---

[617] The time in question is the nine thousand years in the Platonic text, for it is this that constitutes the source of the problem; it is not a statement about how time in general operates. Clearly there must be a gap at one or more points in the ten-thousand-year cycle. These sentences read like an attempt to sum up Porphyry's argument far too briefly, and it is not surprising that uncertainties and textual disputes occur. There is no certainty that Proclus had understood it himself. My translation involves considerable interpretation, in which I differ from other scholars, and should thus be treated with caution. Part of Porphyry's problem is that the Ur-Athenians of the Atlantis-War should perhaps belong to the equivalent point of the cosmic cycle to classical Athenians, which would have placed them ten rather than nine thousand years before them; the other part is derived from the *Phaedrus*, from which (248e) Porphyry accepts the number of nine lives in a ten thousand year cycle. That dialogue clearly demands that there should be a gap in the cycle *after the ninth life*, so that the soul may enjoy a period in its winged condition, when it will attempt to achieve a vision of the place above the heavens.

[618] I am adhering to the MS reading at 18, preserving the negative with Festugière, unlike Schneider, and Diehl.

[619] I.e. the time of nine thousand years does not join up with the next nine thousand, so does not involve the complete cycle.

[620] That the number of nine lives per 10,000-year cycle, each involving a separate 1,000-year period, is derived from *Phaedrus* 248d–249a, we may see by the reference to that dialogue in Iamblichus' criticism at 147.28.

[621] I take it that the modern Athenians here were thought to symbolize souls at the end of a cycle of nine 'lives' and nine thousand years; their next thousand years will therefore be spent in winged condition, removed entirely from terrestrial circumstances. The ancient Athenians would have been starting the cycle.

[622] *in Tim.* fr. 15 Dillon; Proclus himself is clearly a little more sympathetic.

244

Atlantis

of Athena. So the mention of the cycles from the *Phaedrus* is beside the point.[623] But if one must offer an explanation that agrees with Porphyry's approach,[624] one should say that on high the soul lives intellectively and in the way associated with Kronos, but it descends to an awareness of the life that is 'constitutional' in the primary sense,[625] which is associated with Zeus, and then it activates the spirit and lives ambitiously – the spirit being associated with Ares. In addition to this it succumbs to desire and the lives associated with Aphrodite, and finally it emits physical creative principles (*logoi*). All *logoi* are associated with Hermes,[626] and it is ithyphallic Hermes who is the overseer of all physical creative principles. Through these principles it is bound to the body, and when it takes a body it lives first in a vegetative way, being in charge of the food and growth of the body, then appetitively, awakening the generative powers, then spiritedly as it disengages with these things and returns to the spirited life, then constitutionally by moderating the passions, and finally intellectively.[627] So if it completes the return to square one[628] it lives intellectively, and the number ten thousand marks the limit. But while in [the realm of] generation, even if it conducts itself excellently, it lives a life that falls a thousand years short of that figure. The number nine thousand is a symbol of this, one that is fitting for the excellent constitution of the Athenians.

Lexis: details of the text interpreted

Concerning the citizens born nine thousand years ago I shall briefly show you their laws and the finest of their achievements in action. But as for the details of the whole sequence of events we shall get the written records themselves and go through it another time at leisure. (23e4–24a2)

[623] See note on 147.18 above.

[624] An approach, that is, that highlights different lives under the auspices of the five planets. It is difficult to gauge Proclus' level of commitment here. Note that his idea of a Porphyrian approach is to deny that the final stage of the cycle is completed, not to leave spaces between all the millennial cycles as Festugière thinks that Porphyry had done. The term for approach, *epibolê*, is that which Porphyry uses for contiguity in lines 17–18.

[625] The life of the ancient Athenians typified by the control of the passions exercised by reason.

[626] Generally Hermes is the divinity most associated with communication through speech, but it is *logoi* in a different sense that are relevant here.

[627] Proclus depicts an ascent back via similar stages to those of the descent, living vegetatively (Hermes), appetitively (Aphrodite), spiritedly (Ares), constitutionally (Zeus), and intellectively (Kronos).

[628] For the *apokatastasis* see on 87.30.

245

On the *Timaeus* of Plato: Book 1

If you would like to apply this too to the universal arrangement, the **nine thousand years** will show the whole procession up to the cube and to earthly deeds together with the life that pervades all things, while the word **briefly** will show the unification of the plurality of formal principles and their being encapsulated by intellect. For its synoptic character[629] gives us a reflective glimpse of intellective indivisibility, while that which goes forth into multiplicity [gives a glimpse] of the generative power, which multiplies, draws forth, and subdivides the forms through otherness. The word **laws** [gives a glimpse] of how the creation has been divided up in accordance with intelligence,[630] and **finest of their achievements** [gives a glimpse] of the arrangement that is directed to the single end of beauty. For that unified beauty proceeds from the intelligibles into the visible creation. That they will **get the written records** signifies their recourse to the paradigms, which bring to the priest the fulfilment needed for him to pass these things on to Solon. Hence the account will be of a creation that is divided, multiplied, maintained according to intelligence, and extending as far as works on earth, as is possible to comprehend from all that has been said.

So compare the laws with those here; for you will discover here and now many paradigms of those you then had.   (24a2–4)

Just as Socrates outlined his constitution 'under the main heads',[631] so too the priest recalls the laws of the ancient Athenians 'briefly', in order that these may maintain both their subordination to those and their similarity in organization, and with good reason, because those were more universal while these are more particular, and those were the works of the mind while these involve imagination too. The subordination should be observed to the extent that Socrates was outlining a constitution, while this man outlines laws. A constitution is the unifying principle and common bond of the life of its citizens, while law-giving is an order that proceeds to multiplicity and division, the former corresponding to the providential cause, and the latter rather to fate. The similarity [should be observed] to the extent that both claim that they are conveying in a nutshell the multiplicity of what there is to say. So again this too has a grasp of the universe and of the divine causes, for the middle creation is

---

[629] The references are a little vague, but seem to be to the general import of the two phrases under discussion. I do not feel that Festugière's emendation is warranted here.

[630] Festugière rightly draws attention to the allusion to *Laws* 714a, which makes law 'the distribution [*dianomê*] of intelligence' and is about to be quoted at 150.14. This passage was popular in late antiquity (e.g. Olymp. *in Gorg.* 26.3, 47.4). The notion of the creator-god as a law-giving intellect responsible for a distribution occurs at Numenius fr. 13.6.

[631] 19a8, cf. 54.12, the phrase being discussed at 54.27–55.26.

246

Atlantis

dependent upon the first and is assimilated to it, and each is a cause of the All, but the former is so according to unity and a single sameness, and the latter according to the procession and otherness of the things being created – just as the third [creation] is so by reversion. And the first is so by maintaining the 'war' in generation in a heavenly fashion, the second in a secondary and subordinate fashion – just as the third [maintains] the last things of all.[632] So it is with good reason that Critias too is handing down the laws and life of the Athenians 'under the main heads' just like the priest. This much should be grasped here too.

It was images that he called **paradigms** here, since the Saitians participate secondarily in what the Athenians have primarily. For even if the archetypes are first, still it is the images that have first place with respect to our cognition.[633] So just as the things that are secondary in nature are called primary, so too [they are called] **paradigms**. For they serve as **paradigms** to the things that are being recalled by their means, and it is through them that [these things] get to know what is before them.

Here too the Athenian situation is indicating the more universal order, and that of the Saitians the more particular, though both of these stand in the same relation in both particular and universal things. Consequently the constitution that will be handed down belongs to the Athenians' city, though more so to the arrangement of the universe, and the laws that stretch out across the whole cosmos come from Athens. For it is said – and rightly said – that all law is 'the distribution of intelligence', and the Athenians' laws that have been passed in accordance with their presiding deity reflect the distribution of Athenaic intelligence. Such too are the laws in the All, which are determined by the single creative intelligence and the single providential care of Athena.

The Egyptian class structure compared

Firstly the class of priests, which has been separated off apart from the rest . . . (24a4–5)

The fact that all this arrangement is somehow more particular than Socrates' constitution, and more divided than that one through its imitation of the intermediate creation, may be learned from the number and character of the classes in the city. For there had been three classes

---

[632] Festugière notes how Proclus introduces the third creation without warning here, explaining that Socrates corresponds here to the first creation, the priest to the second, and Critias, by retelling things, to the third creation, as we see from the next sentence.

[633] Here Proclus explains an unusual, rather weak Platonic use of *paradeigma* as 'example', by adopting the Aristotelian distinction between what comes first by nature and what does so in our cognitive processes.

247

On the *Timaeus* of Plato: Book 1

there, guardians, auxiliaries, and labourers – for the triad belongs closely
to the creative monad[634] – while here there are double that number,
151 hieratic, military, manufacturing, cultivating, pasturing, and hunting.[635]
That is because the intermediate creation is in possession of the dyadic
element alongside the triadic. Further, while both of these numbers[636]
are proper to Athena, the one comes here *straight from there* – as it is
a triad – and the other comes along with generation. For the hexad is
5 triangular[637] as a result of the triad. By its triangularity and its derivation
from the triad he shows both its subordination and its belonging to the
goddess. For even if the whole of creation participates in Athena, those
that are most filled with her are the first and uppermost things of the
All, the first creation and the first father.

10 In this way you will find, if you take only these classes, that the number
is proper to the goddess. And if you should add the power of caring for
practical wisdom, you will find that the heptad is totally Athenaic. And
this too is something frequently discussed, and the unfeminized character
of the heptad and its derivation from the monad alone are celebrated,[638]
15 and it is above all the third monad and the heptad that constitute an
image of Athena. The former does so through being intellective and
reverting to itself and to the monad, the latter through proceeding from
the father alone. So you could approach things in this way on the basis
of the numbers.

But one should also see which of them is inferior and which supe-
20 rior from the actual quality of the classes. The hieratic is inferior to
the guardian class, which reaches up to the very first cause, just as
[Plato] himself in the *Statesman* subordinated the priests to the statesman and gave them no political power.[639] The military is inferior to

---

[634] This strange statement may be due to the fact that there is a triad of demiurges under
the leadership of a single Father of Demiurges, and to the view that odd numbers
(particularly three) are somehow held together more closely than even numbers.

[635] Much discussion of the list of six Egyptian classes (extending to 24b1) occurs in what
follows; the six are entirely derived from Proclus' understanding of Plato's text, and the
discussion is not informed by the extended knowledge of Egypt in Roman times that
Neoplatonists must have had.

[636] Three and six, the number of classes under each constitution, not two and three.

[637] Because six dots may be arranged in a triangular form.

[638] Underlying all this are two mythical feature of Athena, her having a father alone and so
missing a source of femininity, and her being a virgin so that none makes a woman of
her. Festugière aptly compares II. 236.17–20 and Iambl. *Theol. Arithm.* 71 de Falco; also
relevant is the fact that seven is a prime number, making it indivisible, and impossible
to derive from the multiplication of two numbers other than itself.

[639] 290d–e actually refers to the practice in Egypt of kings involving priests in their deci-
sions, as well as to magistracies in Greece that incorporated a role in sacrificing animals.
The discussion is aimed at showing the closeness of priestly and kingly roles before the

Atlantis

the auxiliary, since this latter class orders things inside the city properly and receives sufficient education, while the former pursues only wars and the deeds of war, and this is the only training that it participates in. The labouring class is divided into the remaining classes, so that it differs in being more comprehensive and by its being somehow dependent on the classes preceding it. Hence it has become clear to us both from the number and from the quality that what is now being handed down is inferior to the constitution of Socrates and would take second place after it.

In the case of that constitution, we were setting out its correspondences with the All in the following way. The guardian class corresponds to the heavenly gods, the auxiliary to the superior powers that attend the heavenly ones and guard the All, and the labouring class to those that conserve enmattered nature and to particular souls; one corresponds to the fixed stars, another to the planets, and another to enmattered things. We were also assuming that even among the heavenly gods themselves all these things were present by analogy.

But it is worth noticing in this case[640] how and in what way these classes are to be taken as present in the All. For the philosopher Porphyry sets it out like this.[641] The priests correspond to the archangels in the heaven which are turned towards the gods whose messengers they are.[642] The military correspond to the daemons who come down into bodies. The pastors correspond to those stationed over the flocks of 'animals', which they secretly explain as being souls that have missed out on human intelligence and have a condition similar to animals – for of humans too there is a particular 'protector'[643] of their flock and certain particular [powers] some of whom watch over tribes, some cities, and some individual persons. The hunters correspond to those that hunt down souls and confine them in the body – for there are some who also enjoy the pursuit of animals, the type that they suppose both Artemis to be and another host of hunt-oriented daemons with her. The cultivators

statesman's art can be decisively distinguished from all others, which have the role of ministering to government (290a). However, it reads as if Proclus has an agenda of his own here, no doubt resenting the political influence of the highest church officials in his own day.

[640] I.e. in the case of the Egyptian classes, as opposed to the Socratic ones just discussed at 152.3–10.

[641] = in Tim. fr. XVII Sodano.

[642] One must bear in mind that 'angel' is simply the same word as 'messenger' in Greek, with archangels being the chief messengers.

[643] Probably an allusion to the Helmsman-god of Plato's Statesman, the shepherd of a previous era, who is introduced at 268c and is the object of inquiry throughout the myth (see 274e–275b).

On the *Timaeus* of Plato: Book 1

25   correspond to those stationed over fruits. The whole of this constitutional scheme of sublunary daemons, distributed into many groups, was
said to be 'manufacturing' (*dêmiourgikos*)[644] by Plato because he was concentrating on a finished product that was either in existence already or
being generated.

However, the divine Iamblichus[645] criticizes the way this was said as
neither Platonic nor true, claiming that 'archangels' were never con-
30   sidered worthy of mention by Plato, and that the military class did not
153   consist of souls drifting into bodies. For one shouldn't involve these in
a classification of gods or daemons,[646] as it is also out of place that we
should place these in a central category and put daemons or gods at
the lowest productive levels. He also denies that 'pastors' refers to those
5   who have missed out on human intelligence and acquired a sympathetic
affinity[647] with animals, for the daemons who have oversight of mortal
nature do not have their own essential nature (*to einai*) from humans.
Nor does 'hunters' refer to those that confine the soul within the body
like a cage, because that is not the way the soul has been attached to the
10   body. And this type of speculation is not philosophical; rather it is rife
with foreign humbug.[648] Nor should the cultivators be taken to refer
to Demeter, for the gods transcend the causes that deal directly with
nature.

Accordingly, after offering these criticisms, he makes the priests correspond, through likeness, to all the secondary substances and powers,
15   as many as honour and serve their causes before them. The pastors [he
makes correspond] to all those in the cosmos who have been allotted

---

[644] Plato's text in fact uses the corresponding verb and noun at 24a5–7, not the adjective,
which needs to be rendered here by something other than 'creative' in the context of
human society. Proclus makes it clear that this use of the term *dêmiourgikos* to cover
this range of occupations is unusual, cf. 153.26–7, but it is by no means certain that
Plato had not intended to be understood as using it in just this way.

[645] = *in Tim.* fr. 16 Dillon, commented upon in Dillon (1973), 282–5.

[646] One should recall that Porphyry had combined the views of Numenius and Origenes by
involving both souls and daemons in his explanation of the Atlantine conflict, 77.6–24.

[647] The term *sympatheia* here refers to the condition of being similarly situated with regard
to the emotional faculties (the *pathê*) as another party (here animals).

[648] It is *barbarikê alazoneia*, indicating something which is (a) alien to Greek traditions,
and (b) full of empty words designed to impress the reader deceitfully. Dillon (1973,
282) rightly finds Iamblichus' protests particularly amusing, given his own interest in
religious ideas with no Greek pedigree. There may, however, be no need to take the
comments as Iamblichan, for the indicative *might* be taken to indicate the inserted
comments of Proclus. While all explanations of the basic Iamblichan claims here use
the indicative (152.32, 153.5, 8–9, 11), as if the connective *gar* were introducing a
subordinate clause, one notes that this slur on the general character of Porphyry's
work is introduced by *oude*, and does not have to be linked with the explanatory clause
that precedes.

Atlantis

dominion over life that sinks into the body and over the irrational powers, and who distribute these in order.[649] The hunters [he makes correspond] to universal[650] powers for adorning secondary things by pursuit of reality, the cultivators who prepare for the germination[651] of the seeds cast from heaven upon the earth, and the military to those who convert all that is godless and bring the divine to victory. That is how the divine Iamblichus puts it. But it is a common point against both that they divide manufacturers into pastors, hunters, and cultivators, instead of producing all four from the one class. For, if one viewed it rightly, one would never subsume the pasturing class or the hunting class *under* the productive.[652]

So perhaps then it is better that we offer our interpretation in the manner of our teacher, supposing the hieratic and military classes to be one dyad, the productive and cultivating to be another, and the pasturing and hunting to be a third, and that we track down their paradigmatic significance on the basis of that kind of arrangement. For the hieratic element is present among the uplifting gods, the military among the protective gods, the manufacturing among those who distinguish all the forms and formal principles among encosmic things, and the cultivating among those who set nature in motion from above and disseminate souls around [the world of] generation. For Plato too calls the fall of the soul into generation a sowing,[653] and sowing belongs most naturally to farmers, just like gathering in the produce of nature. The pasturing element [is present] among the powers that are separately in charge of the various forms of life that are carried around in generation, for in the *Statesman* too he has passed on [the notion of] certain divine pastors.[654] The hunting element [is present] among those that organize all the life-currents within matter, for the theologians are in the habit of calling

---

[649] The verb for distributing, *dianemô*, in its simple form *nemô* also means 'to take out to graze', and is the root behind the term 'pastor' (*nomeus*).

[650] Dillon (1973, 285) makes these identical with the 'young gods' of the *Timaeus*, on the ground that their universality makes them gods rather than daemons; he makes the cultivators and military daemonic servants of these. Dillon sees Iamblichus as resisting a Gnostic or Chaldean system that allows evil daemons, as well as defending the transcendence of the gods.

[651] The term *telesiourgia* is also chosen to convey the notion of the efficacy of a ritual.

[652] See note on 152.27; Proclus denies that Plato's text at 24a7–b1 should be read as offering three examples of the different manufacturers who stick to their own line of business (a5–7), something not unnaturally assumed by early exegetes, who had thus been left with *five* classes in Egypt rather than the six of Syrianus and Proclus.

[653] The sowing metaphor of such passages as *Tim.* 41e and 42d had long been noticed by interpreters, e.g. Numenius fr. 13 with Tarrant (2004).

[654] An allusion to 271d6–7, where *daemones* look after animals that are divided into flocks according to types *like pastor gods*.

On the *Timaeus* of Plato: Book 1

these 'wild beasts'.[655] All these classes belong to the middle creation, the one responsible for reversion,[656] the protective one, the one that manages what is allotted to souls, the one that directs the regenerative species of life, everything that engages in manufacturing and giving form to material things, and the one that organizes the lowest life-currents.[657] Besides all these classes one <must>[658] postulate another contemplative one whose care is wisdom. He will himself laud this one above all,[659] though he mentions the hieratic class first, being a priest. So there are *seven* in all, and the monad has been taken separately from the hexad. The former corresponds to the single intellect that conserves the whole creation of generated things, while the latter [corresponds] to the more particular tribes beneath it, uplifting, protective, informing, life-creating, shepherding civilized life, and subduing the bestial nature.

These things then have been separated from simple things even in the All. And further, it is possible to see them, he says, among humans, firstly among the Athenians, and secondly among the Saitians, as each in accordance with the division of classes goes about its proper work separately. The [words] **from the rest** show this, and **apart**, so that we may understand the unmingled purity of the classes that proceeds from above to the lowest [stages] through subordination.

And after this the situation of the manufacturers, that each goes about his own task, intermixed with no other task, and the situation of the pastors, of the hunters, and of the cultivators. (24a5–b1)

This whole tetractys occupies the third order in the division of classes into three, but it is counted by Plato as second at this point, so that through this too the discourse may imitate the All – in which the lowest element is in the middle, encompassed on either side by more divine ones. For the most enmattered and densest thing[660] reclines in the middle as a result of the creation process, for even so it is only with difficulty that its arrangement is preserved throughout its entirety and protected by all that encompasses it. And it is again added in these words that

---

[655] Festugière, following Diehl, refers to the Chaldean Oracles, fr. 157 des Places (= 60 K), whose relevance is unclear to me; the term 'theologians' would normally refer to Orphic writings.

[656] The language of reversion briefly replaces the language of lifting up higher (154.1, 24).

[657] The order is identical to that which has immediately preceded it, except that the manufacturing class has been placed after both the sowers of souls and the pastors.

[658] Kroll's addition has been accepted by both Diehl and Festugière.

[659] Proclus thinks of 24b7–c3, though there is here no explicit mention of a class to look after this wisdom.

[660] Obviously the earth.

252

Atlantis

the manufacturing element is not intermixed with the others, nor they with it, but each remains on its own and in its own pure state. For this achieves not only precision in their occupations and correctness in their own proper discourse, but also a sympathetic affinity among the citizens, because everybody needs everybody else since each person does not pursue many crafts. The manufacturer will need the cultivator, the cultivator the pastor, this one the hunter, and the hunter the manufacturer, and so each of them, being in need of the rest, will not fail to mix with them. Hence there is sameness along with the difference and separation along with their unification.

Furthermore you have surely noticed that the military class here is separated from all the other classes, people who have been required by the law to concern themselves with nothing other than matters of war. (24b1–3)

The situation as regards their not mixing [trades] and keeping separate applies at all levels, but belongs particularly to the military class. For it is akin to the immaculate order that excises[661] everything enmattered and obliterates error. Hence it is with good reason that matters of war are the concern of this class, for it is on their account that the city remains unused to external and <internal> sources of harm, and this shields it with its own protection, imitating the protective order. For just like the first of the demiurges, so too the middle one has its protective divine power. This is what must be brought to bear from theology. But as for [the term] **law** let us understand it at the universal level as the ordinance that comes from the single creative intelligence, since creational law is prior to encosmic things, sitting by Zeus' side[662] and helping with his arrangement of all the providential power in the All.

Weaponry compared

Furthermore, there is the habit of arming ourselves with shields and spears, with which we have been the first men in Asian parts to be armed, because the goddess revealed this to us just as she did in those regions of yours first. (24b4–7)

The discourse makes the activity of Athena extend from the paradigms at the top down to the lowest classes. For she has things naturally belonging

---

[661] Diehl refers to Chaldean Oracles 53.2 Kroll (= Proclus *in Crat.* 71.17), but, while it does sound as if Proclus has in mind such descriptions of the heavenly order here, it is unlikely that we possess the text that inspired him.

[662] The creator is called Zeus because of the mythical idea that Justice (*Dikê*) sits at his side, alluded to more famously at *Laws* 716a2.

253

On the *Timaeus* of Plato: Book 1

to her, some more universal and some more particular, that partake of her immaculate powers. Also [she has] encosmic classes, set in order across the middle creation-process, corresponding to those things in that they both constrain and are constrained, mastered by Athenaic activities, and remaining ever in the same immaculate condition in the All on her account. This is what one is required to notice generally concerning all this [lemma]. But one should state what this **arming** is, what the **shields** are and the **spears**, and how these things are preconceived within the goddess.

Porphyry calls the shield the body, and for the spear he understands the temper, and these things belong to those who fall into generation and into enmattered things, and they are the instruments not of unflinching preservation but of reproductive life, corrupting the purity of intellect and destroying the rational life.[663] But the divine Iamblichus in his inspired fashion,[664] since all that is divine should act and not be acted upon, so that by acting it might not have inaction similar to matter, and by not being acted upon it might not have a vigorous quality like enmattered things that work when acted upon, supposes that the shields are powers through which the divine remains impassive and immaculate, having hedged itself around with an impenetrable protection. The spears he supposes are powers in accordance with which it passes through all things without touching and acts upon all things, severing what is enmattered[665] and defending the entire generation-producing class.[666] This is first observed in the case of Athena, and explains why her shield and spear have been depicted on her statues too, and she contends against all and remains unswerving as the theologians say[667] and immaculate in the Father. [It is observed] secondly in the Athenaic powers, both the universal ones and the particular ones, for as the Jovian or creative multitude imitates its own monad, and as the prophetic or Apollonian [multitude] imitates the distinctive Apollonian character, so too the Athenaic plurality reflects the immaculate and unmixed character of Athena. Finally [it is observed] in Athenaic souls, for among these too the shield is the invincible and unswerving character of reason, while the spear is that which cuts through matter and rids souls of

---

[663] = *in Tim.* fr. XVIII Sodano.

[664] The adverb *entheastikôs* here signifies the manner of one who is actively *entheos*, motivated by some god within, and hence complements the adjective *theios* that is regularly applied to Iamblichus.

[665] Cf. 155.32–156.1

[666] = Iamblichus *in Tim.* fr. 17, on which see Dillon (1973, 285), who feels that what follows is amplification by Proclus; Festugière, however, appears to regard what follows too as Iamblichan (see 209 n.2).

[667] Cf. 166.2–23 below, where several of these adjectives occur, and *Orph. fr.* 174 is quoted.

Atlantis

demonic or fate-associated affections. Of these weapons the Athenians were allocated a purer share, and the Saitians a secondary one, getting their share in these things too in proportion to their kinship with the goddess.

The wisdom of the goddess and her two cities

And as for wisdom, you see perhaps how much care the law here has taken right from our foundation *up to* having obtained all [branches of learning]. (24b7–c3)

Shortly he will call the goddess both 'wisdom-loving' and 'war-loving'. Accordingly, so that his depiction of the constitution of the Athenians and the Saitians might come to accord with his model,[668] he gave sufficient indication of their training for war in what was said, whereas in these words he presents their attitude to wisdom – so that in the one he might present a reflection of Athena's love of war, and in the other of her love of wisdom. So what is her **wisdom**? It is the study of the whole of hypercosmic and encosmic[669] reality, from which, after the primary goods that are perfective of souls,[670] a certain ease[671] was established for human life, proceeding **as far as mantic and medicine**,[672] and viewing these in one way among the invisible causes, in another at a cosmic level, and in the lowliest way at the level of human practice. Since learning is immaterial and this goddess is transcendent,[673] she accordingly reveals to those that are akin to her all parts of her wisdom, both divine and human. For in the case of mantic one should posit one kind among the intellective gods, another in hypercosmic entities, and another in encosmic ones, and of this [last one should posit] one kind that has come down to us from the gods, another from daemons,

---

[668] I.e. Athena herself.

[669] Accepting with Festugière the supplement of Radermacher.

[670] Apparently an allusion to *Laws* 631b–d, where goods belonging to the soul are distinguished from those belonging to the body.

[671] Reminiscent of the *euporia . . . tou biou* afforded to humans by the gift of fire stolen by Prometheus from Hephaestus *and Athena* at *Prot.* 321e3.

[672] Proclus seems to have chosen to concentrate on these two arts simply because they are mentioned specifically in Plato's text.

[673] While it is not spelled out, I should presume that Proclus is assuming that all immaterial things are able to be shared with others without diminishing what remains with the giver, much as Numenius does (fr. 14 des Places). He also concentrates on showing that knowledge is undiminished in the giver (lines 14–16), regarding it as something divine rather than human, and as therefore able to be shared in a divine manner. Des Places (p. 109) is also prompted to suggest the influence of *Laws* 631b–d, as I have done at 158.4 above. Numenius (fr. 14.19–21) himself draws the parallel with the wisdom proceeding from Prometheus' fire, as I did at 158.6, alluding to *Phil.* 16c.

On the *Timaeus* of Plato: Book 1

and another from the human mind (*dianoia*), which is more dependent on skill (*technikos*) and interpreting images (*eikastikos*).[674] Further, one should posit in the same way the medicine of Paion among the gods, and the subordinate and servile kind that assists the gods among daemons, who are the origin of the preparation of materials and of the means by which the gods reveal themselves. For just as there are many daemons associated with Eros, so also with Asclepius,[675] some allocated the post of attendants, others that of escorts. But in human life [one should posit] the medicine that makes provision on the basis of observation and trial, the medicine in which some relate more closely and others less so to the divine medicine. There is also a mixture of these two branches of wisdom, mantic and medicine, among the Egyptians, because the causes of these seem to have been prefigured in a single divinity,[676] and from the one source several separate streams flow around the cosmos. Let this be our general comment concerning the **wisdom** mentioned here.

Lexis: some details considered

As we move on to explanation of individual details, we shall state that **law** means the pervading order deriving from the single intellect of Athena, **care** means the providence that has travelled from the universals as far as the particulars, and **right from our foundation** shows the *natural* affinity for wisdom of Athenaic souls – for by **right from the beginning** he seems to signify that it is neither introduced nor foreign.[677] But if one were to connect the phrase with the universal order, it seems to me that this **right from the beginning** shows that the arrangement does not proceed from the incomplete to the complete, but that it has always had order and its emergence is linked throughout with goodness.

---

[674] The term *eikastikos* here is difficult, for it cannot mean purely guesswork, which seems to be the contrary of skill; rather, it is likely to imply here the use of mental pictures that require interpretation, and one recalls that it is a feature of *dianoia* at *Rep.* 510d5–511a8 that it uses a kind of image of its own to focus on something higher.

[675] Asclepius, the more recent patron divinity of medicine among the Greeks, is here contrasted with Paion, the divine physician of *Iliad* 5, normally known as Paion (or Paian) Apollo, and the divine and daemonic medicines are then associated with the free and subservient doctors at *Laws* 720a.

[676] Diehl offers Imhotep (Imouthes), while Festugière notes that the same thing could have been said of Apollo.

[677] This seems to be an afterthought added when it was realized that the initial explanation is not stated clearly, hence the repetition of the entire phrase from the lemma.

Atlantis

It is **concerning _all_ the cosmos**, because there are also invisible causes of things arranged in the cosmos, which perfect wisdom studies before these things here, because its character is not technical, as Porphyry says, or suited to the crafts; for that is the gift of Hephaestus, but not Athena, as Iamblichus points out.[678]

It goes **as far as mantic and medicine**, because even of the encosmic gods one ought first to study their other powers, and then in this position [to study] their signification and their health-giving activity; since it has fallen to our lot to manage a body as well, and the future is not clear to us when we are laid low[679] in the body. That is because enmattered life displays a great deal of _possibility_ according to the basic stuff that is carried along in different states at different times.

All other branches of learning of course means geometry, astronomy, calculation, arithmetic, and those akin to these. By establishing all these the **law** lifted the Athenians and Saitians to a remarkable level of wisdom. So much for this.

Porphyry said that medicine too had good reason to come from Athena,[680] because Asclepius is intellect of the lunar order,[681] just as Apollo is intellect of the solar one. The divine Iamblichus criticized these claims,[682] saying that they miserably confuse the substances of the gods, and, to suit the context of the moment, incorrectly distribute the intellects and souls of encosmic things. For Asclepius too should be placed under Helios [the Sun], and should proceed from him into the earthly region, so that, just like the heaven, so too generation through

---

[678] Porphyry _in Tim._ fr. XIX Sodano, Iamblichus _in Tim._ fr. 18; Dillon (1973, 286) seems uncertain whether Porphyry regarded the wisdom referred to in the lemma as technical or craft wisdom, or whether he opposed this view, but he appears to me to offer very good reason to believe that he _sponsored_ the view, and that Iamblichus is here criticizing him. His evidence includes the manner in which the two are cited but not linked, and other extant details concerning Porphyry's views on the sphere of Athena's and of Hephaestus' influence. Furthermore, Iamblichus, in his comments on this section of the _Timaeus_, is largely adopting a _polemical_ attitude towards Porphyry, his sole significant predecessor as a commentator on the details of the Atlantis story.

[679] Reading κατακεκλιμένοις with Festugière, following Praechter, rather than the inferior κατακεκλεισμένοις printed by Diehl.

[680] Porph. fr. XX Sodano. Dillon (1973, 286) finds _eikotôs_ problematic, since it does not look as if Proclus would want to sanction that position by saying that Porphyry had 'good reason' to make his claim. In fact I feel that word order strongly suggests that Porphyry is making a claim about what Plato had said 'with good reason', since _eikotôs_ tends to come first when qualifying the main verb.

[681] Note the connection between Athena and the moon in Porphyry's work, 147.6–11, 165.16–17.

[682] = _in Tim._ fr. 19 Dillon.

On the *Timaeus* of Plato: Book 1

5   secondary participation should be held together by this divinity, being filled[683] by it with proportion and with harmonious blending.[684]

So at that time the goddess, imposing this whole arrangement and system, founded you people first. (24c4–5)

10   The term **whole** indicates the unified embrace within the goddess of all things ordered by her, with neither anything being left out nor plurality being separably contained in her. The word **arrangement** gives an indication of the orderly distribution of Athenaic providence, and the word **system** indicates the unification of these things and their kinship
15   with the one cosmos. Furthermore, **arrangement** signifies the procession of wholes from the goddess, and **system** the reversion to herself.[685] But since some of the things in the All are universal, and some particular, with the former corresponding to monads and the latter to numbers, with both partaking of Athenaic providence, but the universal and monadic
20   doing so in a primary sense, for this reason the present passage allocates the senior and hegemonic role to the Athenians, and the secondary and subordinate one to the Saitians.

Allotment and selection

After selecting the place in which you were born, observing how the
25   **temperate balance of the seasons there would bring men of exceptional wisdom.** (24c5–7)

While the goddess had previously been said to **be allotted** the land, she is now said to **select** it. The two ideas in fact converge, and being **allocated** does not imply a lack of will on her part, nor is her selection a random thing, as it is in the case of the particular soul. That is because
30   divine necessity converges with divine will, a choice with a lot, and
161   choosing with getting allotted something. The identity of this **place**

---

[683] Festugière, influenced by Diehl, sees the nominative participle πληρούμενος (being filled) as pertaining to the earthly region, which appears in the text in the accusative; this is very difficult, and I prefer to see it pertaining to the two parallel nominatives 'heaven' (οὐρανός) and 'generation' (γένεσις). As both partake of the same divinity, both should be filled with analogous qualities.

[684] Festugière speaks of a well-blended climate here, which is fine as applied to meteorological conditions, but, as god of healing, Asclepius must be concerned with the well-blended condition of living bodies too, and I assume that something akin to proportion and blending is also being postulated for the heavens.

[685] Festugière remarks 'pure fantaisie!', but all Proclus wants to suggest is that *diakosmêsis* represents the maintenance of order in separation (*dia-*), while *syntaxis* emphasizes the bringing together (*syn-*) of various elements into a single order.

258

Atlantis

has been stated before,[686] identifying it with space, i.e. place in the genuine sense. For it is in respect of this that the dividing up of divine lots occurs, so that they should be fixed in the same way for ever prior to things that are established in time. But at this time we should add that the soul of the All, which has the formal principles of all things divine and which depends on what comes before itself, imposes upon different parts of space a special affinity with different powers and certain symbols of the various orders among the gods. For this space is suspended immediately after her, and functions as her connate instrument. So she, being a rational and psychical cosmos, brings this too to be a perfect cosmos of space and life through the divine tokens. And space itself, though it is said to be both continuous and unmoved, is still not entirely without variance in itself, bearing in mind that not even the soul of the All is entirely invariant from one part to the next, but part of it is the circle of the Same and part that of the Other. And why speak of the soul? Not even the much-lauded intellect is without variance within itself, though everything in it is of the same colour, as it were – for not absolutely all content of the intellect is of the same potency, but some is more universal, some more particular. Not even this is remarkable. Rather the Demiurge himself has first, middle and last orders within himself. In consequence, as I believe, even Orpheus when he gives an indication of the order of things within him, says:

> Of him indeed is the radiant Heaven his head,
> His eyes are the Sun and against this the Moon,

and so on. If space here had had one substance with no variation, still the power of the soul, the orders of daemons allocated to it, and before these the gods who divide it up in accordance with the order pertaining to creation and allocations required by Justice, would have brought to light a great variation of parts within it. So it is from within that the selection should be considered to arise, resulting from the very substance of the gods, but not the kind of selection that we see in the case of individual souls. The one is substance-related,[687] while the other is determined only on the basis of its present life, the former eternal, the latter temporal. Moreover, one should understand this **place** neither as the earth

---

[686] 138.21–5: 'For the space that receives all the sectors of the cosmos and embraces them within it, and is stretched throughout everything bodily, is immobile, so that by being among things moved it should not itself require yet another place, with an unnoticed regress to infinity.' Cf. 139.9–15.

[687] Proclus means that the very thing that each god is in his or her own right determines what that god selects, while it is not the underlying nature of an individual soul but rather its temporary condition that determines how it makes its choice of life; for the latter *Rep.* 620a2–3 is an important influence.

259

On the *Timaeus* of Plato: Book 1

5   nor as the air,[688] but as the unmoved space that is ever illuminated by
the gods and divided up into Justice's lots. For these material things are
at times ready for participation in the gods, and at times unready, and
before the things that participate *at times* there must be those which ever
10   have the same link with the gods. So that will do for these matters.

Earlier thoughts on the balance of the seasons

As for the **temperate balance of the seasons** that produces wise men,
Panaetius and some other followers of Plato[689] have understood it at
the level of phenomena, supposing that Attica is appropriately constituted for the engendering of wise men because of its seasons being
15   nicely balanced. But Longinus raises difficulties with them, saying that
what they say is not true. On the contrary, there is considerable lack
of proportion in both summer and winter weather in this area. [He
also claims that], even if the area were like that, they would not any
longer be able to preserve [the doctrine of] the immortality of the soul
20   if wisdom grows naturally in them because of the **temperate balance
of the seasons**. For that is the doctrine of people who declare the soul
to be a blend or the perfection of a blend.[690] He [Longinus] himself

[688] Clearly no literal reading can take this place as one in the air, and it is safe to assume
that we are dealing here with the non-literal interpretation of either Porphyry or
one of those who influence him. Interpretations involving a clash of daemons would be
especially likely to fix the 'Athenians' and 'Atlantines' in the air, for the 'battle' is clearly
set in the region through which souls descend at 77.14–15. This is also the region in
which Phaethon's mythical loss of control occurs (cf. 108.8–114.21). It should be noted
that Middle Platonists associated daemons with no element as closely as air (Apuleius,
De Deo Socratis 6–8, cf. Philo *Gig.* 6–9, and by analogy at least Plut. *Mor.* 416e–f).

[689] Some other *Platônikoi*. Patillon and Brisson (2001, 175) somewhat similarly translate 'commentateurs de Platon'. Panaetius, though well-known for his love of Plato
(Glucker 1978, 28–30), always professed to be a Stoic. Indeed, in the second century
BC the term 'Platonic' was not employed for members of any school of philosophy, and
it became popular only in the early years of the Roman Empire – when 'Academic'
still suggested some kind of allegiance to *New* Academic doctrine, now in decline,
while many sought for a term suggesting a commitment to the philosophy of Plato,
usually revealed in the course of interpreting Platonic texts. It is probably the fact
that Panaetius had been cited by Porphyry and Longinus before him *as an authority
on Platonic matters* that causes Proclus to refer to him in this way here. So it would be
philologically rather than philosophically that Panaetius was a 'Platonic', suggesting that it
was Longinus who had been responsible for the term. The text is Panaetius test. 157
Alesse = fr. 76 van Straaten.

[690] Longinus believes that for the soul to be improved by a balance of the elements around
it, then it must itself have the nature of a balance of elements; but this doctrine would
be little different from that of the soul as a harmony (or 'blend', *krasis*, 86b9), said to be
inconsistent with immortality by Simmias at *Phaedo* 85e–86d. For further commentary
on 162.11–27 (= Longinus fr. 36) see Patillon and Brisson (2001), 316.

Atlantis

says that this **temperate balance** does not relate to the quality of the air,[691] but is some unnamed peculiarity of its climate, one that helps to perfect wisdom. For just as there are some waters with prophetic powers, and some places that are unhealthy and ruinous, so too there is nothing remarkable about this kind of peculiarity of a place contributing to wisdom.

Origenes, however, used to refer this **temperate balance** to the circular motion of the heavens, because it is from there that good or poor crops[692] of souls come, as Plato says in the *Republic*.

Proclus on the balance of the seasons

But this person has too partial a hold on the truth, while Longinus inadvertently makes the peculiarity [of Athens' climate] a bodily one, and gets embroiled in the difficulties that Porphyry raises against him.[693] For how does one peculiarity of the atmosphere make people ready for different things? Next, while the same peculiarity still remains, how is it that there is there no longer the same natural gift among the inhabitants? But if the peculiarity is destructible, what can one blame for destroying it? It is better to say that, while the gods divide up the whole of space according to the creational order, every sector of space receives souls that are applicable to it, Areic space the more spirited ones, Apolloniac space the prophetic ones, Asclepiac space the medically-minded ones, and Athenaic space the wise ones. And that this is due to its having a kind of quality from the god allotted it, or rather a power of a certain kind and an attunement to lives of a certain kind. So it is this attunement that he called a **temperate balance**, since in every sector there are many powers, both physical and psychical, daemonic and angelic, and the henad of the god who is allotted each [of them] unites and combines them all, making an unblended unity of them all. Because the Seasons have been

---

[691] That is to say that it is not a climatic feature brought about purely by the surrounding air having a nice balance of hot, cold, wet and dry (as might be suggested by the term for balance, *eukrasia*); rather it involves some special quasi-magical power unknown to the science of the time.

[692] The terms *phora* and more particularly *aphoria* here, both using an *agricultural* metaphor, make it plain that Origenes was attempting to relate his interpretation to *Republic* 546a5, where Plato talks of both souls and bodies, and where the cycles mentioned are not explicitly linked with the heavens. Festugière offers an extended note that fails to explain Origenes' interpretation, which no doubt was built upon earlier Middle Platonist or Neopythagorean understanding of this cryptic speech, which then had considerable attraction for fringe figures such as Dercyllides and Cronius (see *in Remp*. 2.22.20–26.14).

[693] = *in Tim*. fr. XXI Sodano.

261

On the *Timaeus* of Plato: Book 1

allotted by the Father the job of watching over these sectors or lots, the Seasons:

To whom is entrusted the great heaven and Olympus,

as Homer says,[694] and in accordance with whom the attunement of similar souls to locations is also accomplished, on this account he linked this **temperate balance** with **the Seasons,** as it is conserved entirely from that source. So the goddess, noticing how that sector of extended space was continually kept by the Seasons well attuned for the reception of wise souls, chose it. This does not imply that the place existed once without Athena and it was at some time acquired as her lot – for the account demonstrated quite the reverse – but because in extended space itself there are *readinesses* for the reception of divine illuminations, different readinesses in different locations. These were imposed by the universal Demiurge who embraces in a unitary fashion the powers of all the gods after himself, but they are strengthened and perfected, or rather actually proceed, from the gods set in charge of them. So just as in the choice of lives the soul that chooses its own proper life gets things right, in the same way too the soul that is positioned in its own proper place in accordance with its choice of life gets things right more than one sown into another's place. The circular motion of the heaven contributes greatly to this state of affairs, bringing on good or poor crops of souls, but in good harvests [land][695] given to producing **the wise** has an especially good crop, while in cases of failure the shortage there is less. So just as a farmer selects land for the bringing of seed to fruition, knowing that he will do better when there is a good crop, while when there is a poor one he will be affected less by the cycle's downturn on account of the potential of the land, so too the account states that the goddess selected this place because it is productive of **the wise,** so that when there is a good crop it will do better in the production of mindful people, and better when it is poor by falling less far short of a state of locational readiness for life.

But even if he were praising **the temperate balance of the** *observable* **seasons** here, we shall express no surprise, as a balance good for bodily health is one thing, while a balance helping to welcome mindful

---

[694] *Iliad* 5.750; the text is used to give a substantially different slant to the lemma by turning the seasons into the divinities of that name, represented by my capital letter. Since minuscule was not yet employed Proclus had no such means of identifying personifications.

[695] I follow Festugière here. The noun to be understood is far from obvious, but this seems to be the required sense.

Atlantis

souls – which is the kind of balance Attica has – is another. For even if it is not always the same [type of] wisdom, there is still a bit more of it for those who inhabit this land[696] on account of the peculiarity of the place and the seasons' being ready for it. So we suggest this much on these matters.

Miscellaneous additions

On the other hand the divine Iamblichus[697] did not identify **the place** with any corporeal part of extended space, but the immaterial cause, passing right through the earth, which supports bodies in its life and embraces all space within it. For it is into this kind of 'space', he says, that the goddess directs her creative activity, and here that she settles men who are truly good. It is possible to deduce from what is being said whether he is in tune with the details of Plato's language. But if one should step back from this and examine the whole by analogy, one should state that, when this goddess fashions and weaves the All with the Father, she allocated a more perfect lot to wholes and to the things of the better of the two columns of opposites. For these are more mindful than their opposites and more proper to the goddess. How all that is outstanding in wisdom is more Athenaic we shall show directly from the details of Plato's language.

The dual character of Athena – earlier interpretation

So because the goddess is both war- and wisdom-loving she chose this location that would produce the men most similar to herself and settled that first. (24c7–d3)

In these words Plato himself has handed down to us the more precise concept of this most important divinity, the Athenaic, exposing the subtle indications of the theologians for those able to glimpse the vision. Among the interpreters, however, different ones have resorted to different ways of setting it out, some recording their own opinions in a riddling manner, and others openly stating whatever they want, though with no authority

---

[696] One should not forget that Proclus is writing in Athens.

[697] *In Tim.* fr. 20, commented on (with summary of preceding positions) by Dillon (1973, 287–9); it seems likely that Iamblichus is attacking the whole earlier tradition here, and it is notable that Proclus reacts as if this is one of his predecessor's worst excesses.

On the *Timaeus* of Plato: Book 1

in what they said.[698] Porphyry, placing Athena in the moon,[699] says that
souls come down from there with both a spirited and a gentle side.
Consequently they are **both war- and wisdom-loving**, escorts of the
20   initiates at Eleusis, assuming that the family of those who lead the mysteries at Eleusis is from Musaeus of the Moon, and assuming further
that Hermes and the family of Heralds is among them[700] there in the
region of the moon, as he claims. But the divine Iamblichus criticizes
25   these persons[701] as failing to preserve the analogy properly, and he interprets the **war** concerned as that which utterly removed the unordered,
discordant and enmattered nature and **wisdom** as immaterial and transcendent intellection, while this goddess is responsible for both. The
Athenians imitate her through their thoughtful and warlike life, and
30   the Athenaic location is well attuned to the reception of souls of this
type.

The dual character of Athena – Proclus' interpretation[702]

But if it is necessary not only for the approach of these men to become
166   clear but also, before them, for the agreement of Plato's teaching with the
theologians to become clear, one must state things from the beginning as
follows. In the Father and Demiurge of the entire cosmos many unitary
5   orders of gods are revealed, protective, creative, uplifting, conserving,

---

[698] Porphyry, it seems, was one of those who stated his view openly, presumably *following
after* others who expressed things in riddles. For Porphyry's own predecessors it is
easiest to think here of Numenius and Origenes who are named as influences upon
Porphyry regarding Atlantis (76.30–77.24), particularly the former who thought in
terms of souls rather than daemons. However, in view of Plutarch's interest in the moon
as a natural place for souls, best seen in the *De Facie* (943a–5d), and also in religious
rites and daemons (likewise closely associated there with the moon), one should perhaps
consider him as a possible influence on Porphyry – and one less inclined to express his
view dogmatically.

[699] = *in Tim.* fr. XXII Sodano. Festugière observes the close agreement between this and
147.6–11 and 159.25–7 (= frs. XVI, XX).

[700] Not 'according to them', as Dillon translates (1973, 290).

[701] Less probably 'this interpretation' (taking the dative as neuter, not masculine), Dillon
(1973), 125; but the verb *epiplêssô* naturally takes a dative of the person. In any case one
would anticipate there having been for Iamblichus, as there was for Proclus (165.13–
16), more than just Porphyry who indulged in arbitrary interpretation. This fragment
= *in Tim.* 21.

[702] Van den Berg (2001, 41) comments on *Hymn* 7 that the Athena there 'is the Athena
of the life-making triad of hypercosmic gods. This appears from the fact that in *Plat.
Theol.* VI.11, p. 52, 24–7, this Athena is equated with the Athena mentioned in *Tim.*
24c7f. as a lover of war and wisdom. Proclus' exegesis of this phrase in his *Timaeus*
commentary coincides with his treatment of Athena in *H.* VII . . .'

264

Atlantis

and perfective, and one of the principal intellective henads within him is this immaculate and invincible divinity, thanks to whom the Demiurge himself remains unswerving and unflinching,[703] and all things that proceed from him participate in an unyielding power by which he thinks all things in transcendence, removed from all of reality. All the theologians call this divinity Athena, because on the one hand she is born from the head of the Father, and remains in him as creative thought, transcendent and immaterial – that is why Socrates honoured her as Theonoe in the *Cratylus*;[704] and on the other hand because she rose up arms and all,[705] the one who gives immaculate[706] assistance to the one Demiurge in arranging everything and marshalling[707] the entire [force] along with the Father. It is for the former reason that they call her **wisdom-loving**, and for the second reason [that they call her] **war-loving**. For she who embraces all the Father's wisdom is **wisdom-loving**, while she who has uniform authority over all rivalry could with good reason be called **war-loving**. Hence Orpheus too says about her being born that Zeus gave birth to her from his head,

> gleaming with weapons, a brazen bloom to behold.[708]

However, since she had to proceed to the second and third orders as well,[709] she makes an appearance in the person of Korê at the immaculate heptad, and she engenders every virtue from herself and uplifting powers, and she radiates intellect and immaculate life upon those at second

---

[703] For the terminology here (*atreptos, achrantos, adamastos, aklinês*) see 156.29 and 157.11–18; the latter passage again involves 'theologians'.

[704] The *Cratylus* (407a8–c2) has inspired far more than just the name 'Theonoe' here, for Plato already ascribed this kind of interpretation (but without emphasis on transcendence) to 'the ancients' as well as the majority of Homeric exegetes in his own day; and he explains 'Theonoe' as either god's intellective thought (b4) or the thought of divine things (b7), or even as moral thought (b9).

[705] Accepting Festugière's excellent correction of ὅπλων for ὅλων at 166.15.

[706] The term relates, as also 156.18–157.16 and 166.6 above, to the virginal purity of Athena, interpreted in terms of a transcendence free from material influences.

[707] Here the military sense of *tassô* seems irresistible.   [708] *Orph. fr.* 174.

[709] For an earlier account of the way Athena's influence extends into the divine orders below see 140.30–141.13. First in the father; second among the hegemonic gods; third among the twelve rulers; and fourth, revealing *independent* authority, in the heaven, (a) in the inerrant region (Ram, Virgin, etc.), (b) at the sun; (c) at the moon, as monad of a lunar triad. Fifth on the earth, in places like Athens. In this location we hear of her subsequent appearances (after her association first with Zeus), second in the immaculate heptad, third among the independent gods, fourth in the heaven, and fifth beneath the moon. This illustrates the need for careful work on the exact nature of Proclus' system of younger gods, such as that of Opsomer (2003).

On the *Timaeus* of Plato: Book 1

30   level. Hence Korê too is called 'tritogenês',[710] and she is allotted this very
'*koron*' quality, i.e. her purity,[711] from her distinctive Athenaic character. She makes an appearance also among the independent gods, uniting
167 the Lunar order[712] with her intellective and creative light and making it
immaculate as far as acts of procreation are concerned, and also revealing that the one single henad of them is unmixed and free from the
influence of the powers that depend on them. She reveals herself also
in the heaven and beneath the moon, everywhere shielding herself with
5   this double power – or rather providing the cause of both through her
own unified gift. [I make this correction] because her unyielding character is intellective and her transcendent wisdom is pure and unmixed
with secondary things, while there is this one distinctive character of
Athenaic providence that comes right down to the lowest things. For in
circumstances where even those among individual souls assimilated to
10   her shield themselves with an amazing wisdom and display an irresistible
strength, what could one say about those in her chorus who are daemons
or encosmic, independent, or hegemonic members of the divine orders?
All of them receive from this goddess the double characteristic as if from
15   a single spring. Hence the divine poet too, giving an indication of both
aspects of her in the course of his mythical inventions, says:

> Upon the threshold of the Father she spread out the finely woven
> peplos,
> Much embroidered, which she herself had made and toiled at with
> her hands;
20   > While she, donning the tunic of cloud-gathering Zeus,
> Armed herself with gear for the purpose of war.[713]

[710] Unlike Festugière, I keep the lower case, which does not give the adjective the character
of an official name for Korê, and perhaps points to Korê as the third manifestation of
Athena. That enables me to resist the temptation to delete the article before *korê* at
166.29, which would make Athena herself the subject and avoid giving *Tritogenês* as an
epithet to a divinity other than Athena herself. For *Tritogeneia*, a name with various
interpretations in antiquity, is in fact just an ancient name for Athena, while Korê,
as a *name* for a divinity, usually applies to the daughter of Demeter in the Eleusinian
mysteries, elsewhere normally known as Persephone. Athena herself was of course an
unmarried female, and hence a *korê*. As Diehl and Festugière note Korê is later called
Mounogeneia below (457.17), which seems to be in direct conflict with *Tritogeneia* if that
is understood as being derived from *tritos* ('third', hence 'Thrice-Born') as I presume
to be the case here (because of Athena's appearance at three levels).

[711] Diehl accentuates *koron* in such a way as to connect most directly with *korê* (plausibly to
suggest 'unmarried'), but Festugière sees that the accent required is that which makes it
a rare synonym of *katharon* (pure), which is added to explain the term further. Its best-
known use within Platonism was in Plato's *Cratylus*, 396b6, where Kronos is explained
as pure intellect (*koros nous*).

[712] One should remember here Porphyry's association of Athena with the moon; see on
165.16.

[713] The quotation combines *Iliad* 5.734–5 and 8.385–6.

266

Atlantis

For by the peplos, which she makes and bases on her own designs, one should understand her own intellective wisdom, while by the war-tunic of Zeus one should understand the creative providence that cares unflinchingly for encosmic things and constantly prepares the diviner forces to vanquish those within the cosmos. It is because of this, I imagine, that he set her up as an ally of the Greeks against the barbarians, just as Plato makes her an ally of the Athenians against the people of Atlantis, so that everywhere the more intellective and divine forces should conquer the less rational and less respected ones.

It is true that Ares too is fond of war and rivalry, but he is more closely related to separation and division, while Athena both conserves the rivalry and lights the path to unity for those she governs. Hence she has been said to be **war-loving** in respect of her unifying influence, but in his case it is with regard to dividing influence:[714]

> For always are strife, war and battles your loves.[715]

In this case it is because the god drew separation as his supreme lot, but in that case it was because the rival forces are somehow brought together on account of this goddess since the better element prevails – and since even the ancients ranked her alongside Victory on this account.

So if this has been rightly stated, she is **wisdom-loving** qua creative intelligence and qua transcendent and immaterial wisdom, wherefore she is called Mêtis (Counsel) in the company of the gods, and accordingly says about herself:

> I have a name for my counsel and for my benefits.[716]

But she is **war-loving** qua one who conserves the rivalries within wholes and qua invincible and unyielding goddess – wherefore she also keeps Dionysus immaculate,[717] and contends with the Giants along with the Father, and she alone plies the aegis without Zeus commanding it and holds the spear before it:

> With which she tames rows of men,
> Heroes, against whom she of the mighty sire takes offence.[718]

In her graciousness she provides for us a share in her immaculate wisdom and the fulfilment of our intellective power, providing us with

---

[714] One may perhaps be reminded of *Philebus* 23c–d, where 'all things now existent in the cosmos' are mixed of the opposites limit and unlimited, while their mixture is promoted by a cause of mixture and *perhaps* undermined by a cause of separation.

[715] *Iliad* 5.891, addressed by Zeus to Ares.   [716] *Iliad* 13.299.

[717] On her preservation of the heart of Dionysus see *Hymn* 7.11–15, with Van den Berg's commentary (2001), 274–9.

[718] Again the quotation is from two sources, *Iliad* 8.390, and *Odyssey* 1.100.

267

On the *Timaeus* of Plato: Book 1

25 Olympian benefits that elevate the soul, while casting out the Gigantic, generation-producing imaginings, stirring up in us pure and undistorted concepts concerning all the gods, and radiating upon us the divine light from herself.

Other epithets of Athena

For she is 'light-bringer' since she extends the intelligible light in all directions, 'saviour' since she establishes all particular intelligence in the
169 universal intellections of the Father, 'worker' since she is the director of creative works – at least the Theologian says that the Father produced her:

> So that she might become for him the fulfiller of great deeds.[719]

She is 'beauty-worker' since she conserves all the works of the Father in
5 intellective beauty; 'virgin' because she holds before her an immaculate and unmingled purity; '**war-lover**' because she manages the opposing columns in the All and presides over war in its totality; 'aegis-holder' because she sets the whole of destiny in motion and guides its productions.

10 We should have gone on to the other epithets of the goddess, if I didn't feel that I was extending this discussion on account of my own deep involvement in what is being said. So let us turn away from this back to the task before us, and say that Plato called these two gods
15 **wisdom-lovers**, Eros[720] and Athena, not both in the same respect, but the former as an intermediary between two totalities[721] and as one who draws us up to intelligible wisdom, and the latter as an extreme and as the unifying force of creative wisdom. For the Demiurge was:

> Both Mêtis the first parent and Erôs of great delight,[722]

20 and as Mêtis he gives birth to Athena, while as Erôs he is the parent of the Erotic series.

---

[719] *Orph. fr.* 176.
[720] At *Symposium* 203d7 and 204b2–5; his intermediate situation between total wisdom and total ignorance is plain at 203e5 and 204b5. Proclus is certainly correct to distinguish the ways in which the two gods were described by Plato as 'lovers of wisdom'.
[721] Festugière has simply 'intermédiaire dans l'Univers' for μεσότητα τῶν ὅλων, but Proclus is surely thinking of the god's situation between what is ignorant as a whole and what is wise as a whole in Plato.
[722] *Orph. fr.* 168.9 conflated with 169.4.

Atlantis

The Athenians and what they stand for on a universal level

And so you lived under laws of this kind and even more well-governed still, exceeding all humankind in every virtue, as was to be expected of those who were the products of divine parentage and of divine education. (24d3–6)

According to the historical narrative the Athenians' situation was more ancient than that of the Saitians, the foundation of their constitution came earlier, and their laws were closer to Athena. But among their cosmic paradigms too the wholes are prior to the parts, and they have a more divine order, a greater power, and a diviner form of virtue that is genuinely Athenaic.[723] For the genus 'virtue' is proper to this great goddess, seeing that she herself is virtue.[724] For while remaining in the Demiurge she is unchanging wisdom and intellection, and among the hegemonic gods she reveals her power of virtue:

> She is hailed by the noble name of virtue,[725]

as Orpheus says. That is how [we explain] this.

That the more divine things in the All could in the true sense be called **products of divine parentage and of divine education** is evident, for they are both established and perfected – or rather they are always perfect on account of the creative activity of the gods and the immaculate productive activity of Athena. So all that is linked to gods, proceeds from gods, and reverts to gods displays outstanding virtue. This is so at the universal level, since one must also posit divine virtue in the All, and it is also so in human lives in imitation of what is universally so. Hence it is also attributed to the Athenians by the present passage. Making the life of the Athenians one continuous one, it joined up Solon with the ancient Athenians, saying **so you lived**. For their paradigm is one with itself and continuous, since the entire Athenaic series is a single pervasive one passing right through to the lowest things, beginning with the hyper-heavenly arrangements at the top.

The Athenians greatest deed and its paradigmatic significance

Many great deeds of your own city are recorded and admired here, yet of all of them one excels in magnitude and virtue. (24d7–e1)

After promising to give a summary of the laws and deeds of the Athenians (23e5–6) he has actually passed on to their 'laws' already in distinguishing their classes, and he will henceforth give a glowing account

---

[723] Accepting Kroll's emendation, as Festugière too seems to do without comment.
[724] At 166.27 she is the origin of all virtue.   [725] *Orph. fr.* 175.

269

On the *Timaeus* of Plato: Book 1

171 of their deeds, in which the city will be lauded, while its official civic divinity is treated with [silent] respect.[726] But since, even of their deeds, one could give both an enumeration of them on the one hand, and on the other an all-embracing unity through which the entire character of their constitution will be displayed, he announces that he will teach the deed that is greatest and stands out in virtue, [meaning] not

5 one of many, but one prior to the many.[727] For such an approach to discourse is both proper to the All, in which wholes constitute a single continuous life, and to the goddess, who draws together the many rivalries into a single unified whole. So though there were **many great deeds of the city**, it is with good reason that he narrates the single

10 deed that has been written in the temples. For it has also an intellective paradigm, in as much as that which **excels in magnitude and virtue** is also studied in the cosmos, with excellence **in magnitude** reflecting its being universal, and **in virtue** its being intellective. For the universal and more divine things within the cosmos both have many

15 particular operations and constitute a single life and constitution – a constitution according to which they gain the ascendancy over inferior things under the leadership of Athena. That is how this must be stated.

But Porphyry[728] understood all the great and marvellous deeds directed against matter and material characters as being those of souls,

20 using 'material characters' as a term for the daemons. For he says that there are two races of daemons, one souls[729] and the other daemons, and these latter are material powers with a character-forming effect on

---

[726] The verb *euphêmein* at 170.30 means to show appropriate respect in one's speech, whether by reverent speech or by silence. The parallel at 138.27–28 causes Festugière to highlight the former possibility, but the goddess is not directly mentioned in the rest of this dialogue's account of the war with Atlantis, and there appears now to be a contrast between the praise offered to the Athenians and the type of respect that the goddess will receive.

[727] The emphasis is now on demonstrating how what is said in this lemma can reflect the universal order, and order that encompasses these deeds as understood literally, thus ensuring that the story is true in all senses. It seems reasonable to suppose that what is said here must reflect the views of Iamblichus, as (i) the universal-and-particular interpretation is his innovation, and, though Porphyry is criticized below (171.17–22), he escapes mention except in the phrase 'the interpreter after him' (171.23). Only the lines 171.17–23 are printed by Dillon (1973) as *in Tim.* fr. 22, though he inclines towards seeing Iamblichus and Proclus as in agreement throughout the passage, including 171.1–17 (commentary, 291–2).

[728] = *in Tim.* fr. XXIII Sodano.

[729] See *in Tim.* fr. X Sodano, 77.11–12; one type is 'made up of individual souls who have received a daemonic lot'; there had also been a third category of *daemones* here, but they had been divine (perhaps inspired by the frequent use of the term to refer to gods in early Greece) and have no direct relevance to the interpretation of the Atlantis story.

270

Atlantis

souls. And indeed he had to undergo criticism of these doctrines from the interpreter after him.[730]

The Athenians' opponents and what their confrontation represents

For the inscriptions state how great a power your city once   25
stopped when it advanced with aggression against all Europe and
Asia, ... (24e1–3)

Here Plato omits no element of panegyric magnification if one were to understand the war of the Athenians against the people of Atlantis as simple narrative,[731] but neither, in his care, has he fallen short of any   30 theological precision if one should care to cross to universals from particulars and to advance from the images to paradigms.[732] While many certainly were accustomed to go on and on in their Panathenaic speeches[733]   **172** about the Persian invasion force and the Athenian victories by land and sea, stuff with which the new generation of speech-writers[734] have filled

---

[730] This being Iamblichus, of course; *in Tim.* fr. 22. Porphyry's views, no doubt built substantially on those of Numenius except for their avoidance of any suggestion of material soul (Numenius fr. 52. 64–70, where *malignam animam = silvam*), accord perfectly with what is said of them at 77.6–24. Here it is specified that Porphyry was relating Atlantis to the *lowest* of three categories of *daemon*, which is bad and has a corrupting influence on souls.

[731] This kind of observation would seem to be most easily associated with an interpreter who treated the Atlantis episode as an attempt to write history, and to fulfil the stylistic obligations of one composing in that genre. That much would agree with Longinus' 'philological' concerns, and his interest in how best to praise people (see fr. 34 = 90.16–21); from fr. 36 (=162.15–27) one might deduce that Longinus took the literal interpretation for granted, for otherwise he would not have gone to great lengths to make the account of Athens' climate agree with a plausible factual claim; for Longinus as a literalist interpreter see Baltes (1983). Certainly any non-literal interpretation had to be followed through systematically (as Porphyry had done), while Longinus had taken only a passing interest in Atlantis (fr. 37 = 204.18–24). If one were looking for confirmation of Longinus' influence one might seek it in the grammarians' term *enkômiastikos*. This is found only in Book 1, here and at 62.8, where 'one of the older [interpreters]', without endorsement from Proclus, contrasts it with the Socratic style.

[732] Philological considerations continue to 172.14, but the higher significance of the story is then resumed.

[733] It seems impossible that Proclus, or rather the tradition that he follows, should not have Isocrates, as a known rival of Plato, in mind as the author of such a speech. Note the resumption of what might be called 'philological' material.

[734] I.e. those of the so-called 'second sophistic', concerned to display their talents rather than to accomplish any civic purpose; Festugière refers appropriately to the *Panathenaicus* (= speech 1) of Aelius Aristides, an author already cited for his views on the Nile (121.7), and whose works Neoplatonists continued to find it necessary to respond to (Olymp. *in Gorg.* 1.13, 32.2, 36.4–5, 38.2–3, 40.2, 41.3, 11, 45.3). One might note also that Longinus had admired Aristides greatly as an orator (frs. 52, 54).

271

On the *Timaeus* of Plato: Book 1

their speeches too, in his own praise of Athens he does not discuss the Persians or tell of any other similar achievement. Instead he introduces into our region an Atlantic War from somewhere outside it, one with the power to completely obliterate everything, and he records how the Athenians were valiant and victorious in this, vanquishing a power of such size and quality. Since the Persian invasion force set out against the Greeks, and the Athenians in particular, from the east, he himself brought the Atlantic War from the west,[735] so that you could picture the Athenians' city, as if in the centre, chastising the barbarian forces that moved in a disorderly fashion[736] on either side.

Moreover, although in Athenian tradition and in the mysteries the war against the Giants was much discussed, and particularly how Athena won the prize for valour in the battle against them, because she defeated these together with the Titans along with her Father, he did not think it safe to introduce a war directly against gods. That is the very charge that he had been bringing against the ancient poets, and it would have been odd for Critias or Timaeus, after being among Socrates' audience when he found fault with the poets the day before, again to attribute wars and dissension to the gods. So, through the parallel between humans and things divine, he teaches us even of this war before the origin of the cosmos, adopting the Athenians to represent Athena and the Olympian gods and the people of Atlantis to represent the Titans and Giants, for it is possible to study the same things in images as one can in universals. And, so as to remind us of the parallel, he refers his listeners through the name of the Athenians to the Olympian column under Athena's generalship, and through the people of Atlantis to the Titanic gods. For presumably, among the Titanic gods, the very great Atlas is also one. In fact the theologians too say that after the dismemberment of Dionysus, who shows the divisible procession into the All from the indivisible creation, the other Titans were given a different allotment by Zeus, whereas Atlas was stationed in the western regions holding up the heaven:[737]

---

[735] Note how Proclus sometimes writes as if Plato is making a conscious choice in selecting the details of the story, a feature that undercuts the idea that they are determined by history; in cases like this one may ask whether he is not drawing *either* on what had been said by Porphyry and others before him who were unconcerned with any historical truth in the story *or* on Longinus' kind of philologically inspired considerations.

[736] It is difficult to resist the idea of an allusion to the disorderly motion that the Demiurge himself must reduce to order at *Tim.* 30a4–5.

[737] *Orph. fr.* 215; Festugière notes that Kern (p. 236) has included Simpl., *in DC* 375.12–16, in which Atlas is himself one 'of the Titans involved with Dionysus', but, unlike the rest, does not persist in wronging him, inclines towards Zeus, and so receives a different

272

Atlantis

> But by constraints of necessity Atlas holds up the broad heaven
> At earth's very limits.[738]

Furthermore the victory tokens of Athena are celebrated among the Athenians, and they conduct this feast on the assumption that Poseidon was beaten by Athena,[739] the generation-producing defeated by the intellective, and that after the provision of necessities the inhabitants of this land have set out upon the road to life in accordance with intelligence. For they regard Poseidon as presiding over generation and Athena as overseeing intellectual life.

So you have a very great help in achieving this goal from the text at hand. For the Athenians who are named after the goddess correspond to her, while the people of Atlantis, because they inhabit an island and because they are said to be the descendants of Poseidon,[740] maintain their correspondence with this god, so that it is clear from this that the Atlantic War gives an indication of the intermediate creation, in the course of which the second father,[741] brought to fullness by Athena and the other invisible causes, guides the diviner entities to greater power, and enlists under the intellective ones everything multiplied, material, and closer to matter according to their basic nature. For the gods themselves are eternally united, but things managed by them are infected with such division. That's how one must contemplate these things in private.[742]

So that we may adopt some definite guidelines for the analysis confronting us, the habitable regions within the Pillars of Heracles[743] must **174** be made to correspond to the entire superior column, and those outside to the entire inferior one, while this last [must be assumed] to have one

---

fate. Note Festugière's insistence that 'by Zeus' is to be read with what follows, contrary to what is suggested by Diehl's punctuation.

[738] The quotation is from Hesiod, *Theog.* 517–18, who, like his fellow epicist Homer, is often linked by Proclus with Orphic 'theologians'.

[739] In the mythical contest to determine who would have chief honours at Athens, in which Poseidon could offer only a brackish spring as against Athena's olive tree.

[740] At *Critias* 113c2–4; one should not forget that Proclus sees no sharp break between the *Timaeus* and the *Critias*, and should not be expected to refer to it as he would to an entirely separate dialogue.

[741] I.e. Poseidon himself, as second member of the triad of demiurges Zeus (B), Poseidon, Hades (for which cf. 9.16–24), and a generation-worker.

[742] I believe that this is not a comment on the type of interpretation just offered, but is rather part of the help that Proclus wants to offer his pupils on the basis of this passage (cf. 173.15–16 above). Hence this paragraph has been not so much interpretation, but rather a fairly simple lesson in the theology of the Athenian School.

[743] Straits of Gibraltar.

On the *Timaeus* of Plato: Book 1

continuous life that proceeds in a variety of ways. So whether you start with the gods and speak of Olympians and Titans, or with intellect of rest and motion or of same and different, or with souls of rational and irrational, or with bodies of heaven and generation, or if you partition substances in any other way, throughout all the divisions the whole class of people inside the Pillars of Heracles will correspond to the better, and those outside to the worse. For that is where the real 'sea of dissimilarity' is,[744] and all enmattered life and the life which proceeds to extension and multiplicity away from the one. So whether in Orphic fashion you wanted to set the Olympic and Titanic races in opposition and to praise the one side that masters the other; or whether in Pythagorean fashion to see the two opposing columns passing from the top right down to the lowest things with the better arranging the inferior; or whether in Platonic fashion to study 'much unlimited in the All, and much limit', as we have learned in the *Philebus* (30b), and the unlimited as a whole together with the measures of limit bringing about a generation that stretches through all encosmic things, you would be able to grasp one thing from all of these – that the entire composition of the cosmos is joined together in harmony out of this rivalry. And if the noble Heraclitus was looking to this when he said 'War is Father of all', then not even he was speaking strangely.[745]

Porphyry at this point, relating his study to daemons and souls, and at times making mention of the Titanic War of myth, is in some respects persuasive, and in others not, in his approach to the text at hand.[746] The divine Iamblichus,[747] however, taking a line that is surprising because of his attack on others for rushing into too partial an analysis, decided to understand what is being said in no other way than according to its obvious meaning. And yet he certainly gave us in his prefatory comments some encouragement for interpretation of our present type. But may this divine gentleman, who has educated us in so many other matters as well as this, look favourably on us.

---

[744] Proclus alludes to *Statesman* 273d6–e1 (where the phrase depicts a state of disorder that is never quite reached), as he will again at 175.20 and 179.26.

[745] Heraclitus, to whose words (B53) this alludes, was known for his proverbial obscurity.

[746] = *in Tim.* fr. XXIV Sodano. Proclus, believing that the universal patterns that he requires must be able to be found at various levels, hesitates to write off everything Porphyry claims here, being milder than Iamblichus in this regard.

[747] *in Tim.* fr. 23; Dillon (1973, 293) notes that Iamblichus also inclines towards a literal interpretation in fr. 12 (117.18–28). It is a distinct possibility that both Porphyry and Iamblichus suspend their in-depth interpretation for a while (24e4–26b2), as Proclus mentions neither until 194.15, the size of the lemmata increases, and his own treatment is less detailed.

Atlantis

Lexis: the overall interpretation applied to details of the text

As we turn to the interpretation of Plato's language we shall ourselves
see fit to remind ourselves of the guidelines recorded above,[748] and to
align the people of Atlantis with all the universal terms of the inferior
column of opposites. For there are some universals and some particulars in this. The **aggression** relates to their procession, their division
through subordination, and their bordering on matter. For that is what
true limitlessness and ugliness is, for which reason they say that it works
aggression upon what borders upon it and upon what is somehow in it.
The theologian reveals their paradigm in the following terms:

> The ill-planning Titans, with over-violent heart.[749]

The **advance from outside**[750] relates to their secession to a dwelling-
place far from the gods and from the diviner things in the All. For this
from outside does not signify an encircling of forces, but the kind of
being that has passed beyond all that is stable, immaterial, pure, and
unified. The **Atlantic Ocean** relates to matter itself, whether it is as
an 'abyss' that you care to describe it, or as a 'sea of dissimilarity',[751]
or whatever. For matter receives the names of the inferior column of
opposites, being called 'limitlessness', 'darkness', 'irrationality', 'mea-
surelessness', 'principle of otherness', and 'dyad' – just as the Atlantic
Ocean gets its name from Atlantis. In this way, by understanding the
analogies in order, we shall declare that all the inferior column of opposites, both the more universal races with it and the more partial, is
characterized by procession, division, and a move towards matter. In
this way it pervades everything, being reflected in each kind in the way
proper to it and appearing in a corresponding manner in each nature –
divine, intellective, psychical and bodily. Being of this type, it receives
arrangement and order from the better [column], which you could with
good reason call Athenaic because it is immaculate and takes control of
the inferior through its own power. When it is set in order, an end is put
to its division and limitlessness, the race of Titans being held in check
by the Olympian gods, otherness being united by sameness, motion by

---

[748] I.e. 173.28–174.24.

[749] *Orph. fr.* 119; in the term *hyperbios* the latter element (*bia*) is thought to reflect their
aggression.

[750] I place this in bold because Proclus continues as if the lemma had included the words
'advancing from outside, from the Atlantic Ocean'. It may be that the lemma has been
incorrectly recorded.

[751] See on 174.10. The term 'abyss' (literally 'bottomless') is found *as a noun* in religious
and magical literature of the Roman period, and occurs only here in this commentary.

275

On the *Timaeus* of Plato: Book 1

5   rest, irrational souls from the rational ones, generation thanks to things in heaven, and similarly in every case.

Let us not because of this account imagine that one should postulate distinct first principles for things.[752] For we claim that even the two columns of opposites are related. The One is the leading princi-
10   ple of all opposition, as the Pythagoreans too say. But since, after the single cause, the dyad too revealed itself as one of the principles, and among these the monad is superior to the dyad (or, if you prefer to talk in Orphic terms, aether to chaos), the divisions continue in this
15   way both in the gods before the cosmos and in encosmic things right down to the last. In the former case the conserving or creative force comes under one principle, while the generative or life-producing force comes under another, while in the latter the Olympian force comes under the monad and the Titanic under the dyad, and under the senior one
20   come sameness, rest, reason, and form, while under the remaining one come otherness, motion, irrationality, and matter. For the subordination of the two principles proceeds right down to these. But since the One is over and above the first dyad, what seem to be opposites are brought together and ordered in a single arrangement. For there are in the All
25   the twin races of gods, the corresponding divisions of reality, the various kinds of souls, and opposing kinds of bodies, and the inferior are controlled by the more divine. And one cosmos is brought to fulfilment, joined together from opposites, based on 'limiters and unlimiteds' in
30   Philolaus' words,[753] and the nature of its limitlessness accords with the 'unlimiteds' within it that come from the indeterminate dyad, the nature of its limit accords with the 'limiters' that come from the intelligible monad, but what accords with what comes from all[754] of these is a sin-
177 gle, whole, and all-perfect form, being from the One.[755] For it is god who establishes the mixed class, as the Socrates of the *Philebus* says.[756]

---

[752] It is possible, with Festugière, to follow the scholiast in assuming this alludes to Manicheanism, though even Plato was aware of its dualist antecedents.

[753] Philolaus B1.2 DK, which differs somewhat from the 'limit and unlimited' familiar from *Philebus* 23c.

[754] I.e. all 'limiters' and 'unlimiteds' in Philolaus' terms (not just both classes), and that must be the universe.

[755] Rather than adding an article with Diehl and Festugière, I substitute the neuter of the participle (ὄν for ὦν) at 177.1.

[756] Diehl and Festugière refer to 61c, but this involves a prayer to the god of the mixing process, 'whether Dionysus, Hephaestus, or whichever of the gods has mingling as his privilege'; that Dionysus comes first here is obviously because he controls the mixture of wine and water, and has nothing to do with his power to mix limit and unlimited. Rather Proclus has in mind the cause of the mixture from the metaphysical passage itself (23d, 26e–27b, 30b–d), which turns out to be a demiurgic power (27b1), wisdom and intelligence (30c6), and hence part of the nature of Zeus (30d1–3).

Atlantis

The compatibility of historical and symbolic interpretations

For at that time the sea there was navigable; for it had an island in front of the mouth that you call, as you say, the 'Pillars of Heracles'. The island was bigger than Libya and Asia together, and from this it was possible for travellers at that time to cross over to the other islands, and from the islands to the whole mainland on the far side which rings that genuine sea. (24e4–25a2)

That there was such an island, and of this size, is shown by some of those who give the story of the region of the outside sea. For they say that there were even in their own time seven islands in that sea sacred to Persephone, and three other huge ones, that of Pluto, that of Ammon, and in the middle of these another belonging to Poseidon, two hundred kilometres in length.[757] Those living on it have kept alive the memory from their ancestors of the Atlantis that actually came into being, the hugest island there, which over many cycles of time was the overlord of all the islands in the Atlantic Ocean, and was itself Poseidon's sacred island. This is what Marcellus has written in his *Aethiopica*.[758]

But, even if this is right and some such island did arise, it is still possible to take the story about it both as history and as an image of something that arises naturally within the whole universe, both explaining this [island] in terms of what it resembles, and gradually accustoming those who hear of such spectacles[759] to the whole study of encosmic things. For it is possible to study the same correspondences at either a more particular or a more encompassing level. So it is necessary for the instruction to proceed from totalities and to conclude its study with the detail of particular situations.

Do not be surprised then that we are investigating this correspondence to begin with in one way and in general outline, and now in a fashion that is different, but yet the same, with the detail proper to the subject matter. For there is a double column of opposites in the All,

---

[757] The details are such that they could reflect travellers' tales of the Canaries and perhaps the Azores.

[758] Festugière points out that the author is unknown, and suggests confusion with Marcianus of Heraclea, who is known to have written, shortly before Proclus' time, a *Periplous of the Outside Sea*. But Marcellus may well have existed. The title given by Proclus reveals only that it would have been mainly about Africa. Literature about far away places was a particularly disreputable genre, known for the imagination of writers – a feature satirized by Lucian in *A True History*. Pliny, when discussing islands round Africa (6.202), mentions one called Atlantis as still being present, but, remarkably, makes no connection with Plato's story.

[759] Festugière translates 'considérations' and complains that the sense is missing in LSJ. But the idea of the word here is 'wondrous things that somebody has beheld', and it fits the genre of travellers' tales with which we must associate Marcellus.

On the *Timaeus* of Plato: Book 1

as we were saying, beginning with the gods and reaching its limit with matter and the enmattered form, with either of them having some more universal elements and some more particular ones – we said this before too. Some also are in between the two (for the divine races are the most encompassing of all, and the final elements the most individual, while some are in between, the intellective and psychical races).

Lexis: principles applied to details of the geography

So we think it right to first divide the inferior column into three, taking the most universal races in it, the intermediate, and the last. In a position corresponding to the first we place the Atlantines, to the second the other islands, and to the third **the whole mainland on the far side**, and to matter the sea and the Atlantic Ocean. For the whole of the inferior column borders on matter and proceeds towards multiplicity and division, but it still has of itself internal excess and deficiency. That is why he said that the Atlantines set out 'from outside' (24e3), insofar as they are further from the one and closer to matter, and that they inhabit an island **bigger than Libya and Asia**, insofar as they proceed towards mass and extension. For everything that proceeds further from the One gains in quantity as it loses in power, just as those that are compressed closer in quantity have a remarkable power, so that size here signifies subordination, and procession and extension over all. **The sea was navigable** because more universal things proceed down to the last and arrange matter, but when they come to the limit of possible arrangement they stop, and that which remains beyond it is out of range. For the utterly non-existent comes directly after the bounds of existence. The addition of **at that time** is indicative of the fact that the universal causes can pass unhindered even through matter and arrange it, while we cannot always master it, but are submerged in the unlimited and indeterminate nature.[760]

Since the procession of things is continuous, and nowhere is any void getting left, but an orderly lowering in rank is observed coming from the most universal things to the intermediates which both encompass and are encompassed, and from the intermediates to the furthest and most individual, on this account Plato too says that the passage for the people of Atlantis is from Atlantis to **the other islands**, and from these to **the mainland** situated **on the far side**. And Atlantis is one, the other islands are many, and the mainland is largest. For the monad befits individual members of the first kind, number and multiplicity befit the second – for multiplicity comes with the dyad – and largeness befits the third on

---

[760] See note on 117.6–7 regarding the image of the soul's submersion in matter.

278

Atlantis

account of the advance of largeness to the triad.[761] And since the lowest stages of the inferior column of opposites are the most enmattered things, he showed that they are the furthest distant from the better through [the phrase] **on the far side**, and he did not rest content, as in the case of the Atlantines, with calling it 'outside' only, [a term] which demonstrated that they were of the other sector,[762] but he added **on the far side** so that he might give an indication of its extreme subordination. Through its ringing the **genuine sea** he signified its placement in relation to matter and the last of encosmic things. For the **genuine sea** corresponds to what is genuinely *false* or genuine *matter*, which he called 'a sea of dissimilarity' in the *Statesman*.[763]

Furthermore, because it is necessary that these two opposite columns should be divided off from each other, kept free from cross-contamination by the creational boundaries, he said that the **Pillars of Heracles** divided off the inside habitable world from the outside. For it was the strongest point of creational production and the divine division of the kinds in the All, ever remaining steadfastly and manfully the same, that he called **Pillars of Heracles**. For this Heracles is of Zeus' [series]. The one who is divine and precedes him got as his lot the post of guardian of the generative series. So one should assume that the creational division that keeps the two segments of the All apart stems from both.

Symbolism of the confined sea

For things here, as many as are within the mouth of which we speak, resemble a harbour with a narrow entrance; *up to* would most correctly be called 'mainland'. (25a2–5)

Things **within the mouth** gives an indication of the races of the superior column of opposites, because they are turned in upon themselves and delight in what is stable and in the unifying power. For the term **mouth** shows in symbolic fashion the cause that limits and separates the two segments of cosmic things. The **narrow harbour** signifies their compressed, self-directed, orderly and immaterial existence. For through the term **narrow** he is banishing the extended space and spreading associated with the inferior column, while through **harbour** [he signifies]

---

[761] I.e. to three-dimensionality.   [762] I.e. from the other column of opposites.

[763] Proclus' interpretation of 273d5–e1, where the divine helmsman has to resume the helm out of fear that the world become so storm-tossed that it would sink into an infinite sea of dissimilarity; hence this is an imaginary condition of the world, representing an extreme from which it is saved, not an actual one.

On the *Timaeus* of Plato: Book 1

<the stability>[764] that transcends the discordant and disorderly motion of enmattered things. For that is what harbours are like, providing shelter from the disturbances at sea. But even if someone were to say that the ascent to the more intellective and divine elements of the All becomes a **harbour** for souls,[765] not even this person would miss the truth by much.

The size of Atlantis

In this island of Atlantis a great and wondrous royal power was established, *up to* **as far as Etruria.** (25a5–b2)

At this point it is necessary to remember Plato's assumptions about the earth: that he does not measure its size according to the same principles as the mathematicians, but supposes its extension to be somewhat greater, as Socrates says in the *Phaedo*,[766] and that he posits several settlements similar to our own inhabited area. Consequently, even in the outside sea he tells the story of an island and a mainland of such a size. For if the earth has by nature the spherical form overall, it must be like this over the greater part of itself. Yet our inhabited region, with its valleys and peaks, displays a great unevenness. So there are on other parts of the earth levelled plains and an extended area stretching up to a height. For there is a story that Heracles after crossing a great deal of desert land came to Mount Atlas, whose size recorded by those who wrote *Ethiopica*[767] was big enough to touch the ether itself and to cast a shadow to a distance of nine hundred kilometres. For from the ninth hour of daylight the sun is hidden by it until it has completely set. And it is nothing amazing, for even Mount Athos, the Macedonian mountain, casts its shadow as far as Lemnos, which is a hundred and thirty kilometres away.[768] Not only did Marcellus, who wrote the *Ethiopian Inquiry*, report that Atlas was the only mountain that big, but Ptolemy too says that the Mountains of the Moon have an enormous height, and Aristotle says the Caucasus is illuminated by the sun's rays

---

[764] I supply what appears to be needed to fill a likely lacuna in the text. The missing word may possibly be μόνην.

[765] For the imagery of the harbour see Festugière, but the reference to souls at this point strongly suggests that Proclus alludes to Porphyrian exegesis.

[766] 109a–b; it is perhaps remarkable that Proclus takes so seriously a passage that seems to be preparing the way for the myth concerning underground rivers, but, comparing 182.1–2 with 197.18–24, Festugière supplies us with a good reason for him to do so, for he wishes to show that the size attributed to Atlantis is not inconceivable.

[767] Presumably thinking of the Marcellus referred to at 177.20 and 181.15.

[768] An exaggeration. Around ninety kilometres would be closer.

Atlantis

for the third part of the night after sunset and the third part before
sunrise.[769]   20

If somebody were to examine the total size of the earth by using its
high places to determine it, it would genuinely seem to be immense
just as Plato claims, so that we shall have no need of any mathematical
methods to suit our interpretation regarding the earth, nor shall we try
to refute them. For those methods measure it with regard to the area   25
inhabited by us, whereas Plato says that we are living in a hollow while
the earth itself is high up as a whole,[770] something which the sacred
tradition of the Egyptians has also taught. So much for the alleged size   **182**
of Atlantis; we should not be sceptical about it, even if one were to take
what is being said as an historical account only.

The symbolism of the power and influence of Atlantis

Concerning its power – that there were ten kings in it born as five
sets of twins, and that they ruled the other islands, some parts of the   5
mainland, and some parts within the Pillars of Heracles – he gives a
straightforward narrative account in the *Critias*.[771] But in this context,
bearing in mind that the aim is to offer an interpretation of them[772]
insofar as [their meaning] can be transferred to the All, there is talk   10
of their **great and wondrous power** because the decad embraces the
leaders of the two opposite columns, as the Pythagoreans also claim,
when they state that by the decad of opposing forces all things are contained. They are twins, so that there are five dyads after five pairs of   15
twins are born from Poseidon and Cleito, because on the one hand the
arrangement of even this column of opposites accords with the measures of justice, of which the pentad is an image,[773] while its procession

---

[769] Diehl and Festugière refer to *Mete.* 350a31ff.

[770] *Phaedo* 109c3–d8, which is explicit about the first claim, but makes the second in rather
different terms.

[771] The five sets of twins born to Poseidon are mentioned at 113e6–7, and the rule over
Atlantis, other islands, and areas west of Etruria and Egypt at 113e7–114a4, 114c5–6,
and 114c6–7 respectively. By contrast, rule over the mainland is mentioned only here
at *Tim.* 25a8. This sentence has the effect of making the *Critias* the vehicle for the
amplification of the literal account, allowing Proclus to move straight on to symbolic
meanings.

[772] Using the text proposed by Praechter and followed by Festugière, which reads αὐτῶν
for αὐτῷ, which makes this a reference to the kings of Atlantis.

[773] *Pace* Festugière, who takes it to be the 'series', I think it must be justice of which the
pentad is an image, since that is the relationship suggested in Iambl. *Theol. Arith.* 35.6–
40.6, of which Festugière quotes both beginning and end. One might note that Justice
is not consistently associated with this number in Pythagorean texts.

On the *Timaeus* of Plato: Book 1

is by twos,[774] just as that of the superior column is by ones. Yet all are children of Poseidon, because the entire weaving together of opposites and the cosmic war belongs to the intermediate Demiurge. For this god, because he is in charge of the rivalry everywhere, is the instigator of all coming to be, passing away, and motion of every kind. They hold power over Atlantis because they conserve all the foremost and most universal races of the inferior column; and they hold power over other islands because they also presuppose the middle races on account of their own wholeness; and they also hold power over certain[775] parts of the mainland, because they arrange even the final things to the extent that is possible; and they lord it over certain parts of the inside world too because the final races of the superior column are slaves to the first of the inferior column. And there is nothing surprising about this, just as certain daemons too are subject to certain heroes, and particular souls, which have a share in the intelligible, are often slaves to fate. Even among the gods the Titanic order is of this kind, the order to which Atlas too belongs, and the commander-in-chief of these ten kings was also called Atlas, and the name given to the island was his gift, as is said in the *Atlantic Discourse*.[776] But the topmost members of the second column are arranged by the Olympian Gods, whom Athena leads, but they dominate all substance that is subordinate to the gods but belongs to the inferior column, like irrational souls, enmattered solids, and matter itself. And it is probable that Plato called the power of the Atlantines **great and wondrous** for this reason too, that there is a tradition referring to one of this order called Thaumas and another called Bias by the ancient theologians.[777] And perhaps it is also the case that, because the whole of the second column is the offspring in limitlessness – which we claim is a superlatively great power – just as the superior column is the offspring of limit, on this account too he celebrates the power of the Atlantines, just as in the case of the Athenians he celebrates their virtue, which stands for[778] limit; for it is the measure of those who have it. By taking things

---

[774] The absence of the article with the preposition διά suggests to me a meaning such as LSJ A I.5 which gives the interval, not Festugière's 'au moyen de la dyade'.

[775] Reading τινων with Festugière at 182.26.

[776] *Critias* 114a5–b1; the dialogue was often known in antiquity as *Atlanticus*, and, while Proclus seems to use the names indifferently, he may be deliberately using it here to highlight another stage in the passing on of Atlas' name.

[777] *Orph. fr.* 118; but evidence is confined to this commentary, here alone for Bias, but also at 133.9 and III.189.8 for Thaumas.

[778] 'Stands for': the received text's πρό at 183.18, if taken roughly in the sense of LSJ A I.3 (almost 'as a front for'), fits the appended explanation better than when corrected to πρός with Festugière, which would translate 'derives from'.

Atlantis

thus, I believe, we shall, with a natural spontaneity,[779] be able to complete
our analysis according to Pythagorean principles.[780]   20

The description of Atlantis' power as narrative

The description also involves considerable exaggeration, so that he might
display as something greater and more glorious the achievement of the
victors. For he spoke of *power*, amplifying it through the use of the
singular, and he also added **great and wondrous**. Each of the two is
different. For it is **great** irrespective of whether anything else exists,   25
while it is called **wondrous** in comparison with others. And the more
the loser is wondered at, the greater the victor is shown to be. And in
addition to this, by indicating bit by bit the multitude that has been
vanquished by it (25a7–b2), he showed that [power] to be many times
greater, and to exceed all of them together.   30

Atlantine power unified within the straits

All this power, concentrated into one, once attempted to enslave in a   **184**
single swoop your land, our land, and every place within the mouth.
(25b2–5)

He is not saying that there was ever civil war among things divine, nor   5
that the inferior were anxious to master the better. But while we may
assume that these things are true of human beings, the present story
concerns the most universal races in the whole of the second column,
indicating that they pervade all things. For there is, in the heaven and
everywhere else, a separative and motive[781] power, and none of them   10
is without a share [in it].[782] But it is not present among the superior

---

779 The phrase translates *autophyôs*; this implies an intuitively plausible reading, and Festugière rightly compares the quality that Origenes attributes to Plato's writing, and
Proclus then attributes to Origenes' exegesis, at 89.27 and 29, as well as 275.26 below.

780 Proclus is referring to principles of symbolic interpretation, for the use of symbolic
communication is associated with the Pythagoreans at 7.29–30 above, where they are
also supposed to link everything with the intelligibles and transcend the study of the
particular. Note that the intuitive linking of one thing and another, referred to in the
note to 183.19 above, is associated with symbolism in particular by Ammonius, *in Int.*
40.18–22.

781 Reverting to the text with the best authority, after Festugière I note that the idea of
motion is strongly present in the lemma (even though the myth has to depict how
things always are), and that it has just been implied in the verb 'pervade'.

782 I take the genitive αὐτῶν with οὐδὲν rather then ἄμοιρον, and as referring back to
πάντων.

283

On the *Timaeus* of Plato: Book 1

ones[783] in a divided fashion or through multiplication, but [as a power] **concentrated into one** and with **a single swoop**, that is, in a unified fashion and with one continuous life. For just as in the inferior column even the one is multiplied, so in the superior multiplicity is unified. Hence multiplicity is at the same time everywhere and mastered through unification. An image of this is presented by the fact that the Atlantines wish to master all territory in the inside inhabited area [as a power] **concentrated into one**, and that they are nevertheless mastered by the Athenians. For even multiplicity and division, if they are to be studied in the better column, will be studied all the same in a unified fashion and with the upper hand there being held not by multiplicity but by sameness and by the better races in general.

What the Athenians stand for

Then, Solon, the power of your city became conspicuous in virtue and might. (25b5–6)

He set against the Atlantines the power of the Athenians, choosing this name over others as one that fits the middle creation, and he celebrated the better power for its **virtue and might**, so that through the term **virtue** he might give an indication of its appropriation of the wisdom-loving character of Athena herself – for some other theology and not the Orphic[784] alone has called her 'Virtue' – and through the term **might** its appropriation of the war-loving character. He called their power **conspicuous** because it is encosmic and contributes to the creation of sensible things, and it is only to the Atlantines that he attributes power, indeed continuous[785] power, on the grounds that they belong to the order of limitlessness, whereas he says that the Athenians master the power through their overall virtue. For belonging to the column of the limited kind they are characterized by virtue, which brings measure to the passions and employs 'powers'[786] as they should be.

---

[783] We must remember that the superior column is represented by all the places within the Pillars, so that it is precisely here that Proclus sees the Atlantines as appearing in unified fashion and even as being subdued by the influence of unity.

[784] *Orph. fr.* 175, quoted at 170.8 above.

[785] Though the text is difficult, I see no merit in accepting Praechter's suggestion, which Festugière follows. This is comment on Plato's language, and ought, I think, to relate to the idea of the power being 'concentrated into one'.

[786] Proclus makes use of the fact that 'power' is used since Aristotle as 'potency' as opposed to 'actuality', and hence as something to be associated with the forces of matter rather than form.

284

Atlantis

The Athenians and other peoples within the straits

For, because it was foremost of all in bravery and all those arts that concern war, *up to* **it freed them all.** (25b7–c6) 15

Just as we divide the inferior column into three, the first, intermediate, and final terms, so too we shall divide the superior one too into most universal, most individual, and those placed intermediate between them, and in our division we shall make the Athenians correspond to the first, the rest of the Greeks **not yet enslaved** to the intermediate 20 ones, and those already slaves to the last. For according to these paths [of interpretation] the Athenians master the forces of Poseidon, the first master the second, the monadic master the dyadic, and in general the superior masters the inferior. And they preserve eternally the intermediates' [ability] to keep their own order and not be vanquished by the forces 25 of the inferior column on account of their own unity and their enduring kind of power, and they also liberate the enslaved from their slavery, summoning them to unity and stability. For some things are always within matter, others always transcend it, and others still sometimes become subject to the material races, and sometimes are re-enrolled in 30 separable life – very much like the drama we are caught up in, when we are sometimes ranked under the Titanic order, sometimes under the Olympian, sometimes belonging to generation, and at others to the **186** heaven. This privilege belongs to particular souls on account of the ever-unvarying, soul-uplifting providence of the gods. For just as, on account of there being generation-producing gods, souls too descend who serve 5 their will, so it surely is that, on account of the pre-existence of uplifting causes ascent from here also remains possible for our own souls.

Lexis: details of the text explained

This covers the overall intention of the passage before us, but let us go on to explain briefly individual points too. That they were **foremost of all** 10 shows their overall embrace of the first races of the diviner sector, while **in bravery and the arts of war** has the same significance as 'in Athenaic fashion', as they imitate her love of wisdom in **bravery**,[787] and her love of war in **arts of war**. The fact that they **sometimes led the Greeks,** 15

---

[787] I resist the temptation to modify translation of this word to suit Proclus' interpretation to highlight the fact that Proclus is here twisting what Plato says. The term *eupsychia* means bravery or stoutness of heart: though LSJ *claim* it is used once in Plato, *Laws* 791c9, for 'having a good soul' to match the use of *kakopsychia*, the context is still one that concerns bravery. But Proclus *analyses* its linguistic components to get 'goodness of soul', and then leaps to seeing this as referring to the soul's intellectual aspirations only.

285

On the *Timaeus* of Plato: Book 1

and at others faced the danger alone, shows that the first and overall causes do some things along with second or intermediate [causes], and do others by themselves withdrawing beyond their creative activities, and becoming isolated in their operation. For the race of the gods and that after the gods do not equally create, but the creation of the gods penetrates further, because the diviner races operate everywhere, before the things they cause, along with the things they cause, and after them too. It is possible to confirm this from many sources.

The phrase **extreme dangers** indicates the far-reaching creative activity of the first races. The term **trophies** signifies the enrolment of the second column under the first and its being arranged by it, and its being 'turned'[788] so to speak in accordance with the power of it. It also shows that there are permanently established indicators of this turning of the lesser forces, reaching down among the lowest things from the first. For everything that is even among these things ordered, and given form through the subjugation of the material causes, is established as an adequate sign of the domination of the better, which is above all the special purpose of trophies. The reference to **ungrudging freedom** [signifies] the divine and unhindered arrangement from above that penetrates to all, something which the Athenians brought to light for the Greeks by mastering the Atlantines – though rather the Olympian races did so by defeating the Titanic. It is in this way that the creative will reaches its limit and the worse are mastered by the better, among particular things Atlantines mastered by Athenians, and among universal things Titans mastered by Olympians:

> Even though they are strong they come to join up with the better,
> Inexchange for their deadly aggression and haughty bravado,

as Orpheus says,[789] whom Plato emulates when he says that the Atlantines marched with aggression upon the Athenians.

Science, symbolism, and the destruction of Atlantis

But in later time, when there had been giant earthquakes and floods with one particularly severe day and night arising, your whole fighting force was swallowed up together beneath the earth, and in the same way the

---

[788] 'Trophy' (*tropaion*) derives from the same stem as 'turn' (*trepô*). There may also be a hint of the Neoplatonic process of *epistrophê*.

[789] *Orph. fr.* 20, which Festugière, admitting uncertainty, translates very differently. I have tried to interpret the lines in such a way as to emphasize the parallel with a power whose ignoble drives ('aggression', cf. 24d2) are weakened when it pursues a goal that is superior to it, a goal that is viewed as an enemy, but is actually a desirable source of improvement.

Atlantis

island of Atlantis sank beneath the sea and vanished. For this reason even now the sea in that region is impassable and impossible to find a path through, because mud lies in one's way just below the surface, which the island left behind as it came to rest. (25c6–d6)   20

That what is said is consistent with physics is clear to those who are not entirely unversed in physical science. That an earthquake should occur of such a size as to destroy an island of that size, is not remarkable, since the earthquake that took place a little before our time shook Egypt   25 and Bithynia in one day.[790] And that an inundation should follow the earthquake is nothing unexpected, since this always accompanies large earthquakes as Aristotle reports,[791] giving the reason for it at the same time. Wherever an inundation occurs along with an earthquake, a wave is   **188** the cause of this phenomenon. For sometimes the wind that creates the earthquake has yet to pass underground, while the sea is being set in motion by a wind opposed to it; [the wind] rushes on in the opposite direction, but is unable to push [the sea] back on account of the   5 gale pushing it forward; yet by stopping and preventing its advance it becomes cause of a great upsurge being collected under pressure from the opposing wind. [Whenever this occurs,] then indeed, with the sea surging high under the counter-pressure, it plunges down into the earth itself with its concentrated flow unleashed upon it and creates the earth-   10 quake, while the sea washes over the place. This is the manner in which the earthquake occurred in the region of Achaea at the same time as the onset of the wave that flooded the coastal cities of Boura and Helike.[792] So an expert on physics could not discredit this account if he examined   15 it correctly.

Furthermore, that the same place could be passable and impassable or land and sea is one of the things agreed by physicists, as Aristotle too thinks and as the narrative shows. And the same man tells that there is mud[793] in the outside sea beyond the mouth, and that that place is   20 full of shoals,[794] so if **mud . . . just below the surface** signifies 'full of

---

[790] On the 24 August, AD 358, as reported by Ammianus Marcellinus 17.7.1.

[791] *Mete.* 2.8, 368a34–b13, which Proclus now follows until 188.12.

[792] Proclus offers a well-known example of tidal wave destruction on the southern coast of the Gulf of Corinth from 373 BC., which had already been discussed by Aristotle at *Mete.* 1.8, 343b1–4, 2.8, 368b6–13 and Theophr. *Phys. Dox.* p. 490 Diels, as well as Paus. 7, 24–5. The level of reliance on the Peripatetics is a sad reflection on the progress of ancient geophysics.

[793] Plato's discussion of how one might define mud (*pêlos*) at *Tht.* 147a–c warns us that he uses the word typically for water-infused solids that are slippery and can be moulded, as in the making of pottery, earthenware and bricks. We are not dealing with very soft mud here, but with something that will offer a bit more resistance. Indeed, underwater rocks seem to Proclus to offer an explanation for Plato's description.

[794] *Mete.* 2.1, 354a22–3.

287

On the *Timaeus* of Plato: Book 1

shoals' it is not remarkable. For even now they call submerged rocks with water over the top 'surface-reefs'. So why would anybody be bothered making out a detailed case for this?

But we seek proof that these words offer an amazing indication of the whole cosmic arrangement by reminding ourselves of the 'entartarization' spoken of in Orpheus' writing.[795] For he too, when he has given his account of the rivalry-in-creation between the Olympians and Titans, brings to an end the whole account of cosmic arrangement down to the final things of the All, giving even them a share in the immaculate providence of the gods. So knowing this Plato too carries on teaching about the universe through images, consigns these two races to the realm of darkness, and through causing them to disappear in this way imitates the Orphic 'entartarization'. For in order that the last things should be arranged and should enjoy divine providence, it was necessary that both the better column and the inferior one should extend its own power from above right down to the foundation of the cosmos, each of the two in its own proper manner, the one by being shaken [by an earthquake] and sinking **beneath the earth**, which is the equivalent of 'advancing steadily and with solidity',[796] and the other by **vanishing**, which would be the equivalent of becoming enmattered and without order or form. For **beneath the earth** is a symbol of an enduring and stable nature, while **beneath the sea** symbolizes what is easily changed, disorderly, and in flux. For even among the last things their foundation and their generation derives from the better column, while their passing away, interchange, and unharmonious motion come from the worse.

Since these things too are arranged in the course of the completion of the unseen and visible creation, for this reason he says that here too a **severe day and night** arose, with night signifying the unseen causes and day the visible ones, while the severity signifies the impossibility of contending with it, its unyielding nature, and its pervading everything.

Because all these things are brought to completion in accordance with creative powers, earthquakes and inundations have been implicated, which befit the intermediate creation. If he had wanted to indicate Jovian powers or operations, he would have spoken of thunderbolts and tornados,[797] but because he is telling us of Poseidonian creative operations, he has captured their likeness in earthquakes and floods. For they used

---

[795] *Orph. fr.* 122, with *in Remp.* I. 93.22–4.

[796] I preserve Festugière's unexplained quotation-marks.

[797] Again Proclus' notion that the tale would have been told very differently if Plato wanted to reflect different divine truths tends to undermine his own insistence, repeated in a few lines at 190.7–8, that the tale is historically true.

288

Atlantis

to call this god the 'Earthshaker' and the 'One with Sea-dark Locks'. Because time signifies procession in due order or orderly descent, he says this all took place **in later time**. Hence one should not say that the one who obliterated the evidence undermines his subject matter,[798] just like Homer in the case of the Phaeacians or of the wall made by the Greeks. For what has been said has not been invented, but is true, since many parts of the earth are washed over by the sea, and nothing he said happened was impossible. But neither does he report this as a lightweight narrative, but he adopts the story as an indication of the providence that pervades all things, including the last. To sum up then, at the completion of the overall cosmic arrangement, and with the unseen-and-visible creation brought to fullness by the creational fabrications of the Second Father, both the gift of the better part and that of the worse comes even down to the last things. The former masters its materials because of the term **fighting force** and spreads the fertile light of its power because of the phrase **beneath the earth**, while the latter implants the last and most material division and maintains in indeterminacy the motion of Tartarus.[799] And when these things have been arranged it is with good reason that this area of the sea is **impassable and impossible to find a path through** thereafter. For there is no other passage or procession of the races involved

[798] The reference to the Greek wall at Troy, washed away after the war in a huge flood devised by Poseidon in company with Apollo (*Iliad* 12.1–33), warns us not to believe, with Festugière, that this is a contemporary objection to Atlantis. The Greek wall is linked with a witty saying about Atlantis at Strabo 2.3.6: 'He who invented it obliterated it, like the poet in the case of his Achaean wall.' The material derives from Posidonius (F49.297–303 Kidd), and the language (πλάσσω, ἀφανίζω) matches the verbs used by Proclus for 'invent' and 'obliterate'. But that language had been used in a related context at least by Aristotle (Strabo 12.1.36; cf. Kidd (1988), 259), and it seems likely (though less than certain) that Aristotle too had used it in connection with Atlantis. This may have been an oral quip subsequently reported in relevant literature, with Crantor's early commentary on the *Timaeus* (above, 76.1–2) being an obvious possibility, since it is highly likely that Posidonius, who also interpreted part of the work, was familiar with it. What Proclus offers in line 5 seems to be an *interpretation* of the original quip, taking it to *imply* that it is standard practice to arrange for the destruction of one's fictions so as to offer an explanation for the lack of any remaining evidence. The presence of the Phaeacians here adds an extra twist, and is a reference to the destruction of the returning ship after Odysseus had been taken back to his homeland, thus incurring the anger of Poseidon, who is once again the culprit (*Od.* 13.149–87). This disaster together with the threatening mountain overshadowing the town persuades the Phaeacians to stop accompanying stranded sailors. Presumably the idea is that Homer had to do something to explain why Phaeacia disappears from the view of the Greeks, with the land that had routinely been so hospitable and escorted strangers to their destinations never again being heard of. That this piece of scepticism too goes back to Aristotle's remarks is not hard to believe.

[799] Again it is difficult to deny the influence of the indeterminate pre-cosmic motions in the text of the *Timaeus*; see note on 160.5.

289

On the *Timaeus* of Plato: Book 1

in arranging the All. In fact the real 'mud' is that of which Socrates
also makes mention in the *Phaedo* when talking about the underground
places,[800] the region beneath the earth that is dominated by the 'obscure
form'[801] of bodiliness, which it possessed because of the inferior column
settling down in it and advancing to the final point of cosmic arrangement. For the Titanic order also, being driven by Zeus as far as Tartarus,
fills things in that place too with the protection that derives from the
gods.

Summary of interpretation of Atlantis

**So as for what was said, Socrates, by the elder Critias in accordance with
his hearing of Solon, you have heard it put briefly yourself. When you
were speaking about the constitution,** *up to* **for the most part with what
Solon said.**   (25d7–e5)

It has been stated in what went before how the war between Atlantines
and Athenians belongs to the overall construction of the cosmos, and
how the cosmic rivalry is conserved by the intermediate creation in its
advance from the first things above to the last. [In this] the Athenaic
series arranges all things with steadfast leadership and mastery, unfolds
what is detained in matter, and keeps immaculate what transcends matter,
while the other, in a manner appropriate to itself, favours created things
with motion, division and otherness, and proceeds from above to the
end. And we have commented about this at the proper length.

Closing considerations (191.12–204.29)
The status of Critias and of his story

But since the teller of the story was found to correspond with the
god who conserves this rivalry, he is imitating him in a way, and is
ascending, through the referral of the narrative back to its fathers,
via Critias and **his hearing of Solon** to the Egyptians. So this is
also presupposed in his paradigm-figure,[802] who is filled by the first
and fills those that follow him with the creative power. Furthermore,
since he bears the image of the second creation, one that proceeds on

---

[800] 110a5–6, where 'mud' is just one of a list that includes also caverns, sand, and mire.
[801] An allusion perhaps to 49a3–4, where the phrase is applied to the receptacle.
[802] I.e. Poseidon, on whom Critias models himself. His status is already hinted at as early
as 9.17–22, while Festugière prefers to refer us to 88.1–8.

Closing considerations

from another, on this account he says that he was reminded of the story[803] as a result of what Socrates was saying. For this [type of] 'recollection' is not the passing across from images to paradigms,[804] but from universal concepts to more particular happenings. Consequently it also fits with the procession of creation as a whole. For while all things exist in the intelligibles, the creative causes – each according to its own order – have distributed among themselves the creative tasks.[805] Moreover, if you pursue the linguistic details of the text in another manner, the Athenians are being admirably lauded, and the constitution of Socrates is being appropriately celebrated. For this latter has been shown by the life of the Athenians to be possible and to supply the greatest benefits for whomsoever it is adopted by, which was just what Socrates had thought required demonstration in the discussion.[806] But they, by living in accordance with the best type of constitution, have been shown worthy of the greatest admiration. For it is genuinely admirable to be cast in the mould of the first paradigm. Indeed, of encosmic things the more divine, which have received to the highest degree their [paradigms'] whole form are called 'monadic' and are so, whereas enmattered things that have the same form in many inferior [instances] have the lowest rank. Certainly this feature that in the creation process belongs to the gods too, that of attaining one's own proper paradigm to the highest degree, is displayed also by the city of the Athenians when they practise the best-regulated life to the highest degree.

Furthermore, the cycle of favours imitates the cosmic cycle,[807] as the Egyptians were helped by the Athenians through their deeds of war, and the Athenians by the Egyptians through their priestly words. For the

---

[803] A good example of *historia* meaning far less than history, and perhaps no more than a narrative or story; this is important for understanding possible confusions concerning the description of the Atlantis story as *psilê historia*, whose emphasis falls on the lack of any meaning deeper than the literal one, rather than on any truth that the literal meaning must have.

[804] An allusion to the Platonic theme of recollection as it appears particularly at *Phaedo* 74a–76e.

[805] This relates to the 'lottery' of the mythical gods Zeus, Poseidon and Hades, as well as to Proclus' three creations.

[806] E.g. 592a, but cf. *Tim.* 19b–c.

[807] Note how this material is mostly of a straightforward *ethical* character (such as might be expected in a Porphyrian exegesis of prologue material), relating to conduct in repaying favours, but is given cosmic significance by a simple twist. That may suggest that Porphyrian material has been adapted by Iamblichus or Proclus to suit their demand that everything said should have a bearing on the cosmos.

On the *Timaeus* of Plato: Book 1

15 very fact that they kept the achievement recorded was a return of the
favour, but, when you add the instructive narration of their forefathers'
deeds to them, it multiplies the gratitude their repayment displays.

In addition to this, to suggest that their **fortune** was **daemonic** and
makes us think[808] is an indication of the value of Plato's studies, since
fortune and the gift that comes from it is neither blind nor indeterminate,
20 but a power that draws together many disparate causes, arranges things
unordered, and supplies everything with what it has been allotted from
the All.

So why was it, then, that Socrates had **agreed with what Solon said?**
I shall claim that it is because of the cause that draws together many
disparate causes and because of the one goddess who conserves their
25 common intelligence. For because they are Athenaic, they are moved
as if from a single source, their presiding goddess, towards the same
concepts.

Critias' delayed memory

**Yet I did not want to speak up straight away, for with the lapse of time I
could not recall well enough** *up to* **speak only then.**   (25e5–26a3)

30 This must be observed in the All as well, [noting how] prior to partic-
193 ulars the creative cause of what comes to be in time establishes his own
offspring,[809] and how it is only when the founder of generated things
has an intellective grasp of himself, and sees the causes of created things
within himself, that he allows other things to enter the stage from himself. This is so that it may be only when he is sufficient and complete
5 that he grants a share in his own power to secondary things. Thus the
conceiving and the **recalling** and all such things show the embrace of
the creative principles within a single [mind].[810]

Hence I quickly agreed with what you required of me *up to* **I recalled
during the night.**   (26a3–b2)

---

[808] This relates to 25e3–4, in the part of the lemma that is not spelled out in full. It should
perhaps be asked whether Proclus had read δαιμονίας . . . τύχης rather than δαιμονίως
. . . τύχης there.

[809] Festugière translates 'ses pensées' as if reading νοητά for γεννήματα, though it is in
the next line that Diehl reports C's variant reading of νοητῶν for γενητῶν (with the
further variant γεννητῶν).

[810] Proclus comments on the verb ἐνενόησα and the participle ἀναλαβόντα, the former of
which suggests universal concepts to a Platonist, and the latter the recovery of innate
knowledge of the universal.

Closing considerations

Because he remembered in one sense, he promised to fulfil **what was** 10
required, but because he did not remember accurately, he had gone
over the story by himself first, thinking that, for requirements of the
kind that Socrates had made [in asking] to see the constitution up and
running,[811] it was the **hardest task** to find the basis on which one would 15
be able to fulfil the requirements appropriately. That is exactly what
he has done in taking from historical tradition the war between the
Atlantines and the Athenians as something able to show the life that
heralds in the best constitution, and in recalling this **during the night** so
that he could also share it with the participants in the discussion without
stumbling. 20

So let us cross once again from here to the universe. For there too
the creational cause, receiving fullness from the invisible cause[812] – for
there in a primary way resided all intellective causes with which it was
unified at its highest peak – thereby brings his own power into the light in
accordance with their will and judgement. Furthermore, that he should 25
not **speak straight away**,[813] but later on, is a symbol of how the preparation of natural things is being made ready in advance, as the source of
perfection for nature's final products.

You could also speak of an ethical message here, that of being on
the safe side. One should not venture in haste on such accounts without first looking back over the whole task, so that we may, as if from a **194**
bank, publish the statement of account that can genuinely serve as messenger of the accounts that lie within.[814] Furthermore, that he speaks
when he has **recalled** in private imitates the reversion of the creational
principles upon themselves, and also gives an indication of the soul's 5
conscious reversion upon itself, through which it studies the principles
of realities within itself. As for **find a story able to be an appropriate basis for what we want**, it gives an indication of the close
conjunction in the creation process between the phenomena and their
causes.

---

[811] Referring back to 19b–c.

[812] Note that Critias is analogous to the second of the demiurgic triads, and Socrates to
the first.

[813] Proclus has at this point fallen back on elements from the previous lemma, as if offering
a *lexis* that embraces two lemmata simultaneously. Hence I use bold for words from
that lemma too.

[814] I have only slightly updated the metaphor here, which, as Festugière shows, reflects a
topos also encountered in Gregory of Nyssa; the verb translated 'publish' (προφέρομαι),
however, strongly suggests the Stoic contrast between the Stoic *prophorikos logos* that
brings out in speech the *endiathetos logos* embedded in the mind.

293

On the *Timaeus* of Plato: Book 1

On the memory of children

10   **How wonderful a hold on the memory, as the saying goes, our childhood discoveries have *up to* so that it has become permanent like the burnt-in outlines of a non-erasable picture.**   (26b2–c3)

That children are better at memorizing is seen in practice, and might
15   have a number of plausible reasons. One, as Porphyry says,[815] is that the souls of children have no experience of human troubles; so, because they are neither distracted nor hindered by external matters, they have an image-forming faculty[816] that is easily imprinted, though their reasoning
20   faculty is slower because our experiences make this sharp and quick to operate. Another is that in them rational life is more enmeshed in the imagination. Therefore, just as, when the soul responds in sympathy with the body and gets mixed up in it, the body becomes sturdier and livelier,
25   so in the same way the imagination also is strengthened by getting reason, and in being strengthened it receives imprints that are more permanent. It gets a better hold on them because of its own power, just as the body also gets better control of things within its own sphere, being livelier on account of its closer communion with the soul. A third reason over and
30   above these is that the same things appear greater in the imagination of children, or rather that they are more amazed at them, so that they
195   respond more to them. Hence they remember them more. For when things have hurt us a lot or delighted us a lot we store them up in our memory. At any rate they have more effect on us. So just as what suffers more at the hands of fire retains the heat it is given longer, in the same
5   way the image-forming faculty that is more affected by things outside grasps the imprint better. Even so, that of children is affected more on account of the same things appearing greater to us as children. Hence children retain the imprint better, and with good reason because the same things affect them more.

Critias seems to me[817] to be giving an indication of this in stating that
10   it was **with a great deal of pleasure** that he had listened to the narrative

---

[815] *in Tim.* fr. XXV Sodano, which goes down only to line 20, though there is good reason to suppose that Porphyrian influence extends beyond this (cf. Dillon 1973, 293), in my view to 195.8. For this lemma has been used as an excuse for a scholarly *topos* that is easily regarded as a digression, having only a loose relation to the overall *skopos* of the *Timaeus*, and this strongly suggests that its origin is to be sought neither in Iamblichus nor in the school of Syrianus.

[816] Simply translating 'imagination' sometimes obscures the fact that the first text Platonists have in mind when using this kind of language is generally that which introduces 'the painter in the soul' at *Philebus* 39b–40a.

[817] The rare first person singular is used here, as is usual elsewhere in this book, to show that Proclus is conscious of offering a personal view. He has passed beyond what he finds in the commentary tradition stemming from Porphyry.

Closing considerations

from the old man, and that *on this account* it had **become permanent like the burnt-in outlines of a non-erasable picture**. And just as Socrates, in the summary of the constitution,[818] offers us as a reason for remembering the unfamiliarity of the things we hear, so Critias in this passage offers the youth of children. And it is likely that the former is also a reason for the latter case – unfamiliarity a cause of children's memory. For all things seem unfamiliar when they are first encountered by children. And perhaps this too offers an indication of how the reproductive[819] creation of secondary things depends upon the permanent sameness of primary things, in the same way that the cause of memory <offered by Socrates>[820] is also the cause of children's memory as stated by Critias.

But if, in addition to these explanations, one were to persist in the total study of things, let him hear Iamblichus[821] when he says that children's memory gives an indication of the permanent creation, ever new and in its prime, of the formal principles, while the **non-erasable** character of the **picture** – or 'tincture',[822] as both readings exist – [indicates] the ever-flowing and inexhaustible creation, and the **enthusiastic** character of the teacher [indicates] the ungrudging supervision of the younger causes by the elder. For this too has a place, along with the explanations offered.

The cosmic significance of the agreement with Timaeus and Hermocrates

Moreover, first thing in the morning I told just these things to these people here *up to* **or should we find some other topic of conversation instead of it.** (26c3–e1)

Previously Critias was making them participants in the discourse, but now he is encouraging them to share the resource,[823] because among

---

[818] *Tim.* 18c6–8, where sharing wives and sharing children are the unfamiliar ideas in question. Again I prefer not to take *politeia* as the title of a dialogue, but as 'constitution': the subject matter that gave the dialogue its name.

[819] I suspect that γόνιμος here is intended to suggest the reproduction of the species, which will depend for Proclus upon the permanent existence of the archetype of that species.

[820] Supplement proposed by Kroll, and followed by Diehl and Festugière. One must assume, at least, that the sense is correct, and that Proclus is implying that there exists a permanent overall cause of a property *F*, explaining why individuals generated in time may pass through the stage of becoming *F*.

[821] *in Tim.* fr. 24 Dillon; Proclus' remark at 195.30 suggests that he was in no way privileging Iamblichus' ideas in this case.

[822] Some read βαφῆς ('dye') for γραφῆς at 26c3 (cf. Vat. 228 as reported by Burnet).

[823] Συνευπορεῖν. This word picks up the εὐπορεῖεν λόγων μετ' ἐμοῦ in Plato's text at 26c4–5.

On the *Timaeus* of Plato: Book 1

5 their models too[824] all are united at the top and make each other replete with intellectual powers, while in the cosmos they create along with each other according to some divine and universal co-animation (*sympnoia*).[825] In accordance with this, and because of it, all things are present everywhere in the appropriate manner to each, with paradigms of generated 10 things pre existent in the heaven, and images of the heavenly things present in generation.

Since the whole everywhere precedes the parts, this is observable also in the second creation,[826] and on this account he firstly gave a basic outline of the war, and after this he will attempt to teach them in full 15 about the entire constitution of the Atlantines and the origin of their generation, how they turned to injustice, and how the Athenians went into the war: the kind of military resources they had prepared, the kind of embassies they sent, the routes they took, the people who they were 20 aligned with, and all that this entails.[827] It is the case that the unattributed constitution[828] is an imitation of the first creation, so that, hinting at its mystical[829] nature and its prior subsistence in pure rational principles, he says that it has been organized **as if in a myth**, while the attribution 25 to the Athenians as something that was theirs gives an indication of the second creation, in which more particular detail is examined, and further, rivalry, movement, and spatial boundaries. Since the latter constitution is dependent upon the former and follows immediately upon it, he says **they will conform entirely and we shall not be discordant in our claim**.

Socrates agrees on the story

197 **What topic should we rather take up in place of this one, Critias** *up to* **it's not possible.** (26e2–6)

---

[824] The various demiurges to which the characters correspond.

[825] A word common in pythagorizing texts.   [826] That corresponding to Critias.

[827] Festugière refers here to *Critias* 112e, but notes that the dialogue has run out before any details of the Athenian introduction into the war could be given.

[828] The term ἀνυπόθετος is used of the ideal constitution because no physical background conditions are set down with which conformity is necessary, see *Anon. Proleg.* 26.45–58. So one might call this an 'unattributed' constitution, as opposed to the 'attributed' constitution set out in the *Laws*. However, one of the key issues for this distinction appears to be that of private property, which is allowed in the *Laws* but not (for the guardians at least) in the *Republic*.

[829] At 196.21 Festugière proposes a reading that would translate as 'mythical', and so link more directly into the lemma. While he may be correct, the manuscript reading seems quite adequate, and better reflects the status of this paradigmatic constitution.

Closing considerations

Socrates welcomes the topic (*logos*), first because it is pertinent to the festival of the Athenians (the war being an image of warfare throughout the cosmos) and suitable as a hymn for the rite of Athena – for if people have any use for a voice, they should be using it for hymns. Furthermore, since the goddess is the cause of both contemplation and operations, we imitate her operational activity through the rite, and her contemplative activity through the hymn. Secondly, [he welcomes it] as something that will confirm that the constitution is possible. For he himself thought this worth demonstrating in the course of his discussions on it.[830] For on the one hand it was sufficient for him that the shape of the constitution should belong in the heaven and in the individual man. For all things are inside that occur without, and the true law has its beginning in the life within.[831] But on the other hand, if it could be shown that it had once held authority over the Athenians, then its capability is easily demonstrated. So this is what the reasons for that were like.

Then again, we should infer from this passage too that the story of the Atlantines was not a fiction, as some believed, but both a historical study and one with special relevance for cosmic creation as a whole. So even the details he gave about the size of Atlantis should not be condemned as mythical fictions by those who virtually confine the earth to within a narrow strait.[832]

Luck, listening, and their cosmic significance

But with fortune's approval you must speak, and I must listen in turn, keeping silence now in return for yesterday's discourse.   (26e6–27a1)

The position of the Stoics, who say that the wise man has no need of luck, is not shared by Plato. Rather, he wants our thinking activities, whenever they are implicated in material ones in people's progression to the outside, to be inspired by good luck, so that they may ensure

---

[830] Whether the constitution is capable of being realized is an issue raised by Glaucon at 471c (as noted by Diehl and Festugière), but the answer of Socrates hinges on the possibility of philosophers becoming kings (473c–e etc.).

[831] The theory of natural law in antiquity, though finding supporting statements in Plato's *Laws*, Aristotle, and the early Stoa, is explained fully for the first extant time by Cicero in *De Legibus* 1.18–34. In relation to the *Timaeus*, one should remember the law-giving function of the demiurge at 41e–42d, that is already behind Middle Platonic representations of the demiurge as law-giver, as at Numenius fr. 13 and Alcinous 16.2.

[832] Here one should compare 180.25–182.2, designed to explain Critias' extravagant remarks about the size of Atlantis at 24e as well as the actual lemma (25a–b). Proclus there makes appeal to Plato's idea of a mega-earth in the *Phaedo* (109a–110b). The term 'narrow' relates to *Tim.* 25a3, which speaks of the Mediterranean as like a harbour within a narrow entrance.

297

On the *Timaeus* of Plato: Book 1

the progression is fortunate and the activity towards others has divine approval. For just as Nemesis is the overseer of words lightly spoken,[833] so too does good luck guide words for the good of their recipients and of their giver, so that the former may [listen] with consideration and empathy, while the latter renders what is fitting in a divine and capable fashion. So much for the meaning as applied to individuals. As applied to things universal good luck signifies the divine allocation, in accordance with which each thing has received the lot that is proper to itself from the one father and from the creation as a whole. Furthermore, that Socrates should listen to these accounts in silence involves the repayment of a good deed, for they had also done this when he was telling the story of the constitution, so that it wasn't even clear from that work that they had been present. Yet it also shows by analogy how the demiurgic causes, though all are united with one another, still have separate creative roles. For the listening is indicative of their mutual penetration, while that one speaks but the rest are silent signifies the freedom from admixture and impurity with which each, drawing on his own individual nature, creates and engenders secondary things.

The order of the trilogy: Republic–Timaeus–Critias

Then consider the type of arrangement we have made for your entertainment, Socrates *up to* but from then on discuss them as if they were indeed our Athenian citizens. (27a2–b6)

This order makes Timaeus both the top and the mean, for he speaks both after Socrates and Critias and before Critias and Hermocrates. In that way he is a mean, but other ways he's at the top: in his knowledge, and because he engenders the people that Socrates raises and Critias arms. This too is a clear symbol of the universal creation – being a top at the same time as a mean. For it is at once removed from all encosmic things and is present to them all equally, and the topmost parts of the universe are given up to the Demiurge, and also the middle as the Pythagorean account says: that's where they say 'the tower of Zas' is.[834] It makes Critias a mean, having him speak again before Hermocrates, while he has now told his story in outline[835] after Socrates. It is to the middle

---

[833] The origin of the idea, as details of the vocabulary show, is *Laws* 717d.

[834] For this expression, referring somewhat oddly to the central fire, see also 2.106.21–3; *in Eucl.* 90.14. The idea is already attributed to the Pythagoreans by Arist. fr. 204 Rose².

[835] Note that Critias implies that he has given only an outline at 26c6, promising more detail later.

298

Closing considerations

creation that the dyadic nature and the 'whole with parts' belong,[836] just as the whole belongs to the first and the parts to the last. Hence Socrates has handed down the constitution in summary form, while Hermocrates will contribute the specific detail to the story handed down by Critias. So much for the arrangement as a whole.

Somebody might raise the problem about what task could be left to Hermocrates, when Timaeus has explained the origin of these people, Socrates their upbringing, and Critias their achievements. There is nothing to follow on from this. Actually Hermocrates is a partner in Critias' discourse, because the narration of history involved both deeds and words. Critias promised that he himself would give an account of their deeds, but he calls upon Hermocrates too with a view to his sharing his resources[837] in the words – imitating them was difficult, as had earlier been said (19e1–2).[838] Hence in the *Atlanticus* (= *Critias* 121bc) Critias says that Zeus, assembling the gods to deliberate on the penalty to confront the Atlantines, spoke as follows, and terminated his communication, handing over the imitation of speeches to Hermocrates. If he didn't actually go on to the rest of the deeds, that's nothing improbable. For in general, by having the gods summoned *for the chastisement of the Atlantine violence*, he gets everything that follows implied in this: the armament of the Athenians, the expedition, and the victory. Consequently Timaeus engenders the men, Socrates raises them, Critias takes them into action, and Hermocrates makes them speak. One imitates the paternal cause, another the cause that promotes unchanging intellection, another the cause of motion and procession to secondary things, and another the cause that brings back the last things to their origins through the imitation of words. In this way you could interpret this symbolically, and perhaps not over-ingeniously.

One might raise the difficulty of why the *Timaeus* has not been positioned in front of the *Republic*, when the origin of the human race is explained in it along with that of the rest of the cosmos.[839] They have to be born (which the *Timaeus* tells us of), and be educated (which the Socrates of the *Republic* does), and to operate in a manner worthy of their upbringing (which the *Atlanticus* somehow shows). And if he had started

---

[836] As Festugière points out, Critias' story is split into two parts that together comprise a whole.

[837] There is an allusion to the wealth of words that Critias shares with Hermocrates and Timaeus at 26c4–5, but there could be no suggestion there that either would be concerned with words as opposed to deeds.

[838] What makes Proclus confident that the division of labour between Critias and Hermocrates concerned the division of narrative into deeds and speeches?

[839] This difficulty is already responded to by Porphyry at 202.2–8, and is printed as part of *in Tim.* fr. XXVI (Sodano).

On the *Timaeus* of Plato: Book 1

with the end itself and come back to the *Timaeus*, which is by nature the first, we should be able to give the usual explanation, namely that for the purpose of instruction he had first communicated what is first for us yet last by nature.[840] But as things are it looks as if the first has been placed in the middle and the middle first. If this order had been simply passed down to us by the corpus-arrangers,[841] it would be less surprising for us, but as things are it seems that Plato himself is ordering them like this. Certainly the main points of the constitution are here very briefly summarized on the grounds that it has already been treated.

In answer to this objection one should say that if all the subjects were derived from the nature of things that are or have been, then the objection would have to prevail and that Timaeus has not properly been placed second. And if they were all being invented by reason hypothetically, then in that case too one would have to take first what came first by nature. But since Socrates' theme follows reason alone and observes the universal as it shapes the nurture and education of men, while the following ones treat things that are or have been, it is with good reason that these latter are placed with one another, while that of Socrates, which exists in reason alone, has on this account too been placed before the rest. Perhaps Plato also wanted to give an indication of this, that of those things proposed by souls that are divine and turned round towards the divine, all of them at some time come about upon the earth too in accord with certain favourable cyclic revolutions. That's certainly what Critias also will testify to when he says to Socrates:[842] 'And as for the citizens, whom you had in mind, we shall say that they are those genuine ancestors of ours of whom the priest spoke. They are a complete match, and we shall not strike a discord if we say that they are the ones who lived at that time.'

Even if the *Republic* falls short of the *Timaeus* by being partial, by discussing things mortal, and[843] by spending time on the likeness, it is still the case that it excels it in its universality, since it shows how the

---

[840] A standard Aristotelian contrast between the order 'for us' and the order 'by nature'.

[841] Unusually we seem to have a technical term, *diaskeuastês*, for those who, like Aristophanes of Byzantium, Thrasyllus, Dercyllides, and Theon, sought to establish an authoritative order for the dialogues. On them see Tarrant (1993).

[842] While the verb μαρτυρήσει is future, the quotation is from 26d above. This is more likely to indicate that Proclus had prepared these arguments before incorporating them in the commentary, possibly as introductory material for either the *Timaeus* or the *Republic*. One should here note that Porphyry, mentioned shortly at 202.2–8, who is responding to the difficulty raised at 200.4–6, seems to be treating the issues in a context bearing no relation to this lemma (202.3–4).

[843] There is some uncertainty in the text at this point, but the general thrust seems not to be at issue.

Closing considerations

same form of life constitutes justice in the soul, constitution in the state, and creation in the cosmos. Further, its proposed subject of virtue is liberal, though the direction of its action towards the outside requires [the imposition of] cosmic ordering.[844] Hence the *Atlanticus* comes after the *Timaeus*, and the condition of its citizens is evidence of their freely adopted virtue. Plato shows through this too that soul, when it is self-mastering, rises above the entire level of nature and fate, though when it inclines to actions it is mastered by the laws of nature and subject to fate.

Apart from what's been said one should appreciate this point too, that the sequence of these dialogues conforms with the order of human life given in the *Republic*. There too men[845] first were raised and educated through mathematics, next rose to the contemplation of realities, and thirdly descended from that point to the providential care of the city. So it is in accord with this sequence that the *Republic* has been placed ahead of the *Timaeus*, which is ahead of the *Atlanticus*. That's because, once they've been brought up by the *Republic* and raised on high by the *Timaeus*, they will manage such actions as the *Atlanticus* speaks of intelligently in conformity with what they've studied, and live a happy life. At last that is how we have answered the difficulty.

The philosopher Porphyry,[846] however, while dealing with other matters rather than with this problem directly in mind, provided the following route towards a solution. Those who are going to get a real hold on the study of the universe must first have been educated in character, so that by assimilation to the object contemplated it should become properly prepared for the recognition of the truth. This order of the dialogues is an additional proof of this, for those who listen to the discussion in the *Timaeus* must have previously had the benefit of the *Republic*, and, when set in order by it,[847] arrive in that state to hear the doctrines about the cosmos – demonstrating that they have become very similar to the cosmic order of the universe by their education.

Lexis: details of this passage and the next considered

Let us also examine individually the details of the language (*lexis*). Timaeus is here called **best at astronomy**, not as being one who had

---

[844] A case of the *progression* that requires *reversion*, and of *life* that requires *mind*.

[845] A gender-specific term that is essentially a slip, since Plato is keen not to exclude women.

[846] *in Tim*. fr. XXVI (Sodano), which includes the difficulty raised above at 200.4–6 and responded to here.

[847] I.e. when they have received the *cosmos* of the correct constitution.

On the *Timaeus* of Plato: Book 1

investigated the speed of the [heavenly] movements, nor as one who 'measures the sun's course by compiling tables',[848] or wastes time on the works of fate. [He is called this] as one who both 'pursues astronomy beyond the heaven' in the manner of the 'topmost' man in the *Theaete-* 20 *tus*,[849] and studies invisible causes that are also the true stars – whence Socrates did not reveal the human being that we can see, but the one whose true being is founded in reason.[850] [And he is called it] as one who imitates the universal Demiurge, in whom the heaven and all the stars are present intellectively, as the theologian says.[851]

25 He **begins with the generation of the cosmos and ends with humankind**, because the human being is a microcosm, possessing partially everything possessed entirely by the universe, as Socrates demonstrated in the *Philebus*.[852] Certain people had been **exceptionally edu-** 30 **cated** by Socrates, because rather than the whole city he educates the guardians and auxiliaries. In the universe too that which is exceptionally **203** endowed with intelligence is the heaven, which actually imitates intellect by its motion. People are **introduced by Critias according to the law and the tale of Solon**, because Solon too related that the Athenians had once organized themselves in this way and laid down laws on how boys 5 should be inducted into the citizen body (*politeia*), or into the phratries, or into the official lists, and which judges should preside, in one case phratry members and in another other pertinent people.[853] So in personally accepting the hypothesis that those educated by Socrates were Athenians, he followed Solon in the tale and in the law by which certain 10 people are introduced into the citizen body.

It looks as though I am going to be repaid with a full and magnificent banquet of words; so it would be up to you, Timaeus, to make the next speech, apparently: or once you've made the invocation to the gods according to law. (27b)

---

[848] A clear allusion to *Or. Chald.* fr. 107.3 (des Places).

[849] 176c7 and e6; 'topmost' here translates the somewhat poetical image of the *coryphaeus* used by Plato; the impractical nature of such a person, that emerges somewhat comically there, is forgotten.

[850] Cf. 200.24–6, on which Festugière offers a long note.

[851] The standard way of referring to Orphic texts. Festugière refers to the commonplace 'Zeus is sun and moon' encountered at *De Mundo* 401a25 etc., but it seems more logical to think directly of the text quoted in part at 161.24–5 above (*Orph. fr.* 168.10–16), and quoted in Festugière.

[852] On Proclus' doctrine see 5.11–21 above. It is founded in part on *Philebus* 29b–30c, where all things that human beings possess an insignificant and impure sample of are found to be nourished from wonderful universal supplies, including the physical elements, the metaphysical principles of *peras, apeiron, meikton*, and cause, soul, intellect, and wisdom.

[853] The arrangements that Proclus has in mind were those of fifth-century Athens, but the role of Solon himself in establishing such arrangements is dubious.

302

Closing considerations

The **fullness and magnificence** of the repayment give an indication, 15
for those who refer even these words of Socrates to their models, of the
overarching creation process that pervades all things. The **banquet of
words** indicates the realization of the creative forms. The invitation to
Timaeus signifies the reversion of the partial causes to the universal and 20
the invocation of good things from that source. And the **invocation to
the gods** symbolizes the creation process that is linked on high with the
intelligibles.[854] For **according to law** here is not a reference to the kind
of law that ordinary people understand, Italian or Attic law, but the kind
they usually speak in Pythagorean texts – as here: 25

First honour the immortal gods, as is their position by law . . .[855]

Law signifies the divine order, according to which the secondary things
are always linked to what precedes, and receive their fullness from them.
This **law**, starting with the intelligibles, descends to the creative cause, **204**
and proceeds on from there, and is divided about the whole. At the
same time Socrates is revealing through these words that he is asking
for the natural science to be Pythagorean, beginning with the divine 5
cause, and not the kind of cause that he himself rejects in the *Phaedo*,[856]
the one that blinds 'the eye of the soul' by blaming airs and ethers in
Anaxagorean fashion. True natural science must depend on theology,
just as nature depends on the gods, and is divided up according to their 10
overall grades, in order that words too should be imitators of the things
they are supposed to signify.[857] That's why the inventors of myths have
established the tradition that Hephaestus, the one in charge of nature,
was seized with love for Athena, the one who weaves the tapestry of the
intellective forms and is conductor of intellections for all beings within 15
the cosmos.

---

[854] Again reference to Timaeus symbolizing the universal demiurge, whose activities are
directly linked to the next level up, while Socrates symbolizes the demiurge of one of
the parts (the heaven).

[855] *Carm. Aur.* 1, a well-known text in late antiquity.

[856] See *Phaedo* 96a–99d, where a mechanical account of causes is rejected. However, the
freeing of 'the eye of the soul' from the blindness induced by its low-level materialistic
environment is a theme of *Republic* 7, particularly 533d2.

[857] The nature of the name's relation to its original is complex in Neoplatonism; see for
instance *Ammonius: On Aristotle On Interpretation* 40.18–22, trans. David Blank (Duckworth 1996): 'It is no wonder that we want to call the name both a 'symbol' [*symbolon*]
and an 'artificial likeness' [*homoiôma technêton*], for what is imposed unreflectively is
merely a symbol, while what is imposed according to reason resembles symbols in
being able to be composed of now some and now other syllables, but in being appropriate to the nature of what is named it is a likeness, not a symbol.'

303

On the *Timaeus* of Plato: Book 1

Conclusion

At this point the proem of the *Timaeus* is concluded. Severus did not
think it worthy of commentary at all. Longinus[858] said it was not all
superfluous, only the embedded tale of the Atlantines and of the stories told by the Egyptian, so that he used to follow Socrates' request, I
mean **I am here dressed up for it and most ready of all to receive it**,
with Critias' description, I mean **Then consider the type of arrangement we have made for your entertainment, Socrates**. Porphyry and
Iamblichus,[859] though, demonstrated that it was in harmony with the
overall aim of the dialogue, the one in a less complete fashion, and the
other more in the style of a full initiate.[860] Hence, if we too conclude
the book at this point, we shall be providing an arrangement of our own
that accords both with that of Plato and with these people.

---

[858] Longinus fr. 37 (Patillon and Brisson), showing that he did not normally tackle 20c to
27a; that Severus, Platonist of the second century, is mentioned at all is surely due to
either Longinus or Porphyry.

[859] Porphyry, *in Tim.* fr. XXVII (Sodano); Iamblichus, *in Tim.* fr. 25, with commentary in
Dillon (1973), 294–5.

[860] Note the way in which Proclus invites us to imagine a steady development towards the
correct view of interpreting prologues., It seems, however, that the Middle Platonists
and their Neopythagorean contemporaries did not all spurn the introductory material,
and that there had been considerable discussion of the Atlantis story and its status.
For discussion see Tarrant (2000), 39–40 (though n. 42 misinterprets Longinus). No
doubt Porphyry would have picked out Severus as a particularly bad example of a
Middle Platonist who failed to see merit in the prologues, and Longinus as somebody
whose work was well known to him. Porphyry himself found only ethical significance
in the prologues, as may be seen from references above, especially when compared
with *in Parm.* 1.658–9 (where, as is usual in this commentary, commentators are not
named). On the exegetic strategies of Porphyry and Iamblichus in the present work
see Introduction, pp. 44–8.

References

ANNICK, C.-S. (1991) 'Lire Proclus, lecteur du Sophiste', in P. Aubenque (ed.), *Études sur le Sophiste de Platon*, Paris, Bibliopolis, 475–94

ARCHER-HIND, R. D. (1888) *The Timaeus of Plato*. Cambridge University Press

ATHANASSIADI, POLYMNIA (1999) *Damascius: The Philosophical History*. Athens, Apamea

ATKINSON, M. (1983) *Plotinus: Ennead V. 1, A Commentary with Translation*. Oxford University Press

BALTES, MATTHIAS (1976) *Die Weltentstehung des platonischen Timaios nach den antiken Interpreten* I. Leiden, Brill

(1983) 'Zur Philosophie des Platonikers Attikos', in H.-D. Blume and F. Mann (eds.), *Platonismus und Christentum*, Münster, 38–57

BALTES, MATTHIAS et al. (1987–) *Der Platonismus in der Antike*. Stuttgart–Bad Cannstatt, frommann-holzboog

BALTUSSEN, HAN (2003) 'Early reactions to Plato's *Timaeus*: Polemic and exegesis in Theophrastus and Epicurus', in R. W. Sharples and A. Sheppard (2003), 49–71

BALTZLY, DIRK (2002) 'What goes up: Proclus against Aristotle on the fifth element', *Australasian Journal of Philosophy* 80, 261–87

BASTIANINI G. AND DAVID N. SEDLEY (1995) Edition of the anonymous *In Theaetetum* in *Corpus dei papiri filosofici greci e latini*, III: Commentari. Florence, Olschki, 227–562

BECHTLE, GERARD. (1999) *The Anonymous Commentary on Plato's 'Parmenides'*. Bern, Haupt

BEIERWALTES, WERNER (1965) *Proklos: Grundzüge seiner Metaphysik*. Frankfurt

BETEGH, GABOR (2004) *The Derveni Papyrus: Cosmology, Theology, and Interpretation*. Cambridge University Press

BIDEZ, J., ed. (1928) *Proclus: De sacrificio et magia*. Catalogue des manuscrits alchimiques grecs. Brussels, Lamertin

BLANK, DAVID (1996) *Ammonius: On Aristotle On Interpretation 1–8*. London, Duckworth

BOESE, H., ed. (1958) *Die mittelalterliche Übersetzung der Stoicheiosis physike des Proclus: Procli Diadochi Lycii Elementatio physica*. Berlin, Academie-verlag

BOISSONADE, J. F., ed. (1966) Marinus *Vita Procli*. Amsterdam, Hakkert

BRÉHIER, E., ed. (1956) *Plotin: Ennéades*, vol. V. Paris, Les Belles Lettres

BRISSON, LUC (1987a) 'Amélius: Sa vie, son oeuvre, sa doctrine, son style', *ANRW* II.36.2, 793–860

(1987b) 'Proclus et l'Orphisme', in J. Pépin and H. D. Saffrey (eds.), *Proclus: lecteur et interprète des anciens*, Paris, CNRS

References

(1999) 'The Platonic background in the *Apocalypse of Zostrianos*: Numenius and *Letter* II attributed to Plato', in John J. Cleary (ed.), *Traditions of Platonism*, Aldershot, Ashgate

(2000). 'La place des *Oracles Chaldaïques* dans la *Théologie Platonicienne*', in A. P. Segonds and C. Steel (eds.), *Proclus et la Théologie Platonicienne*, Louvain, Presses Universitaires de Louvain, 109–16

(2003) 'Plato's *Timaeus* and the *Chaldean Oracles*', in G. Reydams-Schils (ed.), *Plato's Timaeus as Cultural Icon*, Notre Dame, Ind., University of Notre Dame, 111–51

BROADIE, SARAH (2001) 'Theodicy and pseudo-history in the *Timaeus*', *Oxford Studies in Ancient Philosophy* 21, 1–28

CAMERON, ALAN (1983) 'Crantor and Posidonius on Atlantis', *Classical Quarterly* 33, 81–91

CARBONARA NADDEI, M. (1976) *Gli scoli greci al Gorgia di Platone*. Bologna, Pàtron Editore

CHIESARA, MARIA L., ed. (2001) *Aristocles of Messene: Testimonia and Fragments*. Oxford University Press

CLAY, DISKIN (1999) 'Plato's Atlantis: The anatomy of a fiction', *Proceedings of the Boston Area Colloquium in Ancient Philosophy* 15, 1–21

CLEARY, JOHN J. (2006). 'Proclus as a reader of Plato's *Timaeus*', in H. Tarrant and D. Baltzly (2006), 19–31

CORNFORD, F. M. (1957) *Plato's Cosmology*. New York, Liberal Arts Press

CORRIGAN, KEVIN (1987) 'Amelius, Plotinus, and Porphyry on Being, Intellect and One', *ANRW* II.36.2, 195–203

COULTER, J. A. (1976) *The Literary Microcosm: Theories of Interpretation of the Later Neoplatonists*. Leiden, Brill

DAVIES, J. K. (1971) *Athenian Propertied Families*. Oxford University Press

DENYER, NICHOLAS, ed. (2001) *Plato, Alcibiades*, Cambridge University Press

DES PLACES, É., ed., trans. (1973) *Numénius: Fragments*. Paris, Les Belles Lettres

(1996) *Oracles chaldaïques: avec un choix de commentaires anciens*, 3rd edn. Paris, Les Belles Lettres

DIEHL E., ed. (1965) *Proclus Diadochus: In Platonis Timaeum Commentaria*. Amsterdam, Hakkert. 3 vols. [Reprint of Leipzig, Teubner, text of 1903–5]

DILLER, H. (1957) 'Proklos', *RE* 18.1, 186–274

DILLON, JOHN (1971) 'Harpocration's *Commentary on Plato*: Fragments of a Middle Platonic commentary', *Calif. Stud. in Class. Ant.*4, 125–46

ed. (1973) *Iamblichi Chalcidensis in Platonis Dialogos Commentariorum Fragmenta*. Leiden, Brill

(1977) *The Middle Platonists*. London, Duckworth

(2003) *The Heirs of Plato*. Oxford University Press

(2006) 'Pedantry and pedestrianism? Some reflections on the Middle Platonic commentary tradition', in H. Tarrant and D. Baltzly (2006), 19–31

DODDS, E. R., ed. and trans. (1963) *Proclus: The Elements of Theology*. Oxford, Clarendon Press

References

DUVICK, BRIAN, trans. (forthcoming) *Proclus: On the Cratylus*. London, Duckworth

EDWARDS, M. J. (2000) *Neoplatonic Saints: The Lives of Plotinus and Proclus by their Students*. Liverpool University Press

FESTUGIÈRE, A. J. (1966) *Proclus: Commentaire sur le Timée*. Paris, Vrin
  (1970) *Proclus: Commentaire sur la République*. Paris, Vrin
  (1971) 'Modes de composition des Commentaires de Proclus', in A. J. Festugière (ed.), *Études de philosophie greque*, Paris, Vrin, 551–74

FESTUGIÈRE A. J. AND L. MASSIGNON (1944) *La révélation d'Hermès Trismègiste*. Paris, Librairie Lecoffre J. Gabald

FINAMORE, JOHN, AND JOHN DILLON (2002) *Iamblichus' De Anima: Text, Translation, and Commentary*. Leiden, Brill

GATTI, MARIA LUISA (1996) 'Plotinus: The Platonic tradition and the foundation of Neoplatonism,' in Lloyd Gerson (ed.), *The Cambridge Companion to Plotinus*, Cambridge University Press

GERSH, STEPHEN (2000) 'Proclus' theological methods: The programme of the *Theologica Platonica* 1.4', in A. Segonds and C. Steel (2000), 15–27
  (2003) 'Proclus' *Commentary on the Timaeus* – the prefatory material', in R. W. Sharples and A. Sheppard (2003), 143–53

Gioè, Adriano (2003) *Filosofi medioplatonici del ii secolo DC, testimonianze e frammenti*. Naples, Bibliopolis

GLUCKER, JOHN (1978) *Antiochus and the late Academy*. Göttingen, Vandenhoeck and Ruprecht

GUÉRARD C. (1991) 'Les citations du *Sophiste* dans les oeuvres de Proclus', in P. J. and H. D. Saffrey (eds.), *Études sur le Sophiste de Platon*, Paris, Bibliopolis, 495–508

HADOT, PIERRE (1968) *Porphyre et Victorinus*, vols. i and ii. Paris, Études Augustiniennes
  (1990) 'The Harmony of Plotinus and Aristotle according to Porphyry', in R. Sorabji (ed.), *Aristotle Transformed: The Ancient Commentators and their Influence*, London, Duckworth, 125–140

HALLIWELL, STEPHEN (2002) *The Aesthetics of Mimesis: Ancient Texts and Modern Problems*. Princeton University Press

ISAAC, D., ed. and trans. (1977) *Proclus: Dix problèmes concernant la providence*. Paris, Les Belles Lettres
  ed. and trans. (1979) *Proclus: Providence, Fatalité, Liberté*. Paris, Les Belles Lettres
  ed. and trans. (1982) *Proclus: De l' existence du mal*. Paris, Les Belles Lettres

JACKSON, R., K. LYKOS, AND H. TARRANT, trans. (1998) *Olympiodorus: Commentary on Plato's Gorgias*. Leiden, Brill

JOHANSEN, T. K. (2004) *Plato's Natural Philosophy: A Study of the Timaeus-Critias*. Cambridge University Press

JOHNSON T. M. (1988) *Iamblichus: Exhortation to Philosophy*. Grand Rapids, Phanes Press

JONES, R. M. (1980) *The Platonism of Plutarch, and Selected Papers*. New York

References

KARIVIERI A. (1994) 'The House of Proclus on the southern slopes of the Acropolis: A contribution', in P. Castren (ed.), *Post-Herulian Athens*, Athens, Finnish Institute, I. 115–40

KERN, O. (1922) *Orphicorum Fragmenta*. Berlin, Weidmann

KIDD, I. G. (1988) *Posidonius*, vol. II, The Commentary, Cambridge University Press

KROLL, W., ed. (1899–1901) *Procli Diadochi in Platonis Rem Publicam Commentarii*. Leipzig, Teubner

KUISMA, O. (1996) *Proclus' Defence of Homer*. Helsinki

LAMBERTON, R. (1986) *Homer the Theologian: Neoplatonist Allegorical Reading and the Growth of the Epic Tradition*. Berkeley, University of California Press

LAMBERZ, E. (1987) 'Form des philosophischen Kommentars', in J. Pépin and H.-D. Saffrey (eds.), *Proclus: Lecteur et interprète des anciens*, Paris, CNRS, 1–20

LANG, H. AND A. D. MACRO (2001) *Proclus: On the Eternity of the World*. Berkeley, University of California Press

LEDBETTER, GRACE M. (2003) *Poetics before Plato: Interpretation and Authority in Early Greek Theories of Poetry*. Princeton University Press

LEE, JOHN A. L. (1997) 'Hebrews 5:14 and Ἕξις: A history of misunderstanding', *Novum Testamentum* 39, 151–76

LERNOULD, ALAIN (2001) *Physique et théologie: Lecture du Timée de Platon par Proclus*. Villeneuve d' Ascq, Presses Universitaires du Septentrion

MAKOWSKI, F. (1997) 'L' absent du Timée', *Revue de Philosophie Ancienne* 15, 115–58

MANITIUS, C., ed. (1909) *Procli Diadochi Hypotyposis Astronomicarum Positionum*. Leipzig, Teubner

MANSFELD, JAAP (1983) 'Intuitionism and formalism: Zeno's definition of geometry in a fragment of L. Calvenus Taurus', *Phronesis* 28, 59–74
(1992) *Heresiology in Context*. Leiden, Brill
(1994) *Prolegomena: Questions to be settled before the study of an author or a text*. Leiden, Brill

MANSFELD, JAAP, AND DAVID T. RUNIA (1997) *Aetiana. The Method and Intellectual Context of a Doxographer*, vol. I. Leiden, Brill

MARTIJN, MARIJE (2006) 'The *eikôs mythos* in Proclus' commentary on the *Timaeus*', in H. Tarrant and D. Baltzly (2006) 151–67

MENN, STEPHEN (2001) 'Longinus on Plotinus', *Dionysius* 19, 113–24

MERLAN, PHILIP (1960) *From Platonism to Neoplatonism*, 2nd edn. The Hague, Nijhoff

MORGAN, K. A. (1998) 'Designer history: Plato's Atlantis story and fourth-century ideology', *Journal of Hellenic Studies* 118, 101–18

MORROW G. R., trans. (1970) *Proclus: Commentary on the First Book of Euclid's Elements*. Princeton University Press

MORROW G. R. AND J. M. DILLON, trans. (1987) *Proclus' Commentary on Plato's Parmenides*. Princeton University Press

O' MEARA, DOMINIC J. (1989) *Pythagoras Revived: Mathematics and Philosophy in Late Antiquity*. Oxford, Clarendon Press

References

O'NEILL, WILLIAM (1965) *Proclus: Alcibiades I*. The Hague, Nijhoff

OPSOMER, JAN (2000) 'Proclus on demiurgy and procession: A Neoplatonic reading of the *Timaeus*', in M. R. Wright (ed.), *Reason and Necessity: Essays on Plato's Timaeus*, London, 113–43

(2001a) 'Neoplatonist criticisms of Plutarch', in A. Pérez Jiménez and F. Casadesús (eds.), *Estudios sobre Plutarco. Misticismo y religiones mistéricas en la obra de Plutarco*, Madrid-Málaga, 187–200

(2001b) 'Who in Heaven is the Demiurge? Proclus' exegesis of Plato *Tim.* 28c3–5', *The Ancient World* 32, 52–70

(2003) 'La démiurgie des jeunes dieux selon Proclus', Les Études Classiques 71, 5–49

OPSOMER, JAN AND CARLOS STEEL (2003) *Proclus: On the Existence of Evils*. London, Duckworth

PASQUALI, G., ed. (1908) *Proclus: In Platonis Cratylum commentaria*. Leipzig, Teubner

PATILLON, M. AND L. BRISSON, eds. (2001) *Longin: Fragments, Art rhétorique*. Paris, Les Belles Lettres

PÉPIN, JEAN (2000) 'Les modes de l'enseignement théologique dans la *Théologie Platonicienne*', in A. Segonds and C. Steel (2000), 1–14

PHILLIPS, JOHN F. (1997) 'Neoplatonic exegeses of Plato's cosmogony (*Timaeus* 27c–28c), *Journal of the History of Philosophy* 35, 173–97

PRAECHTER K. (1905) Review of Diehl, *Göttingische Gelehrte Anzeigen* 7, 505–35

(1990) Review of the *Commentaria in Aristotelem Graeca*, in R. Sorabji (ed.), *Aristotle Transformed*, London, Duckworth, 31–54

RANGOS, SPYRIDON (1999) 'Proclus on poetic mimesis, symbolism, and truth', *Oxford Studies in Ancient Philosophy* 19, 249–77

RAPPE, SARA (2000) *Reading Neoplatonism: Non-discursive Thinking in the Texts of Plotinus, Proclus, and Damascius*. Cambridge University Press

RESCIGNO, A. (1998) 'Proclo lettore di Plutarco?' in I. Gallo (ed.), *L' eredità culturale di Plutarco dall' Antichità al Rinascimento*, Naples, D'Auria, 111–41

REYDAMS-SCHILS, GRETCHEN (2001) 'Socrates' request: *Timaeus* 19b–20c in the Platonist tradition', *The Ancient World* 32, 39–51

RICHARD M. (1950) 'Apo phones', *Byzantion* 20, 191–222

RITZENFELD, A., ed. (1912) *Proclus: Institutio Physica*. Leipzig, Teubner

RUNIA, D. T. (1986) *Philo of Alexandria and the Timaeus of Plato*. Leiden, Brill

SAFFREY H. D. (1975) 'Allusions antichrétiennes chez Proclus: Le diadoque Platonicien', *Revue des Sciences Philosophiques et Philogiques* 59, 553–62.

(1990) 'How did Syrianus regard Aristotle?', in R. Sorabji (ed.), *Aristotle Transformed*, London, Duckworth, 173–80

SAFFREY H. D. AND L. G. WESTERINK, eds. (1968–97), *Proclus: Théologie Platonicienne*. Paris, Les Belles Lettres

SCHRÖDER, H. O. (1934) *Galeni in Platonis Timaeum Commentarii Fragmenta*. Leipzig

SEDLEY, DAVID (1997) 'Plato's *Auctoritas* and the rebirth of the commentary tradition', in M. Griffin and J. Barnes (eds.), *Philosophia Togata* II, 110–29

References

(1999a) 'The Stoic-Platonist debate on *kathêkonta*', in K. Ierodiakonou (ed.), *Topics in Stoic Philosophy*, Oxford University Press, 128–52

(1999b) 'The ideal of godlikeness', in G. Fine (ed.), *Oxford Readings in Plato: Ethics, Politics, Religion and the Soul*, Oxford University Press, 309–28

(2002) 'The origins of the Stoic god', in M. Frede and A. Laks (eds.), *Traditions of Theology: Studies in Hellenistic Theology, its Background, and Aftermath*, Leiden, 41–83

SEGONDS, A. AND C. STEEL, eds. (2000) *Proclus et la Théologie Platonicienne.* Leuven and Paris

SHARE, MICHAEL (1994) *Arethas' Scholia on Porphyry's Isagoge and Aristotle's Categories.* The Academy of Athens

trans. (2005) *Philoponus: Against Proclus on the Eternity of the World*, 2 vols. London, Duckworth

SHARPLES R. W. AND A. SHEPPARD, eds. (2003) *Ancient Approaches to Plato's Timaeus.* London, Institute of Classical Studies

SHEPPARD, ANNE (1980) *Studies on the 5th and 6th Essays of Proclus' Commentary on the Republic.* Göttingen, Vandenhoeck and Ruprecht

SIORVANES, LUCAS (1996) *Proclus: Neo-Platonic Philosophy and Science.* New Haven, Yale University Press

(2003) 'Perceptions of the *Timaeus*: Thematization and truth in the exegetical tradition', in Sharples and Sheppard (2003), 155–74

SMITH A. (1987) 'Porphyrian studies since 1913', *ANRW* II.36.2, 717–73

(1993) *Porphyrius: Fragmenta*, Leipzig, Teubner

SODANO, A. R. (1964) *Porphyrii in Platonis Timaeum Fragmenta*, Naples

SOMFAI, ANNA (2003) 'The nature of daemons: A theological application of the concept of geometrical proportion in Calcidius' *Commentary* to Plato's *Timaeus*', in Sharples and Sheppard (2003), 129–42

SORABJI, RICHARD (1988) *Matter, Space and Motion: Theories in Antiquity and their Sequel.* London, Duckworth

(2004) *The Philosophy of the Commentators, 200–600 AD: A Sourcebook*, 3 vols. London, Duckworth

SUMI, A. (1997) 'Plotinus on *Phaedrus* 247d7-e1: The Platonic locus classicus of the identity of intellect with the intelligible objects,' *American Catholic Philosophical Quarterly* 71, 404–20

(2006) 'The Species Infima as the Infinite: *Timaeus* 39e7–9, *Parmenides* 144b4-c1 and *Philebus* 16e1–2 in Plotinus, *Ennead* VI 2 (43) 22', in H. Tarrant and D. Baltzly (eds.), *Reading Plato in Antiquity*, 73–88

TARDIEU, M. (1996) *Recherches sur la formation de l' Apocalypse de Zostrien et les sources de Marius Victorinus, et Pierre Hadot, 'Porphyre et Victorine'. Questions et hypothèses*, *Res Orientales* ix, Bures-sur-Yvette

TARRANT, HAROLD (1979) 'Numenius fr. 13 and Plato's *Timaeus*', *Antichthon* 13, 19–29

(1983), 'The date of Anonymous *In Theaetetum*', *Classical Quarterly* 33, 161–87

(1993) *Thrasyllan Platonism.* Ithaca, Cornell University Press

(2000) *Plato's First Interpreters.* London, Duckworth

References

(2004) 'Must commentators know their sources? Proclus *In Timaeum* and Numenius', in P. Adamson, H. Baltussen, and M. W. F. Stone (eds.), *Philosophy, Science and Exegesis in Greek, Arabic and Latin Commentaries*, ICS BICS Suppl., London, vol. I, 175–90

TARRANT, H. AND D. BALTZLY, eds. (2006). *Reading Plato in Antiquity*. London

TAYLOR, THOMAS (1995) *The Platonic Theology in Six Books*. Frome, Prometheus Trust

TROMBLEY, F. (1995) *Hellenistic Religion and Christianization*. Leiden, Brill

TROUILLARD, JEAN (1983) 'Proclus et la joie de quitter le ciel', *Diotima* 11, 182–92

VAN DEN BERG, ROBERT, ed., trans. (2001) *Proclus' Hymns: Essays, Translations, Commentary*. Leiden, Brill

(2003) '"Becoming like God" according to Proclus' interpretations of the *Timaeus*, the Eleusinian Mysteries, and the Chaldaean *Oracles*', in R. Sharples and A. Sheppard (2003), 189–202

VOGT, E., ed. (1957) *Procli hymni*. Wiesbaden, Harrassowitz

WALLIS, R. T. (1972) *Neoplatonism*. London, Duckworth

WASZINK J. H. (1966) 'Porphyrios und Numenios', in *Porphyre*, Fondation Hardt, *Entretiens* 11, 33–78

WEBER, KARL-OTTO (1962) *Origenes der Neuplatoniker*. Munich

WEST, M. L. (1983) *The Orphic Poems*. Oxford University Press

WHITTAKER, JOHN (1987) 'Proclus and the Middle Platonists' in J. Pépin and H.-D. Saffrey (eds.), *Proclus, Lecteur et interprète des anciens*, Paris, CNRS

WITTWER, ROLAND (1999) 'Aspasian lemmatology', in A. Alberti and R. Sharples (eds.), *Aspasius: The Earliest Extant Commentary on Aristotle's Ethics*, Berlin, De Gruyter, 51–84

ZAIDMAN, L. B. AND PANTEL, P. S. (1992) *Religion in the Ancient Greek City*. Cambridge University Press

English–Greek glossary

This selection of terms is designed to help identify the Greek original of a particular translation. For best effect it should be used in conjunction with the Greek–English index.

above	*anô*	ἄνω
above, from	*anôthen*	ἄνωθεν
activity	*energeia*	ἐνέργεια
affection	*pathos*	πάθος
aim	*skopos*	σκοπός
air	*aêr*	ἀήρ
analogy	*analogia*	ἀναλογία
angelic	*angelikos*	ἀγγελικός
arrange	*kosmein*	κοσμεῖν
arrangement	*diakosmêsis, diakosmos*	διακόσμησις, διάκοσμος
Athenaic	*Athênaïkos*	Ἀθηναϊκός
become	*gignesthai*	γίγνεσθαι
being	*to on, ousia*	τὸ ὄν, οὐσία
bodiless	*asômatos*	ἀσώματος
body	*soma*	σῶμα
chariot	*ochêma*	ὄχημα
cohesive	*synektikos*	συνεκτικός
column (of opposites)	*systoichia*	συστοιχία
complete	*teleios*	τέλειος
conflagration	*ekpyrôsis*	ἐκπύρωσις
constitution	*politeia*	πολιτεία
constitutional	*politikos*	πολιτικός
corporeal	*sômatikos, sômatoeidês*	σωματικός, σωματοείδης
correspond	*analogein*	ἀναλογεῖν
correspondence	*analogia*	ἀναλογία
cosmic	*kosmikos*	κοσμικός
cosmic creation	*cosmopoiïa*	κοσμοποιΐα
craft	*technê*	τέχνη
creation	*dêmiourgia*	δημιουργία
creative	*dêmiourgikos*	δημιουργικός
creator	*poiêtês*	ποιητής
cycle	*anakyklêsis, periodos*	ἀνακύκλησις, περίοδος

312

English–Greek glossary

daemonic	*daimonios*	δαιμόνιος
demiurge	*dêmiourgos*	δημιουργός
depend on	*artasthai, exartasthai*	ἀρτᾶσθαι, ἐξαρτᾶσθαι
descend	*katienai*	κατιέναι
descent	*kathodos*	κάθοδος
destruction	*phthora*	φθορά
destructive	*phthartikos*	φθαρτικός
determine	*aphorizein*	ἀφορίζειν
distinctive character	*idiotês*	ἰδιότης
distinguish	*aphorizein*	ἀφορίζειν
divided	*diêirêmenos*	διῃρημένος
divided, divisible	*meristos*	μεριστός
divinity (abstract noun)	*theotês*	θεότης
dyad	*dyas*	δυάς
earth	*gê*	γῆ
effluence, efflux	*aporrhoia*	ἀπόρροια
element	*stoicheion*	στοιχεῖον
embrace (noun)	*periochê*	περιοχή
encosmic	*encosmios*	ἐγκόσμιος
end	*telos*	τέλος
enmattered	*enylos*	ἔνυλος
eternal	*aïdios*	ἀΐδιος
ether	*aithêr*	αἰθήρ
fall	*ptosis*	πτῶσις
fate	*heimarmenê*	εἱμαρμένη
father	*patêr*	πατήρ
fire	*pyr*	πῦρ
first	*prôtos, prôtistos*	πρῶτος, πρώτιστος
forgetfulness	*lêthê*	λήθη
form	*eidos*	εἶδος
founded in (be)	*hidryesthai*	ἱδρύεσθαι
fulfilment	*apoplêrôsis*	ἀποπλήρωσις
generation	*genesis*	γένεσις
generation-producing	*genesiourgos*	γενεσιουργός
give an indication	*endeiknysthai*	ἐνδείκνυσθαι
goal	*telos*	τέλος
god, goddess	*theos*	θεός
goddess	*thea, theos*	θεά, θεός
good	*agathos*	ἀγαθός
goodness	*agathotês*	ἀγαθότης
guardian (as adjective)	*phrourêtikos*	φρουρητικός
harmony	*harmonia*	ἁρμονία
heaven	*ouranos*	οὐρανός

313

English–Greek glossary

heavenly	*ouranios*	οὐράνιος
hegemonic	*hêgemonikos*	ἡγεμονικός
henad	*henas*	ἑνάς
hieratic	*hieratikos*	ἱερατικός
higher	*hyperteros*	ὑπέρτερος
history	*historia*	ἱστορία
human (adj.)	*anthrôpinos*	ἀνθρώπινος
human (noun)	*anthrôpos*	ἄνθρωπος
image	*eikôn, agalma*	εἰκών, ἄγαλμα
imagination	*phantasia*	φαντασία
immaculate	*achrantos*	ἄχραντος
immaterial	*aÿlos*	ἄυλος
incorporeal	*asômatos*	ἀσώματος
independent (gods)	*apolytoi (theoi)*	ἀπόλυτοι (θεοί)
indeterminate	*aöristos*	ἀόριστος
indication	*endeixis*	ἔνδειξις
infinity	*apeiria*	ἀπειρία
inspired	*entheos*	ἔνθεος
instrument	*organon*	ὄργανον
intellection	*noêsis*	νόησις
intellective	*noeros*	νοερός
intelligence	*nous*	νοῦς
intelligible	*noêtos*	νοητός
invisible	*aphanês*	ἀφανής
irrational	*alogos*	ἄλογος
join	*synaptein*	συνάπτειν
labouring	*thêtikos*	θητικός
limit	*peras*	πέρας
lot	*klêros*	κλῆρος
lot, get as one's	*lanchanein*	λαγχάνειν
maintain	*synechein*	συνέχειν
male	*arrhên*	ἄρρην
matter	*hylê*	ὕλη
measure (noun)	*metron*	μέτρον
measure (verb)	*metrein*	μετρεῖν
messenger (of gods)	*angelos*	ἄγγελος
monad	*monas*	μονάς
moon	*selene*	σελήνη
mortal	*thnêtos*	θνητός
motion	*kinesis*	κίνησις
multiplicity	*plêthos*	πλῆθος
multiply	*plêthuein*	πληθύειν

314

English–Greek glossary

mysteries	*mystêria*	μυστήρια
mystical	*mystikos*	μυστικός
myth	*mythos, mythologia*	μῦθος, μυθολογία
mythical	*mythikos*	μυθικός
name	*onoma*	ὄνομα
narrate	*historein*	ἱστορεῖν
narration	*often = historia*	ἱστορία
natural	*physikos*	φυσικός
nature	*physis*	φύσις
number	*arithmos*	ἀριθμός
official city goddess	*poliouchos thea*	πολιοῦχος θεά
operate	*energein*	ἐνεργεῖν
order	*taxis*	τάξις
otherness	*heterotês*	ἑτερότης
part	*meros* ،	μέρος
partial, particular	*merikos*	μερικός
participation	*metousia*	μετουσία
paternal	*patrikos*	πατρικός
peplos	*peplos*	πέπλος
perfect	*teleios*	τέλειος
perfection	*teleiotês*	τελειότης
period	*periodos*	περίοδος
philosophic	*philosophos*	φιλόσοφος
physical	*physikos*	φυσικός
physical inquiry	*physiologia*	φυσιολογία
plurality	*plêthos*	πλῆθος
portion	*moira*	μοῖρα
pre-exist	*prohÿparchein*	προυπάρχειν
presiding	*prostates*	προστάτης
priestly	*hieratikos*	ἱερατικός
primary	*prôtourgos*	πρωτουργός
principle	*archê*	ἀρχή
proceed, process	*proelthein, proienai*	προελθεῖν, προϊέναι
procession	*proödos*	πρόοδος
procreative	*gonimos*	γόνιμος
productive	*poiêtikos*	ποιητικός
protective	*phrourêtikos*	φρουρητικός
providence	*pronoia*	πρόνοια
psychical	*psychikos*	ψυχικός
purity	*katharotês*	καθαρότης
rank	*taxis*	τάξις
rational	*logikos*	λογικός
readiness	*epitêdeiotês*	ἐπιτηδειότης
reason	*logos*	λόγος

315

English–Greek glossary

receptacle	*hypodochê*	ὑποδοχή
recognition	*gnôsis*	γνῶσις
remain	*menein*	μένειν
representation	*agalma*	ἄγαλμα
reproductive	*genesiourgos*	γενεσιουργός
rest	*stasis*	στάσις
reversion	*epistrophê*	ἐπιστροφή
revert	*epistrephein*	ἐπιστρέφειν
rivalry	*enantiôsis*	ἐναντίωσις
sameness	*tautotês*	ταυτότης
secret	*aporrhêtos*	ἀπόρρητος
seed	*sperma*	σπέρμα
sensation	*aesthêsis*	αἴσθησις
separable, separate	*chôristos*	χώριστος
separation	*diakrisis*	διάκρισις
series	*seira*	σειρά
signify	*sêmainein*	σημαίνειν
solar	*hêliakos*	ἡλιακός
soul	*psychê*	ψυχή
spontaneous	*autophyês, automaton*	αὐτοφυής, αὐτόματον
stable	*monimos*	μόνιμος
subordinate	*hypheimenos*	ὑφειμένος
subordination	*hyphesis*	ὕφεσις
substance	*ousia*	οὐσία
substrate	*hypokeimenon*	ὑποκείμενον
summary	*anakephalaiôsis*	ἀνακεφαλαίωσις
sun	*hêlios*	ἥλιος
superiors	*hoi kreittones*	οἱ κρείττονες
surpassing excellence	*hyperochê*	ὑπεροχή
symbol	*symbolon*	σύμβολον
symbolically	*symbolikôs*	συμβολικῶς
sympathy	*sympatheia*	συμπάθεια
target	*skopos*	σκοπός
theological	*theologikos*	θεολογικός
theology	*theologia*	θεολογία
titanic	*titanikos*	τιτανικός
tool	*organon*	ὄργανον
triad	*trias*	τριάς
underlie	*hypokeisthai*	ὑποκεῖσθαι
unification	*henôsis*	ἕνωσις
universal	*holikos, katholikos*	ὁλικός, καθολικός
unlimited	*apeiros*	ἄπειρος
unmoved	*akinêtos*	ἀκίνητος
unswerving	*atreptos*	ἄτρεπτος

316

English–Greek glossary

unyielding	*ameiliktos*	ἀμείλικτος
vacant (of lots)	*adespotos*	ἀδέσποτος
vehicle	*ochêma*	ὄχημα
virtue	*aretê*	ἀρετή
visible	*emphanês*	ἐμφανής
wisdom	*phronêsis, sophia*	φρόνησις, σοφία

Greek word index

This index is intended to be a help in finding terminology of a technical or otherwise interesting nature, and also proper names. Technical terms found throughout do not have page-references listed. Translations offered are intended to be a good indication of how a term is translated, but because book 1 contains a wide variety of material it has not been possible to standardize translations beyond a certain point.

A

ἄβατος (χώρα), desert land, 181.6
ἀβίαστος, unforced, 93.15
ἀβιάστως, in an unforced manner, 64.25
ἀβούλητος, against one's will, etc., 20.26; 160.28
ἄβυσσος (ὕλη), an abyss (of matter), 175.19
ἀγαθοειδής, of a good sort, 134.1
ἀγαθόν, τὸ, the Good (Form of), 3.6; 3.22–5; 42.23; 45.25; 118.29; 125.22
ἀγαθός, (τὰ) ἀγαθά, good, good things, 22.16; 41.9; 42.27–8; 44.11–17; 45.15; 52.5–8; 113.13; 115.12; 118.1; 133.13; 134.10; 135.18–21; 158.4; 164.8; 168.24; 191.31; 197.25; 198.1; 198.4–5; 203.21
ἀγαθότης, goodness, 25.27; 131.8; 133.6
ἄγαλμα, image, representation, 11.15; 51.25–8; 57.16; 60.16; 99.3; 157.9
Ἀγαμέμνων, Agamemnon, 117.4
ἀγγελικός, angelic, 36.21; 131.27; 136.12; 137.10–12; 163.13
ἄγγελος, messenger, reporter, 92.16; 194.2
ἄγγελοι θεῶν, messengers of the Gods, 152.14
ἀγελαιοκομικά (θεῶν), herd-tending management of the Gods, 99.18
ἀγελάρχης, shepherd, 154.25
ἀγέλη, flock, 152.16–19
ἀγένητος (οὐρανός), ungenerated (heaven), 6.32
ἀγιώτατος (ἱερῶν), most sacred (of temples), 124.17
ἀγλαΐα (τῶν νοήσεων), splendours (of intellections), 87.4

ἄγονος, infertile, 48.1
ἀγχινούστερος, more sharp-witted 2.1
ἀγῶνες, competitions, 89.18
ἀγῶνες διαλεκτικοί, dissension of the dialecticians, 21.13
ἀγῶνες σοφιστικοί, sophistic struggles, 28.18
ἀγωνιστικός, competitive, 21.17–25; (adv.) 21.9
ἀδάμαστος, invincible, 57.18; 166.6; 168.15
Ἀδείμαντος, Adeimantus, 9.1
ἀδέσποτος, independent, vacant (lots), 92.1; 93.17; 145.10; 201.15
ἀδιαίρετος, undivided, 50.3
ἀδιάκοπος, unrelenting, 120.25; (adv.) 120.29
ἀδιαπταίστως, without stumbling, 193.19
ἀδιάστροφος, undistorted, 168.26
ἀδιάφορος, without variance, 161.14–27
ἀδιερεύνητος, outside the inquiry, 1.23; 13.19; impossible to find a path through, 187.18; 190.21
ἄδολος φιλία, straightforward friendship, 24.17
ἀδρανές, τὸ, inaction, 157.1
Ἀδράστεια, Adrasteia, 40.9; 69.26
ἁδρός, fulsome, stout, 62.9; 64.16; 70.21
ἀδυναμία, lack of power, 19.20; 22.11; 22.28; 62.31; 39.2; 114.9–12
ἄδυτον, τὸ, inner sanctuary, 98.16
ἀειμετάβολα, τὰ, ever-changing, 125.10
ἀέναος, ever-flowing, 195.27

318

Greek word index

ἀήρ, air, climate, (sing.) 103.4; 107.3–18; 112.24–9; 117.24; 162.5–163.1; (pl.) 2.14; 99.16; 100.26; 120.18; 137.4; 204.7

ἀέριος, of air, airborne, 112.21; 137.4; 142.5

ἀζωΐα, lifelessness, 41.1

ἄζων (ὄργανον), lifeless (instrument), 12.22

ἀήττητος, undefeated, 57.3

ἀθανασία, immortality, 162.19

ἄθεος, godless, 153.22

ἀθετεῖν, question authenticity, 62.14

ἀθέτησις, a setting aside, 77.27

ἀθήλυντος, unfeminized, 151.14

Ἀθηνᾶ, Athena, 77.4; 78.28; 79.6; 85.13–30; 95.16; 97.13; 103.9–32; 134.25–135.8; 140.23–30; 141.14; 144.9; 145.6–11; 147.1; 150.13–151.15; 156.17; 157.8–159.26; 163.24; 165.17; 166.11; 167.33; 169.14–170.14; 171.16–173.22; 183.7; 185.2; 197.5; 204.13

Ἀθηναϊκός, Athenaic, of Athena, 84.17–28; 134.31–135.2; 141.8; 144.12–24; 147.27; 150.15; 151.12; 156.21; 157.12–17; 159.3; 160.12–9; 163.8; 165.4–29; 166.30–167.8; 170.3–23; 175.32; 185.22–186.12; 191.6; 192.25

Ἀθηναῖοι, Athenians, 4.19; frequent from 74.11

ἀθρούστερος, more widespread, 107.21

Ἄθως, (Mt.) Athos, 181.12

Αἴας, Ajax, 35.4

αἰγίοχος, plying the aegis, 169.8

αἰγίς, aegis, 168.17

ὁ Αἰγύπτιος, the Egyptian(s), (sing.) 102.29; 108.27; 114.26; 127.5–23; 130.2; 135.16; 135.29; 140.23; 204.19; (pl.) 76.4–9; 77.21; 97.17; 98.15; 99.4; 100.26; 101.17–22; 102.11–26; 107.30; 118.2; 119.17–120.16; 121.13–122.18; 123.21; 124.5–20; 127.11; 179.28; 147.9; 158.27; 181.27; 191.17; 192.10–12

Αἴγυπτος, Egypt, 91.11; 93.1–5; 94.29–95.21; 96.4; 97.18; 119.12; 187.25

ἀίδιος, eternal, 2.26; 11.30; 39.15; 57.16; 89.17; 92.7; 105.19; 125.8; 127.6; 130.23; 137.30; 138.3–4; 139.20;

140.17; 141.30; 145.21; (adv.) 132.1; 141.22

ἀιδιότης, eternal nature, 138.11; 141.28

αἰθέριος, of ether, 5.15; 138.26; 142.6; 147.13

αἰθήρ, ether, 176.13; 181.9

αἴνιγμα, riddle, 130.7; 132.22; 134.31

αἰνιγματώδης, of riddling sort, 129.16; (comp. adv.) 165.14

αἰνίσσεσθαι, talk riddlingly, 32.26; 75.22; 108.30; 147.19

αἵρεσις, choice, selection, 160.28; 164.1; also faction, 2.16

αἴσθησις, sensation, 14.22; 102.18; 102.30

αἰσθητός, sensible, 5.19; 11.2–10; 13.3–10; 16.30; 19.12; 22.30; 50.10; 85.1; 105.5; 124.21; 128.12; 142.24–8; 143.16; 144.11; 185.7

αἶσχος, ugliness, 175.10

αἰτία, cause: frequent

αἰών, eternity, 6.28; 39.16; 94.15

αἰώνιος, eternal, everlasting, 38.23; 131.19–26; 162.4; (adv.) 104.11; 108.16; 140.7; 185.24; (comp.) 29.24–6

ἀκάκωτος, undamaged, 111.17

ἀκαλλώπιστος, unembellished, 86.28

ἀκατάληκτος, unceasing, 128.4

ἀκατάτακτος, unordered, 50.3

ἀκατονόμαστος, unnamed, 24.17; 162.24

ἀκίνητος, unmoved etc., 27.9; 39.15; 97.8; 108.4; 124.15; 138.24; 139.2–6; 161.13; 162.6

ἀκλινής, unswerving etc., 157.18; 166.7; 189.24; (adv.) 52.19

ἄκλιτος, unswerving, 157.10

ἀκολουθία, correspondence, consistency, 125.24; 187.21; 201.26

ἀκρόασις, hearing, lesson etc., 9.12; 16.14; 20.29; 21.29–22.24

ὁ ἀκροατής, listener, student etc., 21.4; 21.8; 22.31; 23.11

ἀκροβολισμοί, skirmishes, 61.23

ἄκρος, top, summit etc., 69.15; 70.5; 198.25–199.1

ἀκρότατος, highest, topmost etc., 9.20; 29.23; 168.5; 183.6

ἄκρως, to the highest degree, 192.4–9

ἀκρότης, highest point, pinnacle, 11.17; 24.2; 169.16

ἀκτῖνες, rays, 181.19

319

Greek word index

ἀκώλυτος, unhindered, 187.1; (adv.) 11.24; 100.27; 179.1

ἀλήθεια, truth, 62.26; 80.20; 83.6; 127.8; 130.3; 162.31; 180.21; 202.8

Ἀλκιβιάδης, Alcibiades, 61.13

ἀλλοκίνητος, deriving motion from another, 12.22

ἀλλόκοτος, grating, 68.10

ἀλογία, irrationality, 175.22

ἀλογίστος, irrational, 153.17

ἄλογος, unreasonable, non-rational, 67.8; 145.16; (comp.) 167.30

ψυχὴ ἄλογος, irrational soul, 53.23; 174.6; 176.5; 183.9

τὸ ἄλογον, irrational part, irrationality, 40.25; 176.21

Ἄμασις, Amasis, 97.11; 97.21

ἀμέθεκτος, unparticipated, 10.29

ἀμείβειν μορφάς, change shape, 108.2

ἀμείλικτος, unyielding, 38.18; 166.9; 167.6; 168.15

ἀμέρεια, indivisibility 54.29; 148.27

ἀμερής, undivided, 89.12

ἀμέριστος, undivided, indivisible, 42.29; 95.13; 173.3

ἀμετάβλητος, changeless, unchanging, 58.27; 128.5; 138.14–21; 139.9

ἀμιγής, immaculate, 167.2

ἀμιγὴς καθαρότης, unmingled purity, 48.27; 50.15; 155.1; 169.6; 198.18

τὸ ἀμιγές, unmixed character, 157.16

ἀμιγῶς, in unblended fashion, 163.14

ἄμικτος, failing to mix, 155.24

ἀμιξία, not mixing, 155.31

Ἄμμων, Ammon, 96.18

ἀμοιβή, repayment, return, 25.9; 44.14; 192.16

ἄμορφος, formless, 126.27

Ἀμύνανδρος, Amynander, 87.24; 90.4; 92.31

ἀνάβασις, rising, swelling, 119.18; 120.12

ἀναβλυσθαίνειν, spout up, 119.18; 120.7

ἀναγινώσκειν, read, 35.14

ἀνάγκη, necessity

θεία ἀνάγκη, divine necessity, 160.29

ὑλικὴ ἀνάγκη, material necessity, 42.26

ἀνάγραπτος, recorded, 192.13

ἀναγραφά, recorded, 123.15

ἀναγωγεύς, Upward Leader, 34.20

ἀναγωγή, return, elevation, ascent, 53.11; 79.13; 180.20

ἀναγωγός, leading up, uplifting, etc., 7.30; 38.10; 118.6; 154.1; 154.24; 166.5; 166.28; 168.24; 186.3–6

ἀναδόσεις, return contributions, 74.17

ἀναδρομά, recourse, referral back, 149.4, 191.15

ἀναδύνειν, rise above, 110.26

ἀναθυμίασις, exhalation, 44.25, 110.2–20; 117.22

ἀναίνεσθαι, defy, 138.11

ἀναιρετικός, utterly removing, 165.25

ἀναίτιος, without a cause, 52.7

ἀνακεφαλαιοῦσθαι, summarize, 4.16; 34.31; 200.17

ἀνακεφαλαίωσις, summary etc., 27.26; 30.20; 33.5; 55.19; 72.19; 195.13

ἀνακινεῖν, get under way, 13.29

ἀνακίνησις, stimulation, 30.8

ἀνακρίνειν, inquire of, 100.5

ἀνακύκλησις, cycle, revolution, 28.24; 95.25; 102.7; 108.24; 126.1; 127.26

ἀνάληψις, getting, recalling, 149.3; 193.6

ἀναλογεῖν, be analogous, correspond, 88.2; 89.17; 93.25; 152.13; 174.8

ἀναλογία, correspondence, analogy, 33.9; 33.28; 34.27; 55.10; 57.21–4; 63.2–10; 71.6; 71.21–6; 78.26; 80.2; 91.27; 95.8; 128.13–15; 132.27; 134.20; 152.4–10; 165.24; 172.24–9; 173.20; 175.25; 177.27; 178.1; 198.15

ἀναλύειν, explain away, 129.18

ἀνάλυσις, solution, dissolution, analysis, 76.22; 126.27; 173.28; 174.30; 182.7; 183.20

ἀναμάττεσθαι, take on, 111.2

ἀνάμεστος, replete, 60.17

ἀναμιμνηνσκέσθαι, recollect, remind oneself, 124.7; 175.4

ἀνάμνησις, recollection, 102.32; 123.31; 124.10; 172.29; 191.22

ἀναμνηστικὸν τοῦ ὄντος, reacquainting one with reality, 41.2

ἀνανεοῦν, renew, 39.8; 98.2; 104.26

ἀνανεύειν, rise up above, 58.13

ἀνανέωσις, renewal, rejuvenation, 28.6; 104.5; 126.29

ἀνανταγώνιστος, irresistible, 38.6; 39.6; 167.11; 189.24

ἀναπίνεσθαι, be absorbed, 121.26

ἀναπλήρωσις, fully supplying, 24.24; 26.26

ἀναπλοῦν, reunite, unfold, 38.16; 191.8

320

Greek word index

ἀνάπτυξις, unveiling, 129.15–30
ἀνάρμοστος, incompatible, 69.5
ἀναρρύματα, *anarrhymata*, 88.16
ἀνάρρυσις, Anarrhysis, 88.15
ἀναρτᾶν, attach to, link to, 44.19, 140.13
ἀναστέλλειν, repress, 34.1
ἀνατάσσεσθαι, be stationed, be re-enrolled, 53.30; 185.31
ἀνατείνειν, draw up, 24.10
ἀνατέλλειν, rise up, 120.1
ἀναφορά, transfer, 182.8
ἀναφῶς, without touching, 112.10; 157.6
ἀνεγείρειν, awaken, stimulate, incite, 24.11; 72.29; 86.4
ἀνείδεος, without form, 91.20; 126.26; 189.14
ἀνείλλεσθαι, be confined to, 50.2
ἀνέκλειπτος, unfailing, undiminished, 28.8; 33.21; 44.29; 106.15; 195.27
ἀνεκφοίτητος, not straying from, etc., 6.2; 12.14; 111.20
ἀνέλιξις, unfolding, 29.13
ἀνελίττειν, wheel round, turn back round, 28.26; 105.10
ἀνέλκεσθαι, draw back, 88.16
ἀνενδεής, without lack, self-sufficient, 24.15; 44.13
ἀνεξάλειπτος, indelible, 102.8
ἀνεξαπάτητος, impossible to deceive, 92.18
ἀνεπινοήτως, inconceivable, 3.32
ἀνεπιστήμων, unscientific, 67.11
ἀνθεστιᾶν, give a full return feast, 25.23
ἀνθρώπειον (εἶδος), human (species), 46.3
ἀνθρωπικὸς νοῦς, human intelligence, 152.18; 153.4
ἀνθρώπινος, human, 32.4–11; 33.12; 36.4; 43.27; 44.8; 49.23–4; 64.18; 78.2; 95.26; 125.17; 158.5–16; 170.18; 194.17; 201.21
ἄνθρωπος, human: frequent
ὁ ὄντως ἄνθρωπος, real human being, 83.4
ὁ ἐν ἡμῖν ἄνθρωπος, human within us, 16.16; 117.2
ἀνιέναι, go up, go back, etc.: frequent (as opp. κατιέναι), 29.19; 34.26; 53.21; 58.15; 147.16; 151.22; 191.17
ἀνιέναι, dedicate, 140.16
ἄνοδος, ascent, 54.7; 108.19; 114.20
ἀνταπόδοσις, repayment, 25.29

ἀντιγράφειν, reply (in writing), 31.2
ἀντιδιαιρεῖν, contrast etc., 39.25; 69.3; 152.32; 176.25
ἀντίδοσις, repayment, return favour, 25.8; 43.27; 44.6; 198.12
ἀντίθετος, opposing, 78.7; 78.25
ἀντιλογία, attack on, 174.29
ἀντιμεταλαμβάνειν, swap, 145.18
ἀντιπεριφορά, counter-revolution, 76.24
ἀντιτάττειν, set against, 79.1; 174.12
ἀντίτυπος, intractable, 143.6–9
ἄντοικοι, those who dwell opposite, 120.19
ἀντοχή, clinging closely, 75.10
ἀντωπεῖν πρὸς τὸ φῶς, confront the light (directly), 19.16; 115.4
ἀνυμνεῖν, celebrate, honour, 166.14; 173.9; 191.29
ἀνυπόδετος, unattributed, 196.20
ἄνω, above, etc.: frequent
ἄνωθεν, from above, 8.2; 41.19; 53.9–17; 75.24; 95.10; 98.13; 112.18; 128.11; 130.13; 137.5; 140.29; 142.8; 142.18; 142.29; 143.15; 154.4; 155.2; 156.16; 166.2; 170.24; 174.15; 187.2; 189.10; 191.5–11; 203.22
ἀοριστία, indeterminacy, indefiniteness, 39.4–11; 40.13; 146.21
ἀόριστος, indeterminate, 21.10; 23.6; 38.16; 146.15; 176.31; 179.3; 190.19; 192.19
ἀορίστως, in unspecified fashion, 23.11
ἀπάθεια, dispassionate state, 64.9
ἀπαθής, impassive, immune to influence, 115.23; 157.4
ἀπάντησις, opposition, 81.1
ἀπαξιοῦν, disdain, 68.3
ἀπαρίθμησις, counting, 15.13; 102.28
ἀπατεών, full of deceit, 92.19
Ἀπατούρια, Apaturia, 88.11; 89.8
ἀπεικονίζεσθαι, reflect, mirror, 50.23; 57.10; 60.9; 69.27; 89.24; 118.11; 134.12; 157.16; 158.2
ἀπεικός, improbable, 199.25
ἀπείρατος, untested, unused to, 117.10; 156.3
ἀπειρία, inexperience, 62.18
ἀπειρία, infinity, limitlessness, Unlimited, 22.17; 36.16; 121.20; 130.18–19; 174.18; 175.9; 175.22; 176.2; 176.31; 183.15; 185.8

Greek word index

ἄπειρος, inexperienced, 62.20; 187.22
ἄπειρος, unlimited etc., 47.4; 84.60;
  121.17; 132.13; 138.25; 176.29–30;
  179.3
ἀπεοικέναι, be unlike, 68.11
ἀπέραντος, unbounded, 42.16
ἀπερίγραφον, τό, beyond description, 23.5
ἀπερίληπτος, remaining beyond grasp,
  146.17
ἀπλανής, inerrant, 132.5, 137.5; 141.4
  οἱ ἀπλανεῖς ἀστέρες, the fixed stars,
  76.22–3; 152.8
ἄπλαστος, sincere, 25.4
ἁπλότης, simplicity etc., 29.10; 45.22;
  86.11
ἀποβάσεις τοῦ Νείλου, fluctuations in the
  Nile, 120.23
ἀπογένεσις, passing out of life, 147.22
ἀπόγονος, descendant, child of, 173.19;
  182.19
ἀποδεικτικός, demonstrational, 7.23–8.4
ἀποκαθίστασθαι, return to square one,
  54.8; 148.12
ἀποκατάστασις, return to square one,
  87.30; 101.1; 103.2
ἀποκληροῦν, allot, 192.22
ἀποκόπτειν, do away with, eliminate,
  25.16; 38.2; 157.7
ἀπόκρυφος αἰτία, secret cause, 53.1
ἀπολιμπάνειν, desert, leave, 50.1; 113.3
Ἀπόλλων, Apollo, 78.28; 79.3; 159.27
Ἀπολλωνιακός, Apollonian, 157.14–17;
  163.7
ἀπολογίζεσθαι, recount, 101.17
ἀπόλυτος, liberated, independent, 18.8;
  93.16; 131.5; 141.3; 166.31; 167.13
  ἀπολύτως, without involvement, 88.6;
  91.29
ἀποπίπτειν, miss, 142.15
ἀποπλήρωσις, fulfilment, 25.24; 168.23;
  203.19
ἀποπληρωταὶ τῆς δίκης, administrators of
  justice, 37.27
ἀποπληρωτικός, supplying, 192.21
ἀπόπτωσις, falling away, 22.15
ἄπορος (opp. πορεύσιμος), impassable,
  88.16; 190.21
ἀπορρεῖν, drift away, flow off, 27.10; 28.7
ἀπόρρητος, secret, inexpressible, 30.7;
  49.14; 129.29; 152.17; comp. (adv.)
  21.1

ἀπορροή, outflow, dispersal, 28.24;
  105.33
ἀπόρροια, effluence, efflux, outflow,
  43.5–16; 44.24; 49.10; 60.21; 97.7;
  114.31; 147.12
ἀπόσβεσις, extinguishing, 110.16
ἀποτέλεσμα, finished product, 152.28;
  193.27
ἀποτεμάχεσθαι, be sliced off, 49.23
ἀποτέμνειν, excise, 155.32
ἀποτυποῦσθαι, reproduce, describe,
  66.10; 70.6
ἀποτυφλοῦν, make blind, 115.3
ἀποφαντικός, with affirmation,
  revelationary, 7.31; 8.3; 21.25
  ἀποφαντικῶς, in openly doctrinal
  manner, 21.18
ἀπροαιρέτως, unthinkingly, 118.27
ἀπώλεια, destruction, 28.24; 105.7;
  116.13; 126.28
ἀραιουμένη (γῆ), rarefied (earth), 119.28
ἀραρός, strong, 124.21
Ἀργεῖοι, Argives, 101.7
Ἀργολικὸν γένος, Argive (race), 101.14
Ἄργος, Argos, 101.9
ἀργότερος, slower, 194.19
  ἀργῶς παρεστώς, standing idly by, 73.26
ἄργυρος, silver, 43.6
Ἀρεϊκός, of Ares, Areic, 34.22; 111.6;
  114.15; 148.3; 163.7
ἀρετή, virtue, 19.26; 21.21–22.1; 30.23;
  43.25; 46.1–12; 47.27; 51.18; 56.23;
  64.3; 65.9; 66.26; 73.20; 93.17; 100.3;
  166.27; 170.3–17, 185.4
Ἄρης, Ares, 43.6; 78.29; 79.7; 114.32;
  167.31
ἀριθμητικός, (numbers) for counting, 16.26
  ἡ ἀριθμητική, arithmetic, 41.25; 50.8;
  159.22
ἀριθμός, number 16.21–31; 17.11; 41.24;
  136.20; 147.3
ἀριστεῖς, valiant ones, 172.8
Ἄρκτος, Great Bear, 97.6
ἀρκτῷοι ἀστέρες, the Bear stars, 141.6
  τὰ ἀρκτῷ, the north, 109.27
ἁρμονία, harmony, 7.5; 25.10; 34.15;
  41.20; 79.18; 90.12; 126.29; 143.5
ἀρρενόθηλυς, male-female, 46.20
ἀρρενωπῶς, manfully, 179.32
ἄρρηκτος, unbreakable, impenetrable,
  84.3; 157.4

322

Greek word index

ἄρρην, male, 34.16; 46.18–47.25; 49.21;
110.9–21; 130.24; 131.24
ἀρρήτως, ineffably, 3.32
ἀρτᾶσθαι, depend on, stem from, be
linked to, 82.26; 94.23; 170.15
Ἄρτεμις, Artemis, 79.1–5; 152.23
ἄρτιος, even (number), 21.11–16; 130.26;
131.25
ἀρχάγγελοι, archangels, 152.13; 152.30
ἀρχαιολογία, ancient history,
'archaeology', 101.3–6; 102.4
ἀρχαιότης, antiquity, ancestry, 100.25;
101.14; 103.19; 103.30
ἀρχέτυπον, archetype, 150.3
ἀρχή
μία, single principle, 91.1; 176.11
δύο, two principles (e.g. πέρας, ἄπειρον),
130.18; 132.21; 176.21
ἀρχαί, principles, origins etc., 7.8; 12.2;
27.17; 88.5; 94.26; 128.3; 176.7;
200.2
δημιουργική, creative principle, 100.12
πρῶται, first principles, 91.28; (superl.)
8.3; 108.14
ἀρχηγέται τῆς γενέσεως, ancestors, 83.11
Ἀρχηγέτις, founder-divinity, 98.27–9
ἀρχηγικός, primal, originative, 1.23;
(comp.) 103.28; (adv.) 8.17
ἀρχηγός, chief, 79.14
ἀρχοειδῶς, in an originative way, 8.26
ἀσέβεια, impiety, 122.12
Ἀσία, Asia, 178.21
Ἀσκληπιακός, Asclepiac, 163.8
Ἀσκληπιός, Asclepius, 158.22; 159.26;
160.1
ἄσκοπος, blind, 192.19
ᾆσμα, hymn, 126.10
Ἀσσύριοι, Assyrians, 100.29
ἄστατος, restless, unstable, 37.24; 91.17
ἀστήρ, ἄστρον, star, 141.6; 202.21
οἱ πέντε ἀστέρες, the five planets, 147.15
ἀστρολογία, ἀστρονομία, astronomy,
41.26; 67.4; 103.5; 159.21
ἀσύγχυτος, unblending, uncontaminated,
85.10; 179.28
ἀσυμμετρία, lack of alignment (measure,
proportion), 22.27; 114.29; 115.19;
162.18
ἀσυμμέτρως, in an unbalanced
(disproportionate, unaligned) fashion,
19.11; 91.18; 114.31

ἀσύνδετος, disconnected, 14.13
ἀσφάλεια, being on the safe side, 193.28
ἄσχετος, free of relations, ungoverned etc.,
50.2, 115.25; 138.10
ἀσχολεῖσθαι, be busy with, 2.3
ἀσώματος, incorporeal, bodiless, 11.11;
12.27; 33.18–20; 78.19; 79.2; 164.24;
(adv.) 32.7
ἀτακτότατα, τά, most disorderly parts,
71.23
Ἀτλάντινον ὄρος, Mt. Atlas, 181.7
Ἀτλαντῖνοι, Atlantines, people of Atlantis,
4.19–24; 30.13; 71.7; 75.30–77.17;
128.28; 167.29; 171.29; 172.1–173.18;
178.13f; 179.8; 179.19; 183.12–17;
184.18–185.7; 187.3–6; 191.3;
193.16; 196.15; 197.19; 199.22–6;
204.19
Ἀτλαντίς, Atlantis, 4.12; 76.28; 175.23;
177.17; 179.9–11; 182.1; 182.23;
197.22
Ἄτλας, Atlas, 173.1–5; 181.14
ἄτομος, individual etc., 116.16; (superl.)
178.9; 179.7
αἱ ἄτομοι, (Epicurus') atoms, 59.19
ἄτρεπτος, unswerving, unvarying, etc.,
27.9; 27.31; 38.18–39.6; 41.13–21;
53.26; 111.7; 156.29; 166.8; 170.6
ἀτρέπτως, unflinchingly, 167.25
Ἀττική, ἡ, Attica, 122.10; 162.14; 164.18
Ἀττικός, Attic, 98.28 (= Athenian); 172.15;
203.24
Ἀττικῶς, in Attic dialect, 19.24
ἄυλος, immaterial, 13.29; 89.12; 92.1;
113.13; 158.9; 165.26; 166.13; 168.10;
175.17; 180.14; (adv.) 32.7; 115.32
αὔτανδροι πόλεις, men and all, 121.23
αὐτοβραδυτής, slowness-in-itself, 41.27
αὐτὸ ἕκαστον, each itself, 16.29
αὐτοζῶον, animal-itself, 6.1; 11.8
αὐτοκίνητον, τό, possessing self-motion,
12.22
αὐτόματον, τό, spontaneous, 2.28; (adv.)
2.23
αὐτοτάχος, speed-in-itself, 41.27
αὐτοφυής, spontaneous, from its own
nature, 50.30; 59.13; 60.8; 64.24;
86.27; (adv.) 86.29; 139.27; 183.19
αὐτόχθων, autochthonous, 101.7; 143.32
αὐχμηρός, dry (of style), 83.24
αὐχμώδης, oppressively hot, 122.20

323

Greek word index

ἀφανής, invisible etc., 25.27; 50.22; 53.1; 87.6; 94.23; 96.7; 98.20; 110.7; 144.22; 158.7; 159.9; 173.23; 188.6; 189.20–3; 190.13; 193.21; 202.20

ἀφάνισις, disappearance, 109.28; 189.7

ἀφεστίασις, return feast, 25.23

ἀφηγηματικῶς, instructional(ly), 21.12

ἄφθαρτος, indestructible, 116.9–11

ἀφιστάναι, separate, 21.23; 22.12

ἀφορίζειν, determine, distinguish, divide off, etc., 7.29; 8.25; 22.8; 26.3; 31.5; 36.17; 45.17; 48.16; 55.2; 69.3; 79.8; 125.28; 137.7; 145.6; 150.18; 162.3; (adv.) 154.31

ἀφορμή, encouragement, route towards, 174.32; 202.4

Ἀφροδισιακαὶ ζωαί, lives associated with Aphrodite, 148.4

Ἀφροδίτη, Aphrodite, 18.10; 34.15; 79.17

ἀφρούρητος, unguarded, 145.13

Ἀχαία, Achaea, 188.12

Ἀχιλλεύς, Achilles, 65.29

ἄχραντος, immaculate, 27.31; 52.17–27; 95.16; 104.15; 111.14; 113.29; 133.5; 136.11; 155.32; 156.18–157.16; 166.6; 166.26–167.1; 168.16; 169.5; 170.14; 175.33; 189.4; 191.9; (adv.) 42.6; 132.3; 166.15

ἀχώριστος, inseparable, 10.26–11.22; 12.27; 57.26–58.23; 131.5

ἄψυχος, lifeless, 131.1; (superl.) 11.25

B

βαθύνειν τὸ ἐπίπεδον, give depth to, 146.14

βαπτίζειν, flood, submerge, 117.6; 179.3

βαρύτης, heaviness, 10.10

βαφή, tincture, 195.27

Βενδίδεια, Bendidea, 8.31; 26.12–14; 27.29; 84.27; 85.4

Βίας, Bias, 183.13

Βιθυνία, Bithynia, 187.25

Βοιωτός, Boeotian, 88.12–13

Βοῦρα, Boura, 188.13

τὰ βράχη, surface-reefs, 188.22

βραχυπορώτερα, over a shorter span, 116.20

Βρεττανία, Britain, 112.27

Γ

γαλήνη (νοερά), (intellectual) calm, 21.26; 44.4

γάμοι, ἱεροί, Holy Marriages, 49.14–16

γαῦρος, exalted, solemn, 24.29; 62.9

γειτνιάζειν, neighbour on, 96.17

γειτνίασις, bordering on, 75.9

γενέθλια, birthday, 18.10; 145.24

γενεσιουργός, generation-producing, reproductive etc, 7.3; 34.14; 52.28; 57.20; 77.4; 111.18; 117.5; 126.18; 136.23; 144.28; 148.9; 154.16; 156.29–157.7; 168.25; 173.11; 186.4

γένεσις, generation etc.: frequent

γεννητικός, generative, 3.31; 176.17; 180.2

γένος, kind, etc., 6.8; 50.16; 52.16–27; 53.30; 64.30; 69.8; 77.11–14; 78.8–23; 112.19–20; 136.12; 175.26; 176.25; 178.8–12; 182.24; 184.8; 184.23; 185.30; 186.11; 190.23

γεωμετρικός, geometrical, 8.24

γῆ, earth (as opp. οὐρανός), 43.4–8; 44.28; 45.2; 106.3; frequent from 110.5; (= matter), 110.11; 143.29–114.15; 146.26; (as element) 107.3; 107.15; 112.14–16

Γῆ, Ge, Earth, 7.2–3; 111.28

γήινος, earthly, 5.16; 44.27; 144.2

Γίγαντες, Giants, 85.15; 168.17; 172.27

Γιγάντια φαντάσματα, Gigantic imaginings, 168.25

Γιγαντικὸς πόλεμος, War against the Giants, 172.15

Γιγαντομαχίαι, battles against giants, 38.28

γίγνεσθαι, become, come to be, etc.: frequent

τὰ γιγνόμενα, generation etc. (opposed to τὰ ἀεὶ ὄντα etc.); 2.7–15; 75.21; 76.12; 104.10–17; 113.18–28; 115.8; 123.23; 143.24–6; 192.32

Γλαύκων, Glaucon, 9.1; 82.5–19

γνῶσις, recognition, insight, knowledge etc. 27.4; 69.19; 95.21; 102.24; 104.16; 108.22; 123.30–1; 133.8; 150.4; 202.7

γνωστικὴ δύναμις, cognitive power, 79.11

γόνιμος, (re-)productive, procreative, fertile, 25.16; 36.13; 49.10; 89.26; 195.18

324

Greek word index

γράμματα, writings, 124.31–126.9; 146.2–9; 148.20–149.3; (of souls) 115.17
γραμματεῖον ληξιαρχικόν, official lists, 203.6
γραφικὴ χάρις, grace of writing, 60.2

Δ

δαιμονίδες, daemonesses, 47.16; 50.18
δαιμόνιος, daemonic, of daemons (usually as opp. θεῖος, ἀγγελικός, ἡρωικός) 34.7; 36.27; 39.28; 53.30–54.2; 60.30; 77.11; 110.27 (of souls); 136.12–137.13; 157.19; 163.13; 192.17; (comp.) 113.6
δαιμονιώδης, daemonic, 113.21
δαίμων, daemon: frequent
δεῖνα, ὁ, so-and-so, 15.19
δεκάς, decad, 23.23–4; 87.28; 147.2–3; 182.12–13
Δέλτα, Delta, 95.5; 96.8; 97.4
δεξιότης, cleverness, 35.23
δεξιοῦσθαι, greet, 18.18; 25.20
δεόντως, appropriately, etc., 5.2; 29.17; 40.23; 54.29; 79.29; 105.15; 135.6; 151.25; 185.12
Δευκαλίων, Deucalion, 101.11–16; 122.16; 127.21; 128.22
δεύτερος, second: frequent; as sing. noun, 146.22; as pl. noun, 3.31; 6.1; 19.21; 23.33; 42.7; 44.21; 50.14; 54.19–55.1; 75.5–25; 82.28; 91.16; 92.9; 97.27; 100.11; 108.26; 117.11; 118.22; 132.16; 133.3–11; 146.19; 166.28–167.7; 193.5; 195.19–29; 198.20; 200.1; (adv.) 47.11–16; 50.24; 136.3; 149.30; 150.2; 154.29; 157.11
δευτερουργός, secondary, 93.27
Δήλιον, Delium, 62.19
δηλοῦν, indicate: frequent
δηλωτικός, indicative, 52.20; 198.17
Δημήτηρ, Demeter, 153.11
δημιουργεῖν, fashion, 3.12; 4.28; 5.6; 125.1; 141.9; 155.4; 164.26–30; 196.7
δημιούργημα, creation, 16.22; 143.6; 191.11
δημιουργία, creation, creative activity: frequent
ἡ ὅλη (ὁλικὴ) δ., universal creation, 3.30; 4.3; 12.7; 27.14; 29.7; 30.26;
51.7; 72.24; 84.3; 191.25; 198.10; 198.30
ἡ νέα δ., new creation, 95.14; 95.31; 100.8; 103.8; 104.25; 107.28; 108.23; 124.24–7; 127.14–23; 132.27; 133.23
μία, ἡνωμένη, ἀμέριστος δ. etc., one, unified, or divided creation, 27.30; 32.25; 72.23; 95.13; 114.18; 136.21; 173.3
διρημένη, μεριστή, divided creation, 148.30; 149.6
τρεῖς (etc.), three creations, or first, second, and third creation, 29.10; 60.19; 63.3; 71.6; 71.22; 74.20; 92.22; 95.31; 149.25–6; 154.14; 156.20; 173.21; 182.20; 184.29; 189.27; 191.5; 191.20; 196.12–25; 199.6–7
specific types of creation:
νοερά, θεία, 3.30; 44.30; 95.26
κοσμική, φυσική, 32.12; 33.6
ἐμφανής, 94.13; 149.2; 189.21; 190.14
γόνιμος, 195.19
ἀέναος καὶ ἀνέκλειπτος, 195.28
δημιουργικός, creative, creational: very frequent; also (of persons) manufacturing, 150.28–155.15
δημιουργός, demiurge: frequent
ὁ ὅλος δ., the universal demiurge, 30.29; 38.18; 163.28; 202.23
ὁ τῶν ὅλων δ., (in similar sense) 12.6; 45.16; 63.10
ὁ εἷς δ., the one demiurge, 9.23. 166.16
τρεῖς etc., three demiurges (first, second, third) 12.1–5; 74.15–16; 156.5–6
δημώδης ποιητική, popular poetry-composition, 89.28
διαδύεσθαι, submerge, 107.20
διάθεσις, disposition, description, 28.17; 62.18; 65.20–1; 87.1; 152.18
διαθέτης, organizer, describer, 24.5; 134.11
διαιρετικός, of division, divisive, 67.5; 114.32; 131.25
δίαιτα, life, 44.30
διαιώνιος, eternal, everlasting, 89.16; 127.17; 141.24
διαιωνίως, eternally, 11.26; 33.21; 118.9; 124.18; 138.28; 173.26
διακάθαρσις, purgation, 30.9
διακληροῦσθαι, get an allotment, 173.5
διακλήρωσις, allotment, 40.18, 98.9; 137.7; 141.11; 198.8

325

Greek word index

διακόσμησις, arrangement, 4.21; 25.25; 30.3; 33.14; 38.23; 44.17; 48.22; 54.27; 60.19; 90.29; 91.26; 103.21; 124.14; 136.29; 144.31; 148.22–149.1; 150.12f; 157.29 (= depiction); 159.7; 182.17; 187.2; 188.25–189.3; 190.13–28

διακοσμητὴς τοῦ οὐρανοῦ, arranger of the heaven, 61.3

διακοσμητικὸς νοῦς, intelligence in organization, 34.25

διάκοσμος, arrangement, tapestry, 170.24; 204.14

διάκρισις, separation, division, 63.5; 85.10; 131.8; 155.25–31; 167.32–168.5; 179.31; 184.20

διακριτικός, separative, divisive, 36.14; 184.10

διαλάμπειν, shine (through), 30.23; 61.28

διαλυόμενος, breaking up (of a comet), 109.23

διανοητικόν, τὸ, the reasoning faculty, 194.19

διανοητικὸς ἐνέργεια, thinking activity, 197.30

διάνοια, intellect, view, plan, meaning etc., 9.32; 46.16; 87.14; 109.2; 135.22; 149.17; 158.16; 165.31; 186.8; 192.18

διαπίπτειν, fall short, 64.5

διαπλάττειν, shape, 143.20

διαρρεῖν, be in flux, 118.9

διασκορπίζεσθαι, dissipate, 107.5

διασπασμός, dismemberment (of Dionysus), 173.2

διάστασις, διάστημα, extended space, 163.22–31; 164.23; 180.15

διαστρέφειν τὴν φράσιν, distort the natural expression , 68.8

διατείνειν, (trans.) extend, 10.5; 37.24; 78.4; 143.16; 156.17; 168.28; 189.5–6; (intrans.) extend, pervade, aim at, 40.18; 42.29; 71.11; 80.26; 84.1; 87.2; 94.12; 127.12; 149.7; 150.13

διάφωνος, in disagreement, 1.15

διδασκαλεῖον Ἐλεατικόν, Eleatic school, 20.1

διέπειν, manage, 154.16; 169.7

διερεύνησις, inquiry, 8.28

διήγημα, narrative, narration, 83.20–6; 95.19; 127.4; 129.21–31; 134.15

διηρημένος, divided etc., 2.2; 6.30; 13.2; 27.1; 42.28; 49.29; 96.5; 108.19; 137.3; 148.30; 150.22; 162.7; 173.25; 176.8; (adv.) 60.27; 160.11; 184.12

Δίιος, Zeus-like, associated with Zeus, Jovian, 69.24; 111.7; 148.2; 157.13; 179.33; 189.28

τὸ δικαστικόν, judicial section, 34.19

Δίκη, Justice, 25.31; 34.20; 38.5; 38.24; 161.30–162.9

διοικούμενον, τὸ, what is managed, etc., 11.23; 28.5; 58.21; 75.7; 87.22; 98.30; 104.31; 111.18; 136.18; 138.7–10; 168.1; 173.26

Διονύσιος, Dionysius (of Syracuse), 61.13

Διόνυσος, Dionysus, 77.16; 88.11; 168.16; 173.2

διορίζειν, determine, distinguish, 21.10; 35.19; 40.19; 52.14; 53.13

δοξαστικός, opinion-forming, 21.27

Δορπία, Dorpia, 88.17

δορυφορεῖν, form an escort etc., 28.2; 34.1; 40.7

δορυφορικὴ τάξις, the rank of bodyguards, 111.22

δουλεύειν, be slave to, 3.2; 182.29; 183.1; 185.20–7

δρᾶμα, drama, 185.31

δραστήριος, vigorous, 2.21; 12.24; 60.26; 90.10; 106.33; 110.9; 115.18; 117.16; 157.2; (comp.) 16.10; 79.15

Δρωπίδης, Dropides 82.1; 82.13–18

δυαδικός, dyadic, 151.1; 185.23; 199.6

δυάς, dyad, 16.28; 17.13–29; 36.16; 47.19; 74.2; 78.7; 87.25; 136.20; 146.15; 153.29; 175.23; 176.11–31; 179.14; 182.14–17

δύεσθαι, sink into, become immersed in (matter etc.), 53.27; 83.5

δύναμις, power etc.: very frequent

δύνειν, sink into etc., 10.25; 143.19; 189.12

δυσπαθής, not easily affected, 107.3–4

δυσπαραδεκτότατος, very hard to accept, 49.26

δύσφθαρτος, hard to destroy, 116.10–12

δωδεκάς, dodecad, 136.21–137.11

E

ἑβδομάς, hebdomad, 136.20

ἐγκόσμια, τὰ, things within the cosmos, encosmic things, 4.14; 11.13;

326

Greek word index

13.2–28; 17.12; 34.6; 54.22; 74.22; 87.29; 131.6; 154.3; 156.9; 160.1; 167.25; 171.14; 174.20; 176.15; 177.26; 179.23; 180.12; 192.3–10; 199.1; 204.15
ἐγκοσμίως, in encosmic fashion, 135.13
ἐγκύκλιος κίνησις, circular motion, 138.29
ἐγκωμιαστικός, of the encomium, panegyric, 62.8; 171.27
ἔγχρονος, temporal, in time, 104.11; 125.7; 127.7; 141.30; 162.4
ἕδρα, dwelling place, 143.4
ἑδραῖα στάσις, secure foundation, 97.9
Ἐθήμων, Ethemon, 101.22
εἰδικός, formal, 72.9
εἰδοποιεῖν, give form, 186.30
εἰδοποιός, giving form, 154.17–25
εἶδος, form, species etc.: very frequent
εἴδωλον, image, 58.11; 127.15; 134.22–7
εἰκάς, twentieth, 26.16; 81.16; 85.29
εἰκαστικός, interpreting images, 158.17
εἰκονικής, iconic, through images, 5.19; 8.19; 13.10; 26.10; 30.12; 67.27
εἰκών, image: very frequent
εἱμαρμένοι νόμοι, laws of fate, 136.17
    εἱμαρμένη, fate, 149.22; 169.8; 183.1; 201.18–19
εἱρμός, connecting thread, 89.22
εἱρομένη ζωή, interwoven life, 89.20
εἰσοικίζειν, settle in, be housed in, 5.4; 51.21; 144.14
εἰσοχαὶ καὶ ἐξοχαί, valleys and peaks, 181.4
ἕκαστα, τὰ καθ', the details, 8.27
ἕκαστον, οἱ καθ', individual persons, 152.20
Ἑκατομβαιών, Hecatombaeon, 26.19
ἐκεῖ, (= in the higher realm etc.), 18.3; 36.16; 53.10; 83.5; 132.13; 176.15
ἐκεῖθεν, (= from the higher world etc.), 11.23; 43.5–7, 44.25; 50.24; 52.28; 53.3; 57.12; 103.10; 106.19; 114.30; 162.29; 163.20; 165.17; 203.21
ἐκθεοῦν, divinize, 11.13
ἐκλελυμένη ἐπιθυμία, relaxed spirit, 40.29
ἔκλυτος, slack, 117.16
ἐκμελές, τὸ, poor tuning, 117.18
ἐκνευρίζεσθαι, be weakened, 117.6
ἑκούσιος, voluntary, assenting, 22.13–15; 79.13
ἐκπυροῦσθαι, be consumed by fire, 122.5
ἐκπύρωσις, conflagration, 100.28; 107.7; 107.23; 109.16; 110.5; 113.16; 114.17;

115.32; 117.1; 117.20; 118.4; 118.20; 121.14; 122.11–14
ἔκτασις, extension, 178.26; 180.15
ἐκτροπαί, deviations, 106.5
ἔκφανσις, revelation, 95.28
ἐλάττωσις, reduction, diminution, 23.31; 37.11–15
Ἐλεατικὸν διδασκαλεῖον, Eleatic school, 19.32
Ἐλευσίς, Eleusis, 165.19–21
Ἑλίκη, Helike, 188.14
ἐλλάμπειν, shed light, illuminate, 11.5; 168.1; 190.18; (pass:) 139.22–7
ἔλλαμψις, luminary influence, illumination, 139.18; 142.3; 163.27
Ἑλλάς, Greece, 122.16
Ἕλληνες, Greeks, 70.13; 98.14; 99.5; 100.2; 101.6–9, 102.10; 104.22; 108.21; 167.27; 172.11; 185.19; 187.2
    ὁ παρ' Ἕλλησι μῦθος etc., 95.29; 100.23; 101.3–9; 107.30; 108.28; 109.2
Ἑλληνικός, Greek, 14.30; 73.7
ἐμπνεῖν, breathe life into, animate, 8.7; 11.24
ἐμπύριος, fiery, 112.18–22; 113.12
ἐμφανής, visible etc., 91.26; 94.12; 96.15; 98.20; 106.21; 119.23; 143.4; 144.31; 149.2; 189.20–23; 190.13; 193.23
ἐμφαντάζεσθαι, be reflected in, 95.27
ἐμφαντικός, suggestive, 27.13
ἔμφασις, reflection, impression, 15.12; 36.24; 111.8; 126.20
ἕν, τὸ, the One, 13.24; 78.6–7; 79.19; 87.8–9, 174.12; 176.9–177.1; 178.20–2; 184.15; 193.6
ἐναντίωσις, rivalry: very common after 77
ἐναρμόνιος, harmonious, 41.11; (adv.) 42.7
ἑνάς, henad, 3.28; 14.1; 36.10–16; 42.4; 163.14; 166.6; 167.2; 171.2
ἐνδείκνυσθαι, give an indication of, etc., 7.29; 8.22; 15.14; 19.8; 24.19; 30.1–15; 32.34; 50.25; 53.2; 59.12; 83.10; 84.19; 92.4; 93.22; 98.31; 102.14; 107.30; 113.31; 126.25; 127.9; 132.18; 133.17; 134.9; 157.31; 160.13; 161.23; 167.15; 173.21; 179.21; 180.9; 184.9; 185.3; 194.4–8; 195.9–15; 196.22; 200.30; 201.16; 203.16

327

Greek word index

ἔνδειξις, indication, 17.13; 29.23; 30.8; 54.10; 75.5; 76.11; 80.25; 84.14; 102.7; 130.10; 165.12; 178.31; 188.24; 190.10; 195.18; 196.24

ἐνεικονίζεσθαι, reflect, 91.30

ἐνενηκοντά, the number ninety, 87.29

ἐνέργεια, activity, operation etc.: frequent

ἐνεργεῖν, operate, activate, be in activity etc., 12.23, 26.6; 36.14; 42.5; 54.18; 56.18–24; 57.18–19; 64.10; 67.13; 68.23; 74.6; 131.19–20; 186.22; 200.8

ἐνθεαστικῶς, in inspired fashion, 156.31

ἔνθεος, inspired, divine, 7.27; 54.10; 64.14–28; 80.4; 198.8; (adv.) 198.6

ἔνη καὶ νέα, Old and New, 81.14

ἐνιαῖος, unitary, 41.24; 69.27; 104.13; 130.27; 166.4; (adv.) 127.25; 166.19 (= uniformly)

ἐνιδρύειν, establish in etc., 29.19; 168.29; (pass.) be founded in, 27.8; 133.4; 136.7

ἐνίζειν, unite, unify, 42.3; 135.25; 163.14; 176.4; 184.16

ἔνικμος, damp, 113.11; 117.24

ἐνικώτερος, with greater unity, 137.19

ἔννοια, concept, notion, intention, 10.22; 68.25; 74.24; 148.1; 165.11; 168.26; 191.23; 192.27; 193.5

ἐνοειδής, unitary, 13.26; 27.4; (adv.) 163.29

ἐνοποιός, unifying, 131.25; 180.10

ἑνότης, oneness, 73.6

ἑνοῦν, make one, etc.: frequent ἡνωμένως, in a unified way, 130.22; 184.13–21

ἔνστασις, 51.12; 128.13

ἐνταῦθα, (= in that world etc.), 5.31; 43.16; 71.3; 75.14; 115.32; 176.17

ἐντετακὼς Ἑρμῆς, ὁ, ithyphallic Hermes, 148.6

ἐντεῦθεν, (= from that world etc.), 44.25; 186.7

ἐνύδριος, ἔνυδρος, watery, water dwelling, 112.22; 137.4; 142.4–5

ἔνυλος, enmattered etc., 3.2; 10.14; 37.27; 40.29; 43.9; 50.27; 57.27; 58.12; 89.10; 93.28; 105.8; 105.33; 113.13; 144.2; 152.7–9; 154.12; 156.1; 157.2; 159.19; 162.8; 165.26; 174.11; 178.6; 180.17; 183.9; 189.14; 192.5; (comp.) 78.21; 173.25

ἕνωσις, unification, 4.14–15; 18.4; 32.27; 34.16; 43.20; 48.24; 50.15; 63.6; 78.16; 79.17; 84.20; 129.4; 148.25; 149.19–27; 155.25; 160.14; 167.33; 168.2; 169.17; 171.8; 183.23; 184.17; 185.26–8

ἑνωτικὴ δύναμις, unificatory power, etc., 84.16; 184.11

ἐξαλλαγή, change etc., 14.10; 15.5; 26.3; 51.5; 68.18; 87.10; 99.14

ἐξαλλάττειν, change, vary etc., 14.15; 25.11; 45.3; 68.6; 68.17; 70.15; 99.21

ἐξάπτειν, link, (pass. depend upon), 3.15; 4.3; 7.28; 13.24; 106.19; 111.15; 135.25; 144.22; 163.20; 203.22; ignite, set light to, 110.3–4, 112.20

ἐξαρτᾶν, depend on, be linked with, 3.11; 8.6; 11.23; 53.28; 75.13; 82.24; 111.12; 114.18; 139.28; 142.2; 149.26; 161.6; 162.10; 167.2; 195.19; 203.28

ἑξάς, hexad, 151.5; 154.22

ἔξαψις, igniting force, 110.8

Ἐξηκεστίδης, Execestides, 81.28

ἐξῃρημένως, in transcendent fashion, 39.32; 40.12 (= in exceptional fashion); 104.10; 143.20

ἕξις, disposition etc., 23.7; 41.13; 56.16–23; 68.21–31; 116.4; 201.15

ἐξυμνεῖν, laud, celebrate, 154.20; 183.17

ἐπανακύκλησις, cyclic return, 28.22

ἐπανάληψις, recapitulation, repetition, 4.12; 28.20; 102.5

ἐπάρχειν, govern etc., 137.12; 182.22

ἐπείσακτος, imported, introduced, 42.24; 159.4

ἐπεισοδιώδης, incidental, artificially imported, 50.30; 98.10

ἐπέκεινα, over and above, etc., 12.5; 176.22; 178.29; 186.18

ἐπιβάλλειν, approach, 110.1; 122.18 (notice); 151.18

ἐπιβολή, approach, focus, etc., 7.30; 8.3; 17.3; 32.23 (= grasp); 72.15; 110.22; 147.17 (= contiguity); 147.29

ἐπιδέχεσθαι, admit, 41.18; 106.3; 116.17 (= accept); 125.7

ἐπίκλησις, summoning, 203.21

ἐπικλύζειν, wash over, 188.11–13; 190.8

ἐπικουρητικόν, τὸ, auxiliary, 150.25

ἐπικράτεια, control, dominion, 98.13; 186.31

Greek word index

ἐπιλάμπειν, shed light etc., 41.20; 79.17; 124.28; 133.6; 166.28; 187.2
ἐπιστασία, control etc., 99.19; 138.4–10; 145.17; 153.16
ἐπιστήμη, knowledge, science, 24.23; 25.3; 30.10; 66.20; 73.11; 99.7; 102.30; 127.13; 198.28
ἐπιστημονικός, scientific, 30.5; 67.7
ἐπιστρεπτικός, of reversion, 133.30; 154.15
ἐπιστρέφειν, (trans.) cause to revert, 29.17; 88.4; 95.31; 135.29–31; 136.5–8; 151.17; 200.2; (intrans.) revert, 10.19; 12.15; 44.15; 75.9; 85.7; 170.15
ἐπιστροφή, reversion, 44.20; 45.24; 87.28; 136.1; 149.29; 160.16; 194.4–5; 203.20
ἐπιτηδειότης, readiness, suitability, etc., 25.26; 35.18–22; 51.29–32; 139.23; 140.1–3; 163.27; 164.21
ἐποχεῖσθαι, ride on, 142.6
ἑπτάς, heptad, 137.5; 151.13–16; 166.27
Ἐριχθόνιος, Erichthonius, 101.7
Ἑρμαϊκός, connected with Hermes, 148.5; (adv.) 36.9
Ἑρμῆς, Hermes, 34.18; 46.21; 79.1–10; 148.6; 165.22
Ἑρμοκράτης, 9.3; 15.18; 23.14; 27.15; 59.2; 63.7; 64.12; 68.1, 198.27–199.30
ἔρως, desire, 42.16
Ἔρως, 158.21; 169.14–20
ἔσχατος, extreme, furthest, lowest: frequent
ἑτεροίωσις, otherness, 175.23
ἑτερότης, otherness, 17.21; 21.16; 34.23; 36.17; 40.19; 87.13; 106.13; 132.14; 141.21; 148.30; 149.28; 155.25; 176.3; 176.20; 191.10
ἐτησίαι, etesian, 120.27; 121.21
Εὔβοια, Euboea, 70.15
ἔφορος, presiding (adj.), overseer (noun), etc., 34.15–18; 38.11; 53.4; 77.5; 85.6; 90.11; 98.6; 99.8; 99.19; 106.10; 111.11, 113.9, 126.30; 128.25; 140.18; 144.30; 145.26; 148.6; 150.15; 173.15; 192.27

Z

Ζάλευκος, Zaleucus, 70.18
Ζεύς, Zeus, 18.11; 41.23; 69.26; cf. 199.3 (Ζανός)

ζωδιακὸς (κύκλος), zodiac, 96.24
ζώδιον, sign of the zodiac, 98.22; 108.2
ζωή, life: very frequent
ζωογονεῖν, generate life, 144.4
ζωογονία, animal birth, 79.5
ζωογονικός, life-generating etc., 111.8; 142.21
ζωογόνος, life-giving, 5.15; 11.19; 96.14
ζωοποιεῖν, bring to life, 5.7; 10.21
ζωοποιός, life-creating, 154.25
ζωτικός, vital, lively, etc., 5.3; 12.24; 79.12; 161.12; (comp.) 194.23
ζωώδης, bestial, 16.15

H

ἡγεμόνες, (of gods) leaders, etc., 5.4; 110.28; 111.5; 114.13; 115.28; 137.18; 144.22; 145.15–22
ἡγεμονία, leadership, 98.10; 110.30
ἡγεμονικός, leading, hegemonic, etc., 17.11; 34.24; 42.27; 71.10; 88.5; 131.3; 141.1; 160.21; 167.13; 170.6; (adv.) 191.7
ἠθικός, ethical, 8.1; 15.26; 16.20; 19.29; 24.13; 25.7; 27.22; 32.13; 193.28; (adv.) 117.20; (comp.) 29.31
ἠθοποιός, character-forming, 171.22
Ἡλιάδες, Heliades, 109.15; 113.25
ἡλιακός, solar, of the sun, 43.11; 110.3; 111.12; 112.3–7; 113.12; 113.25; 114.2–6; 115.3; 159.27; 181.19
ἡλιακῶς, sun-wise, 36.9
ἥλιος, sun, 34.20; 43.5; 46.21; 47.10–12; 108.1–9; 141.7–9; 160.2; 181.11
ἡλιοτρόπιον, heliotrope, 111.1
Ἡλίου πόλις, Heliopolis, 101.21
Ἥρα, Hera, 46.27; 79.1
Ἡρακλῆς, Heracles, 68.20; 180.1; 181.6
Ἠριδανός, Eridanus, 109.13; 113.30
ἡρωικός, heroic, 89.22
ἥρως, hero, 66.4; 182.31
Ἡφαίστειος, Hephaestian, 143.23; 144.3; 144.32; 146.28
Ἥφαιστος, Hephaestus, 78.29; 79.13; 142.14; 143.31–144.15; 146.27; 147.7; 159.13; 204.12
Ἡφαιστότευκτος, Hephaestus-wrought 143.1

329

Greek word index

Θ

θαλασσοῦσθαι, be turned to sea, 121.17
Θαλῆς, Thales, 81.9
Θαργηλιών, Thargelion, 26.14; 85.29
Θαύμας, Thaumas, 133.9; 183.13
Θεαίτητος, Theaetetus, 19.32
θεῖος, divine, of the gods: very frequent
θεολογία, theology, 13.29; 141.24; 156.7;
   185.3; 204.9
θεολογικός, theologian 8.13; 13.11; 17.9;
   25.14; 27.30; 171.30; (adv.) 8.5; 29.6;
   130.15
θεός, god, goddess: very frequent
   ἐγκόσμιοι θεοί, encosmic gods, 6.19;
      18.8; 47.7; 78.24; 110.25; 143.1;
      158.13
   ἡγεμονικοὶ θεοί, hegemonic gods
      (=ἡγεμόνες), 5.4; 114.13; 115.28;
      141.1; 170.7
   νοεροὶ θεοί, intellective gods, 47.7–8;
      70.9; 158.13
   Ὀλύμπιοι θεοί, Olympian gods, 85.15;
      172.25; 174.4; 176.3; 183.7; 189.1
   οὐράνιοι θεοί, heavenly gods, 5.7; 34.7;
      42.22; 43.4; 47.22; 57.8; 115.23;
      137.3; 152.5–6
   Τιτανικοὶ θεοί, Titanic gods, 172.32;
      174.4
   ὑπερκόσμιοι θεοί, hypercosmic gods, 4.2;
      47.8; 158.13
   οἱ ὑπὸ σελήνην θεοί, sublunary gods,
      18.8; 166.31
θεότης, divinity, 110.29; 118.6; 156.6;
   160.4; 165.11; 166.7–11
θεσμοὶ τῆς Ἀδραστείας, ordinances of
   Adrasteia, 40.9
Θετταλοί, Thessalians, 101.13
θεωρητικός, contemplative, 154.20; 197.9
θεωρία, study, observation, etc.: frequent
θηρατικός, concerned with hunting,
   150.28; 152.24
θηριώδης, bestial, 154.26
θητεία, labour, 44.2
θῆτες, thetes, 31.31
θητεύειν, labour, 34.4
τὸ θητικόν, labouring (class), 33.29; 39.25;
   150.26; 151.28; 152.7
θνητός, mortal: very frequent
Θρασύμαχος, Thrasymachus, 9.1
θρυλεῖν, talk frequently of, etc., 86.6;
   127.21; 151.13; 172.2; 172.16

τὸ θυμικόν, the spirited part, 33.31; 117.15
θυμοειδής, spirited, 117.1; 165.18; (adv.)
   148.10
θυμός, temper, spirit, 117.9–17; 148.2–3;
   156.27

Ι

Ἴασος, Iasus, 101.10
ἰδιότης, distinctive character etc., 7.25;
   8.8; 8.24; 16.12; 26.3; 36.8–15; 43.10;
   48.25; 54.18; 106.11; 114.13; 132.7–8;
   157.15; 166.31; 167.9
ἱδρύεσθαι, be founded in, fixed in etc.
   (indicating the ground of something's
   existence): frequent; (active) 72.29
ἵδρυσις, foundation, 27.5; 189.17
ἱδρώς, sweat, 63.30; (in a name for the
   Nile) 119.19
ἱερατικός, hieratic, priestly, 119.4; 124.24;
   140.27; 150.27; 151.20; 153.30;
   154.21; 192.12
ἱερατικῶς, in priestly terms, 97.5
Ἴναχος, Inachus, 101.15
ἴνδαλμα, reflective glimpse, 8.20; 133.19;
   148.27
ἰσημερινός, equator, equinox, 96.20–6;
   98.23
ἰσοτελής, equal accomplisher (of Hera), .28
ἱστορεῖν, narrate, tell, etc.: frequent
ἱστορία (opp. μῦθος), history, historical
   writing, narration, 30.13; 46.9; 65.18;
   76.1; 79.30; 81.7; 81.27; 87.19; 89.6;
   92.16–93; 98.1; 100.1; 103.2; 109.9;
   118.3; 129.11; 169.26; 171.28; 177.22;
   188.18; 190.10; 195.10; 199.16
ἱστορικός, historical, 75.20; 145.4; (comp.)
   90.27; (adv.) 109.8; 144.19
Ἴων, Ion, 88.24

Κ

καθαρμός, purgation, 118.21–119.5
καθαρότης, purity, 36.20; 100.26; 118.22;
   156.30
καθάρσια κομίζειν, bring purgatives,
   118.24
καθαρτῆρες, purifiers, 119.1
καθαρτικός, purifying, 38.10; 113.24
καθήκειν, come down (from heavens), 85.9;
   111.11; 158.15; 167.8; 204.1

330

Greek word index

καθῆκον, τό, obligation, 18.31; 19.27; 198.12

κάθοδος, descent, 52.24; 53.2; 54.7; 62.30; 77.14; 89.15; 108.18; 113.28–114.20; 132.4; 146.23

καθολικός, universal, 153.18; 191.23; (comp.) 149.16; (comp.adv.) 63.8

καθ' ὅλου, τὸ (τὰ), universal(s), 32.6–17; 200.25; 201.10

κακία, vice, 22.17; 111.17

Κάλλαισχρος, Callaeschrus, 82.5–14

κάλλος, beauty, 60.12; 71.5; 149.2; 169.4

τὸ καλόν, handsomeness, beauty, the fine, 26.1; 42.23; 129.4

Κανωβικὸς νομός, Canobic nome, 97.20

Κάνωβος, Canobus, 97.20

κατάβασις, descent, 40.29

καταγωνίζεσθαι, contend against, struggle against, 39.9; 157.10; 168.16; 172.18

καταδεέστερος, inferior etc., 21.31; 174.2; 174.16; 175.27; 178.10–16; 183.8; 185.15; 190.27

τὰ καταδεέστερα, inferior things, 131.9; 176.27; 184.6

Κατάδουποι, Catadupa, 121.2–6

κατακλείειν, confine, enclose, 37.13; 152.22; 153.7; 197.24

καταστέλλειν, restrain, check, control, 29.16; 34.10; 38.5; 85.7

κατιέναι, go down, descend, 22.29; 45.11; 52.18; 53.3; 58.15; 71.1; 86.14; 111.16–17; 112.21; 113.f.; 126.16; 144.24; 146.20; 147.16; 148.1; 152.15; 165.17; 186.5; 201.25

κατόρθωσις, correctness, 155.18

κάτωθεν, from below, 119.17; 120.7

Καύκασος, Caucasus, 181.18

Κέκρωψ, Cecrops, 101.15

κέντρον, centre, 32.28; 172.13

κεραύνωσις, thunderbolt, 109.29; 110.16

Κέφαλος, Cephalus, 8.32; 42.21

Κηρύκων γένος, τὸ, family of heralds, 165.22

κίνησις, motion, frequent

Κλεισθένης, Cleisthenes, 88.25

Κλειτώ, Cleito, 182.15

κλῆρος, lot, 34.17–18; 50.25; 51.2; 89.14; 98.13; 98.26–30; 136.11–26; 140.7–8; 160.30–162.7

κληρουχεῖσθαι, acquire a lot, 163.25

κληρουχία, allotment, 137.4; 140.27

κλίμα, climatic region, 122.13–23

κλιματάρχαι θεοί, gods in control of climate, 106.11

Κλυμένη, Clymene, 109.10

κοῖλος, hollow (place), 117.12–26; 120.3

Κολοφών, Colophon, 90.24

κομήτης, comet, 109.22–30

Κόρη, Kore, 166.26–9

κοσμεῖν, arrange etc.: frequent

κοσμητικός, involved in arranging, etc., 174.16; 190.22; 192.21

κοσμικός, cosmic, of the cosmos, 32.13; 33.6; 57.29; 73.8; 78.18; 85.11; 93.25; 95.19; 96.22; 100.4; 103.12; 103.33; 116.14; 122.1; 128.8–11; 130.10–12; 132.19; 134.18–27; 146.10; 159.5; 170.1; 182.20; 189.11; 191.5; 197.5; 201.14

κοσμιότης, orderliness, 31.16; 73.20

κοσμοκράτορες, controllers of the cosmos, 101.2

κοσμοποιία, cosmic creation etc., 3.21; 4.9; 9.17; 12.29; 22.21; 27.17; 71.23; 72.25; 73.18; 75.18; 79.23; 84.8–15; 87.22; 88.6; 134.32; 172.25; 191.4; 197.21

κόσμος, cosmos: frequent

Κουρεῶτις, Koureotis, 88.18; 89.5

κοῦροι, boys, 88.19; 89.3

κρᾶσις, make-up, blend, climate, 99.16; 106.6; 120.18; 162.21

κρατητικῶς, with mastery, 191.7

κρείττονες, οἱ, superiors, superior powers, 49.6; 113.1; 145.13; 152.5; 184.12; 186.31

τὰ κρείττονα γένη, superior races, 45.10

Κρήτη, Crete, 118.24

κριοπρόσωπος, with ram's head, 96.18

Κριός, The Ram, 96.17–9; 98.22; 141.5

Κριτίας, Critias: frequent; his family, 82.2–19; 91.3

Κριτόβουλος, Critobulus, 23.9

Κροῖσος, Croesus, 81.3; 93.4

Κρόνιος, Saturnian, of Kronos, 43.11; 47.2; 103.23; 113.11; 148.1

Κρόνος, Kronos, 34.25; 43.6; 47.1

κρυμώδης, icy, 122.20

κυκλοφορία, circular motion, 28.9; 162.28; 164.4

331

Greek word index

Λ

λαγχάνειν, get as one's lot, etc., 36.22; 78.8; 98.9; 106.12; 111.9; 113.6; 135.27–136.9; 140.17–141.27; 145.6–16; 153.16; 158.23; 159.17; 160.26–161.1; 163.10–16; 166.30; 180.2; 198.9

λέξις, (details of the) lemma, lexis, reading, diction, text, 9.30; 14.2; 30.31; 35.14; 53.12–23; 55.10; 65.10; 87.15; 90.16; 94.5; 122.25; 191.28; 202.15

λήθη (Λήθη), forgetfulness, 41.5; 82.30; 111.27; 123.10; 123.25; 126.12–19; 140.11

Λῆμνος, Lemnos, 181.13

ληξιαρχικὸν γραμματεῖον, official lists, 203.5

λῆξις, lot, portion, domain, 54.2; 54.26; 58.22–7; 77.12; 98.21; 138.9; 142.2–3; 145.19; 147.1; 154.16; 173.5

Λητώ, Leto, 78.29

Λιβύη, Libya, 178.21

λογικός, rational etc., 5.14; 27.25; 34.2; 79.6; 161.11; 174.6; 176.5; 194.21; (adv.) 5.25

λόγος, reason, account, etc., and (in pl.) principles: very frequent

Λοκρίς, Locris (in Sicily or Euboea), 70.12–15

Λοκροί, Locri, 70.1–17

λυμαντικόν, τὸ, injurious, corrupting, 34.1; 77.12

Μ

μαθήματα, mathematics, 41.2; 41.22

μαθηματικός, mathematical, 8.16–22; 181.23

Μακεδονικὸν ὄρος, Macedonian mountain, 181.12

μάνωσις, being rare, 10.10

μεγαλουργοί, οἱ, workers of greatness, 111.16; 113.5

μεγαλουργόν, τὸ, achievement, 64.19–26

μεγαλοφωνία, grandiloquence, 62.15; 64.15–25

μεγαλόφωνος, grandiloquent, 64.4

μέθεξις, participation, 147.27

μειοῦν, diminish, 121.25

μείωσις, decrease, 140.2

Μέλανθος, Melanthus, 88.11–13

μένειν, remain, be fixed, be at rest: frequent

μερικὴ ψυχή, particular soul, individual soul, 5.3; 27.11; 52.22; 54.1–6; 58.16–24; 77.11; 89.14; 90.8; 110.23; 113.23; 115.29; 136.11; 138.12; 140.9; 141.15; 142.1; 152.8; 162.2; 167.10; 183.1; 186.2; passim

μερικὸς νοῦς, particular intellect, 128.9; 168.29

μ. θεοί, δαίμονες, particular gods etc., 27.14; 152.19

μερικώτερος, more particular, more partial, 12.7; 27.14; 32.6; 95.12; 100.11–14; 104.5; 104.16; 116.11; 145.1; 149.16; 150.9; 150.21; 154.24; 156.19; 161.20; 175.26; 191.24; 196.25; (superl.) 178.7; 185.17; (adv.) 99.17; 162.31; 174.29; 177.28; 204.26

μερικῶς, in partial/particular fashion, 5.12–19; 40.1; 43.17; 79.5; 104.12; 104.30; 127.24; 202.27

μερίς, sector, 58.18; 97.5; 138.22; 139.14; 163.6; 179.20; 186.11

μερισμός, division, partition, 11.3; 71.25; 183.28

μεριστός, divided, divisible, 7.30; 36.5; 42.28; 49.24; 58.13; 90.8; 95.13; 173.3

μέρος, part: very frequent

μεσημβρινοὶ τόποι, tropics, 119.25

μεταγράφειν, translate, 76.4

μετάδοσις, share, 18.15; 25.30; 135.21; 168.22

μεταφοραί, metaphors, 59.23; 64.22

μετενσωματοῦσθαι, experience a change of body, 113.3

μετέχειν, participate, share: frequent

μετουσία, participation, 4.4; 18.16; 51.26; 139.4; 140.4–8; 141.18

μετρεῖν, measure, 21.22; 45.21; 145.23; 146.7–8; 148.12; 180.27; 181.25; 185.11

μέτρον, measure, 22.8; 37.24; 45.17–24; 55.1; 130.23; 144.27; 147.27; 157.22; 174.19; 182.16; 183.18; 192.9

μηδαμῶς ὄν, τὸ, utterly non-existent, 178.29

μήπω ὄντα, τὰ, what does not yet exist, 125.2

Μνημοσύνη, Remembrance, 27.4

Greek word index

μοῖρα, portion, share, etc., 45.11; 97.4;
131.11; 139.12; 140.18; 163.28;
180.4–12; 183.1; 190.16
μοιραῖος, fate-associated, 157.19; 202.18
μοναδικός, monadic, 160.20; 185.23;
192.4
μονάς, (mathematical) monad, 16.27;
17.13–27; 21.9–20; 23.29; 24.3; 47.19;
137.13; 160.18; 179.12; 182.18;
(metaphysical) monad, 24.9–20;
87.25–30; 97.25; 141.10; 150.26;
151.15–17; 154.22; 157.14;
176.12–32; 176.32
μόνιμος, stable, etc., 27.5; 92.7; 103.11;
104.6; 105.21; 106.20; 124.21–6;
127.18; 131.25; 146.11; 175.17;
180.10; 185.26; 189.15; 195.19–25;
199.31; (comp.) 29.26; 194.25
μονίμως, in stable fashion etc., 95.22;
102.8; 104.29; 105.2; 108.14; 179.32;
189.13; 191.7
μονοειδής, uniform, 136.16; (adv.) 73.3;
98.30; 166.20
μυθικός, mythical, 167.16
μυθολογία, myth, 87.20; 108.21
μυθοπλάσται, myth-makers, 110.9;
111.30; 204.13
μῦθος, myth etc.: frequent
μυριέτης (-ετής), ten-thousand-year
(period), 147.14–24
μυσταγωγοί, escort of initiates, 165.19
μυστήρια, τὰ, mysteries, 165.21; 172.15
μυστικός, mystical, 14.1; 49.13; 196.21;
(adv.) 7.29; 108.1; (comp.) 21.1

N

Νεῖλος, Nile, 96.8; 96.23–28; 118.2;
119.16–122.3
Νέμεσις, Nemesis, 198.2
Νέστωρ, Nestor, 35.5
Νίκη, Victory, 168.7
Νιόβη, Niobe, 101.8–9
νοερός, intellective, etc.: very frequent
νοερῶς, in intellective fashion, 31.22;
102.8; 135.13; 147.30; 148.12–13;
202.24
νόημα, consideration, thought-object,
17.10; 22.12
νόησις, intellection, etc.: very frequent
νοητός, intelligible: very frequent

νοῦς, intelligence etc.: very frequent
Νύξ, Night, 193.18

Ξ

Ξάνθος (river), Xanthus, 79.14
Ξάνθος (Boeotian), Xanthus, 88.12

O

ὄγκος, magnificence, 64.9; mass, 178.21
οἰκουμένη, (habitable) world etc., 172.6;
179.30; 180.29–181.3; 182.28;
184.18
οἰκειοῦν, relate, link, connect, 92.28; 106.9;
107.9; 158.25
Οἰνόη, Oenoe, 88.13
οἰστικός, producing etc., 162.12; 164.6–12;
191.32
ὁλικός, universal, entire etc.: frequent
ὅλος, whole: often
ὁλοσχερῆ, τὰ, totalities, 177.29
ὁλοτελής, complete, as a whole, 25.24;
90.12; 139.4
ὁλότης, totality, whole, 138.31–139.3;
182.26; 196.11
Ὀλύμπιος, Olympian, 85.15; 168.24;
172.25–30; 174.4–13; 176.3–18;
183.7; 186.1; 187.3–7; 189.1
Ὄλυμπος, Olympus, 73.5; 142.30
ὄμβρια, rain, 120.22
Ὅμηρος, Homer, 15.2; 51.24; 63.26–64.11;
66.6; 73.4; 78.26; 117.4; 129.23;
136.24; 141.25; 163.18; 190.6
ὄμμα τῆς ψυχῆς, eye of the soul, 204.7
Ὁμοακοεῖον, auditorium, 22.8
ὁμοτάγης, of the same rank, 46.23; 49.5;
80.30
ὁμοχροῦς, of the same colour, 181.18
ὄν, τὸ, being, that which is: frequent
τὸ μὴ ὄν, non-being, 38.6
τὰ ὄντως ὄντα, (what is) really real,
13.14; 24.21; 89.12
ὄνομα, name, 15.12; 18.7; 21.4; 39.26;
89.4; 99.5–7; 112.4; 118.11; 119.4;
147.20; 170.8; 172.29; 183.4; 184.28
ὄντως, really, genuinely etc., 8.9; 13.14;
24.21; 83.4; 89.12; 95.30; 100.7;
133.3; 164.27; 170.3; 177.17; 181.21;
192.3; 194.1

333

Greek word index

ὀξυκίνητος, fast-moving, 117.15
ὀπαδοί, attendants, 47.23; 111.23; 131.28; 152.6
ὄργανον, instrument, tool, 12.21–3; 113.14–24; 116.6; 143.21–144.3; 156.29; 158.20; 161.10
organ, organism, 48.2; 51.20–1
Ὀρφεύς, Orpheus, 94.13; 118.23; 123.4; 135.11; 161.22; 166.21; 170.10; 188.26
Ὀρφικός, Orphic, of Orpheus, 12.10; 185.3; 188.7; (adv.) 174.12; 176.13
Ὄσιρις, Osiris, 77.15
οὐράνιος, heavenly: frequent
οὐρανός, heaven: frequent
Οὐρανός, Uranus, 47.3
οὐσία, substance, essence, being etc.: frequent
οὐσιοῦν, found essence (being) in, 12.24, 202.22
οὐσιώδης, substance-related, 162.3
Ὀχαᾶπι, Ochaäpi, 101.22
ὀχετός, stream, 158.29
ὄχημα, vehicle, chariot, 5.5–15; 41.14–21; 112.6; 114.12; 138.26; 139.13; 142.6; 144.13

Π

πάθος, passion, affection, etc., 60.3; 64.8; 67.13; 103.4; 107.18–25; 113.2–16; 138.12; 157.3; 188.2
παίγνιον, plaything, 127.15
παῖδες θεῶν, children of the gods, 111.19–25
παιδευτικός, educational, 34.19
Παιώνιος, of Paion, 158.18
παλαιοῦσθαι, grow old, 104.26
παλιγγενεσία, rebirth, 28.22; 103.15; 126.22; 127.25
παμμεγεθέστατος, hugest, 177.17
πᾶν, τό, the All, the universe: frequent
Παναθήναια, Panathenaea, 26.17–18; 80.25; 84.25–85.27; 135.1
πανδύναμος, all-powerful, 36.6
παντέλειος, all-perfect etc., 25.18; 36.6
παράγειν, produce etc., 3.8–12; 4.31; 39.10; 47.21; 52.15; 103.28
παραδειγματικός, paradigmatic, 2.8; 4.27; 9.21; 11.7; 17.17–21; 33.23; 72.8; 134.21–135.7

παραθαλάττιος, coastal, 188.13
παράθεσις, presentation, 83.20–5; 129.20
παραιρεῖσθαι, deprive, 56.19
παρακτικός, productive etc., 2.29; 193.18
παράλληλος, latitude, 110.12
παράλογον, τό, what is illogical, 80.12
παρατροπή, passing beyond, 6.14
παρεδρεύειν, to sit by one's side, 156.10
παρεισκυκλεῖν, introduce (from a different area), 31.9; 92.13; 204.18
παρεισφέρειν, drag in, 56.27
πάρθενος, virgin, 141.6; 169.5
Παρνασός, Parnassus, 101.12
πάροδος, entry to the stage, 193.4
παροικεῖν, live close, 116.26
παρρησιαστικώτατος, very free of speech, 93.11
Πατενεῖτ, Pateneït (a priest), 101.21
πατήρ, father, 23.10; 49.6; 82.3–6; 97.28; 108.9–109.11; 115.12; 129.28; 191.15;
πατὴρ πάντων etc., as cosmic figure, 3.13; 5.14; 9.16; 17.26; 39.15; 45.16; 46.28; 51.16; 54.9; 57.16; 61.1; 73.30; 75.13; 76.20; 100.9; 134.19–29; 136.13; 137.23; 140.30; 151.9–17; 157.11; 163.16; 164.30; 166.3–17; 174.23; 198.10; (plural.) 58.1; 59.1; 69.29
πατὴρ δεύτερος, second father, 173.22; 190.14
πατὴρ λόγων, (of Timaeus) Father of words, 9.15
πατὴρ μακάρων, (of number) Father of the blessed ones, 16.32
πατρία, fatherhood, 89.1
πατρικός, paternal, of the father, 32.29; 133.23; 166.19; 199.31
παχύς, thick, dense, 112.25; 143.7; 155.11
Πειραιεύς, Piraeus, 8.30–9.9; 20.21–21.3; 26.13–14; 85.7–28
Πεισιστρατίδαι, Pisistratids, 93.6
Πεισίστρατος, Pisistratus, 80.32
Πελασγός, Pelasgus, 101.10
πέντας, pentad, 136.20; 182.17
πέπλος, peplos (robe of Athena), 85.12–14; 134.22–135.12; 167.16–22
πέρας, limit, 11.11; 47.4; 84.6; 128.2; 130.18; 132.13; 148.13; 173.8; 174.17–19; 176.32; 178.28–30; 183.16–18; 187.4

334

Greek word index

περατοειδής, of the limited kind, 185.10
περατοῦσθαι, reach a limit, 178.5
περιεκτικός, embracing, inclusive etc.,
　95.3–11; 105.25; 137.10; 178.8
Περικτιόνη, Perictione, 82.8
περιληπτικός, all-embracing etc., 70.9;
　100.13; 171.2
περίληψις, overall embrace, overview,
　72.23; 186.10
περίοδος, cycle, period, 14.20 (rhet.);
　100.5; 103.24; 108.18–25; 116.13–19;
　126.17; 127.31–128.2; 147.15–21;
　164.10; 177.18
περιοχή, embrace etc., 5.2; 73.14; 98.30;
　104.8; 148.26; 160.9; 175.16; 193.6
περισπᾶν, distract, 194.17
περίστασις, external pressure, 57.1
περιστατικός, under outside pressure,
　circumstantial, 19.3; 56.11
πέριττος, odd (of number), superfluous,
　15.11; 21.11–20; 102.28; 130.26;
　131.24; 204.18
περιφορά, revolution etc., 28.11; 125.23;
　139.24
περίφρασις, periphrasis, 68.14–19
Περσεφόνη, Persephone, 177.13
Πέρσης, Persian, 172.5
Περσικὸς στόλος, Persian invasion force,
　172.2–10
πεφροντισμένος, carefully pondered, 59.15
πηγή, source, spring, 3.28; 17.1 (Doric);
　96.14; 158.29; 167.14; 192.26
πίπτειν, fall, 83.3; 109.14; 113.11
πίστις, proof, 142.19
πιστοῦσθαι, seek proof, 186.23
πλανᾶσθαι, wander, 58.17
　τὰ πλανώμενα, the planets, 152.8
πλανῆτες (pl.), wanderers, 58.6; 76.22–4
　(planets)
πλάτος, plane, 11.12; 37.27
Πλατωνικός, of Plato, Platonist, 12.9;
　56.27; 59.12; 162.13; 166.1; 180.25
πλεονάζειν, take more time over, multiply,
　13.11; 16.13; 37.17
πλῆθος, multiplicity, plurality, number,
　3.27; 4.14; 21.1–16; 23.21–7; 79.19;
　130.22; 148.28; 149.21–3; 174.12;
　178.17; 179.14; 184.16–22
πληθύειν, multiply etc., 23.29; 79.23;
　103.13; 108.15–19; 120.29;
　148.28–149.6; 173.24; 184.15

πεπληθυσμένως, in a multiplied way
　etc., 40.1; 127.24
πληθυσμός, multiplication, 184.12
Πλούτων, Pluto, 177.14
πνεῦμα, wind, 121.22; spirit, life-current,
　139.20; 154.12
ποδηγεῖν, guide, 173.23
ποδηγετεῖν, guide, lead, 8.6; 11.15; 57.13;
　169.8
ποίημα, poem, 88.21; 89.28; 90.24;
　93.23
ποίησις, creation, productive activity etc.:
　frequent; poetry, 90.18–91.10;
　92.30–93.15
ποιητής, creator etc.: frequent; poet,
　18.18; 56.4; 63.15–29; 64.21–8;
　66.16–31; 79.29–80.3; 89.23;
　90.20–91.9; 93.9; 167.15; 172.20–2
ποιητικός, productive: very frequent;
　poetic, 58.23; 63.15; 90.1–22;
　91.5–92.9; 93.22–9; 102.30
　ποιητικὴ αἰτία, productive cause,
　2.8–3.10; 17.17–24; 39.4; 72.9;
　134.24
Πολέμαρχος, Polemarchus, 8.32
πόλεμος, war, 4.19–24; 56.26–57.23;
　61.4–5; 68.7; 73.7; 76.20–77.13;
　78.13–16; 80.4; 85.13; 88.8; 90.8;
　91.23; 92.15; 93.24; 95.18; 107.28;
　128.10–18; 131.10; 134.28–135.15
　149.31; 151.28; 155.28–156.12;
　157.30; 165.25; 167.20–31; 169.7;
　171.29–172.12; 173.21; 174.23–6;
　182.20; 185.14; 193.16; 196.14–197.5
πολιοῦχος θεά, 'city-holding' goddess;
　official city goddess, 98.5–28; 133.19;
　135.23–136.1; 170.31
πολιτεία, constitution, 4.11–12; 13.31;
　21.3; 22.4; 28.13–33.9; 36.4; 44.3;
　49.8; 53.25; 54.15–57.7; 60.5–61.14;
　62.28; 66.24–7; 67.18; 68.22–7;
　72.19–73.14; 76.3–6; 78.12–27;
　128.19–129.6; 132.25; 148.16;
　149.12–20; 152.2; 157.29; 169.27;
　171.3–15; 191.1–33; 193.13–14;
　195.13; 196.15–201.11; environment,
　112.13; citizen-body, 203.5
πολίτευμα, constitutional scheme,
　152.25
πολιτεύομαι, conduct oneself, 62.27;
　66.20; 72.21; 147.11; 148.14; 203.3

335

Greek word index

πολιτικός, constitutional, political, 22.31; 58.7; 61.15; 67.19–20; 69.24; 100.3; 148.1; 151.23–4; (as masc. noun) politician, 51.30; (as fem. noun) political art, politics, 30.21; 67.5; 69.1–18; 71.20; 80.6

πολιτικῶς, constitutionally, 148.11

πόλος, pole, 97.9

πολυειδής, varied, various etc., 53.31; 73.3; 106.5; 108.31; 136.16

πολυθρύλητος, much-vaunted, 101.3

πολυμετάβολος, unstable, subject to frequent change, 58.14; 124.29

πολυπλανής, nomadic, 58.24

πόντος, sea (in metaphors etc.), 113.30; 174.10; 175.20; 178.15; 179.24–6

Ποσειδῶν, Poseidon, 71.9; 78.28–79.3; 136.25; 173.10–19; 177.15–19; 182.15–19; 185.22

Ποσειδώνιος, Poseidonian, 189.29

ποσότης, quantity, 27.12

Πόταμος, River (= Xanthus), 78.29

Ποτίδαια, Potidaea, 62.20

προάγειν, bring forth etc., 71.25; 91.26; 135.30; 148.29; 153.26; 193.24; 199.30

προαναγράφειν, record earlier, 63.21; 175.4

προβεβιώμενα, τά, previously lived existences, 124.10; 126.11

προβολή, offering (of arguments), 79.12

προγονικός, procreative, 49.10

προελθεῖν, proceed, process, 5.14; 11.19; 12.16–21; 85.17; 88.4; 91.20; 110.23; 128.26; 135.17; 139.5; 140.30; 151.18; 157.28; 159.8; 176.22

προευτρεπίζειν, make ready in advance, 143.4; 193.26

προηγεῖσθαι, precede etc., 4.25; 87.21; 133.7; 134.23; 176.9; 196.12

πρόθεσις, aim, 1.4; 1.24; 204.25

προΐδρευμένος, pre-established, 3.7; 98.29; 135.7

προϊέναι, proceed etc., 3.27; 10.4; 11.22; 12.13–20; 27.13–14; 50.20; 56.17; 60.11–20; 87.25; 95.11; 97.1; 98.7; 103.13; 119.22; 134.29; 149.2–21; 155.2; 158.6; 160.2; 163.31; 166.8; 174.3–11; 177.29; 178.17–27; 191.12–20; 204.2

προκατάρχειν, make a start, precede, 18.5; 92.29; 95.12

προκαταστέλλειν, give an escort, 28.2

πρόκλησις, invitation; invocation, 25.29; 27.18; 100.21; 203.21

προσκλητικός, invoking, 100.20

προλαμβάνειν, get a prior grasp etc., 23.26–33; 67.22; 96.1; 98.12; 126.9; 127.27; 134.19; 156.26; 158.28; 173.29; 182.25

προλάμπειν, outshine, 60.13

προμήθεια, forethought, 45.1; 59.19; 113.32; 141.13

providential power, 69.9; 156.11

προνοεῖν, have concern for, 113.28; 138.2

προνοητικός, providential, 18.19; 58.22; 149.21

τὸ προνοητικόν, that which is taking care of, 34.17

πρόνοια, providence,13.25; 26.8; 34.5–11; 40.3; 41.10; 47.15–24; 53.3; 58.26; 74.1–22; 75.7–26; 85.20; 87.26; 99.11; 118.11; 122.3; 134.2; 135.17–136.18; 137.24–138.9; 141.16; 150.18; 159.1; 160.13–19; 167.9–25; 186.3; 189.4–9; 190.11; 201.25; forethought; concern, 44.1; 114.2–16

πρόοδος, procession,13.7–24; 36.20; 87.30–88.3; 103.13; 108.5; 130.14; 134.16; 136.3; 137.20; 141.2; 143.12; 147.3–5; 148.23; 149.28; 160.15; 173.3; 175.7–27; 178.26–179.4; 182.18; 190.11–22; 200.1; advance, progression, 188.6; 197.31–198.1

προοίμιον, proem, 29.9; 204.16

προοιμιώδης, proem-like, 80.9

προπομπεύειν, provide an escort, 34.9

προπομπός, escort, 111.22; 158.22

προσγλίχεσθαι, be over-desirous, 80.27

προσηγορία, name, epithet, 169.10; 175.24

προσλάμπειν, illuminate, radiate upon, 8.8; 162.7; 168.27

προσοχή, attention, 80.10

προστατεῖν, preside over, 145.11

προστάτης, presiding over, in charge of, 77.6; 79.11; 118.31; 137.3; 173.15; 182.21

προστάτις, directing; in charge of, 148.8; 169.1

336

Greek word index

πρόσυλος, close to matter, connected to matter, 50.19; 85.8; 178.16

πρόσωπον, character, (dramatic) participant; 9.28; 72.7; 73.26; 87.19; 129.30

προϋπάρχειν, pre-exist etc., 4.28; 8.26; 27.7; 32.9; 36.15; 38.20; 105.9; 118.28; 186.6; 191.17; 196.10–22

προϋφιστάναι, pre-exist etc., 2.25; 8.17; 33.22; 141.30

προχεῖν, pour forth, 110.14

πρυτανεύειν, preside, 34.22; 88.8; 135.15; 169.7

πρώτιστος, (very) first, 104.29; 112.8; 137.22; 176.22; 183.4–15

πρῶτος, first: frequent

πρωτουργός, primary, primordial, 3.3; 6.21; 17.21; 24.9; 42.1; 93.26; 134.24

πτερορρύησις, loss of feathers, 52.23

πτῶσις, fall, 110.15; 113.30; 115.21; 154.6

Πυθαγορεῖος, Pythagorean, 1.25; 2.30; 7.20–8.14; 15.24–6; 22.8; 23.22; 30.4; 33.8; 124.5; 129.31; 130.16; 136.31; 176.10; 182.14; 183.20; 199.3; 203.25; 204.4; (adv.) 174.14

Πυθαγορικός, Pythagorean, 1.8; 5.22; 7.19–27

πύθμην, foundation, 189.11

πύκνωσις, being dense, 10.10

πῦρ, fire, 104.19; 106.33–112.23; 114.24–119.4; 122.7; 144.3–4; 195.3

πύργος, tower, 199.3

πύριος, fiery, 12.19; 113.23

Πύρρα, Pyrrha, 101.11

Ρ

ῥαπίζειν, strike, 115.13

ῥέπειν, incline, veer (downward), 111.27–112.8; 152.32–153.16; 201.18

ῥητός, rationally expressible, 17.5

ῥίζα, root, 75.17; 97.1

ῥοπή, falling away, inclination, 52.23; 118.27

ῥοώδης, in flux, 189.17

ῥωμαλεώτερον, sturdier, 194.23

Σ

Σάις, Sais (Egyptian city) 95.7–101.21; 140.24–141.14; 145.7

Σαΐτης, Saitian; person from Sais, 98.4; 101.23; 134.14; 144.19–145.2; 145.2; 146.5; 150.2–9; 154.29; 157.21–9; 159.24; 160.22; 169.27

Σαιτικός, Saitic, 95.6–97.19; 97.28

Σαλαμίς, Salamis, 80.31

Σεβεννυτικός, Sebennytic (district), 97.20

Σεβέννυτος, Sebennytos, 97.20; 101.22

σειρά, series, 49.11; 63.5; 85.2; 115.31; 135.25; 142.21; 169.21; 170.23; 180.2; 191.7

Σειρῆνες, Sirens, 41.14

Σεισίχθων, Earthshaker (= Poseidon), 190.1

Σεληναῖα ὄρη, Mountains of the Moon, 121.4; 181.16

σελήνη, moon, 34.13; 43.6; 47.10; 110.29–11.29; 141.9–142.8; 147.11; 161.25; 165.16–22; 167.3

οἱ ὑπὸ σελήνην δαίμονες, sublunary daemons, 152.26

οἱ ὑπὸ σελήνην κλῆροι, sublunary lots, 137.27–30; 139.11; 142.8

σεληνιακός, lunar, 47.13; 81.13; 111.7; 147.8; 159.26; 165.20; 166.32

σημαίνειν, signify: frequent

σημαντικός, signifying, indicative of, 141.28; 159.16; 178.25; 204.11

σημεῖον, sign, 109.25; 124.4; 186.28–31

σῆψις, putrefaction, 107.16

σκοπός, aim, target, 1.18; 4.6; 9.25; 19.28; 30.18; 31.4–7; 43.30; 57.6; 78.1; 92.15

Σόλων, Solon, 80.23–81.17; 86.6; 89.28; 91.4–93.23; 97.21–3; 99.30–102.2; 103.17–31; 108.22–109.4; 127.4–128.16; 133.18–135.22; 149.5; 170.21; 191.16–192.23; 203.3–9

σοφία, wisdom, 165.26–170.6

σοφιστεύειν, be a sophistic teacher, 65.8

σπέρμα, seed, sperm, 51.10–19; 128.1; 143.2–9; 153.21; 164.8

σπερματικοὶ λόγοι, seminal or spermatic principles, 99.18; 143.18

σπήλαιον, cave, 19.14–16

σπορά, sowing, 154.5

στάσις, rest, stability, 78.9; 97.9; 106.12; 124.28; 174.5; 176.4–5; dissension, civil war, 50.28; 93.28; 172.23; 184.5

στερεός, solid, three-dimensional, 77.18; 143.9

στίζειν, punctuate, 31.5

337

Greek word index

στοιχεῖον, element, 7.1; 8.23; 47.4 (with note); 96.21; 105.12–107.8; 112.14–113.9; 126.27; 136.30; 138.31; 178.9; component, 137.6

στόμιον, mouth (of the Mediterranean), 188.19

στομφώδης, bombastic, 64.22

σύγγενης, relative, 40.11; 80.24; 83.9; 94.24

συγκαταβάλλειν, deposit along with, 51.10–19

συγκροτεῖν, strike up, 77.14

σύγχυσις, disturbance, 112.30

συζευγνύναι, yoke, harness etc., 47.14; 49.13; 51.11; 54.21; 154.8

σύζυγος, partner, 97.23

συμβολικῶς, symbolically etc., 7.29; 30.13; 114.7; 130.11; 180.11; 200.3

σύμβολον, symbol, 4.32; 23.32; 27.18; 30.7–14; 51.25; 55.5; 88.1; 94.28; 96.27; 100.7; 104.14; 109.1; 112.10; 125.1; 130.2; 132.21; 142.27; 144.17; 146.19; 147.21; 148.15; 161.8; 189.15; 193.25; 198.30

συμμεταβάλλεσθαι, change together with, 99.25

συμπάθεια, sympathy etc., 36.26; 49.29; 153.4; 155.19; 169.11

συμπαθής, in sympathy etc., 36.25

συμπεραίνειν, terminate, 199.23

συμπεριπολεῖν, spin about, revolve, 71.2; 112.4; 115.24

συμπλήρωσις, completion, 54.20

σύμπνοια, co-animation, integrated life, 44.30; 46.18; 116.5(?); 196.8

συμπροϊέναι, proceed together etc., 46.27; 142.8

συναιρεῖν, summarize, 55.25
    συνῃρημένως, in a nutshell, in concise form, 28.19; 30.27

συνάπτειν, join, fasten etc., 5.22; 9.21; 12.30; 24.2; 25.28; 31.17; 88.5; 126.1; 127.31–128.3; 133.9; 135.24; 204.20

συνάρμοσις, coalition, conjunction, 47.8–26

συναρτᾶσθαι, be linked to, depend upon, 108.7; 137.8; 138.28; 196.7

συνάρτησις, conjunction, 194.8

συνδετικός, with the power to bind, 50.25

συνδιαιρεῖν, divide along with, 139.11

συνδιοικεῖν, assist in managing etc., 71.3; 111.15; 112.5

συνδρομή, conjunction, 140.3

σύνδρομος, keeping time with, 12.24

συνεγγίζειν, border upon, 175.10

συνεκτικός, cohesive, conserving etc., 36.13; 38.13; 91.1; 124.26–125.9; 129.2; 166.5

συνελαύνειν, drive (together), 190.29

συνεσπειραμένος, compressed, concentrated, 29.21; 33.5; 180.13

συνευπορεῖν, share a resource, 196.5; 199.19

συνέχειν, maintain, give coherence, conserve: frequent; hold in check, 176.3

συνήθης, special friend, 83.9

συνθήκη, composition, compact, 59.19–23; 61.21

σύνθημα, code, token, 139.27; 144.15; 161.12

συνοχή, integrity, security etc., 103.16; 106.20; 118.10; 124.28

συνοχικός, conserving, 142.21; 176.16

συντέλεια, perfection, help in achieving, 124.12–125.3; 173.16

σύντομος, brief, concise, 33.5; 61.12; 72.23–73.14

συντρέχειν, coincide, converge, 31.11; 92.1; 116.2; 160.27–9

Συρακόσιος, Syracusan, 71.19

σύστασις, composition, establishment etc., 7.3; 79.14; 104.9; 109.29–110.2; 121.24; 124.19–125.2; 137.16; (company of angels); 139.31; 142.18–143.3, 174.21

συστοιχία, column (of opposites), 4.18; 82.23; 84.1; 97.1; 130.17; 165.2; 169.7; 172.30; 174.1–175.26; 180.9–16; 182.10–29; 185.15–186.25; 189.10–190.25

σύστοιχος, coordinate, 5.17

σχέσις, relation, 99.16; 106.8; 115.25; 141.16; (temporal) condition, 50.2; 77.11; 145.31; getting, 194.25

σχῆμα, shape, figure, 8.23; 60.16; 63.12; 99.20; 105.8; 106.9–17; 130.1; 197.13

σχηματισμός, configuration, 155.6–14

Σωκράτης, Socrates, 2.14–86.15 often; 149.12–18; 162.30; 166.14; 172.21; 177.2; 180.28; 190.24–204.24 often

338

Greek word index

Σωκρατικός, Socratic, 7.23–31; 62.9; 65.23; 152.1
σῶμα, body, 2.28; 5.3; 10.17; 47.18; 60.14–61.8; 77.18–79.2; 108.25; 142.6; 162.32; 175.31; 197.30
σωματικός, bodily, corporeal: frequent
σωματοείδης, bodily, corporeal, 4.29; 8.7; 11.10; 143.3; 164.23
σωματότης, bodiliness, 190.26
σωστικός, able to preserve, salutary, 106.21; 116.5; 118.5

Τ

τακτικός, given to organizing, 154.18
τὰ τακτικά, battle-strategy, 62.19
τάξις, order, rank: very frequent
ταραχή, disturbance, 57.27
Τάρταρος, Tartarus, 190.20–9
ταυτότης, sameness, 50.7; 83.11; 106.13; 124.28; 132.14; 141.20; 149.27; 155.25; 176.4–29; 184.23; 195.20
ταχυκίνητος, fast-moving, 96.19
τελεῖν, initiate, 119.2; belong to, be enrolled in, 183.3–8; 186.1; 186.25
τελειότης, perfection, 23.32; 25.2; 25.29; 29.24; 32.23; 41.8; 42.22; 46.4–6; 108.27; 146.16; 162.21; 193.27
τέλειος, perfect, complete, 21.30; 22.3; 29.5; 55.1; 56.17–19; 69.3; 86.11; 87.21; 89.26; 93.20; 97.27; 139.1; 159.6; 165.2; 170.13; 203.11
τελειοῦν, perfect, 25.28
τελείωσις, perfection, 79.10; 134.1
τελειωτικός, perfective, 124.10
τελεσιουργός, rendering perfect, perfective, 74.22; 87.22–6; 158.5; 166.5
τελεστής, initiate, one giving perfection, 51.22; 144.16
τελευταῖα, τὰ, the last (things), 95.11; 105.19; 178.28; 179.23; 191.6
τελικὴ αἰτία, final cause, 2.9; 4.28; 7.11; 17.17–19
τέλος, end, goal etc., 3.4; 4.10–17; 6.7; 13.18; 29.24; 35.25; 56.25–8; 74.12; 190.28–191.11
τεναγώδης, full of shoals, 188.20–1
τετραγωνικός, square, 21.14; 146.14
τετρακτύς, tetractys, 16.32; 17.23; 155.7
τετράς, tetrad, 21.14; 23.23; 136.20; 137.16

τέχνη, craft etc., 6.16; 10.12–24; 12.11–20; 16.6 (= handbook); 33.1; 59.13; 64.18; 125.6–13; 143.31; 155.21; 159.12; 185.13; 186.12–14
τεχνητόν, τὸ, product of craft, 10.23
τεχνίτης, craftsman, 12.14–19
τήρησις, observation, investigation, 103.4; 124.1–14
τιμαιογραφεῖν, do Timaeus-writing, 1.11; 7.21
Τιτᾶνες, Titans, 77.16; 172.17–173.14; 175.13; 176.2; 187.7
Τιτανικός, Titanic, 172.32; 174.4–26; 176.19; 183.2; 185.32; 187.4; 189.1; 190.28
Τιτανομαχία, battle against Titans, 38.27; 79.27
Τιτυός, Tityos, 111.28
τόπος, place, space, 6.26; 161.3; 169.5–18; 196.26
κίνησις κατὰ τόπον, locomotion, 139.6
τριαδικός, triadic; to the triad, 146.23; 151.2
τριάς, triad, 9.18–19; 16.28–17.29; 21.19; 23.22–24.2; 74.21; 130.23; 136.24–6; 141.10; 146.17; 150.26–151.4; 179.15
τριγωνικόν, τὸ, triangularity, 150.5
τρίγωνος, triangular, 150.4
τὸ τρίγωνον, triangle, 96.17
Τριτογένης, Tritogenês (name for goddesses), 166.29
τριττύς, trittys, 88.26
τροπή, figure of speech, 14.19
τρόπος ὑλικός, material character (= daemon), 171.19–21
τύπος, guideline, imprint, pattern, 16.9; 18.13; 66.21; 68.13; 72.27; 78.2; 173.28; 175.4; 178.2
Τυφῶν, Typhon, 77.16

Υ

ὑγρότης, moisture, 117.6
ὑλαῖος, material, matter-bound, 113.15; 185.30
ὕλη, matter, subject matter, 2.10; 32.4; 32.17; 37.25; 39.4–10; 51.5; 53.21; 58.13–23; 72.12; 83.5; 87.12; 91.17; 96.4; 99.3; 116.6; 117.6–14; 125.19; 126.18; 143.7–25; 157.1–19; 175.8–28; 178.5–179.25; 183.10; 185.29; 191.8–9

339

Greek word index

ὑλικός, material, enmattered, 2.3; 38.2; 42.26; 72.11; 77.19; 79.9–14; 118.26; 143.31; 171.19–21; 186.30

ὕμνησις, laudation, 85.22

ὕπαρξις, substantive existence, subsistence, basic stuff, 13.26; 36.22; 159.20; 180.14

ὑπερδιατείνεσθαι, fight to support, strive to give extra force, 76.27; 102.6

ὑπερζεῖν, overheat, 116.29

ὑπεριδρύεσθαι, be enthroned (or founded) above, 70.12; 96.1

ὑπερκόσμιος, hypercosmic, 3.29–4.2; 13.17; 47.8; 84.29; 108.32; 158.3–13

ὑπερουράνιος, hyper-heavenly, 50.11; 98.8; 170.24

ὑπερούσιος, super-substantial, 131.17–23

ὑπεροχή, surpassing excellence, excess, 19.22; 22.25–23.4; 27.18; 70.3; 171.12; 178.18; 193.23

ὑπερπλήρης, overflowing, 25.17; 134.2

τὸ ὑπερπλῆρες, superabundance, 44.11

ὑπέρτερος, higher, superior, 23.32; 29.6; 51.27; 103.31; 134.17; 144.21–9

ὑποδοχή, receptacle, reception, 49.18–21; 51.4; 54.24; 69.5; 97.2–3; 125.8; 142.30; 163.23–164.18; 165.30

ὑποκεῖσθαι, underlie; be basic etc., 3.23; 26.12–18; 92.22–6; 96.24; 109.16–110.14

τὸ ὑποκείμενον, the substrate, 2.10; 3.16–19; 6.25; 49.20 (pl.); 54.24 (pl.); 143.30; 192.5; the subject matter etc., 68.16; 77.29; 190.5

ὑπόστασις, foundation, basic nature etc., 17.22; 33.20; 53.21; 96.22; 110.27; 125.10; 127.26; 139.17; 173.25; 175.18; 179.23; 201.17

ὑποστάτης, founder, 58.3; 59.1; 193.2

ὑποστατικός, supplying the basis of, 3.32

ὑποτάττειν, rank beneath etc., 111.9; 151.23; 173.24; 201.19

ὑπουργικὴ ἰατρική, servile medicine, 158.19

ὑπουργός, assistant, 113.18

ὑφειμένος, subordinate, inferior, lower; etc., 10.18; 22.2; 23.6; 24.7; 27.6; 32.3–14; 49.7; 50.13; 71.27; 85.3; 86.13; 100.16; 133.25; 137.24; 144.23; 151.20; 152.2; 160.22; 171.16; 182.31; 189.9

ὕφεσις, subordination etc., 22.28; 39.5; 46.27; 71.14; 149.14–30; 151.6; 155.2; 175.8; 176.22; 178.25–179.5; 190.3

ὑφήγησις, teaching, instruction, 7.15; 32.22

ὑφηγητικῶς, instructively, 21.18

ὑφιζάνειν, settle down, 190.27

ὕψος, majesty, 14.12; 64.8–23

ὑψοῦν, give majesty to, 14.20

Φ

Φαέθων, Phaethon, 108.21–110.15; 111.29–115.21; 129.24

Φαίακες, Phaeacians, 190.6

φαινόμενος, apparent, visible, 25.25; 71.3–5; 89.12; 131.11 (manifest); 142.6; 202.21

φαντάζεσθαι, be reflected, 49.19

φαντασία, imagination, 48.12; 149.17; 194.21–30

φάντασμα, imagining, 168.25

φανταστικόν, τὸ, image-forming faculty, 194.19

φανταστικός, imposing, 64.9

φατρία, brotherhood, 89.1

φθαρτικός, destructive, 106.22; 107.13; 115.26–116.15; 125.21; 163.4

φθαρτός, perishable, destructible, 130.23; 163.3

φθορά, (case of) destruction, 102.15; 103.20; 105.4–108.3; 114.15–117.1; 119.4; 122.12; 125.23; 138.12; passing away, 182.22; 189.18

φθορώδης, ruinous, 162.26

φιλόλογος, philologist, 86.24

φιλολόγως, from a philological perspective, 14.7

φιλοσοφία, philosophy, 13.1; 15.28; 26.5; 71.20; 90.1; 129.32

φιλόσοφος, philosophic, philosopher, wisdom-loving, 19.29; 34.2–25; 58.7–20; 64.10; 67.20–1; 69.24–70.28; 86.25–87.1; 90.27; 153.9; 157.27–158.2; 165.6–166.19; 168.9; 169.13; 185.2; 202.2

φιλοσόφως, from a philosophic viewpoint, 109.9

φλέγειν, ignite, 109.13; 110.4–5; 113.22

φοιβόληπτος, inspired by Apollo, 18.17

Φορωνεύς, Phoroneus, 101.8

340

Greek word index

φράτερες, brother, phratry-member,
88.19–89.3; 92.26; 203.5–6
φρόνησις, (practical) wisdom, 34.24;
44.1; 45.26; 67.23; 124.12; 151.11;
154.19; 162.20–6; 164.19; 165.4;
167.10
φρουρητικός, protective; guardian, 38.6;
103.15; 125.9; 154.2–25; 156.5–6;
166.4; 180.1
φυλακίδες, guardianesses, 46.14
φυλή, tribe, 88.24–8
φυσικός, physical, natural, 3.1; 10.3; 12.29;
17.2–4; 19.23–8; 25.8; 27.26; 28.21;
34.11; 48.4; 49.17; 51.3–18; 79.6;
89.25; 93.24; 110.22; 118.3; 134.16;
187.21–2; 201.17–19
ὁ φυσικός, the physicist, 2.8; 6.1–15
τὰ φυσικά, physical things, things of
nature, 2.25; 3.11; 7.14–8.20; 23.2;
51.3–18
τὸ φυσικόν, physical element, 8.12;
31.31; 58.23
φυσικὴ δημιουργία, physical creation,
32.12
φυσικὴ ποίησις, physical creation, 16.23;
61.28
φυσικοὶ λόγοι, physical (creative)
principles, 27.27; 143.17; 148.4–6
φυσιολογεῖν, do natural philosophy, 119.5
φυσιολογία, physical inquiry, account of
nature etc., 1.5–17; 4.26; 13.27; 19.25;
30.4–11; 32.3–5; 83.33; 204.4–8
φυσιολογικόν, natural science, 30.15
φύσις, nature: very frequent
φωτίζειν, shed light, 115.32

X

χαμαιζηλότερος, humbler, 21.30
χαμαιπετής, down to earth, 127.8
χάος, chaos, 176.13
χαρακτήρ, literary character, manner,
7.17; 9.26; 62.10
χαρακτηρίζειν, characterize, 25.18; 42.30;
48.25; 175.28; 185.11
Χαρμίδης, Charmides, 82.7–17
χάσμα, chasm, 107.18
χείρονα, τὰ, the worse, the weaker, the
inferior, 79.18; 131.10; 132.24; 174.9;
185.24; 186.27; 187.5

χθόνιος, earthly, on earth, 142.4; 147.1–4;
148.24–149.7
χίτων, tunic (of the soul), 112.19–113.11
χορεία, dance, 45.3
χορευτής, one in a chorus, 167.12
χορηγία, supervision (as of a chorus),
195.29
χορηγός, leader, promoter (as of a chorus),
34.25; 79.5; 88.3; 199.32
χόρος, chorus, 137.17
χώρησις, separation, 198.17
χώριστος, separate, separable,
transcendent, 10.26; 27.3; 28.4;
58.14–21; 131.5; 165.27–166.9;
185.30

ψ

ψύξις, cold, 122.22
ψυχή, soul, *passim*
  ψυχὴ ἀνθρωπίνη, human soul, 49.24
  ψυχὴ λογική, rational soul, 5.14
  ψυχὴ νοέρα, intellective soul, 12.19
  ψυχαὶ ἄλογοι, irrational souls, 176.5;
    183.9
  ψυχαὶ δαιμόνιαι, daemonic souls,
    110.28; 138.28
  ψυχαὶ θεῖαι, divine souls, 36.11; 41.15;
    52.25; 110.28; 200.30
  ψυχαὶ καλλίονες, finer souls, 77.3
  ψυχαὶ μερικαί, individual or particular
    souls, 5.3; 27.11; 52.22; 54.1–6; 58.16;
    77.11; 89.14; 90.8; 110.23; 136.11;
    138.13; 140.9; 141.15; 142.1; 152.8;
    160.29; 182.31; 186.2
  ψυχαὶ ὅλαι, universal or entire souls,
    27.8
  ψυχαὶ οὐράνιαι, heavenly souls, 41.22
ψυχικός, of soul(s) or psychic(al), 30.9;
47.17; 50.19; 52.25; 53.2; 108.18–25;
142.25; 154.15; 161.11; 163.13;
175.21; 178.10

ω

Ὠκεανός, Ocean, 109.10
ὥρα, elegance, freshness, 14.19; 86.20;
season, 181.10
ὡραΐζεσθαι, use decoration or
beautification, 59.10–28

341

General index

The primary vehicle for finding material within the translation is intended to be the word index and glossary; this index is chiefly designed to help readers locate names, passages, and topics discussed in the introductory material and the notes.

Academy   2–3, 4
Adrastus   32
Aeschylus   66
Alexandria   2
Alexandrian Neoplatonism   11, 23
allegorical interpretation   17, 43, 70–80
Amelius   11, 35, 37–9, 46, 48, 61, 71, 73–4, 83, 106, 169–70
Ammonius, Neoplatonist *Commentary on the De Interpretatione*   15, 303
Ammonius Saccas   36, 43, 44
Anaxagoras   92
Antimachus   184
Antiphon   103
Apaturia   182
Apuleius   35
Archiadas   6, 7
Aristides   216, 271; 36.23–6:   216
Aristocles   114, 179
Aristophanes   66
Aristotle   2–3, 11, 12–13, 26, 50, 62–3, 65, 92, 99–100, 103, 150, 289
   de Longaevitate 465a: 208, 211
   Metaphysics 1083b: 111
   Meteorologica 343b: 287; 351b–352a: 214; 354a: 287; 368a–b: 287
   [*de Mundo*] 400a: 216
Aristoxenus   180
Asclepigeneia   5, 9
Asclepius   4, 6, 7, 76, 256, 258
Aspasius   45–6
Atalante   81
Athena   2, 4, 67, 71, 76–7, 248, 264, 265–6
Athenian Neoplatonism   1, 3, 6, 7, 11, 49

Athens   2–3, 4–5, 6–7, 73, 76
   ancient   60, 76–7, 230 (*see also* Atlantis)
Atkinson, M.   41–2
Atlantis   16, 22–4, 27, 60–84, 95
Atticus, Platonist   30, 31, 33, 34, 35, 61, 192
authenticity   156

Bechtle, G.   46
Bendis   179
biographies (of philosophers)   23
Blank, David   15
Bréhier, Émile   41
Brisson, Luc   39, 46
Buris   81, 287
Byzantium   2

Calcidius   31, 33, 35, 77–8
Callimachus   76
Canon *see* curriculum
Carmen Aureum   111, 303
causation   93–4, 99–100
Chaldean Oracles   9, 12, 13, 47, 48; 33: 106; 36:   133; 70:   105; 107:   302; 108:   96
Chaldeans   5
'character' of Dialogues   51, 100
chariot, of soul   96
Christianity, Christians etc.   3–4, 6, 7, 9–10, 217
Cicero *On Laws* 1.6–8:   63–4
column of opposites   82, 176
commentaries   1, 7, 11, 13–14, 20, 44–6, 47, 50–1, 69
Constantine   6
Cornford, F.   10

342

General index

Crantor 23, 24, 60, 61, 62, 63–70, 75–6, 77–8, 80, 168
Critias, Platonic character 25, 51–2, 55, 58, 69, 82, 164, 165, 247
Critias the Elder 76, 82, 164
Cronius 31, 38, 39
curriculum (Neoplatonist) 13, 47, 48, 51, 52
cycles of time 244, 245

daemons 72–3, 77–8, 80, 260
Damascius, *On First Principles* I.291.23–5: 10–11
Demiurgic Triad 51, 58, 118, 148, 273
Dercyllides 114
Dillon, J. 26, 27
Diogenes Laertius 3.52: 69
division of text 16–19, 21–3, 50
dodecahedron 99
Domninus 3, 9, 23, 24, 203, 217
Duris 76

Earth (goddess) 76
Egypt, Egyptians etc. 5, 30, 63, 66–8, 69–70, 71, 78, 79–80, 190, 214
Egyptian castes 248, 251
Eleatics 114
Empedocles 171, 233
entheastic theology 54
Eratosthenes 75, 216
ethics 45, 73, 78, 80, 110, 132, 165, 197, 213, 291
Eudocia 2

Father of Demiurges 51, 58, 118, 122, 148, 149
Festugière, A.-J. viii, 50
first person singular 203

Galen 32, 33
gender ambiguity 140
geographers 70
Greek wall at Troy 61, 62, 289

Hades 71
Hadot, Pierre 45, 46
haeresis 92
Harpocration 39
Hecate 5
Helice 81, 287
Hephaestus 39, 76, 238, 240

Heraclides Ponticus 70, 75–6
Heraclitus 83; B53: 274; B77: 212
Hermeias 15, 49
Hermocrates, Platonic character 25, 51–2, 55
Herodotus 64, 67, 69
Hesiod *Theogony* 517–18: 273
historia 63–5, 291
historia psile 28, 65
Homer 12, 62, 75, 173
    Iliad 1.104: 212; 5.734–5: 266; 5.891: 267; 7.247–8: 109; 8.385–6: 266; 8.390: 267; 12.1–33: 289; 13.299: 267; 14.382: 145; 15.190–2: 233, 237; 18.400: 243; 20.22: 166; 20.67–74: 171
    Odyssey 1.100: 267; 12.65: 148; 13.149–87: 71, 289
'House of Proclus' 7

Iamblichus 9, 11, 12, 13, 19, 21–2, 38–40, 41, 46–8, 56, 57, 61, 72, 81–4, 117, 165, 166, 222, 264
    de Mysteriis 48
    in Timaeum fragments 107, 111, 113, 119, 124, 149, 170, 176, 187, 213, 215, 226, 241, 242, 244, 250, 251, 254, 257, 263, 264, 270, 271, 274, 295, 304
iconic interpretation 53–4, 59, 187
inspired poetry 173 (*see also* Homer)
introductory topics 49–52, 103
Isocrates 271

Johansen, T. K. 66
Julian, the Apostate 4, 6
Julian, Chaldean 9

Lachares 5
Lang, H. and Macro, A. D. 10
lemmata 15–16
Leonas of Isuria 2
Leontius 2
Lernould, Alain 50
lexis see theôria
life-giving goddess 97
Longinus 35–7, 56, 61, 72–3, 74–6, 108, 125, 126, 129, 145, 149, 150, 153, 157, 160, 161, 177, 178, 180, 184, 188, 197, 224, 225, 260, 271, 304

343

General index

lotteries, divine 232, 291
Lucian 64, 65
Lycia 2

Mansfeld, Jaap 49
Marcellus (travel writer) 277, 280
Marinus 2–3, 4, 7, 9, 14
marriages, holy 143
Maximus of Ephesus 6
Melanthus 182
Middle Platonism 1, 30–5, 36,
   77–8
Moderatus 38
Moon 78, 80, 170

natural law 297
nature, Proclus' concept of 51
Neopythagoreans (*see also* Numenius)
   37, 38
Numenius 31, 33–4, 37, 40, 46, 48, 61,
   65, 71–2, 74, 75, 76, 77–8, 221, 225,
   238, 255, 264

Odysseus 71
Old Academy 26, 28, 60
Olympiodorus (Neoplatonist) 15; *in
   Gorg.* Proem: 51; 41: 23; 46: 83;
   47: 173
One and Dyad 82, 226
Opsomer, J. 55
Origenes, friend of Plotinus 35–7, 56,
   61, 71, 72–3, 74, 76, 77, 178, 180,
   264, 283
   On Daemons 72
Orpheus, Orphics 9, 48, 163, 226, 243
Orphic Fragments 20: 284; 83: 188; 94:
   218; 119: 275; 163: 140; 168–9:
   268, 302; 175: 269, 275; 178: 231;
   215: 272; 354: 209, 212

pagan religion 3–6, 10
Panaetius 260
Panathenaea 120 (*see also peplos*)
Parmenides 107
Parmenides-Commentator 31, 45–6
Patricius 2
peplos 179, 230
Peripatetics 104
Phaeacians 62
Phaethon myth 64, 79–80
Pherecydes 75, fr.4: 225

Philip of Opus 197
Philo of Alexandria 1, 29
Philolaus B1 DK: 276
Plato 23–5, *et passim*
   [?] *Alcibiades I* 114e: 24; 120b: 196
   Apology 21–22: 24
   Charmides 154a–b: 175
   [?] *Clitophon* 52
   Cratylus 396b: 266; 402b–d: 226;
      407a–c: 265
   Critias 1, 25, 55; 106a–109c: 79–80;
      113c: 273; 113e–114c: 281, 282;
      121b–c: 62
   [?] *Epistles* 312d: 42; 312e–313a: 37,
      39–40, 42; 314a: 42; 323d: 42
   Euthyphro 6b–c: 230
   Gorgias 462–6: 160; 466b–468e: 113;
      493a–c: 71; 523a: 173
   Ion 22, 24
   Laws 23, 39, 66, 67, 103; 653a: 185;
      714a: 246; 716a: 133; 720a: 256;
      771b: 236; 803c: 222; 892b: 103,
      104; 896e: 30; 903b–e: 220
   Lysis 211d: 111
   Meno 31
   Parmenides 1, 17, 39–40, 45–6, 49, 107,
      197; 144b: 42; 159b–160b: 143
   Phaedo 14, 30, 31, 92, 62b: 39, 40,
      71; 74a–76c: 291; 91c: 23;
      96a–99d: 303; 109c–d: 281
   Phaedrus 39, 47; 227b: 111; 229d:
      75; 240e: 187; 246a: 146;
      246d–247e: 41, 96; 248–51: 78,
      80–1, 164, 177, 207, 244; 253d–e:
      146; 256a–b: 23, 24; 274e: 183;
      275b: 67; 276c–d: 23, 25
   Philebus 39, 47; 16c: 42; 16d–e:
      143; 26e–30d: 42, 97; 27b: 26;
      29b–30c: 302; 30c: 178
   Protagoras 125; 321d: 125
   Republic 1, 12, 25, 39, 42, 51, 55, 67,
      95, 102; 329e: 51, 136; 369e–370c:
      130; 390b: 92; 393c: 159; 410–12:
      213; 415c: 147; 420b: 189; 509c:
      194; 521d: 135; 534bc: 20; 536a:
      66; 537c: 20; 546a: 261; 592b:
      58, 68; Myth of Er: 71, 74; 617b–c:
      135; 619b–d: 164
   Republic–Timaeus–Critias 23, 25, 51–2,
      70, 298–301
   Sophist 47; 254d–255e: 42

344

General index

Statesman 39, 270–272: 198; 271d: 251; 272c: 26; 273d–e: 274, 279

Symposium 195–8: 179; 203b: 112; 203d–204b: 268

Theaetetus 30, 41; 180d: 226

Theaetetus–Sophist–Politicus 55, 56

Timaeus passim

pleasure (of reader) 73, 75

Plotinus 11, 32, 61, 74

Enneads I.2: 41; III.8: 18; III.9: 41, 43; V.1: 41–2; V.8: 41; VI.2: 42–3

Plutarch of Athens 2, 9, 13, 14, 49, 95

Plutarch of Chaeronea 10, 29–30, 36, 78, 80–1, 212, 264

De Animae Procreatione 29; 1012–3: 27, 30, 79, 80

De Defectu Oraculorum 208, 211

Life of Solon 174; 26–32: 79–80

Porphyry 2, 9, 11–71, 83, 114, 132, 150, 165, 197, 225, 245, 264, 304

De Antro Nympharum 29: 170

Fragments (Smith) 120: 93

in Timaeum fragments 109, 113, 118, 145, 160, 170, 188, 205, 213, 214, 242, 243, 244, 254, 257, 261, 264, 270, 274, 294, 299, 301, 304

Introduction 13

Letter to Anebo 48

Life of Plotinus 2; 3: 37, 38, 43, 72; 14: 32, 35, 40, 44, 180; 16–21: 37–8; 17–20: 36

Poseidon 58, 62, 71, 169–70, 212, 289

Posidonius 28, 63, 78; F49: 62, 81

Potamo of Alexandria 29

Praxiphanes 109

Prayer 138

Presocratics 11, 92, 104

Proclus *passim*

Commentary on the Alcibiades 8, 13, 54

Commentary on the Cratylus 8, 14, 54

Commentary on Euclid Book I 8

Commentary on the Parmenides 8, 13, 17, 22, 24, 658–9: 28, 70; 989.13: 20; 1026.18: 20; 1059–61: 49

Commentary on the Republic 12, 51; II.8: 125, 126

lost commentaries 8, 9

On the Eternity of the World 10

Platonic Theology I.1.6–7: 11, 44, 48; I.4.20: 79; I.5.25–26: 12

works in other genres 8–9

Prolegomena *see* introductory topics

Prolegomena to Plato's Philosophy 21–23: 47, 49

prologues 28, 32, 73, 304

psychology 78, 80

Ptolemy 63

Ptolemy, Platonist 114

Pythagoreans, Pythagoreanism etc. 9, 12, 29, 40, 50, 59, 79, 83, 91, 93–4, 99–100, 111

readiness 145

rhetoric 2

Sais 67

Saffrey, H. D 6

Sedley, D. 27, 70, 75

Seneca

Epistles 65.7–10: 50, 93, 95

Natural Questions 81

Severus 21, 31, 33–4, 61

Simplicius

On Epictetus 13

in Phys. 286.20ff.: 18

Siorvanes, L. 2

skopos 12, 17–20, 47–8, 49–50, 56, 82

Socrates, Platonic character 25, 51–2, 58, 69, 247

Socratic character 100

Sodano, R. 44

Solon 69, 73, 82, 173, 188, 223

Sorabji, R. 15

Speusippus 26–7

Stoics 239

Strabo 2.3.6: 62, 81; 12.1.36: 62, 289

symbolic interpretation 12, 53–4, 79, 101, 124, 173, 187, 283 (*see also* allegorical interpretation)

Syrianus 1, 2–3, 5, 14–15, 49, 56, 81

Commentary on the Metaphysics 49

Tardieu, M. 46

Taurus, Platonist 31

Taylor, A. E. 10

Theaetetus commentary, 30–1, IV: 21, 61

Theagenes 5

Theocritus 67

345

General index

Theodorus of Asine   11, 48, 106
Theodorus of Soli   29
Theodosian Code   4
Theon of Smyrna   176
Theophrastus   28, 70
theôria and *lexis*   15–16
theurgy   6, 48
Thrasyllus   29
Timaeus, of Locri   29, 50, 51, 91, 100
Timaeus, Platonic character   25, 51–2, 55, 58

Timon, of Phleious   75, 91, 100
Titans   78
travellers' tales   277

Van den Berg, B.   264
Victorinus, Marius   46

Xanthus, river-god   171
Xanthus, man *see* Melanthus
Xenocrates   26–7

Zeus   58, 62, 253
Zostrianos   46